China's Cultural Revolution, 1966-1969

AN EAST GATE READER

Reflecting recent proposals by the National Endowment for the Humanities calling for more analysis of primary materials by students, M.E. Sharpe is pleased to announce the East Gate Readers. These readers are primary source textbooks which are expressly designed to afford undergraduate students the opportunity to read and interpret original and varied materials from Asia. These core texts will allow students to fit "raw data" into an overall analytical framework. To help in this process, each volume in the East Gate Readers contains annotations and introductions by an esteemed scholar in the field.

AN EAST GATE READER

China's Cultural Revolution, 1966-1969

NOT A DINNER PARTY

Michael Schoenhals, Editor

An East Gate Book

M.E. Sharpe
Armonk, New York
London, England

An East Gate Book

Library of Congress Cataloging-in-Publication Data

Schoenhals, Michael.
China's Cultural Revolution, 1966–1969 : not a
dinner party / Michael Schoenhals, editor.
p.   cm. — (East gate reader.)
"An East gate book."
Includes bibliographical references and index.
ISBN 1-56324-736-4 (hardcover : alk. paper).
ISBN 1-56324-737-2 (pbk. : alk. paper)
1. China—History—Cultural Revolution, 1966–1969—Sources.
I. Title.   II. Series.
DS778.7.S34   1996
951.05′6—dc20   96-12785
CIP
Printed in the United States of America

The paper used in this publication meets the minimum requirements of
American National Standard for Information Sciences—
Permanence of Paper for Printed Library Materials,
ANSI Z 39.48-1984.

∞

BM (c)   10   9   8   7   6   5   4   3   2   1
BM (p)   10   9   8   7   6   5   4   3   2   1

For Xiaolin

The twentieth century is the century of socialism. From this gigantic struggle among peoples will emerge nations that have shaken off the yoke of a world rule of capitalist oppression.

—Joseph Goebbels, *Das Reich,* 20 April 1944

The fundamental problem to be solved by China's Great Proletarian Cultural Revolution is the eradication of the social foundation of revisionism, the prevention of the restoration of capitalism, and the further consolidation of the . . . socialist system in China.

—Kang Sheng, NCNA, 2 November 1966

Contents

Part II. Effects and Consequences   91

Part III. After the Event 289

Acknowledgments

To the doyen of China's historians of the Cultural Revolution, Professor Wang Nianyi, for his encouragement; to Nancy Hearst, master librarian at the John King Fairbank Center for East Asian Research, for her patient help—and not just with trivia; and to Roderick MacFarquhar, comrade-in-pens, for his inspiration.

To the colleagues who replied so enthusiastically to my Internet query about what a reader like this one ought to look like; to Nils Båth, Per Camenius, Annie Chang, Chi Pingfeng, Nils Olof Ericsson, Britta Kinnemark, Peter and Nettan Nimerius, Liz Perry, Ambassador Petri, Jon Sigurdson, Julia Tung, and Vivian Wagner for providing me with texts and photographs; to Anna, Bengt, Björn, and Håkan for their translations; and to Katharina for her patient typing.

Last but not least, to Doug Merwin, the senior editor at M.E. Sharpe, who first suggested this project.

Introduction

As China changes from a socialist state with socialist characteristics into something that still defies convenient labeling, the Cultural Revolution, as a subject of study, is in limbo. There was a time, not so long ago, when a reader devoted to the Cultural Revolution would have been designed to afford students of political science an opportunity to read up on the dynamics of Maoism and China's pattern of political and social order. But today, political scientists seem largely to have lost interest in events that predate the second coming of Deng Xiaoping. They have exiled Mao, together with his Cultural Revolution, to the academic turf claimed by the historians. And there, of course, the Cultural Revolution is not yet welcome, in part simply because it is assumed that there are no archives on it.

So why, at this stage, should anyone want to put together a reader on such an apparently forlorn subject? Who is going to read it? Is any teacher likely to hand it to her or his students and say, like Hayden White, "Don't worry about labels or schools. Here is a book. Read it. If it helps you in your own work— good; if it doesn't—forget it"?[1] As the Cultural Revolution turns thirty, the present editor's intention is to convince the skeptics among the political scientists as well as the historians that even though the conventions of their disciplines might seem to dictate otherwise, here is a subject that still/already merits your attention. A political science barren in empirical analyses of the past will find it difficult to generate the vocabulary needed to explain the significance of the reordering that seems so palpable in the present—as Vivienne Shue has shown with such persuasive force.[2] And though only a handful of historians appear aware of it, the amount of quasi-archival material on the Cultural Revolution accessible and already in the public domain is massive and growing fast. Hence, there is really

---

[1]Hayden White, "Interview—The Image of Self-Representation," *Diacritics*, Vol. 24, No. 1, Spring 1994, p. 92.

[2]Vivienne Shue, *The Reach of the State: Sketches of the Chinese Body Politic* (Stanford, CA: Stanford University Press, 1988), p. 11.

no valid excuse for letting an event of such magnitude disappear—even temporarily—into the misty academic no man's land that separates one discipline's turf from that of another. We should all seek to explain it.

This reader contains altogether seventy-two primary documents, selected (with some exceptions) from public and classified Chinese sources. It is divided into nine sections representing a modest attempt to prefigure the historical field: first the texts that deal with what Mao Zedong et al. wished would happen; then the texts that account for what took place; and finally the retrospectives and other texts set in the past tense. The topics covered include Party purges, society, culture, economics, and—in an experimental departure—not foreign politics, but mutual perceptions of "us" by them and of "them" by us.

Each section begins with a brief introduction highlighting the significance of the selected documents. A historical chronology and brief biographical sketches provide background on events and personages mentioned in the texts. A list of suggested further readings is included primarily for the benefit of those who do not read Chinese.

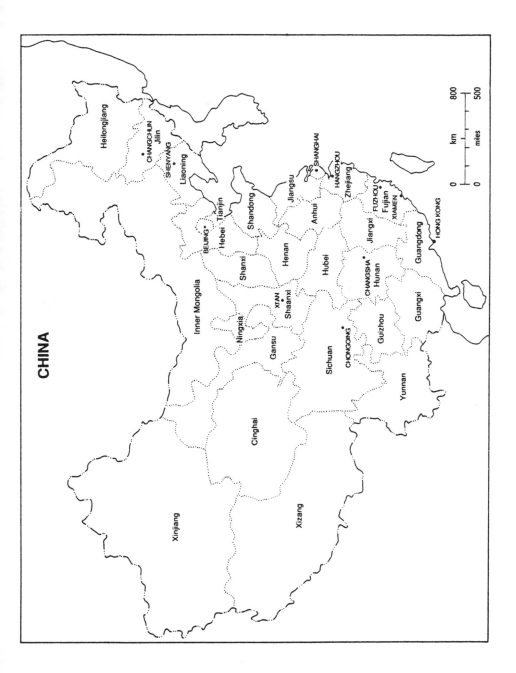

CHINA

Part I

Intentions and Means

A. Pronouncements by Members of the CCP Leadership

One searches in vain for an extended, systematic, and credible explanation by Mao Zedong himself of the goals of the Cultural Revolution. There is no master script to be found, no blueprint, no scenario, no game plan. All there is are random, scattered remarks—some spontaneous, others carefully hedged; some just possibly meant to be taken at face value, others almost certainly intended to obscure rather than elucidate. "Let us toast to the unfolding of a nationwide all-round civil war!" is what at least two guests remember hearing Mao propose on his seventy-third birthday, on 26 December 1966.[1] Was *that* what the Chinese Communist Party Chairman had in mind? Or was his intention (as he was quoted as saying in the *People's Daily* a week later) to achieve "the greatest ever revolutionary transformation of society, unprecedented in the history of mankind"?[2] Were the two goals possibly one and the same? Or one the means, the other the end? We have no firm answers.

The three texts in this section are from the autumn of 1966, a time when the buzz verbs of the Cultural Revolution were "down with," "drag out," "smash, burn, fry, and scorch," and the all-purpose "kill"; and the labels affixed to the movement's victims such creative dysphemisms as "ox-freaks and snake-monsters" and long and ugly "scientific" (so the Party Center insisted) designations like "the biggest handful of Party-persons in power taking the capitalist road." Helping Mao to keep the Cultural Revolution on course were his recently promoted deputy and "closest comrade-in-arms," Lin Biao, and the members of an ad hoc Central Cultural Revolution Group—a dozen or so

---

[1]Chen Boda, cited in Ye Yonglie, *Mingren fengyun lu* (*Famous Men of the Hour*) (Guilin: Lijiang chubanshe, 1992), p. 14; and Guan Feng, cited in *Ye Yonglie caifang shouji* (*Ye Yonglie's Interview Notes*) (Shanghai: Shanghai shehui kexueyuan chubanshe, 1993), p. 119.

[2]*Renmin ribao,* 1 January 1967.

"ideologues" who met regularly under the chairmanship of Premier Zhou Enlai.[3]

In the first text Mao talks briefly about what he wished his audience to believe had been two of his motives in launching the Cultural Revolution: wanting to undo the division of the Party Center into a first and second line of command; and wanting to shake up the Party as a whole in an attempt to reinvigorate it. In other words, to "wreak havoc" with the establishment in an attempt to prevent it from going "revisionist."

The second text is a longer speech by Lin Biao about the whys and wherefores of the Cultural Revolution. It is possibly as close as we shall ever get to an authoritative blueprint for the movement. Mao, we know, had read and approved it prior to delivery, and as CCP historian Wang Nianyi points out, it amounted to the most systematic attempt at explaining the "need" for a Cultural Revolution that any member of the highest leadership had made at that point. "At the time," Wang notes, writing in 1988, Lin "actually seemed quite reasonable and rather moderate in his tone. . . . Consequently, many Party members and cadres accepted his arguments."[4]

The third text is in many ways a mere footnote to history. Still, God resides in the footnotes (or in the details contained therein, as Einstein is said to have put it) and Zhou Enlai's letter is important for that one sacred claim contained therein—that the "*only* criterion of truth" (emphasis added) in the Cultural Revolution was not practice, but "Mao Zedong Thought." In other words, if Mao Zedong could be quoted as saying that "the situation in the Great Proletarian Cultural Revolution throughout the country is not just good but excellent," then so be it.[5] Anyone arguing the opposite was simply deluded, mistaken, or—worse—lying.

---

[3]Zhou, who was himself not a member of the Central Cultural Revolution Group, chaired all of its regular meetings. Wang Li, personal communication.

[4]Wang Nianyi, *Da dongluan de niandai* (*Years of Great Turmoil*) (Zhengzhou: Henan renmin chubanshe, 1988), pp. 110, 112–13.

[5]And he was, of course. Cf. *Liberation Army Daily,* 9 November 1967.

1
"Just a Few Words"

Mao Zedong

Source: Translation of "Zai Zhongyang gongzuo huiyi shang de jianghua" (Talk at the Central Work Conference) (October 25, 1966) in Stuart R. Schram, ed., *Mao Tse-tung Unrehearsed: Talks and Letters 1956–1971* (Harmondsworth: Penguin Books, 1974), pp. 270–74. Reprinted with permission.

I have just a few words to say about two matters.

For the past seventeen years there is one thing which in my opinion we haven't done well. Out of concern for state security and in view of the lessons of Stalin in the Soviet Union, we set up a first and second line.[1] I have been in the second line, other comrades in the first line. Now we can see that wasn't so good; as a result our forces were dispersed. When we entered the cities we could not centralize our efforts, and there were quite a few independent kingdoms. Hence the Eleventh Plenum carried out changes. This is one matter. I am in the second line, I do not take charge of day-to-day work. Many things are left to other people so that other people's prestige is built up, and when I go to see God there won't be such a big upheaval in the State. Everybody was in agreement with this idea of mine. It seems that there are some things which the comrades in the first line have not managed too well. There are some things I should have kept a grip on which I did not. So I am responsible, we cannot just blame them. Why do I say that I bear some responsibility?

First, it was I who proposed that the Standing Committee be divided into two lines and that a secretariat be set up. Everyone agreed with this.[2] Moreover I put too much trust in others. It was at the time of the

---

[1] There are a few minor discrepancies between the translated text and the excerpts quoted in Wang Nianyi, *Da dongluan de niandai (Years of Great Turmoil)* (Zhengzhou: Henan renmin chubanshe, 1988), pp. 113–14. Here Wang has "in view of how Malenkov was no longer able to fend for himself once Stalin had died and how revisionism appeared as a result, we set up a first and second line."

[2] This sentence is missing in all other sources consulted, including Wang Nianyi.

Twenty-three Articles that my vigilance was aroused.[3] I could do nothing in Beijing; I could do nothing at the Center. Last September and October I asked, If revisionism appeared at the Center, what could the localities do?[4] I felt that my ideas couldn't be carried out in Beijing. Why was the criticism of Wu Han initiated not in Beijing but in Shanghai? Because there was nobody to do it in Beijing. Now the problem of Beijing has been solved.

Second, the Great Cultural Revolution wreaked havoc after I approved Nie Yuanzi's big-character poster in Beijing University and wrote a letter to Qinghua University Middle School, as well as writing a big-character poster of my own.[5] It all happened within a very short period, less than five months in June, July, August, September, and October. No wonder the comrades did not understand too much. The time was so short and the events so violent. I myself had not foreseen that as soon as the Beijing University poster was broadcast, the whole country would be thrown into turmoil. Even before the letter to the Red Guards had gone out, Red Guards had mobilized throughout the country, and in one rush they swept you off your feet.[6] Since it was I who caused the havoc, it is understandable if you have some bitter words for me. Last time we met I lacked confidence and I said that our decisions would not necessarily be carried out. Indeed all that time quite a few comrades still did not understand things fully, though now after a couple of months we have had some experience, and things are a bit better. This meeting has had two stages. In the first stage the speeches were not quite normal, but during the second stage, after speeches and the exchange of experience by comrades at the Center, things went more smoothly and the ideas were understood a bit better.

---

[3]I.e., when Mao put forward his new twenty-three-point directive for the Socialist Education Campaign in January 1965 and Liu Shaoqi refused to accept it.

[4]Wang Nianyi has "if revisionism appeared in Beijing, what should be done?"

[5]A translation of the big-character poster "What Are Song Shuo, Lu Ping, and Peng Peiyun Up To in the Great Cultural Revolution?" is in *Survey of China Mainland Press,* No. 3719, 16 June 1966, pp. 6–8. A translation of Mao's "Letter to the Red Guards of Qinghua University Middle School" is in Stuart R. Schram, ed., *Mao Tse-tung Unrehearsed: Talks and Letters 1956–1971* (Harmondsworth: Penguin Books, 1974), pp. 260–61. A translation of Mao's big-character poster "Bombard the Headquarters" is in *Current Background,* No. 891, 8 October 1969, p. 63.

[6]Wang Nianyi has ". . . throughout the country. There are all kinds and all sorts of Red Guards and in Beijing alone there are three, four headquarters. In one rush they swept you off your feet."

It has only been five months. Perhaps the movement may last another five months, or even longer.

Our democratic revolution went on for twenty-eight years, from 1921 to 1949. At first nobody knew how to conduct the revolution or how to carry on the struggle; only later did we acquire some experience. Our path gradually emerged in the course of practice. Did we not carry on for twenty-eight years, summarizing our experience as we went along? Have we not been carrying on the socialist revolution for seventeen years, whereas the Cultural Revolution has been going on for only five months? Hence we cannot ask comrades to understand so well now. Many comrades did not read the articles criticizing Wu Han last year and did not pay much attention to them. The article criticizing the film *The Life of Wu Xun* and studies of the novel *Dream of the Red Chamber* could not be grasped if taken separately, but only if taken as a whole. For this I am responsible. If you take them separately it is like treating only the head when you have a headache and treating only the feet when they hurt; the problem cannot be solved. During the first several months of this Great Cultural Revolution—in January, February, March, April, and May—articles were written and the Center issued directives, but they did not arouse all that much attention. It was the big-character posters and onslaughts of the Red Guards that drew your attention; you could not avoid it because the revolution was right on top of you. You must quickly summarize your experience and properly carry out political and ideological work. Why are we meeting again after two months? It is to summarize our experience and carry out political and ideological work. You also have a great deal of political and ideological work to do after you go back. The Political Bureau, the provincial committees, the prefectural committees, and county committees must meet for ten days or more and thrash out the problems.[7] But they mustn't think that everything can be cleared up. Some people have said, "We understand the principles, but when we run up against concrete problems we cannot deal with them properly." At first I could not understand why, if the principles were clear, the concrete problems could not be dealt with. I can see some reasons for this: It may be that political and ideological work has not been done properly. When you went back after our last meeting, some places did not find time to hold proper meetings. In Henan there were ten secretaries. Out

---

[7]"Political Bureau" should read "[Regional] Bureaus of the Center."

of the ten there were seven or eight who were receiving people. The Red Guards rushed in and caused havoc. The students were angry, but they did not realize it and had not prepared themselves to answer questions. They thought that to make a welcoming speech lasting a quarter of an hour or so would do. But the students were thoroughly enraged. The fact that there were a number of questions that they could not immediately answer put the secretaries on the defensive. Yet this defensive attitude can be changed, can be transformed so that they take the initiative. Hence my confidence in this meeting has increased. I don't know what you think. If when you go back you do things according to the old system, maintaining the status quo, putting yourself in opposition to one group of Red Guards and letting another group hold sway, then I think things cannot change, the situation cannot improve. But I think things can change and things can improve. Of course we shouldn't expect too much. We can't be certain that the mass of central, provincial, prefectural, and county cadres should all be so enlightened. There will always be some who fail to understand, and there will be a minority on the opposite side. But I think it will be possible to make the majority understand.

I have talked about two matters. The first concerns history. For seventeen years the two lines have not been united. Others have some responsibility for this; so have I. The second issue is the five months of the Great Cultural Revolution, the fire of which I kindled. It has been going on only five months, not even half a year, a very brief span compared to the twenty-eight years of democratic revolution and the seventeen years of socialist revolution. So one can see why it has not been thoroughly understood and there were obstacles. Why hasn't it been understood? In the past you have only been in charge of industry, agriculture, and communications, and you have never carried out a Great Cultural Revolution. You in the Ministry of Foreign Affairs and the [Central] Military Commission are the same. That which you never dreamed of has come to pass. What's come has come. I think that there are advantages in being assailed. For so many years you had not thought about such things, but as soon as they burst upon you, you began to think. Undoubtedly you have made some mistakes, some mistakes of line, but they can be corrected and that will be that! Who wants to overthrow you? I don't, and I don't think the Red Guards do either. Two Red Guards said to Li Xuefeng: "Can you imagine why our elders are so frightened of the Red Guards?" Then there were Wu Xiuquan's four children, who belonged to four different factions.

Some of their school friends went to his home, several dozen at a time, and this happened quite a few times. I think that there are advantages in making contact in small groups. Another method is to have big meetings, 1,500,000 meeting for several hours. Both methods serve a purpose.

There have been quite a few brief reports presented at this meeting. I have read nearly all of them. You find it difficult to cross this pass and I don't find it easy either. You are anxious and so am I. I cannot blame you, comrades, time has been so short. Some comrades say that they did not intentionally make mistakes, but did it because they were confused. This is pardonable. Nor can we put all the blame on Comrade Shaoqi and Comrade Xiaoping. They have some responsibility, but so has the Center.[8] The Center has not run things properly. The time was so short. We were not mentally prepared for new problems. Political and ideological work was not carried out properly. I think that after this seventeen-day conference things will be a bit better.

Does anyone else want to speak? I guess that's all for today. The meeting is adjourned.

---

[8]Wang Nianyi has "There are reasons too, for why these two comrades made mistakes."

2
"Why a Cultural Revolution?"

Lin Biao

Source: "Lin Biao tongzhi zai Zhongyang gongzuo huiyi shang de jianghua" (Comrade Lin Biao's Talk at the Central Work Conference) (October 25, 1966), first circulated on November 9, 1966, in CCP Central Document *Zhongfa* [1966] 542 (classified "crucially secret"). Our translation is of the reprint in People's Liberation Army Armored Force Political Department, ed., *Wuchanjieji wenhua dageming shengli wansui* (*Long Live the Victory of the Great Proletarian Cultural Revolution*) (Beijing, 1969), pp. 152–68.

I want to speak mainly about two things: one is the need for a cultural revolution and the other is how a cultural revolution is to be carried out. In other words, is it necessary to have a cultural revolution and if so how is it to be done? These questions are related, and I shall emphasize the need for a cultural revolution.

This conference has lasted for seventeen days and has been very successful. From beginning to end it has been led by Chairman Mao personally. It is in actuality a continuation of the Eleventh Plenum of the Central Committee and has aimed at further clarifying the question of the two lines.

During the last several months the Great Cultural Revolution has been characterized by great enthusiasm at both ends and a lack of enthusiasm in the middle, including some stubborn resistance even. At one point the situation was quite tense. After seeing what was happening, Chairman Mao suggested that everybody be invited to a discussion. The meeting was originally meant to last for three days, but then it went on for seven days, and now already more than two weeks have passed. In the course of discussion, the situation has become clearer and clearer, as has everybody's thinking. It has become possible to grasp Chairman Mao's line and to persist in this line. Consequently, this has been a very necessary conference.

There has been great enthusiasm at two ends: one end represented by Chairman Mao's leadership and the other end by the masses.

The broad masses have been most vigorous and dynamic. Beginning in the schools and continuing in society, the impact of the movement has spread from the cultural sphere to the economy, politics, and throughout all spheres of society. The gains—the political gains in particular—have been considerable. A number of persons in authority who have taken the capitalist road have been dragged out from within the Party. Many bourgeois reactionary "authorities" in society have been discredited, and many hidden counter-revolutionary elements and bad elements have been ferreted out. Many counter-revolutionary cases have been solved, and arms, radio transmitters, gold, etc., have been uncovered. But what is most important is that ideologically, the movement has truly touched people's souls. This is a profound great revolution that has shattered the old ideology and established a new ideology on a massive scale. Drastic changes have taken place in the face of society and in the mental attitudes of people. In this movement, Chairman Mao's thoughts have been extensively propagated and popularized. They have become deeply engraved in the minds of people and have exerted a tremendous didactic impact upon the young and upon society in general. In the course of the movement, many young people will grow up to become dependable successors of the revolution.

During the period of the Great Cultural Revolution, our social production has not suffered, as certain comrades had feared. On the contrary, production has increased. It stands to reason that a cultural revolution should accelerate production, and this has also been borne out by the facts.

Our movement has set an unprecedented example in the world. In regard to anti-revisionism, this action on the part of China has great didactic potential.

At the top there is Chairman Mao. Everybody has seen it quite clearly how from beginning to end, this movement has been unleashed and led by the Chairman. With tremendous energy and resolve, Chairman Mao took it upon himself to unleash a large-scale mass movement. An ordinary working-class party leader could not possibly have shown such great energy and resolve. Only a great Marxist-Leninist such as Chairman Mao—with his extremely rich fighting experience and his profound Marxist-Leninist wisdom—would have dared to unleash such a dynamic and totally earth-shaking revolutionary mass movement. Some comrades under Chairman Mao's leadership have also been most effective in consistently supporting and implementing Chairman Mao's line.

Just now I said that there had been some stubborn resistance in the middle. It was similar to what was described in the Center's Circular of May 16 [1966] as "most Party committees concerned have a very poor understanding of the task of leadership in this great struggle and their leadership is far from conscientious and effective."[1] All the time up to just prior to this meeting, that was the situation. But, there was a difference in degree and in some places the situation was more serious than in others. In some places, it also changed more quickly than in others. In some cases, there was conscious resistance, but in most cases there was not—merely a failure to perceive and understand what was going on. Only these last two days has everyone come to realize clearly that the situation was

---

[1]"Circular of Central Committee of Chinese Communist Party" (May 16, 1966), *Peking Review,* No. 21, 1967, pp. 6–9.

caused by two things.[2] On the one hand, there were local and ideological causes. But more importantly, there were a few leaders at the Center, namely Liu Shaoqi and Deng Xiaoping, who pursued a different line, a line that was the opposite of Chairman Mao's. This is how Chairman Mao described the Liu-Deng line in his big-character poster: "Having the reactionary stand of the bourgeoisie, they have enforced a bourgeois dictatorship and struck down the surging movement of the Great Cultural Revolution of the Proletariat. They have stood facts on their head and juggled black and white, encircled and suppressed revolutionaries, stifled opinions differing from their own, imposed a white terror, and felt very pleased with themselves. They have puffed up the arrogance of the bourgeoisie and deflated the morale of the proletariat. How vicious they are!"[3] After these last few days, you comrades have already become quite aware of this root cause.

Generally speaking, what we call culture encompasses ideology, social consciousness, world outlook, customs and habits, political viewpoints, legal viewpoints, artistic viewpoints, motion pictures and drama, sculpture, literature, the educational system, etc. So why is there a need for a cultural revolution? The decisive factor prompting us to launch a revolution in the sphere of social consciousness is the fundamental change that has occurred in the economic base of our society.

Where does ideology come from? Marxism-Leninism Mao Zedong Thought has always maintained that ideology comes from matter and that social consciousness derives from social existence, e.g. from the economic base of society and the system of ownership in society. Since Liberation, the proletariat has held political power, and the system of ownership in our society has changed fundamentally. We confiscated, turned over to the peasants, and later collectivized the land belonging to the landlords. These were two changes that took place in the system of ownership in agriculture: Landlord ownership became

---

[2] Lin is alluding here to the fact that two days earlier, Liu Shaoqi and Deng Xiaoping had presented their self-criticisms to the conference. A translation of Liu's self-criticism is in Harold C. Hinton, ed., *The People's Republic of China 1949–1979: A Documentary Survey* (Wilmington: Scholarly Resources, 1980), pp. 1620–23. A translation of Deng's self-criticism is in *Classified Chinese Communist Documents: A Selection* (Taipei: Institute of International Relations, National Chengchi University, 1978), pp. 236–44.

[3] See Document 1, note 5.

individual peasant ownership, and after that it became collective peasant ownership. The bourgeois system of ownership passed through various transitional stages to become a socialist system of public ownership. Now we are preparing the abolition of fixed interest payments. Since changes have occurred in the economic base, our social consciousness, which is part of the superstructure, must also change accordingly in order to catch up. Unless it catches up, we shall be obstructing the consolidation of the socialist system of ownership and slowing down progress. In other words, we will prevent new social productive forces from developing and make the consolidation of the fruits of revolution impossible. The result will be the restoration of capitalism and the subversion of the people's democratic dictatorship, which protects the system of public ownership. The socialist system of public ownership will be overturned, and China will become ruled by revisionists and retrogress to a semi-feudal and semi-colonial status. Thus to carry out a Great Cultural Revolution or not is a major political question that will decide whether or not proletarian political power can be consolidated and the fruits of revolution can be developed. It is a major political question that will decide the success or failure of our revolution.

The revolution of the proletariat and the class struggle carried out by the proletariat has three aspects: one aspect is political, another is economic, and a third is ideological.

To overthrow a regime by means of war is a violent act. We succeeded in routing the Guomindang in 1946–49 (naturally, we had already spent many years [fighting them] before that). We achieved victory, seized political power, established our own state, and established the dictatorship of the proletariat. The revolution in the system of ownership, i.e. the revolution to abolish the feudal system of ownership and the bourgeois system of ownership, took less time. But on the other hand, on another front, we shall need to spend more time, and the struggle there will see more twists and turns. I am referring to the ideological sphere, where the struggle will take longer than it took to seize political power and to change the system of ownership. Next year will mark the fiftieth anniversary of the revolutionary victory in the Soviet Union. And yet, how much bourgeois ideology have they eliminated and how much proletarian ideology have they fostered? One result, after these fifty years, is that after the death of Stalin, instead of forging ahead, they retrogressed toward revisionism, toward new forms of bourgeois restoration, and toward a capitalist system manifesting itself to varying degrees in new guises. Yugoslavia was the first country where a bourgeois restoration occurred. In addition, not only in the Soviet Union but in a number of "socialist" countries, one or two decades after victory, they failed to grasp this facet of struggle, and as a consequence there were signs of the revolution stagnating and retrogressing, and of restoration. If we do not grasp this point, the development that has occurred in the Soviet Union and Yugoslavia will also take place here. The Soviet Union has existed for fifty years, but it is now ruled by revisionists. Unless we constantly and persistently grasp the Cultural Revolution, that will also be the outcome here. Therefore Chairman Mao said: "You should pay attention to affairs of state and carry the Great Proletarian Cultural Revolution through to the end." Chairman Mao regards the Great Cultural Revolution as an important state affair and as politics. While revising the minutes of the forum on literature and arts in the armed forces in March this year, Chairman Mao agreed to include a reference to all class struggles being political struggles, hereby reiterating this classic viewpoint of Marxism-Leninism and regarding it as an important state affair and as a political question.[4] Unless we firmly grasp the cultural revolution and unless we carry the Great Proletarian Cultural Revolution through to the end, we too will end up changing our color midway.

That we normally grasp economic construction firmly is good. Nonetheless, with regard to destruction and construction in culture and in the ideological sphere, not all comrades have grasped the situation as firmly and emphasized these tasks as strongly as Chairman Mao. There are people who feel that this is an extra burden. They maintain that everything is all right and ask why does there have to be a cultural revolution? In fact, since we gained political power, on the one hand, we have had to undertake economic construction; but on the other hand, from a long-range point of view, it is even more important to undertake ideological construction. Ideology has a tremendous impact upon political and economic developments. Old ideology serves the old economic base and reflects the demands of the reactionary classes, thus obstructing the development of society; new ideology serves the

---

[4]A translation of the text referred to here, the so-called "Summary of the Forum on the Work in Literature and Art in the Armed Forces, which Comrade Jiang Qing Convened at the Behest of Comrade Lin Biao," is in Hinton, pp. 1416–21.

new economic base and reflects the demands of the progressive classes, thus exercising a progressive and accelerating impact on the development of society. As soon as the masses are in the grip of progressive ideology, that ideology will become a tremendous material force propelling the development of society forward. This is why we should destroy on a massive scale (and not just on a small or medium scale) the old ideology and establish a new ideology. We should establish on a massive scale the ideology of our Chairman Mao, who represents new ideology, the people's ideology, the proletariat's ideology, communist ideology, Marxist-Leninist ideology, and ideology strong enough to stand up against old ideology. This is a point that many comrades have failed to grasp firmly. They have failed to grasp firmly what should be destroyed on a massive scale and what should be established on a massive scale. After these last few days, you all know about the attitude taken toward the dissemination of Mao Zedong Thought by Liu and Deng among the comrades working at the Center. You also know about the attitude taken in the past by Lu Dingyi's Propaganda Department. That was infuriating and simply intolerable.

After seizing political power, with respect to our domestic tasks, we must, apart from suppressing the opposition of the exploiters and engaging in economic construction, carry out cultural construction. Not only we, but all ruling classes in history have engaged in destruction and construction in the cultural field. There is no state and no ruling class that would allow the propagation of an ideology that is opposed to its class stand. One must insist on one's own ideology in order to consolidate one's political and economic systems. Though the ruling ideology of each epoch in history would appear to have represented the outlook of the entire society, it actually represented only the interests of the ruling exploiting classes. The ideology of the ruling class in each epoch was an ideology that merely represented the interests of that ruling class. In the past the ideology of the laboring people did not occupy a governing status; moreover, most laboring people have for a long time been fooled and deceived. Our Party is one of Marxism-Leninism Mao Zedong Thought. According to the theories of Marxism and Mao Zedong Thought, there must be a complete break with the old systems of ownership and a complete break with old traditional ideas. We have the power and the obligation to establish the ideological rule of the proletariat.

Although we have by now achieved a governing status, both economically and politically, we have not yet completely attained a governing status ideologically. We have overthrown the old classes economically and politically, but in the sphere of ideology the ways of the old classes still predominate. Consequently, it is necessary for us to develop this struggle on the ideological front unrelentingly and persistently. After many decades Stalin had still not resolved this struggle. We are lucky and it is a great honor for us to have Chairman Mao raise this matter for us in good time to resolve.

It would seem as if instead of a few decades it might take a century or even centuries to eliminate the old ideologies. Naturally, antagonism between old things and new things will continue to exist in future society for two hundred years, three hundred years, four hundred years, one thousand years, or even ten thousand years. There is bound to be struggle in the ideological sphere in which the new will oppose the old and the old will linger and refuse to exit the historical stage. Though the nature of the situation will be different from the kind of class struggle we are waging today, there will still be a commonality in that the new will defeat the old.

It is likely there will be ideological contradictions and ideological struggles in the future. Thus, this struggle in culture and in the sphere of ideology will be a protracted struggle and by no means a simple matter.

Our form of struggle is sometimes one of denunciation in the press, as in the case of the denunciation of *The Life of Wu Xun* and *Studies of the "Dream of the Red Chamber,"* the denunciation of the reactionary ideology of Hu Shi and Hu Feng, the denunciation of Yang Xianzhen, and the denunciation of Wu Han, Deng Tuo, Jian Bozan, Zhou Yang et al.[5] These were all movements of profound significance personally led by Chairman Mao. But when things develop to a certain stage, it becomes necessary to mobilize all of society in a dynamic mopping up and elimination operation, as has happened in the last five months. This kind of a movement, this kind of a battle, should create a solid foundation after about half a year or maybe one year. The function of this kind of movement can by no means be replaced by denunciations in the press and is quite extraordinary and powerful. This movement is

---

[5]For a comprehensive account of some of these events, see Merle Goldman, *Literary Dissent in Communist China* (New York: Atheneum, 1971).

a major innovation, although there may be some overlap between big and small campaigns.

What is the essence of old culture and old ideology? We can use a great many words to express it and call it old culture, old ideology, poisonous weeds, ox-monsters and snake-demons, reactionary authorities, old academia, old morals, old art, old laws, old educational systems, old world outlook, etc. The most essential oldness of these things lies in them being old in one particular respect, namely as parts of the system of private ownership. In short, they are old in one word and that word is "self" (si). What, then, is new about new things and new ideology? They are also new in one word and that word is "public" (gong).

The history of human society prior to the invention of writing had lasted for a long time, at least half a million years. Some scientists say that the earth was formed maybe six billion years ago. Nonetheless, since the rise of civilization, in these past millennia, there have only been class societies—like slave society, feudal society, and capitalist society. What did these societies all have in common? The system of private ownership. It already has a history of several millennia. While there may be a dozen different ideologies of exploiting classes, they all have one thing in common, and that is they all defend the system of private ownership.

Our present society is one of a socialist system of public ownership, in which everything—land, factories, and the means of production— belongs to the public (guigong). Under these circumstances, in order to consolidate this system, it is necessary to eliminate the old culture of the bourgeoisie and other exploitative classes and to eliminate the old ideologies that serve to uphold and restore the system of private ownership. The existence and influence of the ideology of the exploiting classes will in the end inevitably restore the old political power protecting the system of private ownership. Those who are opposed to the destruction of old culture and old ideology are bound to suppress the revolution and suppress the masses. If we want to consolidate the socialist system—its economic system and its political system—we must advocate a concept of public-mindedness, i.e. we must create a new man to construct a new society, a man with a communist spirit. What is a man with a communist spirit like? He is like Zhang Side, Norman Bethune, Liu Hulan, and Lei Feng, who have all been praised by our Chairman Mao. Other such men are Ouyang Hai, Jiao Yulu,

Wang Jie, and Liu Yingjun, all of whom are men of communism and men of a new kind.[6] We need new men like these to build our new society, and we must gradually transform the people in our society into men of this kind.

What is communism? In a certain sense, communism is for the public. Communism can also be called the "ism" of public (*gong*) property (*chan*). The kind of people we need to foster are what Chairman Mao called people who are divested of base interests and who are men of morality. We must foster the kind of men who have a new morality and, as Chairman Mao has said, are totally devoted to the people, devoted heart and soul. These are the people of communism. Their opposites are the people centered on "self," who are only interested in their own gain, fame, power, status, and with being in the limelight. Such people are egocentric and oblivious of the masses and the laboring people. In short, they care only about themselves. In class society, each person belongs to a specific class. He either belongs to this class, to a certain stratum or group within this class; or he belongs to that class, to a certain stratum or group within that class. There is no such thing as an abstract, independent individual. To care only about oneself is a purely bourgeois worldview. Bourgeois individualism is to promote one's own interests at the expense of others. In order to become wealthy themselves, they do not care if millions of other people go bankrupt. To look at the world from a "self"-centered viewpoint is to look at the world from a bourgeois point of view; it is not to look at the world from a proletarian point of view.

What we need is to foster people dedicated to the "public." Here too we have different class characteristics. The "public" we have in mind is the public of the people, the public of the proletariat, and the public of socialism and communism. There have been a great many public-minded people of this type in our Party since its founding and now there are even more of them. Where Chairman Mao's thought has been further popularized, the number of people like this has become even greater. Since the workers, peasants, soldiers, and educated youth began studying Chairman Mao's works on a great scale, ever so many good people have emerged and ever so many good things have occurred.

---

[6]For a convenient introduction to these "men of a new kind," see Pär Bergman, *Paragons of Virtue in Chinese Short Stories during the Cultural Revolution* (Stockholm: Föreningen för Orientaliska Studier, 1984).

In building our country, there have been two lines. One has been to one-sidedly emphasize matter, machinery, and mechanization and things like material incentives, like in the Soviet Union. The other has been the line that Chairman Mao has led us in taking.

Chairman Mao has led us in creating a new nation, which, besides being engaged in mechanization, is engaged more importantly in revolutionization and in leading mechanization with the help of revolutionization. In comparing machines with men, the latter are naturally more important. Chairman Mao tells us that man is the most precious thing in the world. Militarily, weapons are important, but they are not the decisive factor. The decisive factor is man. This is a Marxist viewpoint, a truly Marxist viewpoint. Machines can be transformed into productive forces only through human effort. A machine on its own is only a heap of iron. Machines are created and used by man. No man, no machines. Machines without men are useless. Machines represent a potential productive force, but in order to be transformed into an actual productive force, they must be combined with men. Only then can they become actual productive forces.

Machines are nothing but artificial organs. Unlike other animals, our hands have become "tools" of liberation. Right now all kinds of machines are in fact merely organs producing in our place, after having replaced, helped, and strengthened our hands. Thus all these machines exist to strengthen our organs and as a matter of fact to strengthen man's ability. They are centered around man. To neglect man is to neglect the greatest productive force of all. Politically, it is to neglect the force of making revolution, of rising in revolution.

Ours is a country different from those led by revisionists. They lopsidedly engage in mechanization, while we engage in revolutionization as well as mechanization. We allow revolutionization to lead mechanization. Chairman Mao already at an early date proposed that the Liberation Army needs to be revolutionized as well as modernized. You can see that he did not mention merely one "ization" but two. That was in the case of the Liberation Army, but it holds true for the whole country as well. In other words, we must on the one hand engage in mechanization and on the other hand in revolutionization, and ultimately the latter must lead the former.

The question may be put as follows: How should we rate the importance of the Great Proletarian Cultural Revolution? Is it really necessary? Is it an extra burden or is it something within our duties? If it is within our duties, then not to undertake it is tantamount to neglecting our duties. Under the dictatorship of the proletariat, the state has three great tasks: i.e., political construction, economic construction, and ideological construction. In the past we emphasized the first two, but there is also the additional one of ideological construction or cultural revolution which has not yet comprehensively unfolded. It must be realized that without the successful unfolding of a cultural revolution and ideological construction, the fruits we have gained in the first two great constructions will be lost. Thus, it is incumbent on us to emulate Chairman Mao's launching of a cultural revolution on a massive scale. Chairman Mao's theories are to be found in his works. His books provide the necessary basis for our studies. There are also a great many writings of Chairman Mao that have not found their way into the books but which we must study as well. We should do as Chairman Mao does. In both theory and practice, and both in Marxist theory as well as in his personal talents, Chairman Mao is not only superior to us in all respects, but he is also the world's greatest contemporary Marxist-Leninist. We must use Chairman Mao's example as our measuring stock and attempt to catch up with, emulate, and learn from him. We should rate the importance of the Great Cultural Revolution very highly and regard it as an important state affair, a political matter, an important part of the class struggle, and an important battle front. This is the only proper way.

Because the Cultural Revolution is a political struggle between the proletariat and the bourgeoisie, there will inevitably be a struggle between two lines. You have all come to see this two-line struggle clearly these past two days.[7] One line is that represented by Liu and Deng. It represses the masses and is opposed to making revolution. The other line, boldly advocated by Chairman Mao, has faith in the masses, relies on, and mobilizes the masses. This is also the mass line of the Party and the proletarian revolutionary line. One is the mass line, the other is the anti-mass line. This, then, is the sharp conflict between two lines inside our Party. For a short period of time, the line of Liu and Deng was almost dominant and was implemented all over the country. Nevertheless, in the final analysis, Chairman Mao's line will always be victorious, because it is the truth.

---

[7]See note 2 above.

Chairman Mao said: "The people, and the people alone, are the motive force in the making of world history." This sentence is quite classic and the most succinct and essential summary of the Marxist theory of historical materialism. The theory of historical materialism explains the progressive development of the history of the people and the masses as the progressive development of the living forces of production. Only thus can there be a social revolution, a change in the system of ownership, and a change in production. The masses are the progressive motive force at every stage in history, the most basic as well as the most constant force. The masses are numerous and their power is great. More people, more wisdom. You suggest something, he suggests something. With many people coming up with solutions, there is greater wisdom and creativity.

The revolutionary movement of the masses is naturally right (*tianran helide*). While there may be segments and individuals among the masses who deviate either to the "left" or to the right, the main current of the mass movement always accords with the development of society and is always right. Therefore we should have faith in and rely on the creativity of the masses. At the beginning of this movement we did not set forth very many regulations. Chairman Mao said time and again that we did not make up the Red Guards, but they were created by the masses and then turned into a nationwide phenomenon. Many things are started by the masses. First, we should be the pupils of the masses, learn from them, concentrate and promote their views, and only then make ourselves the teachers. To come from the masses and to implement among the masses has consistently been Chairman Mao's ideology and method.

The youth of this generation are children we have fostered during the seventeen years since our revolutionary victory. By now they are about twenty years old, and most of them are ideologically aware. Nurtured by Mao Zedong Thought and under the leadership of a correct revolutionary line, they are quite receptive to the new, proletarian world outlook. In the course of the cultural revolution, we must have faith in this group of young friends. They are daring young generals whose daring spirit is most precious. Quite a few problems we were unable to solve—quite a few "long-standing, big, and difficult" problems—they, by means of their daring, clarified and resolved just like that.

There are still a considerable number of comrades who are afraid of the students and the masses, and they have this or that kind of fear. Since Comrade [Chen] Boda has already given us plenty of examples I shall not repeat them.[8]

It says in the "Decision Concerning the Great Proletarian Cultural Revolution" of the Eleventh Plenum of the Central Committee that the persons in charge in many units fear there will be chaos.[9] Quite a few people indeed do fear chaos. But actually, this chaos affects only the enemy and not ourselves. Sometimes, we do create some minor problems for ourselves as well.

Chaos has a dual nature—this is something that Chairman Mao said a long time ago. It has a good side and a bad side. We must not see only the bad side and ignore the good side. Moreover, what's bad can be transformed into what's good.

That the general situation should descend into chaos is out of the question. Our armed forces stand firm, and production is on the rise. How much chaos can some students and young people engaged in a cultural revolution cause? They cannot possibly cause major chaos. This is how we view the chaos issue. This is our "outlook on chaos."

Chairman Mao said: "A revolution is not a dinner party, or writing an essay, or painting a picture, or doing embroidery; it cannot be so refined, so leisurely and gentle, so temperate, kind, courteous, restrained, and magnanimous." There are bound to be deviations, perhaps few, perhaps many. Nevertheless, the mainstream is good, and one need not be afraid. If you are that worried about small chaos now, you will be facing even bigger chaos in the future, when the ox-monsters and snake-demons rebel against the proletariat, rebel against us. This time I asked Comrade Xie Fuzhi to prepare a document that would illustrate the accomplishments of the Red

---

[8]Lin is referring here to Chen Boda's address to the Central Work Conference on 16 October, entitled "Wuchanjieji wenhua dageming zhong de liangtiao luxian" (The Two Lines in the Great Proletarian Cultural Revolution). First circulated on 9 November 1966 as CCP Central Document *Zhongfa* [1966] 543, it is reprinted in People's Liberation Army Armored Force Political Department, ed., *Wuchanjieji wenhua dageming shengli wansui (Long Live the Victory of the Great Proletarian Cultural Revolution)* (Beijing, 1969), pp. 288–307.

[9]See Document 4, point 3: "Put Daring Above Everything Else and Boldly Arouse the Masses."

Guards, and I also sent some people to look at their exhibits.[10] In fact, those people were prepared to rebel against us, and had even prepared for a "change in the weather." Some of them hold on to their old land deeds as if they represent the difference between life and death. They paste them up if they are torn, and photograph and preserve them. Why do they want to keep such things? The reason why they keep them in secret can only be that they figure when the Guomindang and the imperialists return, they can claim that this house belongs to them or that land belongs to them. In vain they believe they will be restored to rule. Although the exploiting classes have been overthrown, these people are still alive; in their minds they are very reactionary and they are full of hatred toward the people. Inside our Party, there are also people hoping to be restored to rule. Peng [Zhen], Luo [Ruiqing], Lu [Dingyi], and Yang [Shangkun] are such types, who contemplate in vain the launching of a counter-revolutionary coup. If we had not undertaken this Cultural Revolution or if we had not gone after them, they would have come to attack us. Right now there are many rumors, reactionary handbills, and reactionary anonymous letters expressing hatred toward the revolution. These are all signs of people hoping to be "restored to rule." When the time is ripe, these nasty types will come out and stir up trouble and rebel against the people. Some of these types take advantage of the organizational principle that "the lower echelon obeys the superior" to give orders to usurp political power and to change our social system. In actuality, they have been attacking us. Therefore, we must go for them and strike at them. If we do not attack them, they will attack us. This is why we say that there are great lurking perils. The Soviet Union had been in existence for forty years; but with the emergence of Khrushchev the entire country changed its color.

We must not fear chaos, but must put daring and not fear above everything else. Otherwise we shall commit errors, great political errors. Not to have faith in the masses is a great error. The Liu-Deng line does not believe in the masses, nor does it believe in Chairman Mao.

---

[10]Lin is referring to *Reference Document* No. 4, "Smashing the Old World to Pieces, Letting the Flowing Water Carry Away the Pieces Like Fallen Flowers," printed and distributed at the Central Work Conference. See Wang Nianyi, *Da dongluan de niandai (Years of Great Turmoil)* (Zhengzhou: Henan renmin chubanshe, 1988), p. 100.

Instead of believing in the masses, they believe only in themselves, in those who share their ideology, in the bourgeois world outlook, and in the bourgeois line.

Did not Chairman Mao raise the matter of preserving one's revolutionary integrity late in life? There are no other means of preserving one's revolutionary integrity than these: One is to have faith in Chairman Mao, the second is to have faith in the masses, and the third is to have a correct attitude toward oneself. This is in effect to observe Chairman Mao's five requirements of successors. Chairman Mao's first requirement of a proletarian revolutionary successor is that he believe in Marxism-Leninism, which is to believe in Chairman Mao and to believe in Mao Zedong Thought. Mao Zedong Thought and Marxism-Leninism stand in unity and differ only with respect to the time at which they emerged. Mao Zedong Thought is even more highly developed Marxism-Leninism.

The second requirement of proletarian revolutionary successors, according to Chairman Mao, is to serve the people. The third requirement is to unite with the great majority. The fourth requirement is to practice the system of democratic centralism. All these are part of having faith in the masses. Since the masses are the creators of history, we must not think that we are superior to them. In fact, what we may claim is only greater seniority. As far as genuine wisdom or moral character is concerned, it is doubtful whether we are on the same level as comrades like Lei Feng and Zhang Side. Therefore, although some comrades may be exalted in status and senior in qualifications, this does not imply that their thinking is more profound or their talents are greater than others. It may be said that there is indeed ever so much wisdom among the masses. You must not underestimate the students simply because they are only in their twenties. I have come across some who are truly bright and who are far more articulate than some of us in our fifties, sixties, seventies, or eighties.

Chairman Mao has said that the fifth requirement of proletarian revolutionary successors is that they must have a correct attitude toward themselves. How should one look at oneself? By dividing one into two. One may have some merits, but certainly one also has shortcomings. One should develop one's merits fully in order to contribute to the revolution. In regard to one's shortcomings, one should struggle continuously to adapt to the needs of the revolution. We must consider ourselves as parts of a revolutionary force and at the same time regard ourselves as objects of revolution. While making revolution, we must also make revolution within ourselves. Otherwise the revolution will not be successful. First of all, we must break out of our old habits and not just keep our own selves in mind. To see only to oneself is a limitation. A Marxist-Leninist must absolutely be able to transcend this kind of limitation. A different kind of limitation is to think only of which faction (*shantou*) do I belong to and to care only for that faction and nothing else. Some of our comrades think only of their own units, and are oblivious of the rest of the population in China and the world. This too is a limitation. Nor should we feel that we are special just because our present status is higher. We must liberate ourselves from this concern with our selves, with our limitations, and with our immediate unit. We must take the bigger unit and the totality into consideration. Chairman Mao says that the proletariat has to liberate not only itself, but the rest of mankind as well. Unless all of mankind is liberated, it will be impossible for the proletariat to achieve complete liberation. Consequently, we must endeavor to break all kinds of limitations imposed upon us.

The most important thing with respect to the preservation of one's revolutionary integrity late in life is to implement the five requirements of revolutionary successors as laid down by Chairman Mao. In a word, this means that we must have faith in Chairman Mao, have faith in the masses, and we must handle ourselves correctly.

Chairman Mao said: "We must have faith in the masses and we must have faith in the Party. These are two cardinal principles." This must be so now. We must have faith in Chairman Mao and have faith in the masses, for otherwise we shall not be successful in anything we do. To preserve one's revolutionary integrity late in life is indeed a very serious matter and not something that is necessarily easy. There are people who have engaged in revolution for thirty, forty, or fifty years, and they have reached the ages of fifty, sixty, seventy, or even eighty, and yet it is an open question whether they will be able to preserve their revolutionary integrity to the end. There are quite a few who have slipped in the last few years and failed to preserve their integrity. It is incumbent upon us to carefully and meticulously preserve our integrity in order to set an example for posterity. If we do not have faith in Chairman Mao and the masses, and if we are overly self-confident, then we will not be able to preserve our integrity.

The erroneous line in this cultural revolutionary movement was initiated primarily by Liu and Deng, but it was implemented in far too many places. This is a problem that concerns many comrades, and, of course, it should be dealt with in a discriminating fashion. There is a difference between initiating and implementing a policy, and between what is serious and what is light. Our general appraisal is that a majority of comrades were not self-conscious and did not at all intentionally resist Chairman Mao's line. In most cases it was a question of understanding and not a question of opposing the Party, socialism, and Mao Zedong Thought. We are all quite aware of this. The majority of our Regional Bureau secretaries, provincial Party secretaries, and municipal Party secretaries are good old fellows. There is the occasional bad guy, but a majority is good. Of course, you too have your responsibilities. The erroneous line was implemented to a varying extent in different regions, and your responsibilities are all different. In each case, the individual problem must be handled properly, without any over- or underestimation. People are often prone to forget that quantitative changes can cause qualitative changes. They look upon different quantities as being equal quantities and upon different qualities as being equal qualities. For instance, water freezes at zero degrees; it changes into water when the temperature rises above zero and into steam when the temperature passes a hundred. As the temperature changes, it changes into different things. Thus we should accord differential treatment to cadres at various levels instead of treating them uniformly. There are some serious cases and some light ones, but on the whole it is largely a question of understanding. There is only a small handful that has resisted Chairman Mao's correct line.

As long as our comrades strive to grasp Mao Zedong Thought, master the policies of the Party Center, have faith in the masses, and adopt a correct attitude toward the deviations and mistakes that may occur in their own work, they will be able to rectify them, perform their own tasks well, and come to work in a good mood and thus enable the entire Party under the banner of Mao Zedong Thought to unite even better and further.

3
"Mao Zedong Thought Is the Sole Criterion of Truth"

Zhou Enlai

Source: Translation of "Gei Shoudu dazhuan yuanxiao hongweibing geming zaofan zongbu de xin" (Letter to Capital University Red Guard Revolutionary Rebel Headquarters) in *Chinese Studies in Philosophy*, Vol. 25, No. 2, Winter 1993–94, pp. 15–16.

Students and fighters of the Revolutionary Rebel Headquarters of Red Guards in the Capital's Institutions of Higher Education:

Yesterday I gave a speech at a Red Guard mass rally organized by your headquarters in which I made one rather incomplete remark.[1] I now correct and complement that remark of mine as follows:

Immediately after "which you consider to be correct, and consider to be the truth, you may adhere to for some time," it should say "If in discussions or in practice, if you yourselves or someone else has proven that indeed they are wrong or partially wrong, then you should admit your mistakes and rectify them. If it has been proven that indeed they are correct or partially correct, then you should continue to adhere to those words or actions which are correct." This is, as Chairman Mao often teaches us, the principle of "adhering to the truth while rectifying one's mistakes." In the course of this Great Proletarian Cultural Revolution of ours there can be only one criterion of truth, and that is to measure everything against Mao Zedong Thought. Whatever accords with Mao Zedong Thought is right, while that which does not accord with Mao Zedong Thought is wrong. This is why Comrade Lin Biao tells us to "read Chairman Mao's works, obey Chairman Mao's words, and act according to Chairman Mao's instructions." This is something you must bear in mind constantly.

It is my hope that you shall be able to pass on these words to the Red Guards and revolutionary teachers and students.

Great Proletarian Cultural Revolutionary greetings,

Zhou Enlai

27 September [1966]

---

[1]A transcript of Zhou's speech is in Douzheng shenghuo bianjibu, ed., *Wuchanjieji wenhua dageming ziliao huibian* (*Collected Materials on the Great Proletarian Cultural Revolution*) (Beijing: Hebei Beijing shifan xueyuan, 1967), pp. 215–20.

B. Official Policy

Like most political initiatives launched by the CCP after 1949, the Cultural Revolution did not really *begin* with the announcement of a "resolution" in the national media. By the time the formal decision of the Central Committee (Document 4) appeared in the *People's Daily* on 9 August 1966, the movement had already been under way for some time—in secret at first, as Mao had plotted in Shanghai to remove the mayor of Beijing and make the national capital safe for "extensive democracy"; then publicly, in the form of a student movement so "noisy and boisterous" as to provoke complaints from resident foreign diplomats no longer able to fall asleep.[1]

The texts translated in this section represent but a fraction of the steady stream of orders, decrees, decisions, directives, "reference materials," editorials, etc., issued by the central authorities to set or alter the parameters of the movement. Unlike Mao's own "supreme instructions," the language in these bureaucratic communications is dry, formalistic, and repetitive. The CCP Chairman claimed he did not enjoy reading such "officialese" and on one memorable occasion—when speaking about a telegram sent, in his own name, by the CCP Central Committee to the Albanian Party of Labor—he even told Zhang Chunqiao "I never read such crap (*piwen*)."[2]

The birth of the Red Guard movement cannot be traced to a decree from Mao or the Party Center—it was a spontaneous event. But the ex-post-facto endorsement given it in the pages of *Red Flag* (Document 5) and *People's Daily* contributed directly to its remarkable growth. Young and restless Red Guards, out to "destroy the old world and build a new world," played highly visible roles on China's political stage throughout the autumn and winter of 1966. Military (Docu-

---

[1]Letter to Swedish Ministry of Foreign Affairs from the Swedish ambassador to China, Lennart Petri, dated 16 June 1966, in the Ministry Archives, File HP 1 XK.

[2]The telegram was issued in Mao's name but had actually been penned by Wang Li. Information from an official source.

ment 6) and public security organs were expressly forbidden from interfering with their "revolutionary acts of rebellion."

In January 1967, the Cultural Revolution entered a new phase, one of "revolutionary power seizures from below." The existing political structure had become paralyzed and the time appeared ripe to replace it with something better and "redder." There was some talk of instituting a system of general elections, like that of the Paris Commune. Mao, meanwhile, ordered the military and public security forces to rejoin the movement to suppress and punish anyone found "attacking or slandering our great leader Chairman Mao and his close comrade-in-arms Comrade Lin Biao" (Document 7) and to "give firm support to the revolutionary masses of the Left" (Document 8).

Although the "broad masses" were granted unprecedented political freedoms, it was not as if they were enjoying true democracy. Far from it: A variety of restrictions applied, for instance, to their freedom of association. "You may not," Zhou Enlai insisted, "bring people together from all over to set up your own independent nationwide, trans-provincial organization, because then what you will have done is to have created a political party."[3] The gist of Zhou's argument was repeated in policy documents banning nationwide organizations (Document 9), organizations formed specifically to lobby on behalf of the most underprivileged strata of the working class (Document 10), and so-called "ethnic mass organizations" (Document 11). China's peasants were simply asked to concentrate on spring cultivation and to desist from "rebelling" against rural Party cadres, most of whom were said by the Party Center to be "good or comparatively good" (Document 12).

In March 1967, *Red Flag* announced that so-called "three-in-one" organs made up of People's Liberation Army officers, revolutionary cadres, and representatives of the "masses" would replace the Party and government organs of the past (Document 13). The name given these new "provisional organs of power" was Revolutionary Committee. With the Party organization in tatters and the "masses" divided and

---

[3]"Zhou zongli di yi ci jiejian Neimeng si fangmian daibiao tanhua jiyao" (Record of Premier Zhou's First Meeting with Representatives of the Four Sides in Inner Mongolia) (10 February 1967), Dongfanghong zhandou zongdui, ed., *Zhongyang guanyu chuli Neimenggu wenti de youguan wenjian he Zhongyang fuze tongzhi jianghua* (*Documents and Central Leaders' Speeches Concerning the Center's Resolution of Problems in Inner Mongolia*), 2 vols. (Huhehot: Neimenggu shifan xueyuan, 1967), Vol. 1, p. 11.

circumscribed in their political freedom, the Revolutionary Committees became dominated by the PLA. The army was presented as the political model from which the rest of society was to "learn" (Document 14). As the months wore on, the Red Guards were sent back to school (Document 15), then demobilized, and finally dispatched to an uncertain future in China's countryside (Document 16). Meanwhile, by order of the Center, the CCP embarked upon the tortuous procedure of "rebuilding" itself (Document 17).

After April 1969, when the CCP finally convened its Ninth Party Congress and elected a new Central Committee, Western observers began to speak of the Cultural Revolution in the past tense. A distinct chapter in the history of the People's Republic of China had—so it seemed—been concluded. In fact, in some of its nastiest aspects, the movement was still far from over. Although scenes of screaming Red Guards dragging dunce-capped officials in front of kangaroo courts were a thing of the past, China was still far from a kinder, gentler place. Behind closed doors, the persecution of those who had resisted Mao's "greatest ever revolutionary transformation of society" continued unabated. The section ends with a translation of the top-secret circular *Zhongfa* [1970] 3, which marked the beginning, in 1970, of the so-called "One Hit Three Anti" (*yi da san fan*) campaign. According to conservative official estimates, this campaign led to the discovery of more than 1.84 million (and arrest of more than 284,800) "renegades," "special agents," and "counter-revolutionary elements" between February and November 1970.[4]

---

[4]Wang Nianyi, *Da dongluan de niandai* (*Years of Great Turmoil*) (Zhengzhou: Henan renmin chubanshe, 1988), p. 337.

4

Decision Concerning the Great Proletarian Cultural Revolution

CCP Central Committee

Source: Peking Review, No. 33, 1966, pp. 6–11. This decision was adopted by the Eleventh Plenum of the Eighth CCP Central Committee on 8 August 1966 and published in the *People's Daily* the next day.

1. A New Stage in the Socialist Revolution

The Great Proletarian Cultural Revolution now unfolding is a great revolution that touches people to their very souls and constitutes a new stage in the development of the socialist revolution in our country, a deeper and more extensive stage.

At the Tenth Plenary Session of the Eighth Central Committee of the Party, Comrade Mao Zedong said: To overthrow a political power, it is always necessary, first of all, to create public opinion, to do work in the ideological sphere. This is true for the revolutionary class as well as for the counter-revolutionary class. This thesis of Comrade Mao Zedong's has been proved entirely correct in practice.

Although the bourgeoisie has been overthrown, it is still trying to use the old ideas, culture, customs, and habits of the exploiting classes to corrupt the masses, capture their minds, and endeavor to stage a comeback. The proletariat must do just the opposite: It must meet head-on every challenge of the bourgeoisie in the ideological field and use the new ideas, culture, customs, and habits of the proletariat to change the mental outlook of the whole of society. At present, our objective is to struggle against and crush those persons in authority who are taking the capitalist road, to criticize and repudiate the reactionary bourgeois academic "authorities" and the ideology of the bourgeoisie and all other exploiting classes and to transform education, literature and art, and all other parts of the superstructure that do not correspond to the socialist economic base, so as to facilitate the consolidation and development of the socialist system.

2. The Main Current and the Zigzags

The masses of the workers, peasants, soldiers, revolutionary intellectuals, and revolutionary cadres form the main force in this Great Cultural Revolution. Large numbers of revolutionary young people, previously unknown, have become courageous and daring pathbreakers. They are vigorous in action and intelligent. Through the media of big-character posters and great debates, they argue things out, expose and criticize thoroughly, and launch resolute attacks on the open and hidden representatives of the bourgeoisie. In such a great revolutionary movement, it is hardly avoidable that they should show shortcomings of one kind or another, but their main revolutionary orientation has been correct from the beginning. This is the main current in the Great Proletarian Cultural Revolution. It is the main direction along which the Great Proletarian Cultural Revolution continues to advance.

Since the Cultural Revolution is a revolution, it inevitably meets with resistance. This resistance comes chiefly from those in authority who have wormed their way into the Party and are taking the capitalist road. It also comes from the old force of habit in society. At present, this resistance is still fairly strong and stubborn. However, the Great Proletarian Cultural Revolution is, after all, an irresistible general trend. There is abundant evidence that such resistance will crumble fast once the masses become fully aroused.

Because the resistance is fairly strong, there will be reversals and even repeated reversals in this struggle. There is no harm in this. It tempers the proletariat and other working people, and especially the younger generation, teaches them lessons and gives them experience, and helps them to understand that the revolutionary road is a zigzag one, and not plain sailing.

3. Put Daring above Everything Else and Boldly Arouse the Masses

The outcome of this Great Cultural Revolution will be determined by whether the Party leadership does or does not dare to boldly arouse the masses.

Currently, there are four different situations with regard to the leadership being given to the movement of the Cultural Revolution by Party organizations at various levels:

(a) There is the situation in which the persons in charge of Party organizations stand in the vanguard of the movement and dare to arouse the masses boldly. They put daring above everything else, they are dauntless communist fighters and good pupils of Chairman Mao. They advocate the big-character posters and great debates. They encourage the masses to expose every kind of ghost and monster and also to criticize the shortcomings and errors in the work of the persons in charge. This correct kind of leadership is the result of putting proletarian politics in the forefront and Mao Zedong's thought in the lead.

(b) In many units, the persons in charge have a very poor understanding of the task of leadership in this great struggle. Their leadership is far from being conscientious and effective, and they accordingly find themselves incompetent and in a weak position. They put fear above everything else, stick to outmoded ways and regulations, and are unwilling to break away from conventional practices and move ahead. They have been taken unawares by the new order of things, the revolutionary order of the masses, with the result that their leadership lags behind the situation, lags behind the masses.

(c) In some units, the persons in charge, who made mistakes of one kind or another in the past, are even more prone to put fear above everything else, being afraid that the masses will catch them out. Actually, if they make serious self-criticism and accept the criticism of the masses, the Party and the masses will make allowances for their mistakes. But if the persons in charge don't, they will continue to make mistakes and become obstacles to the mass movement.

(d) Some units are controlled by those who have wormed their way into the Party and are taking the capitalist road. Such persons in authority are extremely afraid of being exposed by the masses and therefore seek every possible pretext to suppress the mass movement. They resort to such tactics as shifting the targets for attack and turning black into white in an attempt to lead the movement astray. When they find themselves very isolated and no longer able to carry on as before, they resort still more to intrigues, stabbing people in the back, spreading rumors, and blurring the distinction between revolution and counterrevolution as much as they can, all for the purpose of attacking the revolutionaries.

What the Central Committee of the Party demands of the Party committees at all levels is that they persevere in giving correct leadership, put daring above everything else, boldly arouse the masses, change the state of weakness and incompetence where it exists, encourage those comrades who have made mistakes but are willing to correct them to cast off their mental burdens and join in the struggle, and dismiss from their leading posts all those in authority who are taking the capitalist road and so make possible the recapture of the leadership for the proletarian revolutionaries.

4. Let the Masses Educate Themselves in the Movement

In the Great Proletarian Cultural Revolution, the only method is for the masses to liberate themselves, and any method of doing things on their behalf must not be used.

Trust the masses, rely on them, and respect their initiative. Cast out fear. Don't be afraid of disorder. Chairman Mao has often told us that revolution cannot be so very refined, so gentle, so temperate, kind, courteous, restrained, and magnanimous. Let the masses educate themselves in this great revolutionary movement and learn to distinguish between right and wrong and between correct and incorrect ways of doing things.

Make the fullest use of big-character posters and great debates to argue matters out, so that the masses can clarify the correct views, criticize the wrong views, and expose all the ghosts and monsters. In this way the masses will be able to raise their political consciousness in the course of the struggle, enhance their abilities and talents, distinguish right from wrong and draw a clear line between the enemy and ourselves.

5. Firmly Apply the Class Line of the Party

Who are our enemies? Who are our friends? This is a question of the first importance for the revolution, and it is likewise a question of the first importance for the Great Cultural Revolution.

Party leadership should be good at discovering the Left and developing and strengthening the ranks of the Left, and should firmly rely on the revolutionary Left. During the movement this is the only way to isolate thoroughly the most reactionary rightists, win over the middle, and unite with the great majority so that by the end of the movement we shall achieve the unity of more than 95 percent of the cadres and more than 95 percent of the masses.

Concentrate all forces to strike at the handful of ultrareactionary bourgeois Rightist and counter-revolutionary revisionists, and expose and criticize to the full their crimes against the Party, against socialism and against Mao Zedong's thought so as to isolate them to the maximum.

The main target of the present movement is those within the Party who are in authority and are taking the capitalist road.

Care should be taken to distinguish strictly between the anti-Party, anti-socialist Rightists and those who support the Party and socialism but have said or done something wrong or have written some bad articles or other works.

Care should be taken to distinguish strictly between the reactionary bourgeois scholar despots and "authorities" on the one hand and people who have the ordinary bourgeois academic ideas on the other.

6. Correct Handling of Contradictions Among the People

A strict distinction must be made between the two different types of contradictions: those among the people and those between ourselves and the enemy. Contradictions among the people must not be made into contradictions between ourselves and the enemy; nor must contradictions between ourselves and the enemy be regarded as those among the people.

It is normal for the masses to hold different views. Contention between different views is unavoidable, necessary, and beneficial. In the course of normal and full debate, the masses will affirm what is right, correct what is wrong, and gradually reach unanimity.

The method to be used in debates is to present the facts, reason things out, and persuade through reasoning. Any method of forcing a minority holding different views to submit is impermissible. The minority should be protected, because sometimes the truth is with the minority. Even if the minority is wrong, they should still be allowed to argue their case and reserve their views.

When there is a debate, it should be conducted by reasoning, not by coercion or force.

In the course of debate, every revolutionary should be good at thinking things out for himself and should develop the communist spirit of daring to think, daring to speak, and daring to act. On the premise that they have the same main orientation, revolutionary comrades should, for the sake of strengthening unity, avoid endless debate over side issues.

7. Be on Guard against Those Who Brand the Revolutionary Masses as "Counter-Revolutionaries"

In certain schools, units, and work teams of the Cultural Revolution, some of the persons in charge have organized counter-attacks against the masses who put up big-character posters against them. These people have even advanced such slogans as: Opposition to the leaders of a unit or a work team means opposition to the Party's Central Committee, means opposition to the Party and socialism, means counter-revolution. In this way it is inevitable that their blows will fall on some really revolutionary activists. This is an error on matters of orientation, an error of line, and is absolutely impermissible.

A number of persons who suffer from serious ideological errors, and particularly some of the anti-Party and anti-socialist Rightists, are taking advantage of certain shortcomings and mistakes in the mass movement to spread rumors and gossip, and engage in agitation, deliberately branding some of the masses as "counter-revolutionaries." It is necessary to beware of such "pick-pockets" and expose their tricks in good time.

In the course of the movement, with the exception of cases of active counter-revolutionaries, where there is clear evidence of crimes such as murder, arson, poisoning, sabotage, or theft of state secrets, which should be handled in accordance with the law, no measures should be taken against students at universities, colleges, middle schools, and primary schools because of problems that arise in the movement. To prevent the struggle from being diverted from its main objective, it is not allowed, whatever the pretext, to incite the masses to struggle against each other or the students to do likewise. Even proven Rightists should be dealt with on the merits of each case at a later stage of the movement.

8. The Question of Cadres

The cadres fall roughly into the following four categories:
    (a) good;
    (b) comparatively good;

(c) those who have made serious mistakes but have not become anti-Party, anti-socialist Rightists;

(d) the small number of anti-Party, anti-socialist Rightists.

In ordinary situations, the first two categories (good and comparatively good) are the great majority.

The anti-Party, anti-socialist Rightists must be fully exposed, hit hard, pulled down, and completely discredited and their influence eliminated. At the same time, they should be given a way out so that they can turn over a new leaf.

9. Cultural Revolutionary Groups, Committees, and Congresses

Many new things have begun to emerge in the Great Proletarian Cultural Revolution. The cultural revolutionary groups, committees, and other organizational forms created by the masses in many schools and units are something new and of great historic importance.

These cultural revolutionary groups, committees, and congresses are excellent new forms of organization whereby under the leadership of the Communist Party the masses are educating themselves. They are an excellent bridge to keep our Party in close contact with the masses. They are organs of power of the Proletarian Cultural Revolution.

The struggle of the proletariat against the old ideas, culture, customs, and habits left over by all the exploiting classes over thousands of years will necessarily take a very, very long time. Therefore, the cultural revolutionary groups, committees, and congresses should not be temporary organizations but permanent, standing mass organizations. They are suitable not only for colleges, schools, and government and other organizations, but generally also for factories, mines, other enterprises, urban districts, and villages.

It is necessary to institute a system of general elections, like that of the Paris Commune, for electing members to the cultural revolutionary groups and committees and delegates to the cultural revolutionary congresses. The lists of candidates should be put forward by the revolutionary masses after full discussion, and the elections should be held after the masses have discussed the lists over and over again.

The masses are entitled at any time to criticize members of the cultural revolutionary groups and committees and delegates elected to the cultural revolutionary congresses. If these members or delegates prove incompetent, they can be replaced through election or recalled by the masses after discussion.

The cultural revolutionary groups, committees, and congresses in colleges and schools should consist mainly of representatives of the revolutionary students. At the same time, they should have a certain number of representatives of the revolutionary teaching staff and workers.

10. Educational Reform

In the Great Proletarian Cultural Revolution a most important task is to transform the old educational system and the old principles and methods of teaching.

In this Great Cultural Revolution, the phenomenon of our schools being dominated by bourgeois intellectuals must be completely changed.

In every kind of school we must apply thoroughly the policy advanced by Comrade Mao Zedong of education serving proletarian politics and education being combined with productive labor, so as to enable those receiving an education to develop morally, intellectually, and physically and to become laborers with socialist consciousness and culture.

The period of schooling should be shortened. Courses should be fewer and better. The teaching material should be thoroughly transformed, in some cases beginning with simplifying complicated material. While their main task is to study, students should also learn other things. That is to say, in addition to their studies they should also learn industrial work, farming, and military affairs and take part in the struggles of the Cultural Revolution as they occur to criticize the bourgeoisie.

11. The Question of Criticizing by Name in the Press

In the course of the mass movement of the Cultural Revolution, the criticism of bourgeois and feudal ideology should be well combined with the dissemination of the proletarian world outlook and of Marxism-Leninism, Mao Zedong's thought.

Criticism should be organized of typical bourgeois representatives who have wormed their way into the Party and typical reactionary bourgeois academic "authorities," and this should include criticism of various kinds of reactionary views in philosophy, history, political economy, and education, in works and theories of literature and art, in theories of natural science, and in other fields.

Criticism of anyone by name in the press should be decided after discussion by the Party committee at the same level, and in some cases submitted to the Party committee at a higher level for approval.

12. Policy toward Scientists, Technicians, and Ordinary Members of Working Staffs

As regards scientists, technicians, and ordinary members of working staffs, as long as they are patriotic, work energetically, are not against the Party and socialism, and maintain no illicit relations with any foreign country, we should in the present movement continue to apply the policy of "unity, criticism, unity." Special care should be taken of those scientists and scientific and technical personnel who have made contributions. Efforts should be made to help them gradually transform their world outlook and their style of work.

13. The Question of Arrangements for Integration with the Socialist Education Movement in City and Countryside

The cultural and educational units and leading organs of the Party and government in the large and medium cities are the points of concentration of the present Proletarian Cultural Revolution.

The Great Cultural Revolution has enriched the socialist education movement in both city and countryside and raised it to a higher level. Efforts should be made to conduct these two movements in close combination. Arrangements to this effect may be made by various regions and departments in the light of the specific conditions.

The socialist education movement now going on in the countryside and in enterprises in the cities should not be upset where the original arrangements are appropriate and the movement is going well, but should continue in accordance with the original arrangements. However, the questions that are arising in the present Great Proletarian Cultural Revolution should be put to the masses for discussion at the proper time, so as to further foster vigorously proletarian ideology and eradicate bourgeois ideology.

In some places, the Great Proletarian Cultural Revolution is being used as the focus in order to add momentum to the socialist education movement and clean things up in the fields of politics, ideology, organization, and economy. This may be done where the local Party committee thinks it appropriate.

14. Take Firm Hold of the Revolution and Stimulate Production

The aim of the Great Proletarian Cultural Revolution is to revolutionize people's ideology and as a consequence to achieve greater, faster, better, and more economical results in all fields of work. If the masses are fully aroused and proper arrangements are made, it is possible to carry on both the Cultural Revolution and production without one hampering the other, while guaranteeing high quality in all our work.

The Great Proletarian Cultural Revolution is a powerful motive force for the development of the social productive forces in our country. Any idea of counterposing the Great Cultural Revolution to the development of production is incorrect.

15. The Armed Forces

In the armed forces, the Cultural Revolution and the socialist education movement should be carried out in accordance with the instructions of the Military Commission of the Central Committee and the General Political Department of the People's Liberation Army.

16. Mao Zedong's Thought Is the Guide for Action in the Great Proletarian Cultural Revolution

In the Great Proletarian Cultural Revolution, it is imperative to hold aloft the great red banner of Mao Zedong's thought and put proletarian politics in command. The movement for the creative study and application of Chairman Mao Zedong's works should be carried forward among the masses of the workers, peasants, and soldiers, the cadres and the intellectuals, and Mao Zedong's thought should be taken as the guide to action in the Cultural Revolution.

In this complex Great Cultural Revolution, Party committees at all levels must study and apply Chairman Mao's works all the more con-scientiously and in a creative way. In particular, they must study over and over again Chairman Mao's writings on the Cultural Revolution and on the Party's methods of leadership, such as *On New Democracy, Talks at the Yan'an Forum on Literature and Art, On the Correct Handling of Contradictions among the People, Speech at the Chinese Communist Party's National Conference on Propaganda Work, Some Questions Concerning Methods of Leadership,* and *Methods of Work of Party Committees.*

Party committees at all levels must abide by the directions given by Chairman Mao over the years, namely that they should thoroughly apply the mass line of "from the masses and to the masses" and that they should be pupils before they become teachers. They should try to avoid being one sided or narrow. They should foster materialist dialectics and oppose metaphysics and scholasticism.

The Great Proletarian Cultural Revolution is bound to achieve brilliant victory under the leadership of the Central Committee of the Party headed by Comrade Mao Zedong.

5
In Praise of the Red Guards

Red Flag Commentator

Source: *Peking Review,* No. 39, 1966, pp. 15–16. This commentary first appeared in *Red Flag,* No. 12, on 17 September 1966.

The revolutionary people throughout China are now vying with each other in praising the Red Guards.

The revolutionary initiative of the Red Guards has shaken the whole world.

The Red Guards are something new that has emerged in the tempest of the Great Proletarian Cultural Revolution; they were born and are growing up in the Great Proletarian Cultural Revolution.

The Red Guards have been nurtured in their growth by Mao

Zedong's thought. The Red Guards say, and say it well: Chairman Mao is our red commander, and we are the young, red soldiers of Chairman Mao.

What our Red Guards love most of all is to read Chairman Mao's works and follow his teachings, and their love for Mao Zedong's thought is most ardent. They carry with them copies of *Quotations from Chairman Mao Zedong*. They take as their highest obligation the study, dissemination, application, and defense of Mao Zedong's thought.

In the Great Proletarian Cultural Revolution, which was personally started and is being personally led by Chairman Mao, the Red Guards have resolutely carried out courageous and stubborn struggles against those in authority who take the capitalist road and against all ghosts and monsters, and they have become the path breakers in the Great Proletarian Cultural Revolution.

After the publication of the "Decision of the Central Committee of the Chinese Communist Party Concerning the Great Proletarian Cultural Revolution," which was drawn up under his personal direction, Chairman Mao, the great leader, and Comrade Lin Biao, his close comrade-in-arms, reviewed the Red Guards in the Chinese capital on 18 August. With the direct encouragement of the great supreme commander Chairman Mao, the Red Guards and other revolutionary organizations of the young people set going a new high tide in the Great Cultural Revolution.

Coming out of their schools and into the streets, the tens of millions of Red Guards formed an irresistible revolutionary torrent. Holding aloft the red banner of the invincible thought of Mao Zedong and displaying the proletarian, revolutionary spirit of daring to think, to speak, to act, to break through, and to rise up in revolution, they are cleaning up the muck left over by the old society and sweeping away the rubbish accumulated over thousands of years of history.

The Red Guards have done many good things and put forward many good suggestions. In accordance with Chairman Mao's teachings, they have achieved brilliant results in the struggle to eradicate the old ideas, culture, customs, and habits of the exploiting classes and to foster the new ideas, culture, customs, and habits of the proletariat.

The Red Guards are the shock force of the Great Proletarian Cultural Revolution. Their revolutionary actions have roused revolutionary fervor among the masses, bringing about a vigorous mass movement on a still greater scale. Such a sweeping revolutionary mass movement has engulfed in the vast sea of the revolutionary masses the handful of persons in power who have wormed their way into the Party and have taken the capitalist road. Without such a large-scale mass movement, it would be impossible to destroy the social basis on which the handful of bourgeois Rightists rests and to carry through the Great Proletarian Cultural Revolution thoroughly and in depth.

The Red Guards are a new phenomenon on the eastern horizon. The revolutionary youngsters are the symbol of the future and the hope of the proletariat. Revolutionary dialectics tells us that the newborn forces are invincible, that they inevitably grow and develop in struggle and in the end defeat the decaying forces. Therefore, we shall certainly sing the praises of the new, eulogize it, beat the drums to encourage it, bang the gongs to clear a way for it, and raise our hands high in welcome.

Our Red Guards have performed immortal meritorious deeds in the course of the Great Proletarian Cultural Revolution. Chairman Mao and the Central Committee of the Party enthusiastically praise their soaring revolutionary spirit, and the broad masses of workers, peasants, and soldiers enthusiastically acclaim their revolutionary actions.

The revolutionary actions of the revolutionary young fighters are indeed excellent! Their meritorious deeds in the Great Cultural Revolution will go down forever in the revolutionary history of the proletariat.

The Red Guards are learning to swim by swimming, are learning to make a revolution by taking part in it. What they demand of themselves is not only to have the daring to struggle and make revolution, but to be good at struggle, good at revolution. On the basis of the experience they themselves have gained in practice, they are now further studying the sixteen-point decision of the Party's Central Committee concerning the Great Proletarian Cultural Revolution, grasping it, and applying it.

Having received the warm praise of Chairman Mao and the broad masses of the workers, peasants, and soldiers, the revolutionary young fighters are now reminding themselves to guard against conceit and rashness and to learn modestly from the People's Liberation Army and the masses of the workers and peasants. They are determined to raise their political consciousness still further and heighten their sense of organization and discipline in accordance with the "three-eight" working style of the People's Liberation Army and the Three Main Rules of Discipline and the Eight Points for Attention.[1] They are resolved to temper themselves in the furnace of revolution so as to become revolutionary fighters of the type of Lei Feng, Wang Jie, Mai Xiande, and Liu Yingjun, to become Communists who are utterly devoted to others without any thought of self, to become the successors to the revolutionary cause of the proletariat.

Different classes take different views of the revolutionary actions of the Red Guards. The revolutionary classes regard them as extremely good, while the counter-revolutionary classes look upon them as extremely bad.

Revolutionary people throughout the world have applauded these revolutionary actions and paid high tribute to the Red Guards. On the other hand, the imperialists, the reactionaries of all countries, the modern revisionists, and the Chiang Kai-shek bandit gang are cursing the Red Guards in the most venomous language. They have vilified the Red Guards as "young fanatics" and attacked their revolutionary actions as "violating human dignity," "destroying social traditions," and so on and so forth.

Chairman Mao has taught us that to be attacked by the enemy is not a bad thing but a good thing. It is still better if the enemy attacks us wildly and paints us in the worst colors and without a single virtue. It is indeed a great honor for the Red Guards that they have been attacked wildly by the class enemies at home and abroad.

"Young fanatics!" Invariably the enemies of revolution are extremely hostile to the revolutionary enthusiasm of the masses, and they smear it as "fanatical." And it is precisely what the enemy hates that we love. Not only must the revolutionary young fighters maintain their

---

[1]The "three-eight" working style of the PLA refers to the three phrases and eight characters written by Mao Zedong to describe the working style that officers and men were exhorted to adopt. The three phrases are: correct political orientation, a simple and arduous working style, and flexible strategy and tactics. The eight characters are *tuanjie, jinzhang, yansu,* and *huopo,* and translated into English they mean "united, alert, earnest, and lively." The Three Main Rules of Discipline are: (1) obey orders in all actions, (2) do not take even a needle or thread from the masses, and (3) turn in everything captured. The Eight Points for Attention are: (1) speak politely, (2) pay fairly for what you buy, (3) return everything you borrow, (4) pay for anything you damage, (5) do not hit or swear at people, (6) do not damage crops, (7) do not take liberties with women, and (8) do not ill treat captives.

exuberant revolutionary enthusiasm, they must also further display their soaring revolutionary spirit.

"Violating human dignity!" The Red Guards have ruthlessly castigated, exposed, criticized, and repudiated the decadent, reactionary culture of the bourgeoisie, and they have exposed the ugly features of the bourgeois Rightists to the bright light of day, landing them in the position of rats running across the street and being chased by all. So they shout: "This violates human dignity." To speak frankly, we should not only violate their "dignity" but knock them down so that they can never rise up again.

"Destroying social traditions?" You are right. The Red Guards do want to destroy the traditions of the landlords and the bourgeoisie. The revolutionary young fighters want precisely to make a clean sweep of the remaining viruses of feudalism, eliminate the germs of capitalism, and dig out the evil roots of revisionism. Only by utterly destroying the various old traditions of the exploiting classes is it possible to carry on and develop the revolutionary traditions of the proletariat.

In accordance with the directives of Chairman Mao and the Party's Central Committee, the young Red Guard fighters are concentrating all forces to strike at the handful of bourgeois Rightists, and their main target is those in power within the Party who are taking the capitalist road. In doing so, they are removing the time bombs planted in China by imperialism and revisionism. Therefore, it is quite natural that the imperialists and revisionists should feel shocked, enraged, and bitter about the revolutionary actions of the Red Guards.

That mouthpiece of the reactionary classes Pope Paul VI helplessly blurted out that for them the revolutionary actions of the Red Guards were "a sign of death and not a sign of life." Yes, indeed. The revolutionary actions taken by the revolutionary young fighters are a sure sign of final destruction for the class enemies at home and abroad. And our Red Guards are a symbol that the revolutionary cause of the proletariat is prospering and has unlimited vitality.

Like the red sun rising in the east, the unprecedented Great Proletarian Cultural Revolution is illuminating the land with its brilliant rays.

Long live the Red Guards armed with Mao Zedong's thought!

Long live Chairman Mao, our great teacher, great leader, supreme commander, and great helmsman!

6
Regulations Forbidding the Use of Military Force to Suppress the Revolutionary Student Movement

PLA General Staff and General Political Department

Source: These regulations ("Guanyu juedui buxu dongyong budui wuzhuang zhenya geming xuesheng yundong de guiding") were ratified and circulated by the CCP Center on 21 August 1966 in the form of Central Document *Zhongfa* [1966] 416 (classified "crucially secret"). Our translation is based on the text reproduced in People's Liberation Army National Defense University Research Institute for Party History, Party Building, and Political Work, ed., *"Wenhua dageming" yanjiu ziliao ("Great Cultural Revolution" Research Materials)* (Beijing, 1988), Vol. 1, pp. 90–91.

When students recently took to the streets to demonstrate in Guilin, Xi'an, Lanzhou, Baotou, and other places, local Party and government organs asked for contingents of armed soldiers to be mobilized to protect their premises. In Guilin, an entire armed battalion has apparently been mobilized for contingency use. In other places, demands have been made for carloads of soldiers to be sent to factories and schools to talk to and dissuade the students from demonstrating. As a result, the relationship between the army and the students has become quite tense, and some students and masses have engaged the soldiers in arguments and put up big-character posters. Teachers and students in some schools have sent a stream of telegrams to the Central Military Commission claiming that revolutionary teachers and students are being surrounded by the army. The situation has already pitted the army against the revolutionary students, and we must regard it with the utmost seriousness. Consequently, we have drawn up the following regulations:

1. No part of the armed forces may under any circumstance suppress the revolutionary student movement by force, much less open fire at the students. Even to fire blanks at the students is a serious political error against which serious disciplinary action will be taken.

2. If the local Party and government authorities invite the army to join the National Day celebrations, the army may with permission from the Party Committee of the Military Region allow a limited number of

men to take part, but they must not under any circumstances bear arms.

3. Regardless of the circumstances, the local Party and government authorities may mobilize the army only with the permission of the Central Military Commission.

4. The army should not become involved when students clash with other students or with the masses. Definite cases of active counter-revolution such as manslaughter, arson, poisoning, destruction of property, and theft of state secrets should be handled according to law by local public security organs. In such cases, if the power of the public security organs is insufficient and if requests for help are made, the army may provide assistance.

5. The army should not send soldiers to factories and schools to engage in propaganda and dissuasion.

6. The army should not put up big-character posters criticizing the local schools, factories, or government organs. The army should warmly welcome the [critical] big-character posters directed at it appearing in local schools, factories, and government organs.

7. Any person who attempts to avoid the struggle by escaping to and hiding on military premises should be asked to go back to where he came from and not be given a hiding place.

All units must earnestly respect and implement the above regulations.

7
Regulations on Strengthening Public Security Work in the Great Proletarian Cultural Revolution

CCP Center and State Council

Source: These regulations ("Guanyu zai wuchanjieji wenhua dageming zhong jiaqiang gongan gongzuo de ruogan guiding") were issued on 13 January 1967 as Central Document *Zhongfa* [1967] 19. Our translation is based on a copy of the text as printed by the Beijing Politics and Law Institute "Politics and Law Commune" on 16 January 1967 in the form of a 15 × 21–inch public notice.

The Great Proletarian Cultural Revolution is a movement for promoting extensive democracy under the command of Mao Zedong Thought and the conditions of proletarian dictatorship. It has aroused the revolutionary activism of the broad masses. The situation is excellent. Without the dictatorship of the proletariat, it is not possible to practice extensive democracy among the masses of the people. The public security organs are an important tool of the dictatorship of the proletariat. They must adapt to the needs of the situation and progress of the Great Proletarian Cultural Revolution, take appropriate measures, strengthen dictatorship over the enemy, safeguard the democratic rights of the people, and protect the normal progress of full and frank airing of views, big-character posters, debate, and exchange of revolutionary experience. For this purpose, it is specially provided that:

1. Definite cases of active counter-revolution such as manslaughter, arson, poisoning, hostage-taking, causing traffic accidents, assassination, storming prisons or detention facilities, illicit foreign contacts, theft of state secrets, and other acts of subversion should be punished according to law.

2. To send counter-revolutionary anonymous letters, to post or distribute counter-revolutionary handbills in secret or in public, or to write or shout reactionary slogans attacking or slandering our great leader Chairman Mao and his close comrade-in-arms Comrade Lin Biao constitutes an act of active counter-revolution and should be punished according to law.

3. Protect the revolutionary masses and their organizations, protect the Left, and strictly prohibit armed struggle. It is unlawful to attack the revolutionary mass organizations or to assault or detain the revolutionary masses. In general, the Party and government leadership and the revolutionary mass organizations are to respond by engaging in criticism and education. Leading offenders who have beaten representatives of the popular masses to death, assailants who have committed serious offenses, and persons manipulating events from behind the scenes are to be punished according to law.

4. Landlord, rich-peasant, counter-revolutionary, hooligan, and Rightist elements; persons subject to education through labor or ordered to remain in [labor] camps (plants) after the completion of their sentences; reactionary party or league hard-core elements; intermediate and minor heads of reactionary religious sects and professional [reactionary] religious practitioners; members of enemy

and puppet armies (above the rank of company commander), governments (above the rank of *bao* chief), police forces (above the rank of sergeant-major), military police forces, and secret services; elements who in spite of having completed their assigned education through labor have not been satisfactorily reformed; speculators; and family dependents of executed, imprisoned, publicly supervised, or escaped counter-revolutionary elements who cling to their reactionary stand may under no circumstances travel to exchange revolutionary experience, change their names, or worm their way into revolutionary mass organizations with a fabricated personal history. Nor are they allowed to engage in manipulation or agitation from behind the scenes, much less set up their own organizations. Such elements committing subversive acts are to be severely punished according to law.

5. In general, anyone who utilizes extensive democracy or other means to spread reactionary utterances is to be struggled against[1] by the revolutionary masses. In serious cases, the public security organs should work in concert with the revolutionary masses to conduct timely investigation and when needed take action according to the circumstances.

6. If the personnel of party, government, military, and public security organs distort the above regulations and fabricate facts to suppress the revolutionary masses, they must be investigated and dealt with according to law.

The above regulations should be propagated among the broad masses. The revolutionary masses should be called upon to assist and supervise the public security organs in carrying out their duties, to uphold revolutionary order, and to ensure that the personnel of public security organs are able to carry out their duties in a normal way.

These regulations may be widely posted in the cities and in the countryside.

---

[1]"Struggled against" is a term commonly used to mean public denunciation and humiliation, and physical abuse, at an ad hoc mass rally.

8

Decision to Provide the Revolutionary Masses of the Left with the Firm Support of the People's Liberation Army

CCP Center, State Council, Central Military Commission, and Central Cultural Revolution Group

> *Source:* This decision ("Guanyu renmin jiefangjun jianjue zhichi geming zuopai qunzhong de jueding") was announced on 23 January 1967 in Central Document *Zhongfa* [1967] 27. Our translation is based on the text in CCP Central Committee General Office and State Council General Office Joint Cultural Revolution Reception Office, ed., *Wuchanjieji wenhua dageming youguan wenjian huiji* (*Collection of Documents Concerning the Great Proletarian Cultural Revolution*), 5 vols. (Beijing, 1967–68), Vol. 1, pp. 64–68.

To all Central Committee Regional Bureaus, all military regions, all provincial, municipal, and autonomous regional Party Committees and People's Councils and, through them, to the Party Committees and People's Councils at various levels and the military districts and military subdistricts:

Under the leadership of Chairman Mao, the Great Proletarian Cultural Revolution has entered a new stage. The main characteristic of this stage is that the proletarian revolutionaries have formed great alliances to seize power from the handful of Party-persons in power taking the capitalist road and the diehard-elements clinging to the bourgeois reactionary line. This struggle to seize power is a general counter-attack of the proletariat against the frantic attacks over the last seventeen years by the bourgeoisie and its agents within the Party. This is a nationwide, all-round class struggle and a great revolution in which one class overthrows another.

The People's Liberation Army is a proletarian revolutionary army personally created by Chairman Mao. It is a most vital tool of the proletarian dictatorship. In this great struggle of the proletariat to seize power from the bourgeoisie, the People's Liberation Army must firmly take the side of the proletarian revolutionaries and resolutely support and help the proletarian revolutionary Leftists.

Recently, Chairman Mao directed: The People's Liberation Army should support the broad masses of the Left. From now on, the demands of all true revolutionaries for support and assistance from the army should be satisfied. The so-called "non-involvement" of the army is bogus, as the armed forces have been involved already for quite some time. The question is not one of involvement or noninvolvement, but one of choosing sides and of deciding whether to support the revolutionaries or the conservatives, or even the Rightists. The People's Liberation Army should actively support the revolutionary Leftists.

All commanders and fighters of our armed forces must resolutely carry out Chairman Mao's directive.

1. All past directives concerning the army's noninvolvement in the local [i.e., civilian—Ed.] Great Cultural Revolution and other directives that violate the above spirit are null and void.

2. Active support must be rendered to the broad masses of revolutionary Leftists in their struggle to seize power. When genuine proletarian Leftists ask the army for help, the army should send troops to actively support them.

3. Counter-revolutionaries and counter-revolutionary organizations who oppose the proletarian revolutionary Leftists must be resolutely suppressed. Should they resort to force, the army should strike back with force.

4. This directive reaffirms that the army must not be an air-raid shelter for a handful of Party-persons in power taking the capitalist road and diehard elements clinging to the bourgeois reactionary line.

5. The whole army should be given a penetrating education on the struggle between the proletarian revolutionary line represented by Chairman Mao and the bourgeois reactionary line represented by Liu Shaoqi and Deng Xiaoping.

This directive should be transmitted word for word to every PLA fighter.

9
Public Notice Banning Nationwide Organizations

CCP Center and State Council

Source: This public notice was issued on 12 February 1967 in the form of Central Document *Zhongfa* [1967] 47. Our translation is based on the text reproduced in CCP Central Committee General Office and State Council General Office Joint Cultural Revolution Reception Office, ed., *Wuchanjieji wenhua dageming youguan wenjian huiji* (*Collection of Documents Concerning the Great Proletarian Cultural Revolution*), 5 vols. (Beijing, 1967–68), Vol. 1, pp. 154–56.

In this Great Proletarian Cultural Revolution, a number of so-called nationwide organizations have appeared in Beijing and elsewhere. None of them have come about through great alliances based on nationwide democratic elections of genuine revolutionaries, from lower levels to higher levels. Instead, they have been formed by small numbers of people banding together temporarily. A tiny number of these organizations have been set up by landlord, rich-peasant, counter-revolutionary, hooligan, and Rightist elements. The CCP Center and the State Council have therefore decided as follows:

1. The Center does not recognize any so-called nationwide organizations. All such organizations should disband immediately. Their members should immediately return from Beijing, or elsewhere, to where they came from and take part in the movement in their own units.

2. The public funds that these organizations have obtained under various pretexts should be demanded back in full by the units that approved the initial payment. An account, to be audited by the unit that approved payment, must be made of the money spent prior to the receipt of this notice. Articles purchased must be retrieved, except those consumed. Money drawn after the receipt of this notice may not be spent. Anybody absconding with money is to be prosecuted and punished according to law.

3. If it turns out that any of these organizations have been engaged in counter-revolutionary activities, their members must inform the public security organs, which in turn will be responsible for investigating and handling the matter.

The above has hereby been announced.

10
Public Notice Concerning Workers' Organizations

CCP Center and State Council

Source: This public notice was issued on 17 February 1967 in the form of Central Document *Zhongfa* [1967] 55. Our translation is based on the text reproduced in CCP Central Committee General Office and State Council General Office Joint Cultural Revolution Reception Office, ed., *Wuchanjieji wenhua dageming youguan wenjian huiji* (*Collection of Documents Concerning the Great Proletarian Cultural Revolution*), 5 vols. (Beijing, 1967–68), Vol. 1, pp. 179–82.

1. The joint notice issued by the National General Rebel Corps of Red Laborers, Ministry of Labor, and All-China Federation of Trade Unions on 2 January 1967 is illegal and should be canceled.[1] All documents passed by provincial and municipal Labor Bureaus on the basis of the joint notice issued by the three organizations are null and void.

2. The systems governing the employment of temporary workers, contract workers, rotation workers, and outside contract laborers are rational in some cases and quite irrational and erroneous in other cases. The Center is presently studying ways of reforming these systems depending on actual conditions. Before the Center makes a new decision, the established methods are to be followed as usual.

3. Temporary workers, contract workers, rotation workers, and outside contract laborers employed by various enterprises and units are to enjoy political rights equal to those enjoyed by permanent workers, staff members, and other functionaries, and have the right to participate in the Great Proletarian Cultural Revolution.

4. Those temporary workers, contract workers, rotation workers, and outside contract laborers who were branded "counter-revolutionary" for criticizing the leadership during the initial period of the Great Proletarian Cultural Revolution should be acquitted of their charges, and those who were dismissed for the same reason should be allowed to

---

[1]For a discussion of the joint notice and the radical changes to China's labor system proposed by the National General Rebel Corps of Red Laborers, see Xiaoxia Gong, "Repressive Movements and the Politics of Victimization: Patronage and Persecution during the Cultural Revolution" (Ph.D. diss., Harvard University, Dept. of Sociology, 1995), pp. 257–65.

return to their former jobs and work according to their former contracts. They should be paid the wages owed to them.

5. The ranks of temporary workers, contract workers, rotation workers, and outside contract laborers must be purged of landlord, rich-peasant, counter-revolutionary, hooligan, and Rightist elements (not referring to family background) clinging to a reactionary stand. Persons who assume the name of a revolutionary organization to swindle and bluff others must be exposed resolutely.

6. Temporary workers, contract workers, rotation workers, and outside contract laborers need not form independent organizations. The National General Rebel Corps of Red Laborers and its branches all over the country are to disband. Members of the revolutionary masses who had joined this organization may join the revolutionary mass organizations in their own enterprises, units, or localities.

This notice is to be displayed in public throughout the country.

11
"No Ethnic Mass Organizations"

CCP Center and Shaanxi Ankang District Committee

Source: "Zhonggong Zhongyang guanyu Shaanxi Ankang diwei wenge bangongshi laidian de pishi" (CCP Center Comment/Instruction on Telegram from Shaanxi Ankang District Committee Cultural Revolution Office), first circulated as Central Document *Zhongfa* [1967] 112 on 29 March 1967. Our translation is based on the reprint in Baotou Municipal Revolutionary Committee Propaganda Group, ed., *Wuchanjieji wenhua dageming wenjian huibian* (*Collected Documents from the Great Proletarian Cultural Revolution*) (Baotou, 1968), p. 178.

To Party Committees at all levels, military region and district Party Committees, and provincial and municipal Revolutionary Committees:

We are now transmitting to you the text of a telegram from the Shaanxi Ankang District Committee Cultural Revolution Office, hoping that you will pay attention to this matter and strengthen education concerning ethnic policy.

Chairman Mao teaches us: The ethnic struggle is, ultimately, a matter of class struggle. The Center is of the opinion that in order to promote a great alliance of proletarian revolutionaries and the unity of the various nationalities, and in order to prevent bad people from exploiting ethnic sentiment to create ethnic disputes, it is inadvisable in the course of this Great Proletarian Cultural Revolution to set up separate ethnic mass organizations in the various regions or to give mass organizations ethnic designations. Organizations of this nature that already have come into existence should be called upon to disband of their own accord. Their members may on a voluntary basis join other revolutionary mass organizations in their own work units or systems.

[Original] appendix: *Telegram from the Shaanxi Ankang District Committee Cultural Revolution Office*

To the Office of the Central Cultural Revolution Group:

Ours is not a region where there are many Muslims, and yet a top-to-bottom Muslim Revolutionary Rebel Command has been set up here. Furthermore, the District Committee United Front Department recently issued notifications to county-level United Front Departments asking Party organizations everywhere to work out and decide upon effective measures in support of rebelling revolutionary Muslims, and calling upon Party Committees in Muslim residential areas to resolutely implement and carry out [these measures]. We are of the opinion that this action is detrimental to the strengthening of ethnic unity, detrimental to the interests of the working class as a whole, and detrimental to the establishment of Great Alliances according to systems and sectors. Please issue instructions as quickly as possible on how to deal with organizations like these.

Shaanxi Ankang District Committee
Cultural Revolution Office
17 March 1967

12
Letter to Poor and Lower-Middle Peasants and Cadres at All Levels in Rural People's Communes All Over the Country

CCP Central Committee

Source: Peking Review, No. 9, 1967, p. 6. Circulated on 20 February 1967 as Central Document *Zhongfa* [1967] 58.

Poor and Lower-Middle Peasant Comrades!

Comrade Cadres Doing Rural Work:

The poor and lower-middle peasants are the main force taking firm hold of the revolution and promoting production in the countryside. At the start of the present spring cultivation, Chairman Mao and the Party's Central Committee call on you to take firm hold of the revolution and promote production conscientiously, mobilize all forces, and set to immediately to get the spring cultivation done well.

Cadres at all levels in the rural people's communes must be good at consulting with the poor and lower-middle peasants and all the laboring masses to get an upsurge going in spring cultivation.

The Party's Central Committee believes that the overwhelming majority of cadres at all levels in the rural people's communes are good or comparatively good. Those comrades who have made mistakes should also work hard in the spring cultivation so as to make amends by good deeds for their mistakes. As long as cadres who have made mistakes act in this way, the poor and lower-middle peasants should show understanding and support them in their work. The attitude to be taken in criticizing them must be that of "learning from past mistakes to avoid future ones and curing the sickness to save the patient," which Chairman Mao has always taught.

Landlords, rich-peasants, counter-revolutionaries, bad elements, and Rightists are categorically not permitted to be unruly in word or deed, to sabotage production or the unity among the working people, or to incite factional disputes. They must diligently continue to reform themselves through labor under the supervision of the poor and lower-middle peasants.

Former cadres removed from office in the "four clean-ups" movement must take an active part in labor and remould themselves. They are not allowed to counter-attack in revenge.

We recommend that you consider convening immediate conferences of cadres from the three levels of the people's commune, production brigade, and production team to arrange the work of spring cultivation. These conferences must be well prepared. The conference period should be short, preferably a day or two.

We also recommend that you convene production team meetings of all commune members to discuss the work of spring cultivation.

At the same time, we also recommend that units of the People's Liberation Army stationed locally and military organizations at all levels should make great efforts to support and help with the work of spring cultivation.

Unite under the guidance of the great thought of Mao Zedong!

Work to seize victory in the spring cultivation!

(This letter should be read and posted in the villages.)

> The Central Committee of the Communist Party of China
> 20 February 1967

13
On the Revolutionary "Three-in-One" Combination

Red Flag Editorial

Source: Peking Review, No. 12, 1967, pp. 14–16. This editorial first appeared in *Red Flag,* No. 5, on 30 March 1967.

Chairman Mao has pointed out that in those places and organizations where power needs to be seized, the policy of the revolutionary "three-in-one" combination must be carried out in establishing a provisional organ of power that is revolutionary and representative and has proletarian authority. This organ of power should preferably be called a revolutionary committee.

This policy is the political and organizational guarantee for the victory of the proletarian revolutionaries in their struggle to seize power. The proletarian revolutionaries should understand this policy correctly and implement it correctly.

The revolutionary "three-in-one" provisional organ of power should be formed by leaders of revolutionary mass organizations that truly represent the broad masses, the representatives of the People's Liberation Army units stationed in the area, and revolutionary leading cadres. None of these three bodies can be excluded. It is wrong to overlook or underestimate the role of any one of them.

As a result of the vigorous mass movement of the Great Proletarian Cultural Revolution during the past half year and more, the masses have been fully mobilized, and large numbers of up-and-coming representatives of the revolutionary masses have emerged. The revolutionary masses are the base of the proletarian revolutionaries' seizure of power from the handful of the persons in the Party who are in authority and taking the capitalist road. They are the base of the revolutionary "three-in-one" provisional organ of power.

True proletarian revolutionaries and up-and-coming representatives of the revolutionary masses have performed immortal exploits in the Great Proletarian Cultural Revolution. They are the new rising forces nurtured by Mao Zedong's thought, and they embody the general orientation of the revolution.

This struggle to seize power from the handful of persons in the Party who are in authority and taking the capitalist road is a mass movement from below under the leadership of the Central Committee of the Chinese Communist Party headed by Chairman Mao. In the revolutionary "three-in-one" provisional organ of power, it is imperative to give full play to the role of leaders of the revolutionary mass organizations and to take full account of their opinions, and never regard them simply as secondary, because they are the representatives of the broad revolutionary masses. If their role is not recognized or if it is underrated, in effect, the revolutionary masses as well as the Great Proletarian Cultural Revolution are negated. If they are excluded or regarded as secondary, it is impossible to establish a provisional organ of power that is revolutionary, representative, and has proletarian authority; it is impossible to have a revolutionary "three-in-one" combination.

In all great revolutionary mass movements, it is scarcely avoidable to have shortcomings and make mistakes. It is necessary to see clearly the essence, the mainstream, and the general orientation of the revolution. In this Great Proletarian Cultural Revolution, the shortcomings and errors of the leaders of revolutionary mass organizations who truly represent the masses are a question of one finger among ten, and a problem that arises in the course of progress. As proletarian revolutionaries, we should recognize that their general orientation is correct, that they have many strong points and we should learn from them modestly. As for their shortcomings and errors, we should warm-heartedly, patiently, and painstakingly help them. It should also be noted that many revolutionary mass organizations have pointed out themselves the wrong tendencies existing in their own organizations and have proposed ways of correcting them as a result of their creative study and application of Chairman Mao's works. Such revolutionary consciousness and initiative is praiseworthy. It is precisely the revolutionary masses themselves who have proposed eliminating self-interest in their own thinking while seizing power from the handful of persons in the Party who were in authority and taking the capitalist road.

In the final analysis, the question of one's attitude toward leaders of revolutionary mass organizations that truly represent the masses taking part in the "three-in-one" provisional organ of power is a question of one's attitude toward the masses, toward the mass movement itself. It is also an important indication of whether the proletarian revolutionary line represented by Chairman Mao can be carried out or not. We must at all times remember Chairman Mao's teachings: "The masses are the real heroes," "the masses have boundless creative power," "the people, and the people alone, are the motive force in the making of world history." If alienated from the revolutionary masses, it is certain that no organization or individual is able to carry out the proletarian revolutionary line represented by Chairman Mao.

The vigorous mass movement of the Great Proletarian Cultural Revolution of more than the last half year has been a severe test for the ranks of our cadres. The handful of persons in the Party who were in authority and taking the capitalist road has been exposed. At the same time, the majority of our cadres have proved to be good or comparatively good. The concept of excluding and overthrowing all cadres is absolutely wrong. It is necessary to point out that the masses are not to be blamed for this. To exclude and overthrow all cadres indiscriminately is the view advocated by those several people who put forth the bourgeois reactionary line, and this was precisely what they did. The poisonous influence has not been wiped out of the minds of certain comrades, and therefore they have, to a certain extent, committed similar mistakes without being conscious of them.

In every place, department, enterprise and unit there are great numbers of revolutionary cadres. This is also true even for some places or departments where those in authority taking the capitalist road have been entrenched, but the revolutionary cadres there were suppressed over a long period. We must be aware of this.

The role of the revolutionary cadres in participating in the "three-in-one" provisional organ of power must be given full consideration. They should and can play the role of nucleus and backbone of the organ. Of course, they can do this only by integrating themselves with the masses and by following the mass line in work.

Provided those cadres who made mistakes criticize their own mistakes and correct them, draw a clear-cut demarcation line between themselves and the handful of persons in the Party who are in authority and taking the capitalist road, between themselves and the bourgeois reactionary line, and really stand on the proletarian revolutionary line represented by Chairman Mao, they should be united in accordance with the principle of "early or late, all who make revolution merit equal treatment," proper jobs should be arranged for them, and many of them can be allowed to participate in the provisional organ of power.

However, those who persist in their mistakes, and who do not draw a clear-cut demarcation line between themselves and the people in authority taking the capitalist road, between themselves and the bourgeois reactionary line must not be imposed on the masses and arbitrarily pushed into the "three-in-one" provisional organ of power. Otherwise, this would not be the revolutionary "three-in-one" combination, to say nothing of the seizure of power from the handful of persons in the Party who are in authority and taking the capitalist road; a new reversal would occur, and those in authority taking the capitalist road who had been overthrown might even regain power.

We must be vigilant against those who distort the principle of revolutionary "three-in-one" combination and, on the pretext of forming the "three-in-one" combination, carry out eclecticism, conciliation, and the combining of two into one, and furthermore, in a hundred and one ways, pull in the persons in the Party who are in authority and taking the capitalist road. This is trying to fish in troubled waters, usurp the fruits of the Great Proletarian Cultural Revolution and carry out counter-revolutionary restoration. All revolutionary masses and all revolutionary cadres must resolutely resist, oppose, and smash the conspiracy of the class enemy.

The great People's Liberation Army is the mainstay of the dictatorship of the proletariat. Chairman Mao's call on the People's Liberation Army to actively support the masses of the revolutionary Left is a matter of great strategic significance.

Experience proves that participation by representatives of locally stationed People's Liberation Army units in the revolutionary "three-in-one" provisional organ of power has played an extremely important role in successfully accomplishing the task in the struggle to seize power.

With the participation of cadres of the People's Liberation Army in the "three-in-one" provisional organ of power and with the support of the PLA, the forces of the local proletarian revolutionaries will become still stronger. The class enemy fears the People's Liberation Army and the revolutionary "three-in-one" combination in which PLA cadres take part the most. They try by every means to manufacture rumors and fabricate stories in a vain attempt to sow dissension between the revolutionary masses and the People's Liberation Army, and to incite those among the masses who do not know the truth to direct the spearhead of their struggle against the People's Liberation Army. Such class enemy intrigues must be fully exposed and firmly smashed.

The Chinese People's Liberation Army is an extremely revolutionized army of the proletariat, unmatched in the world. Chairman Mao Zedong has said: "The sole purpose of this army is to stand firmly with the Chinese people and to serve them wholeheartedly." It is precisely because of this that all revolutionary mass organizations and revolutionary masses have faith in the People's Liberation Army and warmly support the participation by representatives of the local army units in the revolutionary "three-in-one" provisional organ of power. At various levels, in those departments where power must be seized, representatives of the armed forces or of the militia should take part in forming the "three-in-one" combination. This should be done in factories and rural areas, in financial, trading, cultural, and educational departments (universities, middle schools, and primary schools), in Party and government organizations, and in people's organizations. Representatives of the armed forces should be sent to the county level or higher, and representatives of the militia should be sent to the commune level or lower. This is very good. If representatives of the armed forces are not sufficient, their posts can be left vacant for the time being and filled in the future.

The attitude toward the People's Liberation Army is actually the attitude toward the dictatorship of the proletariat, and it is an important criterion for distinguishing whether a person is of the genuine revolutionary Left or not.

In certain places, some comrades in the local army units may commit temporary mistakes in giving their support because of the intricate and complex conditions of the class struggle. When such problems occur, the genuine revolutionary Left should explain, with good intentions and in the proper way, the conditions and state their views to the leading members of the army units. They should absolutely not adopt an openly antagonistic attitude and still less should they direct the spearhead of their struggle against the People's Liberation Army. Otherwise, they will commit gross mistakes and do things that sadden our friends and gladden our enemies, and they will be used by the class enemy.

The People's Liberation Army has made important contributions in supporting the proletarian revolutionaries in their struggle to seize power. All commanders and fighters must follow Chairman Mao's teachings, closely rely on the broad revolutionary masses, learn from them modestly, be their students before acting as their teachers, be good at discussing matters with them, and carry on deep-going and careful investigations among them. In doing so, they will be able to give the proletarian revolutionaries very powerful support in their struggle to seize power and bring still closer ties between the army and the people, and, on their part, the army units will get new tempering and improve in the course of the struggle.

The "three-in-one" provisional organ of power must be revolutionary, representative, and have proletarian authority. This organ of power must resolutely carry out the proletarian revolutionary line represented by Chairman Mao and firmly oppose the bourgeois reactionary line. It must not be "combining two into one" or eclectic. Only thus, can this organ be representative and speak for the broad revolutionary masses and revolutionary cadres. Only thus, can it have proletarian authority, exercise powerful centralized leadership on the basis of the most extensive democracy, impose effective dictatorship on the class enemy, and smash every kind of scheme for counter-revolutionary restoration on the part of the handful of persons in the Party who are in authority and taking the capitalist road and the ghosts and monsters in society.

A big question now confronting the people of the whole country is whether to carry the Great Proletarian Cultural Revolution through to the end, or to abandon it halfway. All revolutionary comrades must keep a cool head and not get confused. "With power and courage to spare we must pursue the tottering foe and not ape Xiang Yu the conqueror seeking idle fame."[1] At present, we should especially keep this teaching of Chairman Mao's in mind.

[1]Lines quoted from Mao Zedong's poem "The People's Liberation Army Occupies Nanjing" (April 1949).

14
Learn from the Liberation Army in Political Work

Anonymous

Source: This unusual record of an almost stream-of-consciousness-like approach to political work comes from a booklet (*Xuexi jiefangjun zhengzhi gongzuo jingyan*) put out by the Industry and Transport Political Department of the Beijing East City District Temporary Party Committee in January 1967. We have attempted as far as possible to preserve the layout of the original (e.g., its extensive use of arrows, boxes, borders, etc.) in order to give the reader of the translation a "feel" for how the intended readership might have been expected to read it.

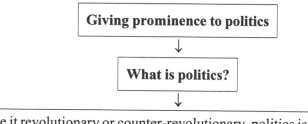

Be it revolutionary or counter-revolutionary, politics is always a struggle of one class against another and not merely the activity of a few individuals.

↓

> ## What is meant by giving prominence to politics?
> ↓

When we give prominence to politics, we give prominence to proletarian politics and firmly grasp the class struggle of the proletariat against the bourgeoisie; which is to say we give prominence to Mao Zedong Thought and put Mao Zedong Thought in command; which is also to say that top priority is put on political work in everything we do.

The Five Principles of giving prominence to politics
↓

First: Practice the living study and living application of the works of Chairman Mao and in particular stress their "application," hereby turning Chairman Mao's books into the supreme instructions guiding everything we do within the armed forces.

Second: Persist in the Four Firsts and pay particular attention to grasping Living Thought in a major and intense way.[1]

Third: Leading cadres must enter deeply into the basic levels and intensely grasp the Four Good Company movement, see to it that the basic levels are in good shape, and at the same time make sure that the cadre style of leadership is up to scratch.[2]

Fourth: Daringly promote truly outstanding fighters to crucial positions of responsibility.

Fifth: [Reward] technical skills mastered to perfection through strenuous practice and close-up and night-time combat skills.

The great strategic significances of giving prominence to politics
↓

1. Giving prominence to politics has been put forward according to the laws of development of socialist society and the economic foundation

---

[1]As enunciated by Lin Biao in the early 1960s, the "Four Firsts" are: the human factor, political work, ideological work, and living thought.

[2]A "Four Good Company" is good in political and ideological work, in the "Three-Eight Work Style" (see Document 5, note 1, p. 46), in military training, and in its arrangement of daily life.

of socialist society. It has been put forward on the basis of the fact that classes and class struggle still exist in socialist society.

2. Giving prominence to politics is at the root of our attempts to further revolutionize and modernize our armed forces.

3. Giving prominence to politics is at the root of our preparations to crush the U.S. imperialists engaged in a war of aggression.

4. Giving prominence to politics is at the root of our opposition to and prevention of modern revisionism and our guarantee that our armed forces will never deteriorate.

5. Giving prominence to politics is a glorious tradition of our armed forces.

How to give prominence to politics
↓

---

1. To hold even higher the great red banner of Mao Zedong Thought and to even more successfully promote a high tide of the living study and living application of Chairman Mao's works throughout the armed forces.

2. To strengthen class education and at all times and in all situations not forget class struggle.

3. To carry out and implement the long-term policy of involving the entire Party in military work and strengthening the absolute leadership of the Party over the armed forces.

4. To persist in the mass line and carry forward the Three Great Democracies.[3]

5. To realize the Five Principles [of giving prominence to politics] in the movement to build Four Good Companies and to grasp Living Thought in a major and intense way.

6. To strengthen our cadre corps in order to guarantee, from an organizational standpoint, the implementation of the Five Principles; to promote modesty and prudence and to oppose conceit and arrogance.

---

[3]As applied in the PLA during the civil war, the "Three Great Democracies" are: politically, officers and men help each other to understand goals; economically, soldiers take part in running their own mess; and militarily, all share knowledge and express their own views.

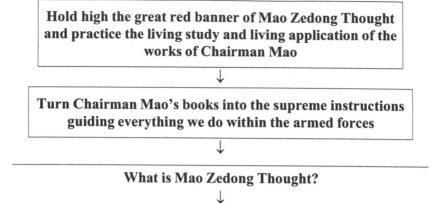

Mao Zedong Thought is the ideology of class struggle. Mao Zedong Thought is the pinnacle of Marxism-Leninism in the present era. It is the ultimate and most living Marxism-Leninism, the compass guiding the Chinese people's revolution and socialist construction, a powerful ideological weapon in opposing imperialism and modern revisionism, and a powerful ideological weapon in the revolutionary struggle of all the peoples of the world.

Why study Mao Zedong Thought?
↓

To study Mao Zedong Thought is an important safeguard to continuously raise one's class consciousness, to resist the corrosive influence of bourgeois thinking, to further the revolutionization of one's thinking, and to do one's work well. It is a major fundamental undertaking allowing us to carry our country's socialist revolution and socialist construction through to the end and guarantee that our Party and our state will never deteriorate or change their color. It is the key sign of having realized the "Four Firsts," the ideological foundation of the fostering of a Three-Eight Work Style, and the basic guarantee for building Four Good Companies.[4]

All in all, Mao Zedong Thought is our "grain, arms, and steering wheel."

---

[4]For an explanation of "Three-Eight Work Style," refer to Document 5, note 1 (p. 46).

The basic contents of the study of Mao Zedong Thought
↓

To study Comrade Mao Zedong's most unswerving proletarian stand and most thorough revolutionary spirit; to employ the viewpoint and method of dialectical materialism and historical materialism to investigate, analyze, and resolve matters; to employ the most living and most clever combat techniques in the revolutionary struggle; and to have a frugal work style of going deep into the realities of life and staying in close touch with the masses.

What are the ways of studying Mao Zedong Thought?
↓

1. Study Chairman Mao's works;
2. Study the Party's policies and resolutions and Chairman Mao's instructions;
3. Study Comrade Mao Zedong's great practice of integrating theory and practice;
4. Study the glorious tradition of our armed forces.

The basic method of studying Chairman Mao's works
↓

Study them with problems in mind.	Living study and living application and integration of study and application.	When instant results are needed, first set up a pole and see its shadow.
↓	↓	
1. Study what is relevant to the ongoing movement and political education;	Lei Feng's study formula: "Problem—study— practice— summary."	

2. Study what is relevant to the kind of work you are doing;	The experience of the Good Eighth Company:[5]
3. Study what is relevant to present or emerging ideological problems.	"One: read; Two: discuss; Three: compare; Four: Act." Formula: Apply—study—apply.

Eight relationships that must be resolved well in the course of study

↓

---

1. The relationship between work and study;
2. The relationship between collective study and individual study;
3. The relationship between cadres' own studies and organizing soldiers' studies;
4. The relationship between transforming one's ideology and improving one's work;
5. The relationship between living study and living application on the one hand and reading the *Selected Works of Mao Zedong* from cover to cover on the other;
6. The relationship between studying Chairman Mao's works and the long- and short-term policies of the Party;
7. The relationship between studying Chairman Mao's works and vocational studies;
8. The relationship between long-time planning and short-time arrangements.

> **Hold high the great red banner of Mao Zedong Thought and persist in the Four Firsts**

↓

---

[5]The "Good Eighth Company" refers to a PLA company stationed on Nanjing Road in Shanghai that was hailed as an exemplary unit "successfully withstanding the quintessence of bourgeois corruption and decadence" from the old world-renowned cosmopolitan city in China.

What is meant by the "Four Firsts"?

↓

The "Four Firsts" are four principles for correctly solving four relationships in the area of political work. They are:

The human factor comes first in the arms (matter)/men relationship

Arms are an important factor in war but not the decisive factor. The human factor and not that of matter is decisive

Political work comes first in the all-kinds-of-work/political work relationship

There is all kinds of work to be done in the armed forces, but leading it all should be political work. Political work is the lifeline and the basic guarantee of all work

Ideological work comes first in the practical work/ideological work relationship

Both these kinds of work must be done, but the stress should be on ideological work. Ideological work is the most fundamental and most essential aspect of political work

Living Thought comes first in the book learning/Living Thought relationship

Books must be read, but the important thing is to have a command of Living Thought and to integrate book learning and practice

Why must one persist in the "Four Firsts"?

↓

To persist in the "Four Firsts" is the way to build a modern revolutionary armed force.

1. To persist in the "Four Firsts" is to persist in putting Mao Zedong Thought in command and to persist in Chairman Mao's army building and political direction.

2. To persist in the "Four Firsts" is the foundation on which rests the reinforced revolutionization and rapid modernization of our armed forces.

3. To persist in the "Four Firsts" is an objective necessity in view of the intensity of domestic and international class struggle.

How does one persist in the "Four Firsts"?

↓

Whether or not one is able to persist in the "Four Firsts" is first of all a matter of understanding. With a different understanding comes a different zeal and a different way of organizing one's task, as well as a different degree of efficiency.

1. An ability to persist in the "Four Firsts" is gained through the process of protracted struggle and many setbacks.

2. As far as cadres doing political work are concerned, the ability to successfully realize the "Four Firsts" depends on factors like understanding, work-style, and method, and, generally speaking, primarily understanding.

3. The main criteria for the successful realization of the "Four Firsts" at the grassroots level are:

| **1.** Has political ideological work been given priority over all other kinds of work? | **2.** In work of every kind is Mao Zedong Thought the guiding principle and have all the long-term and short-term policies and instructions of the Party Center and the Central Military Commission been implemented? | **3.** Is every single person indeed taking part in political ideological work? |

The aim of persisting in the "Four Firsts" is to:

↓

Fully mobilize man's subjective initiative in order to make our armed forces extremely proletarian and extremely militant.

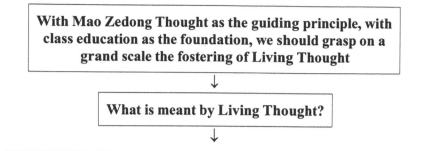

With Mao Zedong Thought as the guiding principle, with class education as the foundation, we should grasp on a grand scale the fostering of Living Thought

↓

What is meant by Living Thought?

↓

It is as Comrade Mao Zedong has said ever so often, the integration of the universal principles of Marxism-Leninism with the practical realities of the Chinese revolution, "from the masses, to the masses," and "concentration and perseverance." In other words, it is "the need not to stop at the level of what is only in the books."

**Why must one grasp the fostering
of Living Thought?**

1. To grasp Living Thought is the most central aspect of the "Four Firsts" and amounts to using Mao Zedong Thought to answer all kinds of practical ideological questions.

2. People's thought develops and changes with the uninterrupted development and change of things.

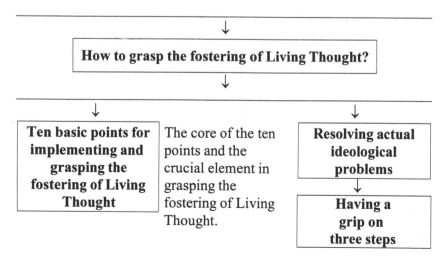

↓

How to grasp the fostering of Living Thought?

↓

↓

Ten basic points for implementing and grasping the fostering of Living Thought	The core of the ten points and the crucial element in grasping the fostering of Living Thought.	**Resolving actual ideological problems**
		↓
		Having a grip on three steps

1. Living study and living application of Chairman Mao's works—taking Mao Zedong Thought as the guiding principle.

2. Starting out from class education—with class education as the basis.

3. Proceeding from the actual situation while taking a firm grasp of top and bottom.

4. Grabbing the buds and doing first work first.

5. Persisting in education and persuasion, convincing by argument.

6. Beginning at the level of the majority and gradually moving upwards.

↓

Grasping top and bottom →

↓

What is meant by grasping top and bottom?

↓

The top refers to the long-term and short-term policies of the Party Center and Central Military Commission and Chairman Mao's instructions.

The bottom refers to the actual ideological trends in the armed forces and existing actual problems.

Why grasp the top and bottom?

↓

Grasping both top and bottom is a basic principle of leadership, as both top and bottom have an objective existence. The top is the leadership's direction, and unless it is grasped one will go astray.

↓

Timely discovery; true clarification; correct resolution.

The step of tying things together.

Building up an ideological working team relying on core elements and the Party and youth league organization.

The five interrelationships of ideological work

↓

1. The difference and interconnection of ordinary solutions and concrete solutions.
2. The difference and interconnection of the piecemeal solution and total solution of ideological problems.
3. The difference and interconnection of ideological problems and activity problems.
4. The relationship between resolving ideological problems and resolving practical problems.

7. Integrating the political ideological movement and ordinary educational activities.

8. Each and every one takes part in ideological work.

9. Integrating ideology in the lead and attention to the resolution of practical problems.

10. Making use of living teaching and living methods.

The bottom is the foundation of leadership, and unless it is grasped there will be nothing to lead, and work will be in vain.

5. The relationship between grasping practical ideological problems that are part of carrying out a task and problems that are of an ordinary day-to-day nature.

15

Notification Concerning the Resumption of Classes to Make Revolution in Universities, Middle Schools, and Elementary Schools

CCP Center, State Council, Central Military Commission, and Central Cultural Revolution Group

Source: This notification ("Guanyu da, zhong, xiaoxue fuke nao geming de tongzhi") was issued on 14 October 1967 as Central Document *Zhongfa* [1967] 316. Our translation is based on the text in CCP Central Committee General Office and State Council General Office Joint Cultural Revolution Reception Office, ed., *Wuchanjieji wenhua dageming youguan wenjian huiji* (*Collection of Documents Concerning the Great Proletarian Cultural Revolution*), 5 vols. (Beijing, 1967–68), Vol. 4, pp. 87–89.

To all provincial, municipal, and autonomous regional Revolutionary Committees (including Preparatory Groups) and Military Control

Commissions; all military regions and districts and, through them, to the organizations of the masses:

1. All universities, middle schools, and elementary schools throughout the entire country are to resume classes immediately.

2. All schools must conscientiously implement Chairman Mao's directives about combating selfishness and repudiating revisionism.

3. All universities, middle schools, and elementary schools are to engage simultaneously in teaching and [educational] reform. Chairman Mao's thoughts about educational revolution are to be implemented in the teaching process, and plans for a revolution of the contents and system of education are to be drawn up step by step.

4. Each school is to comply with Chairman Mao's directive of 7 March 1967 and according to the principles of revolution and on the basis of an organizational structure consisting of classes, grades, and departments achieve a revolutionary great alliance and set up revolutionary "three-in-one" leading bodies.[1]

5. A majority of teachers and cadres in the schools are good or comparatively good. With the exception of landlord, rich-peasant, counter-revolutionary, hooligan, and Rightist elements, persons who committed mistakes in the past should be permitted to come forward and return to work, assuming they have understood their errors and rectified them.

6. All universities, middle schools, and elementary schools should immediately start actively preparing to enroll new students.

(This document is to be posted in schools everywhere.)

---

[1]Mao's directive of 7 March stipulated that the People's Liberation Army should give students and teachers military and political training. A translation is in *Current Background,* No. 852, 6 May 1968, p. 851.

16

Notification Concerning Work Assignments for University Graduates in 1968

CCP Center, Central Cultural Revolution Group, State Council, and Central Military Commission

Source: This notification ("Guanyu 1968 nian dazhuan yuanxiao biyesheng fenpei wenti de tongzhi") was issued on 15 November 1968 as Central Document *Zhongfa* [1968] 158. Our translation is based on the text in Hubei Provincial Revolutionary Committee, ed., *Wuchanjieji wenhua dageming wenjian huibian* (*Collected Documents from the Great Proletarian Cultural Revolution*) (Wuhan, 1969), Vol. 3, pp. 1158–67. The original notification also included a report, not translated here, from the Beijing Municipal Revolutionary Committee on the assignment of jobs to graduates from universities in the capital.

The Center has decided that students graduating from universities in 1968 are to begin receiving their work assignments in mid-November. You are hereby notified as follows:

1. When assigning work to graduates, you must hold the great red banner of Mao Zedong Thought even higher, firmly implement and carry out Chairman Mao's proletarian revolutionary line, firmly implement and carry out all the latest in a series of directives concerning revolution in education issued by our great leader Chairman Mao, thoroughly criticize the counter-revolutionary revisionist educational line represented by Liu Shaoqi, destroy the old bourgeois educational system, and eradicate its influence.

2. In response to our great leader Chairman Mao's teaching "We encourage intellectuals to go among the masses, to the factories, and to the rural areas in particular . . . to be re-educated by the workers, peasants, and soldiers," the assignment of work to graduates should reflect the firm implementation of the long-term policy of catering to the needs of the rural areas, catering to the needs of the border regions, catering to the needs of factories and mines, and catering to the needs of the grassroots. In general, graduates must become ordinary peasants or ordinary workers. A majority must become ordinary peasants. University graduates must resolutely take the road pointed out by Chairman Mao of integrating with the masses of workers, peasants, and

soldiers, and of accepting re-education from the workers, peasants, and soldiers. They must resolutely obey the assignments given by the Party and the state and must not insist upon being given work corresponding to their disciplines. At the time when work is to be assigned, graduates who are members of Revolutionary Committees or who are leading members of mass organizations should play exemplary roles and set examples for others to follow.

Provincial, municipal, and autonomous regional Revolutionary Committees may continue to send graduates to work as ordinary peasants in PLA farms and state farms. In addition, they may also in accordance with actual local conditions and in a planned way organize their participation in the battle to reshape nature, e.g. the transformation of saline-alkali land and the launching of water conservancy projects. Conditions permitting, part of the graduates may also be sent to rural people's communes (teams) to go to work, on an experimental basis, in production teams.

3. Our great leader Chairman Mao teaches us: "Revolutionary Committees must exercise unified leadership," and "In order to make the proletarian revolution in education a reality, there has to be working class leadership." Provincial, municipal, and autonomous regional Revolutionary Committees are to exercise unified leadership over graduate work assignments in their respective localities. In schools where Worker-Soldier Mao Zedong Thought Propaganda Teams have been stationed, graduate work assignment is, without exception, to be led by the Propaganda Teams. In schools where Revolutionary Great Alliances have already been achieved or where Revolutionary Committees have already been set up, this propaganda team leadership is to take the form of a "three-in-one" School and Department Graduate Work Assignment Leading Group on which workers, soldiers, revolutionary cadres, students, and revolutionary teachers are to be represented. In schools where Revolutionary Great Alliances have not yet been achieved, where there is no Revolutionary Committee, or where the Revolutionary Committee is not yet firmly in power, propaganda teams are to exercise direct and total control over graduate work assignments, with the leading member of the team assuming responsibility for organizing an ad hoc leading group on which revolutionary cadres and students are to be represented. In schools in which no Worker-Soldier Mao Zedong Thought Propaganda Teams are stationed, graduate work assignment is to be led by the Revolutionary

Committee if one exists, by the Military Control Committee if one exists in schools where there is no Revolutionary Committee, and by the higher-level Revolutionary Committee or Military Control Committee in schools where there is neither a Revolutionary Committee nor a Military Control Committee.

4. All localities, all departments, and all schools must give prominence to proletarian politics, energetically strengthen political ideological work, and organize Mao Zedong Thought Study Classes in the course of executing graduate work assignment tasks. Receiving units are to warmly welcome the graduates to take part in productive labor and should not discriminate against them. Students who have shortcomings or who commit this or that blunder should be provided with help and education and should not be retaliated against. The broad masses of workers, poor and lower-middle peasants, PLA soldiers, and revolutionary cadres should with awareness shoulder the glorious task of fostering the younger generation with the help of Mao Zedong Thought.

5. The payment of salaries to students who graduated in 1968 is to commence in December. That is also the month from which the time of their employment is to be calculated. Calculation is to be in accordance with the procedure described in the State Council's "Notification Concerning the Disbursement of Salaries to 1968 University Graduates" of 27 June 1968.[1]

For as long as there is no reform of the salary system, the salaries of students (including graduate students) who graduated in 1966, 1967, and 1968 are without exception to be temporarily set at the level of temporary workers and there will be no [automatic] change in status to that of a regular worker with a fixed grade after one year.

6. The number of students graduating from universities all over the country in 1968 is approximately 150,000. Of these, some 98,000 will be assigned jobs by the various localities and departments themselves. Some 55,900 will be given unified assignments across the country by the Center. The State Planning Commission's proposed plan for the unified countrywide assignment of work to university graduates in

---

[1] State Council Document *Guofawen* [1968] 59: "Guowuyuan guanyu 1967 nian dazhuan yuanxiao biyesheng gongzi fafang banfa de tongzhi," in Chinese People's Liberation Army Nanjing Unit No. 825, ed., *Wuchanjieji wenhua dageming wenjian huibian* (*Collected Documents from the Great Proletarian Cultural Revolution*) (N.p., 1969), pp. 461–62.

1968 will be sent out, after ratification by the Center, by the Commission. The provinces, municipalities, autonomous regions, and various departments must resolutely implement it and promptly draw up plans for allocation, as well as inform the relevant units and schools to send out and receive the graduates. Graduates who have been sent to units in accordance with the plan may not—without the permission of the provincial, municipal, or autonomous regional Graduate Work Assignment Leading Group—be refused employment or be sent back to the schools from which they came. Students meant to graduate in 1969 should normally not be allowed to graduate ahead of time in 1968.

7. The task of assigning work to those who graduated in 1968 is to begin in November by putting the plan for the recipient units into practice and by dispatching graduates. All graduates should be in place at their recipient units by the end of December. In this way it becomes possible to speed up the process whereby graduates go among the worker-peasant masses to be given a re-education, take part in actual productive labor, take the workers and peasants to be their teachers, and themselves assume the role of the humble students of the revolutionary masses. No jobs will be assigned to those who do not report for work within the prescribed time limit, unless there are exceptional circumstances and special permission has been granted by the provincial, municipal, or autonomous regional Graduate Work Assignment Leading Group.

8. The Revolutionary Committees of the provinces, municipalities, autonomous regions, and various departments are themselves to formulate, implement, and carry out plans in accordance with the above principles for those university graduates who are to be assigned work by the localities and various departments.

9. Other matters relating to the assignment of work to university graduates not dealt with in this notification continue to be governed by what is stipulated in the Center's "Notification Concerning Work Assignments for University Graduates in 1967" of 15 June 1968.[2] The provinces, municipalities, autonomous regions, and various departments may in the course of the actual implementation [of the present

---

[2]"Zhonggong Zhongyang, Guowuyuan, Zhongyang junwei, Zhongyang wenge guanyu 1967 nian dazhuan yuanxiao biyesheng fenpei wenti de tongzhi," in Hubei Provincial Revolutionary Committee, ed., *Wuchanjieji wenhua dageming wenjian huibian* (*Collected Documents from the Great Proletarian Cultural Revolution*) (Wuhan, 1969), Vol. 3, pp. 1010–17.

notification] and to the extent that it is necessary formulate supplementary regulations according to local conditions.

17
Opinions and Questions Concerning the Reconsolidation, Revitalization, and Rebuilding of the Party Organization

CCP Center and Central Cultural Revolution Group

Source: These opinions and questions ("Guanyu zhengdun, huifu, chongjian dang de zuzhi de yijian he wenti") were distributed on 2 December 1967 in the form of Central Document *Zhongfa* [1967] 366. Our translation is based on the text reproduced in CCP Central Committee General Office and State Council General Office Joint Cultural Revolution Reception Office, ed., *Wuchanjieji wenhua dageming youguan wenjian huiji* (*Collection of Documents Concerning the Great Proletarian Cultural Revolution*), 5 vols. (Beijing, 1967–68), Vol. 5, pp. 138–46.

To all provincial, municipal, and regional Revolutionary Committees (including Preparatory Groups) and Military Control Commissions; Party Committees of military regions and districts:

We are now distributing these "Opinions and Questions Concerning the Reconsolidation, Revitalization, and Rebuilding of the Party Organization" in the hope that you will solicit comments on them and, in order to permit us to revise them, pass on your comments to the Center before the end of the year.

(Distribute down to the county/regiment level.)

OPINIONS AND QUESTIONS CONCERNING
THE RECONSOLIDATION, REVITALIZATION,
AND REBUILDING OF THE PARTY ORGANIZATION

The reaction of a vast number of Party members and revolutionary masses to the Party Center's "Comment/Instruction on the Revitalization of the Regular Activities of the Party Organization in Units that

Have Set Up Revolutionary Committees" was quite positive.[1] Everyone agreed that this directive from Chairman Mao and the Party Center was very timely and very wise, that it expressed concern and care for the vast numbers of Party members, that it was a major event in the political life of the entire Party, and that it was yet another great victory for Chairman Mao's revolutionary line.

1. On Using Mao Zedong Thought to Reconsolidate, Revitalize, and Rebuild the Party Organization

Comrades have stressed that the resumption of regular activities of the Party organization by no means is a revival of the old ways and old system from before the Great Proletarian Cultural Revolution. Instead, we must hold high the great red banner of Mao Zedong Thought and employ Mao Zedong Thought to reconsolidate, revitalize, and rebuild the Party organization; thoroughly denounce the Liu-Deng revisionist Party-building line; and build our Party into a vanguard organization imbued with vitality, composed of the progressive elements of the proletariat, and capable of leading the proletariat and the revolutionary masses in the struggle against the class enemy. This is the most fundamental principle that absolutely must be observed when reconsolidating, revitalizing, and rebuilding the Party organization.

2. On Ideological Work in the Process of Reconsolidating, Revitalizing, and Rebuilding the Party Organization

In the process of reconsolidating, revitalizing, and rebuilding the Party organization, it is imperative that a good job is done of ideological and educational work among Party and non-Party proletarian cultural revolutionary rebel comrades. Comrades have proposed: (a) conducting Mao Zedong Thought Study Classes wherein the living study and living application of Chairman Mao's works is employed to raise ideological consciousness and resolve ideological questions; (b) mobilizing the

---

[1]CCP Central Document *Zhongfa* [1967] 328 ("Guanyu yijing chenglile geming weiyuanhui de danwei huifu dang de zuzhi shenghuo de pishi") issued on 27 October 1967. Reprinted in People's Liberation Army National Defense University Research Institute for Party History, Party Building, and Political Work, ed., *"Wenhua dageming" yanjiu ziliao* (*"Great Cultural Revolution" Research Materials*) (Beijing, 1988), Vol. 1, pp. 600–1.

masses on a grand scale to discuss and modestly listen to the opinions of the proletarian revolutionary rebels, to improve the relationship between the Party and the masses, and to once and for all overcome the notion that Party members are somehow a cut above other people, as well as the notion shared by proletarian revolutionary rebels that Party members will take revenge on them; (c) that those Party members who have committed errors must "combat selfishness and repudiate revisionism" as the key link and conscientiously engage in self-criticism, so as to be forgiven by the revolutionary masses.

3. On the Conditions, Scope, and Policy Limits of Reconsolidating, Revitalizing, and Rebuilding the Party Organization

What are the conditions to be satisfied by a unit prior to the resumption of regular activities by the Party organization?

A majority of comrades are of the opinion that in accordance with the Center's instructions, all units that have set up Revolutionary Committees or Revolutionary Committee Preparatory Groups may resume the regular activities of the Party organization.

What kind of person should no longer participate in the regular activities of the Party organization?

a. "Those persons who have proven to be renegades or special agents and those who in the course of the Great Proletarian Cultural Revolution have performed very badly, yet show no remorse whatsoever" should no longer take part in the regular activities of the Party organization.

b. A majority of comrades are also of the opinion that those persons who are suspected of being renegades or special agents but whose cases have not yet been settled should temporarily be excluded from taking part in the regular activities of the Party organization. Once their problems have been resolved, one should decide whether or not to allow them to take part.

c. Party members who have committed serious errors, who have performed very badly in the course of the Great Proletarian Cultural Revolution, and against whom the revolutionary masses have major objections, should be excluded from the regular activities of the Party organization for as long as they have not admitted their errors, presented the revolutionary masses with a self-critical examination of their own mistakes, and been forgiven by the revolutionary masses.

What are the conditions for taking in new Party members? A summary of major shared proposals follows:

a. New Party members should be accepted on the basis of Chairman Mao's five criteria for successors and Vice Chairman Lin's three criteria for selecting and promoting cadres, and while importance should be attached to class background, one should also look at the person's ideological and political performance and whether or not he is loyal to Marxism, to Leninism, to Mao Zedong Thought, and to Chairman Mao's revolutionary line.[2]

b. Performance in the course of the Great Proletarian Cultural Revolution: Proletarian revolutionary rebels loyal to Chairman Mao who have come to the fore in the Great Proletarian Cultural Revolution and who have been tested and tried in the course of the movement may be admitted into the Party.

c. The Party should admit those progressive elements of the proletariat who are imbued with vitality, have a strong proletarian rebel spirit, and who have daringly charged and shattered enemy positions in the class struggle. The Party should admit, in particular, progressive elements from among the workers, poor peasants, and Red Guards. The "docile tool theory" and the notion that "obedience," "hard work," "professional competence," etc., are criteria for admission into the Party must be thoroughly denounced, as must the Liu-Deng Party-building line of not paying attention to proletarian political ideology and revolutionary integrity.

d. Right now there are a number of probationary Party members who have not yet been formally admitted, and those among them who satisfy the criteria and whose time of probation has passed may be admitted into the Party.

On what grounds are members to be thrown out of the Party?

a. Renegades, special agents, and class alien elements are without exception to be thrown out of the Party.

b. Arch-unrepentant counter-revolutionary revisionist elements are to be thrown out of the Party.

---

[2]Mao's "five criteria" were that a revolutionary successor should be: (1) truly Marxist-Leninist; (2) determined to serve the people of China and the great majority of the people in the world; (3) able to unite with and lead the proletariat; (4) able to listen to the masses; and (5) willing to criticize himself and to correct mistakes in his work. Lin's "three criteria" were that a good cadre should: (1) hold high the red banner of Mao Zedong Thought; (2) engage in political ideological work; and (3) possess revolutionary vitality.

c. Spiritless and useless Party members totally devoid of revolutionary vitality who simply do not qualify should either be expelled or asked to withdraw from the Party.

d. Persons who have remained probationary Party members for an extended period of time and who do not qualify [as members] should no longer enjoy the status of probationary Party members.

e. In the course of the Great Proletarian Cultural Revolution movement, in some units, some Party members have been expelled by popular demand. Those who fall within the above categories should remain expelled, while those who do not should—after education and after having been forgiven by the revolutionary masses—have their Party membership reinstated.

4. On the Question of Setting Up Party Nuclei

Most comrades argue that as far as the Party's organizational leadership is concerned, there should within each Revolutionary Committee be a Party nucleus that exercises leadership. At the grass roots level, there should be branches and small groups.

The nucleus must be set up by proceeding from higher to lower levels, through interlevel and inside-outside cooperation, and after ample deliberation and democratic consultation. [Its composition] must be reported to and ratified by higher levels.

18
Instructions on Cracking Down on Counter-Revolutionary Destructive Activities

CCP Center

Source: These instructions ("Guanyu daji fangeming pohuai huodong de zhishi") were issued on 31 January 1970 in the form of Central Document *Zhongfa* [1970] 3. Our translation is based on the text reproduced in an official compilation of documents from the Cultural Revolution published in 1981.

Since the Ninth National Party Congress and inspired by our great leader Chairman Mao's great appeal to "heighten vigilance; protect the motherland" and "prepare for war," the entire Party and millions upon millions of soldiers and civilians throughout the entire country, their fighting spirit aroused, have rallied closely together, "grasping revolution while promoting production, promoting work, promoting war-preparedness," and the situation is excellent. But class enemies at home and abroad have not resigned themselves to defeat. The Soviet revisionists are at present intensifying their collusion with the American imperialists and are conspiring to launch a war of aggression against us. Domestic counter-revolutionary elements have seized this opportunity to create disturbances. The two are echoing each other at a distance. This is a new trend in the class struggle at present, and it merits attention.

A tiny handful of counter-revolutionary elements hanging on in vain to the armed might of the imperialists, revisionists, and reactionaries in the hope of regaining their lost paradise are intensifying their destructive activities. Some are spreading war hysteria, fabricating rumors to mislead the masses; others are stealing state secrets and offering their services to the enemy; some are using the opportunity to demand a reversal of verdicts and refuse to submit to surveillance; others link up in secret, plotting to riot; some engage in graft, embezzlement, and speculation and sabotage the socialist economy; and others sabotage the rural resettlement of school graduates and the grassroots transfer of cadres. Although these people are merely a tiny handful, they stop at no evil and the damage they inflict is very grave. There is nothing strange about this. Chairman Mao teaches us that although after Liberation we rooted out a number of counter-revolutionary elements and there are no longer that many left, there are still counter-revolutionaries, and new ones are likely to emerge. Given that classes and class struggle still exist in socialist society, it is by no means odd that class enemies at home and abroad avail themselves of every opportunity to stir up trouble. It is merely a reflection of the law-bound nature of the struggle between the two classes, the two roads, and the two lines. At present the class struggle at home and abroad is extremely fierce, and counter-revolutionary elements will inevitably jump out into the open or arrive on missions from abroad to engage in destruction and disturbance. Consequently, we must heighten our vigilance.

In order to prepare for war, strengthen our national defense, strengthen the dictatorship of the proletariat, and protect the glorious achievements of the Great Proletarian Cultural Revolution and in compliance with our great leader Chairman Mao's teaching "Counter-revolutionaries must be suppressed whenever they are found," it is imperative to resolutely crack down "surely, accurately, and relentlessly" on all forms of destructive activities by counter-revolutionary elements. Therefore:

1. Go all out to fully mobilize the masses. Survey, examine, and implement everything with war-preparedness in mind and make the masses see clearly that a crackdown on counter-revolutionary destructive activities is an acute class struggle; a struggle to crack down on the "fifth column" of the imperialists, revisionists, and reactionaries; a struggle to crack down on the Soviet revisionists' schemes of aggression; and in fact also an important aspect of our preparations for war. Call upon the broad masses to inform against, expose, uncover, and denounce counter-revolutionary elements and in this way ferret out the hidden enemy.

2. Stress the main point. The main point is to crack down on active counter-revolutionaries. Resolutely put down (*zhenya*) those active counter-revolutionary elements who collude with the enemy and betray the nation, conspire to revolt, gather military intelligence, steal state secrets, commit murder and physical assault, commit arson and poison people, counter-attack to settle old scores, viciously slander the Party and the socialist system, plunder state property, and disrupt the social order.

3. Strictly distinguish between the two different kinds of contradictions, draw a clear distinction between ourselves and the enemy, and consider in each case the degree of seriousness. Different crimes should be handled differently and in accordance with the principle "The chief criminals shall be punished without fail, while those who are accomplices under duress shall go unpunished." Resolutely execute (*shadiao*) those counter-revolutionary elements who are swollen with arrogance after having committed countless heinous crimes and against whom popular indignation is so great that nothing save execution will serve to calm it. Those whose crimes are serious but against whom popular indignation is not great may be sentenced either to death sentences with a two-year reprieve or to imprisonment for life. Those whose crimes are quite serious, and who therefore must be sentenced, may be given set terms of imprisonment, while those whose crimes are less serious may be handed over to the masses for tight surveillance. In the course of struggle, implement the policy of "leniency to those who

confess and severity to those who resist," so as to spur them on to make a clean breast of their crimes and take the initiative to atone for their crimes.

4. Do well at propaganda and mobilization, on a grand scale and extensively. The masses should be involved in the discussion prior to execution and sentencing, so as to make sure that "every household is informed and everyone has understood." Execution and sentencing should be carried out at mass rallies: the sentence should be announced publicly and carried out immediately. Only in this way will the people be gratified and the enemy made to tremble. However, the number of persons executed must not be excessive and should represent only a tiny minority. The number to be imprisoned should not be large, and those to be put under surveillance should be a majority. Cases should be handled with accuracy regardless of whether the sentence is execution, imprisonment, or surveillance. The evidence must be conclusive and the sentencing appropriate. The masses must always be involved in denunciation and struggle, and it [sic] must be struggled until it collapses and denounced until it sinks. This is the only way in which the aim of the dictatorship of the masses can be attained.

5. Retain unified control over the limits of authority to approve sentences. According to the regulations of the Center, executions may be approved by the Revolutionary Committees of the provinces, municipalities, and autonomous regions who are to report on them to the Center for the record. Permission to urgently dispose of important criminals may be requested and obtained directly from the Center by telegram.

6. Strengthen leadership. The leadership assumes responsibility and everyone joins in the practical work. Practical direction should be provided, in depth and enforceable. Investigation and research are to be strengthened so as to make sure that everyone knows what's what, and "the lists of names of people to be arrested and executed must be rigorously examined." Heighten vigilance and prevent class enemies from taking revenge. In particular, take strict precautions against those who employ bourgeois factionalism to muddle the demarcation line between the enemy and ourselves. In those places or units where a Great Revolutionary Alliance has not yet been fully achieved organizationally and ideologically, one should first by way of a cleansing of the class ranks eliminate those counter-revolutionary elements who have wormed their way into the ranks.

The leadership over public security work by Revolutionary Committees and Military Control Commissions at all levels must be strengthened, and a public security contingent boundlessly loyal to Chairman Mao must be formed.

Each locality is expected to earnestly discuss and conscientiously implement these instructions upon receiving them.

(This document is distributed only down to the leading nuclei at the province/corps level. The province/corps level will arrange for its contents to be transmitted orally to lower levels. This document may not be reprinted or redistributed, much less be published in the Party press, broadcast, or circulated in any form.)

Part II

Effects and Consequences

C. Purging the Party

Inside as well as outside China, the Cultural Revolution is now and then described as a political movement in which the Communist Party brought untold suffering upon the Chinese common people (*baixing*). This convenient characterization overlooks the fact that millions of Party members themselves became victims of the movement. The purge of the Party—the vicious attack, humiliating denunciation, and physical abuse of cadres accused of treachery or of "taking the capitalist road"—did as much to define Mao's "revolutionary transformation of society" as did the persecution of ordinary citizens.

Accounts of the Cultural Revolution invariably highlight the role of Red Guards in the attack on Party cadres. What has not always been sufficiently appreciated by outsiders, however, is the extent to which the seemingly "spontaneous" violence inflicted upon leaders by the previously led was covertly managed and manipulated by Mao and the members of his inner circle. The history of one of the best known university Red Guard organizations shows the extent to which the activities of this particular group involved repeated contacts with and received direct official endorsement from the CCP Center (Document 19).

Of the roughly two million Party cadres who had their past and present examined for signs of heresy or treachery, less than half a dozen (e.g. only those who immediately prior to their demise had been members of the Politburo Standing Committee, like Liu Shaoqi and Deng Xiaoping) were at Mao's insistence spared the ordeal of so-called "face-to-face" struggle by Red Guards.[1] Liu Shaoqi's wife Wang Guangmei was not so lucky, and an edited extract from her "interrogation record" (Document 20) is a thought-provoking document. Humiliated but far from humbled, Wang manages to put up a spirited defense against the accusations hurled at her.

Kang Sheng was a member of Mao's inner circle deeply implicated in the purge of the Party. As an acknowledged expert in sinister prac-

---

[1]Liu, Deng, and Tao Zhu were "struggled" against inside the Zhongnanhai compound by Central Committee General Office staff and members of the Central Guard regiment.

tices (he had been trained in counter-intelligence techniques in the Soviet Union at the time of Stalin's Great Purges) Kang would now and then share his expertise with Red Guards and military officials. His talk to a delegation from Jilin (Document 21) on the topic of "examining cases"—the official euphemism for the state-sponsored terror against officialdom—suggests a paranoid and truly evil mind at work.

The final text in this section (Document 22) takes us beyond the public spectacle of "persecution at the hands of the masses" to the still only incompletely understood world of special prisons and torture of political opponents led by the so-called Central Case Examination Group, a tribunal chaired by Zhou Enlai and answerable directly to the Party Chairman.[2] Here the treatment accorded Vice-Premier Bo Yibo is chronicled by his official biographers on the basis of contemporary prison records. Bo was a cadre (one of more than sixty) who on the eve of the Sino-Japanese War had been told by the CCP Center to publicly renounce communism in order to be released from a KMT prison; thirty years later, the fact that he had obeyed orders was held against him and described as an act of "treachery."

---

[2]See Michael Schoenhals, "The Central Case Examination Group, 1966–1979," *The China Quarterly,* No. 145, March 1996, pp. 87–111.

19
"Annihilate Every Renegade"

Nankai University "Weidong" Red Guards

Source: Excerpt from The History of the Great Proletarian Cultural Revolution at Nankai University, Writing Group of the Red Guard Congress, Nankai University "Weidong" Red Guards, ed., *Tianfan difu kai er kang—Ji Nankai daxue wuchanjieji wenhua dageming (Heaven and earth are moved with emotion—a record of the Great Proletarian Cultural Revolution at Nankai University)* (Tianjin: Nankai daxue "Weidong" hongweibing zongbu zhengzhibu, 1968), pp. 173–78.

On August 5, 1966, our greatest leader, Chairman Mao, wrote a great historical document that would come to be known throughout the world for its tremendous power, namely, the article "Bombard the Headquarters: My First Big-Character Poster."[1]

"Bombard the Headquarters!" That was the key salvo, the shot that led to the complete and thorough burying of the bourgeois headquarters headed by Liu Shaoqi, China's Khrushchev! It was the shot that shook up the whole world! It was a salvo that opened up a whole new chapter in human history! It was in the noise of this earthshaking shot that the conspiratorial clique of Liu Shaoqi, that big renegade and traitor who has hidden himself inside the Party for as long as thirty years, was exposed!

The document *Zhongfa* [1967] 96, printed and distributed by the Office of the Central Committee of the Chinese Communist Party, clearly points out:

> In August, 1966, after Chairman Mao wrote the big-character poster, "Bombard the Headquarters" at the Eleventh Plenum of the Eighth Central Committee, we, in accordance with the directives of Comrade Kang Sheng, launched an investigation into the issue of how Bo Yibo, Liu Lantao, An Ziwen, Yang Xianzhen, et al., had been able to get out of prison by way of so-called "simple procedures." We investigated and read all the newspapers that were published in Beiping at the time,

[1] English translation in *Current Background,* no. 891, 8 October 1969, p. 63.

inspected the files on all the members of this group, and extensively investigated all the people who were involved in this matter, as well as all the official personnel who were related to the case. Subsequently, certain Red Guard organizations provided a number of additional clues [that were followed]. The results of our investigation demonstrated that, in fact, Bo Yibo et al. had not simply gotten out of prison by performing a "simple procedure"; instead, they were let out after they had given themselves up, betrayed the Party, and turned against the Party by signing and putting their fingerprints to a "Public Renunciation of Communism" which was then published, and by performing what was called a "turning over a new leaf" ceremony.[2]

During this period [in 1966], Comrade Kang Sheng personally summoned and interrogated the big renegades Xu Bing, Yang Xianzhen, Liu Xiwu, Liao Luyan, and others, and took personal charge of investigating the circumstances surrounding how, in 1936, Bo Yibo and sixty other renegades surrendered and gave themselves up to the enemy and got out of the prison known as the "Beiping Soldiers' Self-Examination Institute."

"A clap of thunder of immense power cracks open the doors to a new universe; The East Wind, blowing over ten thousand li, sweeps away all the remnant clouds." In that heaven-shaking thunderous cannon shot that was sounded in our great leader Chairman Mao's "Bombard the Headquarters," and carried along on the crest of the red storm of the Great Proletarian Cultural Revolution, from the very beginning, the conspiratorial clique of the big renegade Liu Shaoqi was seized and dragged out into the open by the command headquarters of the proletariat. . . .

In August and September of 1966, news that the Case Groups or-

---

[2]The full title of the document referred to here is "Zhonggong Zhongyang guanyu yinfa Bo Yibo, Liu Lantao, An Ziwen, Yang Xianzhen deng ren zishou panbian cailiao de pishi" (Comment/instruction of the CCP Center concerning the printing and distribution of materials documenting the voluntary surrender and defection by Bo Yibo, Liu Lantao, An Ziwen, Yang Xianzhen, et al.). The quoted passage is from one of the document's numerous appendixes, a report from the Peng Zhen Case Group Office entitled, "Preliminary Investigation into the Matter of the Voluntary Surrender and Defection of Bo Yibo, Liu Lantao, An Ziwen, Yang Xianzhen, et al." The rare full text of this appendix is reprinted in an untitled collection (cover missing) of documents from the "Cleansing the Class Ranks" campaign (pp. 22–23) held in the library of the John King Fairbank Center, Harvard University, Cambridge, Massachusetts.

ganized by the Center and Comrade Kang Sheng had found out, through their investigations, [the truth about] the problem of the surrender and betrayal [of the Party] on the part of Bo Yibo, An Ziwen, Liu Lantao, Yang Xianzhen, and others, reached a number of organs at the Center, such as the Ministry of Agriculture.

Subsequently, a number of people in charge of personnel and organization work in the old Ministry of Agriculture made known to the masses what they knew about the circumstances relating to this renegade clique. The document "Report Concerning the Circumstances of How the Capitalist-Roader Power Holders Led by Liao Luyan Carried Out Class Vengeance in the Ministry of Agriculture (Third Draft)," issued by the Party Group of the old Ministry of Agriculture on September 23, 1966, pointed out: "The political background of these power holders (such as Liao Luyan) is problematic. Liao Luyan was himself an element who betrayed the Party and gave himself up [to the enemy]." It also said: "Liao Luyan: He is from a trader capitalist background. He was captured and arrested [by the enemy] in 1930 and was in prison for a time along with Peng Zhen, An Ziwen, and others. Then he surrendered to the enemy and betrayed the Party, by making an open declaration to that effect in the newspaper." This report was made public at a mass rally of the Ministry of Agriculture at the time.

At the end of September 1966, Liao Luyan returned from the countryside to Beijing for the anniversary of the founding of the People's Republic. On October 2 and 3, the masses of the Ministry of Agriculture dragged Liao Luyan out for struggle and demanded that he give an honest account of the matter related to his surrendering to the enemy and getting out of prison. At the time Liao had no recourse but to explain the circumstances under which he had surrendered to the enemy. He said it happened in late August, early September 1936, in the "Beiping Soldiers' Self-Examination Institute." He also said that, [at the time, he went by] his original given name, Liao Guangjiu. Then, on October 4, some of the masses in the Ministry of Agriculture went forthwith to the Beijing Public Library to check on the newspapers that had been published by the enemy government in places such as Beiping, Tianjin, and Ningbo around the time in question. On October 5 they discovered, in an issue of the newspaper *Huabei ribao* (North China daily), which was published by the enemy government at the time, the "Open Notice of Renunciation of Communism" which these renegades had made. They immediately took photographs of this material and reported the matter to the higher authorities while at the same time making this case public within the ministry. On the same day they also organized themselves to struggle and denounce the big traitor Liao Luyan.[3]

At the same time, the State Economic Commission, the First Ministry of Light Industry, the Ministry of Education, and other units also conducted investigations into the matter of the surrender by other renegades such as Bo Yibo, Zhou Zhongying, Kong Xiangzhen, and Yang Xianzhen.

"We will wipe away all harmful pests; Be Invincible."[4]

Once the little generals of the Red Guards found out from the organs of the central government, such as the Ministry of Agriculture, how people like Bo Yibo, An Ziwen, Yang Xianzhen, and Liao Luyan had surrendered to the enemy and betrayed the Party, they were utterly enraged. With their boundless loyalty, their boundless adoration, their complete and unbounded faith in and boundless love for their great leader Chairman Mao, they threw themselves into an unprecedentedly large-scale people's war to surround and annihilate the conspiratorial clique of that big renegade Liu Shaoqi. Starting in late October and early November 1966, numerous revolutionary Red Guard organizations around the country—in places like Xi'an Jiaotong University, Jilin Teachers' University, the East Is Red Group at Beijing Agricultural University, the Three Red Flags Faction at China People's University, the East Is Red Group of the Beijing Geological Institute, the Jinggangshan faction at Qinghua University, the Red Flag group at the Beijing Aeronautical Institute, the August 13 faction at Tianjin University, and both the Weidong Red Guards and the August 18 Red Rebel Regiment here at Nankai University—carried out major work to nab and bring renegades and traitors to account. The young militant Red Guards, carrying with them the treasured book, crossed over mountains and streams, underwent all sorts of hardships, and they were able to drag out, one by one, that small handful of renegades against the Party and the secret agents of the enemy who had wormed their way into the ranks of the revolution. By doing so, they made an immortal

---

[3]In March 1967, the CCP Center circulated a photograph of the original newspaper notice as one of the appendixes (this one classified "absolutely secret") to CCP Central Document *Zhongfa* (1967) 96.

[4]Lines quoted from Mao Zedong's poem "To Comrade Guo Moruo" (January 1963).

contribution to the cause of the Great Proletarian Cultural Revolution.

"If we are to enumerate truly great people, we need to focus [not on the past, but] on today."[5]

The Weidong Red Guards of Nankai University, with their boundless loyalty to Chairman Mao's proletarian revolutionary line, threw themselves heroically, without reserve and without regard for their own safety, into the life-and-death battle with the big renegade Liu Shaoqi's clique. They stormed the front lines and totally routed the enemy. In doing so they fully epitomized the heroic spirit of daring to struggle, daring to be victorious, fighting with the greatest valor in the face of all odds and hardships, and never yielding no matter what the setbacks may be. In so doing they acted as typical representatives of the revolutionary Red Guards nurtured and succored by Mao Zedong Thought.

After they discovered, in early November 1966, in the Beijing Library, in a faded and aged issue of the *Huabei ribao* published under the auspices of the enemy government, the "Open Notice of Renunciation of Communism" of Zhang Yongpu (Bo Yibo's alias), Xu Ziwen (An Ziwen's alias), and the others of the gang of eighty-three [*sic*] renegades, the Weidong warriors, with their boundless sense of responsibility toward our great leader Chairman Mao and the cause of revolution, dedicated themselves to the task at hand and, breaking through every blockade thrown in their way by the representatives of the bourgeois reactionary line, began to carry out their meticulous and arduous work of investigating the affairs of the [counter-revolutionary] clique of the big renegade Liu Shaoqi.

On November 12, 1966, Nankai University became engulfed in an atmosphere of White Terror created by the frenetic counteroffensives unleashed by those of the bourgeois reactionary line. The North wind was howling ominously, and the dark clouds were roiling over the campus. It was on this very day that the warriors of Weidong posted, on Nankai University's campus, the big-character poster "Unmasking the Inside Story of the Big Renegade Clique" in which they made public the list of the names of the eighty-three traitors, which included the names of Bo Yibo and An Ziwen, among others, as well as a copy of the renegades' "Open Notice of Renunciation of Communism" and the time it was published. This revolutionary big-character poster

---

[5]Lines quoted from Mao Zedong's poem "Snow" (February 1936).

pointed out the following for the first time, clearly and unequivocally and on the basis of serious investigative work and scientific analysis:

> Where was the root of this renegade clique? It was in the Northern Bureau [of the Party] at the time! And who, one might then ask, was the boss behind the scenes? It was none other than the biggest party person in power taking the capitalist road. "We must dig up and eliminate this black root at all costs! We must drag out and seize this back stage boss!" The big-character poster went on, in the final section, to call on "all comrades who truly care about the destiny of this nation, unite and work together with one mind and spirit and strength and follow the clues hidden for us in the names of Gao Yangyun, Bo Yibo, Liao Luyan, An Ziwen, Yang Xianzhen, Li Chuli, Liu Lantao, Kong Xiangzhen, Xu Bing, and Peng Zhen—until we are able to dig up that black root that lies at the bottom of all this! We swear to defend Chairman Mao to the death! We swear to defend the Great Mao Zedong Thought to the death! We swear to defend to the death this proletarian country of ours, so that it may never change its color!"

This revolutionary big-character poster, whose spearhead was directly pointed at the largest handful of capitalist roaders in the Party, clearly pointed out who and what stood behind the scenes propping up the big renegade clique. The poster reflected the noble and heroic spirit of the Weidong Red Guards in their pledge to wage bloody battle against Liu Shaoqi's big renegade clique, to the death. When it was posted, it immediately created shock waves throughout the entire Nankai University campus, and also attracted the attention of revolutionary rebel factions and their comrades-in-arms throughout the country.

On November 13 the Weidong warriors published another big-character poster entitled, "An Appeal to the Revolutionary Masses Throughout the Nation: Seize the Renegades!" With it, the Weidong fighters once more expressed their heroic ambition and steadfast resolve to thoroughly destroy the Liu Shaoqi Big Renegade Clique and to stand firm, never to give up, not even in death, until this goal has been accomplished.

On November 19 the Weidong warriors published, in their "Investigation Report on the Renegade Clique," the aliases, real names, and current official positions and titles of some forty big renegades—out of the sixty-one who had surrendered to the enemy in the "Beiping Soldiers' Self-Examination Institute" back in 1936—whose cases have already been thoroughly brought to light, and preliminarily clarified the circumstances under which Liu Shaoqi had instigated and instructed them to surrender to the enemy and turn coat against the Communist Party. In this investigative report, the Weidong Red Guards once again iterated the following, unequivocally and clearly: "The declaration of their renunciation of the Party was made under directions and instructions from Liu Shaoqi, and they were put up to it by the Northern Bureau, which had usurped the name of the Central Committee."

"He who is not afraid of death by a thousand cuts dares to unhorse the emperor."[6]

Under the guidance of the invincible Mao Zedong Thought, this group of revolutionary "nobodies," who were originally unknown and students from Nankai University who were not well recognized, once again declared war on the "Colossus of the Day"—Liu Shaoqi! They declared war on Liu Shaoqi's Big Renegade Clique!

---

[6]Lines from the novel *Dream of the Red Chamber,* here most likely quoted from Mao Zedong's "Speech at the Chinese Communist Party's National Conference on Propaganda Work" (March 1957) in which Mao had cited them to characterize "the dauntless spirit needed in our struggle to build socialism and communism."

20
Interrogation Record: Wang Guangmei

Qinghua University "Jinggangshan Regiment"
Red Guards

Source: The "South Sea Wall" Combat Team of the Capital Red Guard Congress, Qinghua University "Jinggangshan" Regiment, ed., *Sanshen dapashou Wang Guangmei (pipan cailiao)* (*Thrice Interrogating Big Pickpocket Wang Guangmei (Denunciation Materials)*) (N.p., n.d.), pp. 1–7, as reprinted in *Red Guard Publications* (Washington D.C.: Center for Chinese Research Materials, 1975), Vol. 17, pp. 5547–63.

The place: Qinghua University central building, 7th floor
The time: Around six-thirty A.M. [10 April 1967]

INTERROGATOR: Why did Liu Shaoqi call the movie *Secret History of the Qing Court* "patriotic"?[1]

WANG GUANGMEI: I never heard comrade Shaoqi referring to the movie as being "patriotic"! Comrade Shaoqi definitively would not have said anything like that. I have faith in Chairman Mao; Chairman Mao will investigate the matter and find out what really happened. (The students want her to put on the dress she wore while in Indonesia, but Wang Guangmei refuses.[2])

INTERROGATOR: You must put on that dress!

WANG: I will not!

INTERROGATOR: You have no choice in this regard!

WANG (drawing in her horns and pointing at her own dress): This is good enough for receiving guests.

INTERROGATOR (sternly): Receiving guests? You are being struggled against today!

WANG: I am not going to put on that dress. It is not presentable.

INTERROGATOR: Why then did you wear it in Indonesia?

WANG: It was summer at that time, and I wore it in Djakarta.

INTERROGATOR: Why did you wear it in Lahore?

WANG: I am not going to put it on, whatever you may say.

---

[1]The movie, shot at the end of the 1940s, dealt with the Reform Movement of 1898 and the Boxer Uprising. According to Cultural Revolutionary accounts, it "eulogized the royalists while slandering the revolutionary mass movement and the heroic struggle of the people against imperialism and feudalism." It was the subject of the first major public salvo against Liu, Qi Benyu's "Patriotism or National Betrayal?—On the Reactionary Film *Secret History of the Qing Court*," translated in Harold C. Hinton, ed., *The People's Republic of China 1949–1979: A Documentary Survey* (Wilmington: Scholarly Resources, 1980), pp. 1686–96.

[2]This refers to Liu Shaoqi's state visit to Indonesia in the spring of 1963, during which on one occasion Wang Guangmei had worn a traditional Chinese *qipao*.

INTERROGATOR: Let me tell you: you are being struggled against today. You'd better be careful if you are not honest with us!

WANG: Even if I have to die, that doesn't matter.

INTERROGATOR: Death? We want to keep you alive. Put it on!

WANG: Would it not be better for us to discuss things seriously?

INTERROGATOR: Who wants to discuss things with you? Let me tell you: You are being struggled against today!

WANG (angrily): On no account can you encroach upon my personal freedom.

INTERROGATOR (amid the sound of laughter): You are the wife of a Three-Anti Element, a reactionary bourgeois element, and a class-alien element.[3] You will not be given an iota of small democracy, let alone extensive democracy! Dictatorship is exercised over you today, and you are not free.

WANG (interrupting): Who says I am the wife of a Three-Anti Element?

INTERROGATOR: We do.

WANG: I will not put on that dress, come what may. If I have committed mistakes, I am open to criticism and struggle.

INTERROGATOR: You are guilty of crimes! You are being struggled against today, and you will also be struggled against hereafter. Put it on!

WANG (evasively, pointing at the fur coat she is wearing): This is already good enough for receiving guests. It was a gift from Afghanistan. They had this in mind when they said that I was fashion-minded.

---

[3]A "Three-Anti Element" is someone who is allegedly anti-Party, anti–Mao Zedong Thought, and anti-socialist.

INTERROGATOR: We want you to put on the dress that you wore in Indonesia.

WANG: That was summer. There is winter clothing for winter, summer clothing for summer, and spring clothing for spring. I cannot put on a summer dress now. If I must wear a dress for spring, I can send someone to bring me one.

INTERROGATOR: Rubbish! We know nothing about such bourgeois stuff as what is good for summer, winter, or spring, for receiving guests or for travel.

WANG: Chairman Mao has said that we must pay attention to the climate and change our clothing accordingly.

INTERROGATOR (amid laughter): What Chairman Mao was referring to was the political climate. With your standpoint, even though you are now wearing a fur coat, you are likely to freeze to death.

INTERROGATOR: Let me ask you: Didn't you wear that dress when you were in Lahore although it was colder at that time than it is now? Put it on! It will do so long as you will not freeze to death. Are you going to put it on?

WANG: No.

INTERROGATOR: All right! We'll give you ten minutes. Watch what happens at a quarter to seven. Try to defy us by not wearing that dress. We mean what we say. (Wang remains silent.)

INTERROGATOR: Wang Guangmei: What's your opinion of Liu Shaoqi's fall from grace?

WANG: It is an excellent thing. In this way, China will be prevented from going revisionist.

INTERROGATOR: One day we are also going to drag out Liu Shaoqi and struggle against him. Do you believe us?

WANG: You just go on with your struggle; just carry on . . . (silent)

WANG: You members of the Jinggangshan Regiment are thoroughly revolutionary. Except, the form of struggle which you employ is no good. Could you not find a more sophisticated form of denunciation?

INTERROGATOR: Pay no attention to what she says! We shall see what you look like when your ten minutes are over.

WANG: You . . . I can ring someone up and ask for a spring dress.

INTERROGATOR: That won't do!

WANG: This dress is made of silk. It is too cold!

INTERROGATOR: Put it on and wear your fur coat on top of it.

INTERROGATOR: "Small wonder flies freeze and perish."[4]

WANG: If I were really opposed to Chairman Mao, I would deserve to freeze to death.

INTERROGATOR: You *are* opposed to Chairman Mao.

WANG: I am not against him now, and I will not oppose him in the future.

INTERROGATOR: No more nonsense with her. . . . Seven minutes left!

WANG: (silence)

WANG: How about my putting on that pair of shoes (pointing to the pair of pointed shoes she had brought with her)?

INTERROGATOR: That is not enough! You must wear everything.

WANG: You don't have the right.

INTERROGATOR: We have this right! You are being struggled against today. We are at liberty to wage struggle in whatever form we may want to, and you have no freedom. You might as well forget about

---

[4] A line quoted from Mao's poem "Winter Clouds" (1962).

your vile theory of "everybody being equal before truth." We are the revolutionary masses, and you are a notorious counter-revolutionary old hag. Don't try to confuse the class demarcation line!

(At the time limit set, the [Jinggangshan] "Ghostbusters" (*Zhuo-guidui*) begin to force Wang to put on the outlandish dress.)

WANG: Wait a moment. (They ignore her. Wang Guangmei sits on the floor and refuses to allow them to slip the dress on her. Eventually she is pulled to her feet and the dress is slipped on her.)

INTERROGATOR: Have you got it on now? (Wang Guangmei had said that the dress was too small for her.)

WANG: You have violated Chairman Mao's instruction about not struggling against people by force.

([RED GUARDS] Reading in unison [from Mao's "Little Red Book"]: "A revolution is not a dinner party, or writing an essay, or painting a picture, or doing embroidery; it cannot be so refined, so leisurely and gentle, so temperate, kind, courteous, restrained, and magnanimous. A revolution is an insurrection, an act of violence by which one class overthrows another.")

WANG: You violate Chairman Mao's instructions by saying . . . (Wang Guangmei is interrupted and forced to wear silk stockings and high-heeled shoes and a specially made necklace. She is photographed.)

WANG: My point is that you are using coercion. Chairman Mao says that nobody is allowed to strike, abuse, or insult another person.

INTERROGATOR: Nonsense! It is you who have insulted us. By wearing this dress to flirt with Sukarno in Indonesia, you have put the Chinese people to shame and insulted the Chinese people as a whole. Coercion is called for when dealing with such a reactionary bourgeois element as you—the biggest pickpocket on the Qinghua campus! ([Red Guards] Reading in unison [from Mao's "Little Red Book"]: "Everything reactionary is the same; if you don't hit it, it won't fall.")

WANG: One day we shall see if I am indeed "reactionary" or not!

INTERROGATOR: What! Are you trying to reverse the verdict? (Everybody begins listing her crimes.)

WANG: (denies the accusations) I wish you would make a proper investigation.

INTERROGATOR: Let me ask you: Who is responsible for the policy of "Hitting at a great many in order to protect a handful"?[5]

WANG: In any case, certainly not I. . . . A true revolutionary must dare to stand forth and take responsibility for what she has done.

INTERROGATOR (points out that she told Liu Shaoqi last evening that Kuai Dafu had "Hit at a great many in order to protect a handful")

WANG: This is not true.

INTERROGATOR: Do you want to cross-examine the witness? You said this at six o'clock last evening.

WANG (embarrassed): I welcome you to try to influence the attitude of the members of my family. (Because Wang's daughter is unwilling to face her mother, the cross-examination is put off.)[6]

INTERROGATOR: Of course we want to influence the attitude of the members of your family . . .

INTERROGATOR: What was the intention behind the work teams?

WANG: Work teams were dispatched with the consent and according to the decision of the Politburo Standing Committee at the time. Of course the principal responsibility is Liu Shaoqi's, as Chairman Mao was absent. I am the only person whom Liu actually dispatched himself in person.

INTERROGATOR: How many of the revolutionary masses have been branded as counter-revolutionaries by you alone? How many persons have you victimized?

WANG: We have not branded a single person as counter-revolutionary.

---

[5]This refers to the alleged practice of the work teams that entered China's schools in June 1966.

[6]Wang's stepdaughter Liu Tao was a student at Qinghua University. A translation of her long denunciation of her stepmother is in Hinton, pp. 1639–53.

INTERROGATOR: There is no way for you to deny the fact that you "hit at a great many in order to protect a handful"!

WANG: Facts are facts, and conclusions should be drawn according to facts. *That* is Mao Zedong Thought.

INTERROGATOR: Wrong! The standpoint is the most important thing. Taking the reactionary stand, you see only the dark side of the revolutionary masses and are opposed to the Great Cultural Revolution. The facts we have studied and collected are different from yours.

WANG: Now some people want to shift the responsibility to others. . . . A person should dare to acknowledge facts, if he is a genuine revolutionary Leftist. It is wrong to "Doubt everything." Who was it that advocated "doubting everything"?[7]

INTERROGATOR: You have doubted all revolutionary things and attacked all of the revolutionary masses and cadres.

WANG: In any case it was not my idea to "doubt everything," much less was it Liu Shaoqi's. We are opposed to "doubting everything."

INTERROGATOR: You are opposed to the revolutionary masses who doubt you. You mortally fear those who have their doubts about you.

WANG: I am a Communist and fear nothing. I am not afraid of death by a thousand cuts . . .

INTERROGATOR (shouting a slogan): Down with the Three-Anti Element Wang Guangmei!

WANG: Since you think in this way, I will one day . . .

INTERROGATOR (citing facts: Wang lit a cigarette for Sukarno and brought disgrace upon the Chinese people.)

---

[7]The slogan "doubt everything" (*huaiyi yiqie*) is intimately associated with Tao Zhu, who in the autumn of 1966 had made an ambiguous remark that was interpreted by some Red Guards as implying that even Mao Zedong himself could be "doubted."

WANG: I am of the opinion that I have nothing to be ashamed of. At the farewell banquet that day, he sat next to me, and as the hostess . . . I should respect the Indonesian customs.

INTERROGATOR: To hell with you! We know nothing of those foreign conventions. You flirted with such a bad fellow as Sukarno.

WANG: At that time Sukarno was quite progressive . . . in diplomacy . . .

INTERROGATOR: So tell us, how many students did you brand as counter-revolutionaries? There are quite a few of us here.

WANG: In any case, we only criticized people and did not brand them as counter-revolutionaries.

INTERROGATOR: Who told you to oppose what you called "sham Leftists"?

WANG: Not Liu Shaoqi. It was the work team, Ye Lin and Yang Tianfang, who asked me. They said that Kuai Dafu had written a comment calling for a power seizure.[8] They also gave a very distorted description of the situation, and on the basis of what they said, I agreed.

INTERROGATOR: Did Liu Shaoqi issue any instructions?

WANG: Liu Shaoqi issued very few instructions concerning Qinghua University.

INTERROGATOR: Who authorized you to sell vegetables in the university canteen? You were fishing for political capital.

WANG: That was after Chairman Mao had asked Liu Shaoqi: "Why is it that Wang Guangmei does not live together, eat together, and work together with the masses any longer, the way she did during the Four

---

[8]The "comment" refers to a few lines that Kuai had scribbled at the bottom of a big-character poster by one Liu Caitang on 21 June 1966. Kuai had suggested that the Qinghua students ask themselves if the work team really represented their interests. If not, he said, they might themselves have to carry out a second "power seizure."

Cleanups?" The Chairman said: "She can participate in labor . . . in this way she will be able to accept criticism." I heard this and was moved. So I went to work.

INTERROGATOR: Then you should work honestly! Why did you go to three different mess halls to sell vegetables?

WANG: Was it not because my exposure to the masses was not wide enough that I went to three different mess halls? (The masses expose the facts.)

WANG: Liu Tao also criticized me for this, and I have been thinking about it.

INTERROGATOR: So let's hear it: Who was it that came up with "Hitting at a great many in order to protect a handful"?

WANG: Really, it wasn't Liu Shaoqi.

INTERROGATOR: Who branded Kuai Dafu a counter-revolutionary?

WANG: It had nothing to do with Liu Shaoqi. Also, he was almost certainly not branded. (After the students cite facts to refute her, Wang Guangmei becomes incoherent and begins contradicting herself. At first she affirms that nobody had been branded, but then she says: "I told the work team that it was not good to oppose Kuai Dafu in this way." Hereafter she says: "I said that we must not prematurely brand people as counter-revolutionaries.")

INTERROGATOR: What do you think of the criticism of the book *Cultivation*?[9]

WANG: The book is idealist and fails to discuss the class struggle, and on this point I agree with the statement made in the *Red Flag* commentator's article. Subjectively, on the other hand, I don't agree with the claim that it opposes Mao Zedong Thought. It merely represents an insufficiently transformed worldview.

---

[9] I.e. Liu Shaoqi's *How to Be a Good Communist,* a book dealing with the need to maintain absolute loyalty to the Party and to overcome bureaucratic and individualistic tendencies, mainly by practicing "self-cultivation." The book had been re-issued in 1962.

INTERROGATOR: What do you think of comrade Qi Benyu's article criticizing *Secret History of the Qing Court*?

WANG: That is a movie of national betrayal from beginning to end. Comrade Qi Benyu's criticism is quite profound and thorough. Liu Shaoqi never said that the movie was patriotic. He and I watched it together, and he saw only the first half of it; when the sun came out, you couldn't see very clearly. He did not say anything. He definitely did not comment on it. We watched it together, so I know. He said nothing. Definitely.

INTERROGATOR: So according to what you say, Liu Shaoqi did nothing wrong?

WANG: He is responsible. In 1952, Chairman Mao did tell him that the movie was one of national betrayal. As a senior leader, it was a major error on his part not to organize a denunciation of it.

INTERROGATOR: What kind of major error is that? That's only an oversight in work.

WANG: It may have been an oversight, or it may have been a major error.

INTERROGATOR: So what you're saying is that comrade Qi Benyu is a rumor monger!

WANG: It may have been somebody else who made this comment in Liu Shaoqi's name

INTERROGATOR: Very well! Last evening you said: "Qi Benyu was once in the same Party branch with me. I know him." Only later, when we pressed further, you said that "Qi Benyu is a good comrade." Now you have revealed your true nature.

WANG (brazen-facedly): Rubbish. I said it on my own initiative and not because you were pressuring me.

INTERROGATOR: Do you think that Qi's article is correct or not? Chairman Mao has read it!

WANG: Is that so? Has Chairman Mao read it? I still think that one has to proceed from what is good for the revolution and from the facts. Chairman Mao has to be told the facts the way they are.

INTERROGATOR: Are you clear as to whom comrade Qi Benyu's article is directed against?

WANG: Then he really does refer to Liu Shaoqi.

INTERROGATOR: What do you think of the questions raised by comrade Qi Benyu?

WANG: Liu Shaoqi is only responsible for some of those things.

INTERROGATOR: So you're saying that *Red Flag* is spreading rumors? That Liu Shaoqi is not a person in authority taking the capitalist road?

WANG: I have faith in Chairman Mao and in the masses. In the past I made mistakes because I did not have enough faith in him. I have worked by Liu Shaoqi's side for more than a decade, and I feel that not everything [in the article] tallies with the facts. A lot of it has nothing to do with Liu Shaoqi. It never occurred to me directly that he is the biggest Party-person in authority taking the capitalist road.

INTERROGATOR: So what was telling the clique of renegades to surrender to the enemy all about?[10]

WANG: It was not [Liu] who instructed them to do that. It was a responsible comrade's proposal. [Liu merely] agreed.

INTERROGATOR: Who was he?

WANG: I refuse to say.

INTERROGATOR: You're shielding someone! Hurry up and tell us.

WANG: (after pondering for some time) It was Ke Qingshi who proposed it; Liu Shaoqi agreed.[11]

---

[10]This refers to the incident of the "Sixty-One Renegades." See Document 22.

[11]The ultimate responsibility was Zhang Wentian's, who, as the then general secretary of the CCP, had approved the controversial decision to publish admissions of "surrender" to the KMT in the media. In this way, the release of hundreds of senior CCP cadres was secured.

INTERROGATOR: (angrily) Don't you dare slander the revered comrade Ke!

WANG: It does not matter what I say, you still won't believe me. You may carry out an investigation, OK? I'm telling you, Wang Qian is a scoundrel who spreads rumors and gives vent to personal spite.[12] Don't be fooled! I don't care if you don't believe me . . .

INTERROGATOR: Wang Guangmei, tell us how you feel about Liu Shaoqi being the biggest Party-person in power taking the capitalist road?

WANG: Subjectively, my understanding is not yet up to that level. In any case, before the Eleventh Plenum of the Eighth Central Committee, the Chairman entrusted Liu Shaoqi and the Central Secretariat with many tasks, and if anything happened, [Liu] would of course have been responsible. But now he has had to step aside and is no longer responsible and no longer in power! At the time of the "reactionary line," he traversed a stretch of the capitalist road.[13]

INTERROGATOR: Only at the time of the reactionary line? That's all?

WANG: Of course not. Anyone who makes an error in line will have traversed a stretch of the capitalist road. . . . (The students tell her to put on the necklace.)

INTERROGATOR: Tell me this! Comrade Jiang Qing had told you not to wear the necklace when you were abroad. Why did you have to wear it?

WANG: Comrade Jiang Qing only told me not to wear the brooch but said nothing about the necklace. But the question is one and the same.

INTERROGATOR: You are talking nonsense! You are a Three-Anti Element.

---

[12]Wang Qian was Liu Shaoqi's fourth wife (Liu had divorced her in 1947) and the mother of Liu Tao. When the Cultural Revolution began, she was living on the campus of China People's University, in Beijing.

[13]The time of the "[bourgeois] reactionary line" refers to the initial period of the Cultural Revolution, prior to Mao's return to Beijing, during which Liu Shaoqi had been left "in charge" by Mao.

WANG: I am not! . . .

INTERROGATOR: We intend to struggle against you reactionary bourgeois element and big pickpocket on the Qinghua campus.

WANG: I am not what you say I am; I am a Communist Party member.

INTERROGATOR: Don't try to denigrate our Party. Haven't you done enough filthy things already? What did you do during the Four Cleanups in Taoyuan?[14]

WANG: How much do you know about the Four Cleanups? From whom did you get your information? You have spent no more than five days at the grass-roots level, while I stayed there for almost one year. I understand things better than you do. You must investigate things in real earnest.

INTERROGATOR: To hell with you! Your Taoyuan experience is notorious enough. You'll soon hear of it.

WANG: Taoyuan's experience is good and not bad. But there were shortcomings and mistakes . . .

WANG: I admit I have committed Rightist-opportunism errors!

INTERROGATOR: You were "left" in appearance and "right" in essence, waving the Red Flag to oppose the Red Flag!

WANG: I leaned to the Right.

INTERROGATOR: You leaned to the Right? If you'd been any more Leftist, we would all have been dead by now! "Hitting at a great many"—and you mean to say you leaned to the Right?

WANG: I've seen those materials and they're extremely biased. . . . (The masses are enraged, and they dress her up for a photograph. She is led away to be struggled against.)

---

[14]Wang had spent the winter of 1963–64 taking part in the Four Cleanups in Taoyuan Brigade, Hebei, and her experience had been written up for emulation in a major CCP Central Document. During the Cultural Revolution, Wang's "Taoyuan experience" (*Taoyuan jingyan*) was widely denounced as an example of "Leftism."

WANG: You are making every effort to make me look ugly.

INTERROGATOR: This is what you have been all the time. Why feel shy about what you have done. All we do is restore your true identity. (Wang Guangmei is ready to "go to prison" and has brought with her a towel, a toothbrush, and other things.)

INTERROGATOR: Wang Guangmei! Are you afraid?

WANG: Why should I be? I am not afraid. A Communist has nothing to fear. (As she is about to go downstairs, her shaking hands are unable to put things in the proper place.)

WANG: I want a glass of water.

WANG: Where is that PLA comrade? Old Ma, I want a tranquilizer.

INTERROGATOR: Are you afraid?

WANG: My mind is calm. I have to take medicine because I am sick. My nerves are no good. (She gasps for breath.)

INTERROGATOR: Wang Guangmei's hands are trembling.

WANG: There is some trouble with my hands. I am not afraid, and I am very calm in mind. (Wang Guangmei asks for two tranquilizer tablets, but the PLA comrade gives her only one.) All right. I'll take one as you say. (As she is dragged out, she becomes downcast and turns pale. She drags her feet step by step and again asks for a tranquilizer.) Where is the PLA comrade? I want some more medicine.

INTERROGATOR: Didn't you say you were not afraid? Paper tiger!

WANG: I am not afraid, and I am willing to go through with the meeting, but I have been running a fever these past few days. Liu Shaoqi is also sick, and I have nursed him a number of days. (She then purses her lips, and the veins stand out on her hands.)

INTERROGATOR: What have you in mind now?

WANG (in a low voice): I am now ready to face the criticism, repudiation, and struggle of the masses.

21
On Case Examination Work

Kang Sheng

Our translation of this lecture given to representatives of "mass" organizations, case examination groups, and the PLA in Jilin Province on 8 February 1968 is based on the excerpt published as "Kang Sheng tongzhi tan zhuan'an gongzuo" in Chinese Academy of Sciences Revolutionary Committee, ed., *Xuexi wenjian* (*Study Documents*), Vol. 2 (April 1968), pp. 10–12.

Comrades who are involved in the work of examining special cases must, first of all, master and hold firmly to Mao Zedong Thought. Second, they must have a clear and correct class viewpoint. What they are dealing with are one traitor [after another], and the longer they deal with something like that, the greater the likelihood of their minds becoming confused, and, slowly, maybe their own ways of thinking, their own ideology, will become affected. One day you find out about a traitor here, and the next day you deal with another traitor over there; and in the meantime, all the material is concentrated here, in your hands; O good gracious! The Chinese Communist Party is such a great, glorious and correct party; how could things have become so dark, so black all over? [Maybe it is] no longer quite so great, glorious, or correct[?] ([Original editor's comment] Some omissions here.) Unless you have a rock-solid firm and steadfast standpoint, slowly your own viewpoint and standpoint can be shaken, and you will begin to waver. [What you see is] Liu Shaoqi turns out to be a renegade, and Peng Zhen too; Yang Shangkun was in secret and illicit communications with a foreign government, and An Ziwen, too, was a traitor. After you have read [all the material on these cases], everywhere you turn your eyes, things are black all over; what greatness, what glory, is there to talk about? This is why I say unless your class viewpoint is clear and firm, you are liable to waver. After you have worked with case examinations for a good part of the day, you might ask yourself:

Is it just that? Am I wasting my energy? The answer, I tell you, is: No. You are not wasting your energy. I have long held two sets of ideological preparedness myself [for this sort of work]. One is that the cases I deal with are indeed renegades; and the other is that they turn out not to be. When one investigates and examines the material, given that people's ideas are bound to be a bit subjective, when you are trying to nab a renegade, your mentality is likely to be biased in that direction, and you are likely to feel: That fellow must be a renegade. If, on the other hand, you are somewhat ideologically numbed, or insensitive in your thinking, you might lean to the other side in your thinking. That is why we absolutely must seek the truth from facts (*shishi qiushi*). For this reason, too, in dealing with those cases we must link up with the masses. The Center has made a commentary on the case of the sixty-one renegades; have you seen it?[1] In this matter, which entails responsibility for a person's political life, the Center takes a very cautious attitude. Owing to the complexities of the environment and circumstances, it is possible that there could be mistakes; and sometimes it is unavoidable that mistakes would be made. In the examination of cadres at Yan'an, for instance, there were mistakes made, and subsequently, those cases were reversed and corrected. And after the Liberation of the entire country, when the matter was reviewed, it has been proven that in the vast majority of cases, the examination of cadres at Yan'an had been correct. Sometimes, there could also be mistakes in the reversal of verdicts; this is because conditions evolve and change and are not always the same, and so this matter calls for investigation and study. In this matter we must adhere firmly to policy. On the issue of people switching from Youth League to Party [membership]: In this matter, we must remember that the history of the Party

---

[1]The reference is to Central Document *Zhongfa* [1967] 96: "Zhonggong Zhongyang guanyu yinfa Bo Yibo, Liu Lantao, An Ziwen, Yang Xianzhen deng ren zishou panbian cailiao de pishi" (Comment/Instruction of the CCP Center Concerning the Printing and Distribution of Materials Documenting the Voluntary Surrender and Defection by Bo Yibo, Liu Lantao, An Ziwen, Yang Xianzhen, et al.). Reprinted under the "sanitized" title, "Comment/Instruction of the CCP Center Concerning the Printing and Distribution of Materials Documenting the Release from Prison of Bo Yibo, Liu Lantao, An Ziwen, Yang Xianzhen, et al.," in People's Liberation Army National Defense University Research Institute for Party History, Party Building, and Political Work, ed., *"Wenhua dageming" yanjiu ziliao* (*"Great Cultural Revolution" research materials*) (Beijing, 1988), Vol. 1, p. 344.

has evolved from period to period, and has not remained the same. You must not look at the past from today's standards. In terms of people switching from membership in the Youth League to Party membership in history overall, sometimes, in a war environment, when someone switched from the Youth League to the Party, he did not follow fixed procedures but soon began to take part in the work of the Party, and attend the Party's meetings—and so he became a member of the Party. Then there is the [matter of the] probation period. It was only when, after the War of Resistance Against Japan, when the [Youth] League was abolished, that there was a period of probation. So, in regard to this matter, things were very different from one historical period to another. Furthermore, there is then the question of people having surrendered [to the enemy], the question of turning against the Party, and the question of people having been arrested or captured [by the enemy]—the circumstances are all very complicated. On the one hand we must have a firm standpoint and uphold the principle that whenever someone confesses or gives up something to the enemy it is tantamount to treason. However, under such a principle, we must still analyze the situation specifically and concretely, understanding that there may be different conditions and circumstances. That is why when you conduct the investigation and examination you must pay great attention. That is why those of us involved in case examination work must, first of all, have a firm grasp of the Chairman's Thought; we must look at problems dialectically, and we must not be subjective. Secondly, we must be clear, correct and firm in our class viewpoint, and we must never, not for a minute, waver in our trust in the Party. Thirdly, we must have a firm grasp and command of policy. Case examination work is difficult and strenuous. One should acknowledge that there have already been very great accomplishments and successes. In the Northeast, you have accomplished a great deal in this regard. The success in Heilongjiang [province] with regard to investigating and examining cadres has been very great, and the Center has already approved and circulated their report.[2] In Shenyang, under the

---

[2]Kang appears to be referring to Central Document *Zhongfa* [1968] 25, of 5 February 1968, entitled "Zhongyang zhuanfa Heilongjiang sheng geming weiyuanhui 'Guanyu shenwa pantu gongzuo qingkuang de baogao' " (Center circulates Heilongjiang Provincial Revolutionary Commitee's "Report on work of digging deep to pull out renegades") and reprinted in an untitled collection (cover missing) of documents from the "Cleansing of the Class Ranks" campaign (pp. 27–29) held in the library of the John King Fairbank Center, Harvard University.

leadership of the Shenyang Military Region, all groups and factions have joined together to carry out the investigation and examination together, and the success has been remarkable. In this regard, you here in Jilin haven't done enough. That is why, as Revolutionary Committees are established, it becomes necessary to grasp this matter firmly. You must continue to grasp this matter, on the basis of [and learning from] the experience of the special case groups, following the experience of Heilongjiang and Liaoning, and you must continue to pursue it in greater depth. From here on out, case work will be very important work. You must not get involved in incessant debates and quarrels over cadres in connection with these cases. Instead, you must heighten your awareness of what the enemy's conditions are. On this point, you comrades of the Northeast must be particularly vigilant. In my opinion, in the past, you have been involved in too much factional fighting over factional interests and in promoting armed struggle, while falling behind in your awareness of the enemy's activities. The enemy has been able to make use of [your] factionalism; and it has given him something to hide behind. You should give thought to what it is that you are facing. In your area, in the past, there was a Japanese imperialist regime, then there was the Guomindang, and then U.S. imperialism; in addition to that you are also faced with the espionage activities of the Soviet and Korean revisionists. In fact, the activities of revisionist Korean secret agents have a long history in your area. Recently, we have come to know that the Korean revisionist regime is organizing treasonous activity among our people through its embassy—I'm quite sure that there must be such activities in your area. The Soviet revisionists have also been in your area for a very long time. This is something that must alert you and make you heighten your vigilance. Don't think that if the cadres are liberated, the work of the case groups will have been a waste of time and effort. If you do just that, your awareness of the enemy's activities will become diluted and weakened. Also don't let the same thing happen to you once a great alliance and unity has been brought about or when a Revolutionary Committee has been established; instead your sense of what the enemy may be up to must be strengthened, intensified and heightened. In many places, as soon as the Revolutionary Committee had been established, the enemy followed on its heels immediately. You must pay attention and be vigilant, and you must dig out the Soviet revisionist secret agents, the

Korean revisionist secret agents, and all the renegades. Learn from Heilongjiang and Liaoning. You have already done a great deal of work; you have come to grasp and understand quite a few circumstances and you have learned and acquired many skills; in the future, once the Revolutionary Committee is set up, you will become its backbone cadres. Remember, the enemy is very cunning. Didn't I say that last time? Last time, I spoke of the example where the Northeast Institute of Industrial Engineering in Liaoning took care of someone called Hou Zhi, and I criticized the way they had handled the matter. My criticism was not that it was wrong to deal with Hou Zhi or to arrest her; rather, my criticism had to do with them not turning her over to the organs of the proletarian dictatorship. What we had there was a veteran secret agent for Soviet revisionism—she had studied and practiced to become a secret agent for a long time in the Soviet Union. Not only did young people not understand clearly the issue at stake; even some cadres were unable to get to the bottom of her situation. She had many false fronts and disguises. First she masqueraded as an anti–Wang Ming progressive; then she masqueraded as a veteran revolutionary loyal to the Party, and she made use of her image as a veteran cadre to attack the proletarian headquarters. Thirdly, she masqueraded as a victim! She claimed that her husband had been eliminated and purged at the time when the Soviet Union purged counter-revolutionaries. In fact, what happened was that she betrayed her husband, and now she turns around and claims that the Chinese Communist Party had not helped her resolve the problem. Finally, she masqueraded as someone who confesses to having made some mistakes, and then uses the opportunity to spread even more poison. In a situation like that, you simply couldn't get to the bottom of her real problems. The Northeast Institute of Industrial Engineering interrogated her. Let me tell you, the more they interrogate her, the more poison she will spew forth. That's why I told them that they must immediately hand her over to the dictatorship. I was not suggesting at all that they made a mistake in grabbing Hou Zhi. In fact, I suppose she is not the only one of her kind in the Northeast who is a secret agent who has received training at the hands of Soviet revisionists, is she? The Soviet revisionists have trained many secret agents now operating in our country; the Mongolian revisionists are promoting treasonous activities among our people and so are the Korean revisionists. The Soviet revisionists are sending secret agents to China. You must also heighten your vigilance against infiltration by Japanese secret agents and the secret agents of the Guomindang. Those of you who are involved in the investigation and examination of special cases will find your training to your advantage when weeding out traitors and secret agents. Then there are the people who followed Gao Gang! And don't forget Wang Xiaoci! The situation is very complicated! Well, let me just discuss these few issues with you. I hope that you will liberate your thinking and ideology somewhat, and liberate the cadres. I would like to remind you, comrades, to pay attention to this: Last year, in the letter he wrote to the Red Guards, Chairman Mao said that it is only when the proletariat has liberated the entire human race that it can eventually liberate itself.[3] Also last year, when Chairman Mao commented on the experience of organizing military training in the Yan'an Road Middle School, he raised this very same issue again.[4] I discussed this matter with delegates from Jiangsu: Unless and until the cadres are liberated, the Revolutionary Committee cannot be established, and you yourselves will not be liberated. There is a huge pile of business that goes with establishing a Revolutionary Committee: Reports have to be written; the Central Cultural Revolution Group has to discuss the matter; the Chairman and Vice-Chairman Lin have to give their approval; and then there is a whole list of things to do. If the cadre problem stands in the way, you will lose time and miss the opportunity. But don't be discouraged simply because you misjudged one single cadre. The Great Cultural Revolution is by no means over yet! You need to get rid of your factionalism—don't have one person propose one thing and someone else propose something altogether different, because if you get entangled in those things in that way, problems will never get resolved. You must take the Chairman's Thought and implement it in your own actions. You should discuss this. I would like to say this to you comrades: Don't always believe that your own documentation has to be absolutely correct; and by the same token, don't always think that other people's material must be wrong—this is the correct attitude to have when investigating and examining [the cases of] cadres, or else you will become subjective and one-sided, and unable to look at prob-

---

[3]English translation in Stuart R. Schram, *Mao Tse-tung Unrehearsed* (Harmondsworth: Penguin Books, 1974), pp. 260–61.

[4]A translation of Mao's directive is in *Current Background,* no. 852, 6 May 1968, p. 851.

lems dialectically. "One divides into two" is a complex matter; today I do not intend to say much about this; in any case, everything exists. Chairman Mao has spoken about this problem specifically and specially. You should all read *On Contradiction.* In terms of material, don't absolutely believe that your own material is correct; the material that you have put together yourself is likely, in content, to lean to your side. One more problem, and that is that you cannot rely entirely on, or believe completely, verbal confessions and testimony. Don't believe one-sidedly or prejudicially is what I say; and, under certain conditions, also analyze what the "other side" has to say—even if it is something they maintain themselves, we must analyze it. Don't believe your own material and information entirely, and don't believe confessions and testimonies entirely either. All factions and groups must do the same. Even our own information and material has to be negated over and over again; as for verbal confessions and testimonies, we absolutely cannot believe them completely.

22
"Bo Yibo Has an Attitude Problem"

Wu Linquan and Peng Fei

Source: Excerpt from *Caolan chunqiu* (*Springs and Autumns in Caolan*) (Beijing: Renmin chubanshe, 1988), pp. 248–56.

On February 9, 1967, under the manipulation and control of Kang Sheng and his confederates, a large rally was held at the Beijing Workers' Stadium to criticize and struggle against Bo Yibo. When he appeared, Bo had around his neck a large iron plaque on which had been written all sorts of charges against him. Nevertheless, he held his head high, and walked with proud and unbowing strides. Without waiting for those presiding over the rally to announce the charges made against him, he walked up to the microphone first, and announced in a loud voice: "Comrades! Comrades! I would like to speak . . ."

Seeing that the situation was not going in their favor, the Red

Guards rushed up and grabbed Bo Yibo by the hair. They pressed his head down and shouted: "Down with the big renegade." Then they dragged him to the rear of the stage and resumed declaring the rally commenced.

Suddenly, however, Bo Yibo again raised his head and once more rushed to the microphone, crying in a loud voice: "I am not a traitor! I am a member of the Communist Party!"

Shouting: "Nonsense!" the Red Guards rushed over again and ferociously grabbed hold of Bo Yibo's hair, dragging him away, frantically yelling into the microphone: "He is a dog, crawling out of the Guomindang's den for dogs!"

Disregarding the pain and any concern for safety, Bo Yibo raised his head again and spoke loudly: "Every step I have taken since I left the Guomindang's prison has been carried out in accordance with the directives of the Party Central Committee; Chairman Mao knows all about this."

The stadium was in utter chaos, resounding with shouts and loud denunciations; there was no way the rally could continue. So after having been held for only three minutes, this criticism and struggle rally was adjourned amid total confusion.

Not long after that rally, in early March 1967, Bo Yibo was transferred to a prison outside Desheng Gate [in Beijing]. He was framed with many forced charges, all of which claimed that he deserved to die many times over for his crimes. He was labeled "a backbone general for the Liu-Deng Black Headquarters," "a core element of the Liu Shaoqi Renegade Clique," "a big traitor," "a counter-revolutionary revisionist element," "a Three-Anti element," and so on. With a ponderous black plaque hanging from his neck, he was subjected every day to the brutal and barbarous criticism and struggle in large "meetings" as well as to the stern torture and torment for confession by his Case Group. The heroic and triumphant struggle that he had led members of the Communist Party in waging inside the enemy's prison in the 1930s was now turned against him and became a charge against him; also seen as one of his crimes was the fact that, during the War of Resistance Against Japan, he and his comrades-in-arms cooperated with Yan Xishan in establishing a national united front against the Japanese and thus made outstanding contributions to swiftly developing and enlarging the forces of the revolution—that, too, was now seen as one of his crimes. Indeed, the fact that, after Liberation of the entire country, he was appointed Vice Premier of the State Council and contributed greatly to leading and guiding the socialist economic reconstruction throughout the nation became one of his "unpardonable crimes." Everyone—from the Red Guards in the colleges and universities and schools to the "rebel factions" in government organs and enterprises and business units—wanted a piece of Bo and wanted to seize him for criticism and struggle.

In the early summer of 1967, along with Peng Zhen and Liu Ren, Bo Yibo was dragged to the No. 27 Rolling Stock Plant in Changxindian to be criticized and struggled against. While there, they were incarcerated in a hut made of sheet metal. Under the intense summer sun, the place was like a high-temperature indoor oven. They were given no food all day, and not even a mouthful of water to drink. All they got was a merciless beating by people who struck them continuously with metal pipes or wooden cudgels wrapped in rubber. Bo Yibo's upper vertebrae were injured by the beating; his pain was so severe that he could not sit up or stand up straight. In the evening, when he was dragged back to his prison cell, he could no longer stand the agony and asked to be treated for his wounds and injuries. The guard sarcastically refused to do anything, saying: "Isn't it a wonder that people like you would have the guts to hope someone would treat your illness; you should be counting yourself incredibly fortunate that you're not dead yet!"

At the time the "Bo Yibo Case Group" was ordered to write up, every day, a *Trends and Situation Report* in which it would record the conditions of that day's interrogations or criticism-and-struggle activities, and submit it to Kang Sheng and the Case Examination Group, and then adopt new and novel actions of persecution [depending on the feedback those reports generated]. Let us read from those *Reports* that were filed in the summer of 1967, and let our story be corroborated by the gory narratives written by those very people in their own hand at the time.

The *Report* filed on July 5, 1967, for instance, included the following: "Bo Yibo, whether at the struggle meetings or on any other day, has never been honest with us. On July 5, he wrote, on sheets of newspaper: 'This morning I was seized and taken out to be struggled against by the Economic Commission in bldg. no. 72. This was organized by another group of people at the Economic Commission. . . . Hu XX resorted to force and physical violence, and he tore my clothes.

Well, there was nothing much to that; when I came back, I was able to sew the clothes back into shape myself. Actually, today, they would not even allow me to piss in the bathroom. Now, is this an accident? Or is something being planned?' "

Another *Report* contains the following passage: "On [July] 6 [1967], Bo Yibo wrote on the newspaper: 'This afternoon, at the Beijing Workers' Stadium, the Beijing Municipal Government convened a big gathering to smash the Liu-Deng-Peng-Bo Counter-Revolutionary Revisionist Capitalist Restoration Trust. I was dragged off to attend this rally, and so was Zheng Tianxiang. . . . I received another round of severe beatings today. I am now covered with wounds and injuries, and my clothes are all in tatters. At one point, because I became dizzy and moved my body a couple of times, I was hit with fists and kicked over and over again. This sort of random beating . . . is a small matter for me as an individual; it's just that I can't help feeling bad about the fact that even now people are still resorting to this kind of physical violence. It is not so much a matter of suffering these injustices—after all, I have now become accustomed to this sort of thing.' "

"On August 7 [1967], (Bo Yibo) wrote on the newspaper: 'This morning a meeting was held at the Ministry of Forestry, where they criticized me for all the monstrous crimes I had committed in the area of forestry. Those involved in the criticism and struggle said they had to teach me a severe lesson. Whenever I said that I could not remember something, there would be a confrontation during which they would all shout in my face and yell for me to be beaten.' . . . 'On the afternoon of the seventh, a meeting was held somewhere between Lugouqiao and Changxindian. We started on our way at 2:00 P.M. and arrived at 3:00 P.M. The meeting was scheduled for 5:30 P.M. Before the meeting started a large number of people were summoned there to carry out 'armed struggle' first. They were ferocious. They yelled fiercely at us: What the hell did you think you were doing? Damn you! You piece of shit! You big traitor! Liu Shaoqi, is he your father? . . . I thought it was all somewhat ridiculous, just willful and deliberate provocation. At first I said a few things in response, telling them I was not a renegade or traitor, and so on . . . but later I just kept my mouth shut and said nothing. That bunch of rebels then said: Fine, we'll just see you at the meeting. Were it not for Chairman Mao forbidding armed struggle, damn it, we'd beat you to death! Then the meeting—Peng Zhen and Jia Tingsan were also dragged out for this occasion. I was guarded by three people. One of them suddenly said: Let's give him something to remember! Let's put him on an airplane! So two of them tied my hands behind my back—in fact, it was much more than that; what they did was not only tie my hands behind my back, they simply twisted my arms until my arms were dislocated, and the fellow in the back, his specialty was kicking me all the while, grabbing my hair and pressing my head down. Most unbearably painful of all this was when my arms were being twisted out of joint, and then having them push me and drag me along at a fast pace, while kicking and hitting me all the while. They took turns guarding me, three fellows to each turn in rotation, and about ten minutes each turn. Altogether they changed six times, six shifts. This meant that I was tortured in this way every two minutes. My two arms were held behind my back, twisted, and when they 'put me on the jet plane' they forced me to keep my legs wide apart, while pressing my back down as far as it would go, but keeping my head up and at attention. Then they took turns pulling my hair while kicking and beating me. After the meeting, they kept on kicking me all the way from the 'stage' to the car. The 'struggle' today not only gave me a headache and made me dizzy and faint, but resulted in terrible pain in my wrists and in my arms. They were so painful I am unable to lift my hands or arms. In regard to suffering these kickings and beatings and humiliation, . . . at first I thought all that was perhaps just a matter of some misunderstanding that they had against me, and it wasn't much to withstand such torment. However, after what happened today, I am beginning to see that the Party's policy seems to be changing, that it intends to use this method to bring you down entirely.' "

"On August 8 [1967], [Bo Yibo] wrote on a piece of newspaper: 'After yesterday's beating, my stomach illness flared up again last night; the pain was unbearable. I was unable to sleep for even fifteen minutes; this afternoon, the pain got even worse. In particular, my wrists and my arms are in pain. My motions are now entirely limited, and I can no longer hold a pen steadily. How can I write a confession?' "

"On August 16 [1967], [he] wrote on a piece of newspaper: 'Yesterday there were two rounds of criticism-struggle. Today, things were quiet and peaceful all the way to 6:30 in the afternoon. I was just beginning to formulate some ideas about how I would write up the inspection report when suddenly they told me to have dinner earlier. (That was a signal that I would have to suffer through another struggle session.) Anyway, we took off at 7:00 P.M. The meeting was being held at the auditorium of the Beijing Petroleum Institute, and was convened by the various units of the petroleum industry system. The subject of the meeting was "Down with Bo Yibo" "Defend the Red Banner of Daqing." It was also of the nature of an armed struggle. Whenever something was said that did not fit the facts and I was told to acknowledge it, and when I tried to explain, they started beating me. I was put on an airplane, twisted, choked, kicked and hit with fists. I tried, at one time, to use persuasion, and I said: Can it be so easy? To overthrow someone? The Central Committee, I said, advocates overthrowing someone politically, theoretically, and ideologically, [but not physically]. . . . Not only were my attempts at moral persuasion entirely without effect, but the beatings became even more ferocious. Me and my big mouth.'"

"On August 23 [1967], [Bo Yibo] wrote on a piece of newspaper: 'Today I was also dragged out twice. In the morning it was by the Case Group; in the afternoon it was the Struggle Against Bo [Yibo] Rally of the Eighth Ministry of Machine Building, to denounce me for my crimes on the agricultural-machinery front. . . . For the last four months, I have been dragged out to suffer a struggle almost every day. To date, it has been the ninety-sixth time. . . . This week we set a record of eight struggles within the same week.'"

"On August 31 [1967], [Bo Yibo] wrote on a piece of newspaper: 'This afternoon a rally to struggle against Peng [Zhen], Bo [Yibo], Liao [Luyan], and Ma [Wenrui] was held in the Table Tennis Arena. This month I have been dragged out for struggle at rallies twenty-six times and that has set a record for a month. Last night, when the Case Group interrogated me, they told me to hurry up and submit my self-criticism report. I told them that in recent days I did not have any time to write anything. . . . I was reprimanded and denounced by the Case Group for that.'"

The day-in, day-out criticism-struggles and the incessant interrogation tortured Bo Yibo. Nonetheless, in order to give a factual account and true explanation of the circumstances, he dragged his badly wounded and bruised body off its feet and, taking more than two days' time, wrote up his first document [about his situation]—a piece of writing that was more than twenty thousand characters long. In this document he described in detail the heroic deeds of several dozen members of the Communist Party when, in Caolanzi Prison, they carried out a struggle [against the Guomindang enemy] resolutely; he described the entire course of events in which they left that prison, acting in accordance with the instructions of the Party Central Committee, and he also described the circumstances in which, in 1943, he reported to Chairman Mao about this issue in the caves of Yan'an. In this document Bo wrote, clearly and firmly: "I am not a traitor nor a renegade. None of these several dozen comrades of ours was a traitor. The Party Central Committee and Chairman Mao himself have affirmed our loyalty to the Party."

[He went on to write here:] "[Some time] after we were released from the prison, I had the opportunity to report [on this matter] to Chairman Mao. I was elected to serve as a member of the Central Committee in 1945 and have served in that capacity since then. Later I was elected an alternate member of the Politburo; how could I be a renegade or a traitor [to the Party]?" Beneath Bo's lines about having reported to Chairman Mao, Kang Sheng, with calculation and dark intentions, put in pencil a thick, black bar. When he saw that nothing was coming out of all the criticism-struggle, Kang immediately dispatched three men in military uniforms, accompanied by a couple dozen thugs, to deal with Bo Yibo. They seized Bo Yibo, and dragged him up to the interrogator's desk. There they sternly and severely announced: "When you people left that prison, you were carrying out Liu Shaoqi's black directives. Now, through investigation and proof, we have found Liu Shaoqi to be a big traitor and renegade. Since you carried out his black directives, that, of course, makes you a traitor also! Tell us: How did Liu Shaoqi and Deng Xiaoping collude with you? What have you done for them personally? When you people crawled out of that Guomindang den for dogs, is it not true that you even thanked the prison warden for the instructions and teaching he gave you?"

With extraordinary anger and indignation, Bo Yibo rebutted: "All that is nothing but fabrication and false accusations! I strongly protest!" Speaking sternly, with a sense of justice, he then asked the interrogator to answer his questions: "It was in accordance with the directives of the Party Central Committee, and in accordance with the [Party's] principle of the individual obeying the interests of the organization, the subordinate obeying the orders of the superior, and the minority obeying the will of the majority, that we managed, through the connections of the National United Front in the War of

Resistance Against Japan and through strategic means that combined firm resolve with flexibility, to leave the Guomindang's incarceration in that prison; how could that be considered the act of traitors? What is the purpose of labeling as traitors all those underground workers who had the misfortune of being thrown in jail in a white area and who suffered the persecution of the enemy? Comrades Liu Shaoqi and Deng Xiaoping have both long been in charge of responsibilities [at the highest level of government] in the Central Committee; how can carrying out their instructions be construed as collusion?"

Under such questioning, the interrogator flew into a rage from shame and, in uncontrollable anger at Bo, howled thunderously: "Who the hell do you think you are?" Then he abruptly grabbed and pulled at Bo Yibo's hair, but Bo resisted, angrily, and said: "These methods that you people are using are nothing but methods of suppression, of repression. They do nothing but demonstrate that you people are entirely unreasonable and act without justification, and I most strongly object to what you are doing!"

"So, you object, do you?" Suddenly a fist struck the back of Bo's head, and he stumbled forward. The man standing in front of Bo stepped up and landed a heavy blow on Bo Yibo's chest, sending Bo reeling backward. The fellow to his left pushed him powerfully with both hands, while the man to his right shoved him violently. There was Bo Yibo, surrounded, in the middle, greeted with fists, kicks, chokes, and shoves from all sides and angles, beaten until he slumped unconscious to the floor, then he was carted back to his cell.

The interrogator gave him three days within which to write up a piece answering the three charges specified during that latest interrogation; he was told that until he finished writing up the material, he would not be allowed to sleep.

Bo Yibo made up his mind then that he would uphold the truth resolutely, no matter what. He decided he had to adhere strictly to the facts; he could not bring himself to say anything that violated his conscience. So he did not write a single word; instead, he put his head down on the desk and took naps. The desk was then taken away. He sat on a long bench, and then the bench was also removed. He laid down on the bed. Four burly fellows barged into the room; two of them grabbed his hands, the other two picked up his feet. One, two, three, they yelled, and then tossed Bo into the air and let him fall heavily onto the hard cement floor. Bo's back became swollen; his internal organs all were in shock and seemed to have been tossed out of their proper places. He saw stars. The leader of the squad rushed up and boxed Bo's ears repeatedly until Bo once again fainted and slumped to the ground. The "Defend Mao–Defend Lin Red Guards" shouted slogans at the top of their voices and hauled in two big buckets of water that they poured in Bo's face. The unconscious Bo Yibo lay there on the floor, soaked in a puddle of cold water more than an inch deep for a day and a night. The arthritis he had contracted years ago in that Guomindang prison now flared up abruptly. Every joint in Bo's body ached and became inflamed, and was as painful as if a knife or an arrow had pierced through them. Still Bo refused to write down a single word [of confession].

Thus brutal torture, attempts at extracting a confession by force, by humiliation, and by hunger, were all visited on Bo Yibo's body. Kang Sheng's thugs sometimes made him stay awake several days and nights in a row, trying to force a confession out of him. At other times they tried to compel him into compliance with the pressures of hunger and thirst. He was given only a small steamed bun and a bowl of plain water soup with a few strands of cabbage floating in it for every meal; when on the rare occasion he was allowed a meal of machine-processed rice, it was only half a bowl. His hands, now tortured to the extent that they trembled all the time, could no longer hold a pair of chopsticks steadily, and he was unable to bring the kernels of rice to his mouth. Instead the rice would fall to the floor, and Bo would have to stoop down or grovel on the ground, and with his shaking hands, pick up the rice kernel by kernel and put each into his mouth. The hunger sapped his body of all energy, and he became weak and flaccid all over his deteriorating frame. Even more intolerable, however, was the shortage of water. He was given only half a jar of water a day. So he had to resort to not washing his face, not brushing his teeth, nor rinsing out his mouth, and saving the water only for drinking and quenching his thirst. Here he was, in a jail cell that was damp and moist on the floor, and yet his eyes, his throat, his lips and tongue were all burning and parched to a crisp. The illness, the pain, the injuries, the humiliation all made him age quickly. His eyes became dull; he became like an old man who had lived through centuries. Yet Bo endured and withstood the incessant suffering with his incomparably firm resolve and steady perseverance. He was determined to stay alive so he could claim justice for the truth and for the case of the wrongful charges brought against those sixty-one people.

For the sake of upholding the truth and [maintaining the principle of] seeking truth from facts, Bo Yibo waged a stubborn and persistent resistance struggle against his persecutors. This left the thugs [sent to deal with him] with no way out. On September 11, 1967, the "Bo Yibo Case Group" wrote a report to Kang Sheng, in which it said: "Since last January, the various revolutionary mass organizations of the industrial and transportation and communications systems have carried out altogether more than a hundred criticism-struggles against the big traitor and counter-revolutionary revisionist renegade Bo Yibo. . . . The Case Group, for its part, has also focused several times on interrogating and examining him concerning his past history of capture and arrest by the enemy. To this date, however, Bo Yibo has remained stubborn in his resistance; his attitude is extremely bad and he refuses to admit to any wrongdoing. After the criticism-struggle [meetings] and after the interrogations, he would often write things on pieces of newspaper that he had read, in which he would spew out a lot of nonsense and give vent to his discontent . . . He makes the ridiculous claim that he is 'entirely and undyingly loyal [to the Party],' that 'his past is clear,' that he 'has been completely faithful to the Party.' . . . He has smeared the revolutionary masses' exposure and criticism of him as '[nothing but] speculation,' and 'a lot of trumped-up charges.' . . . He also claims that 'when I was released from prison in 1936, it was because Liu Shaoqi allowed us to follow the necessary procedures,' and that. . . . 'after I was released from prison I reported [this matter] to Chairman Mao . . . ' He has been rebuffing his questioners and interrogators openly in the meetings and contradicting them."

In *Trends and Situation Report No. 29* the Case Group wrote: "At 18:20 hours on August 5 Bo Yibo was reading the newspaper indoors. When he read Chairman Mao's big-character poster 'Bombard the Headquarters,' he appeared to get very angry, and he flung the newspaper to the floor."

In the *Report* filed on December 5 of the same year, the Case Group wrote: "In the morning of November 17 (Bo Yibo) turned on his semiconductor transistor radio. When he heard the broadcast about the contents of the criticism against Peng Dehuai and Luo Ruiqing, he abruptly turned the radio off."

The January 17, 1968 *Report* contained the following: "19:00 hours on the eleventh, (Bo Yibo) was listening on his semiconductor transistor radio. When he heard the broadcast concerning the criticism of the writings of China's Khrushchev, he abruptly turned the radio off. After awhile, he turned the radio back on to listen to other programs."

The Case Group said, in an "issue" of the *Report* on October 24, 1967, "Bo Yibo wrote on a piece of newspaper: Today, in the afternoon, the Beijing Electrical Machinery Plant held a rally to struggle against Bo. Also brought out for struggle and criticism at the meeting were Wan Li, Zheng Tianxiang, and Lu Heng. All the contents of all the speeches made had to do with affairs in Beijing municipality itself. In particular, the speech made by that fellow from the service company had nothing whatsoever to do with me. The fellow that made the speech talked about the old Beijing Municipal [Party] Committee, and he did not even mention my name a single time. What I have become is a 'model teacher by negative example'; no matter what kind of a meeting it may be, and no matter whether it may have anything to do with Bo Yibo, as long as they can drag me to the platform, it is okay with them. Those people who are shouting slogans just seem to have to shout 'Down with Bo Yibo' several times. At such moments, Bo Yibo would respond, with particularly apparent indignation: The more you people struggle against me and criticize me, the more spirit I will have. No matter what time you call on me, I will come to your meetings, even if I am sick, I'll be there!"

Nonetheless, being human, who can be without sensations, feelings, emotions, or thought? Least of all a member of the Communist Party, someone who has steadfastly and so dedicatedly fought, for several decades, for the sake of the great cause of Liberation? Could he, in the face of such extremes of topsy-turvy logic, such reversals of right and wrong, of black and white, in the face of these circumstances that have plunged the Party and the nation into such extraordinary chaos and crisis—would he not be burning in his soul with worry and anxiety, would his mind not be filled with a million disturbed thoughts? Often, after coming back from one of those criticism-struggle rallies and sitting in his cell facing those four dark and bare prison walls, he would, understandably and inevitably, "sigh and groan," "be depressed and low," and he would be found "sitting quietly, without a sound, as if concentrating his spirit on something, his eyes staring blankly into the darkness" or sometimes "weeping bitterly, with tears pouring." Naturally, all these situations were reported to the higher "authorities" as "recent developments."

Bo Yibo had a wife and seven children. Although he was forced to be separated from them, how could he completely suppress his intense longing for them? In those long nights of sitting by himself, "he would bring out photographs that had been taken of him with his children, and he would pore over them carefully for a long while, all the time sighing, perhaps, and muttering to himself: Ah, forget it, go to sleep." This, too, was observed by those who kept an eye on him day and night and was written into their *Reports.*

Sometimes Bo would casually, and at random, express his naturally irrepressible longing [for his family] in what he wrote on those pieces of newsprint that he had read. For example, there was this "entry": "My home has been ransacked. I still have six children at home who are not yet of adult age, and they cannot yet be counted on to lead life independently. But now they have to worry about me instead of my taking care of them. A few days ago, they brought things from home for my use, and these are all things they need themselves. I feel so ashamed and so sorry." "Yesterday was New Year's Eve. I spent it at the table tennis pavilion. I had to wait in the women's toilet for three hours, and [the struggle-rally] in the main pavilion itself took three hours. Today, New Year's Day; they had dumplings for lunch this morning, but I was unable to swallow anything . . . This is something that has never happened to me in the last forty years, maybe even the last sixty years. . . . These last few days are really so very difficult . . . , I keep seeing images of them [members of my family] in my mind. . . . Young little no. 7, do you still write letters asking Xilai to buy fire-crackers? Actually, now that I recall this matter, it seems amusing."

After much repeated pleading, Bo was finally permitted to write a letter to his children, which he did on August 1, 1967. In that deeply moving letter, he wrote:

> I have been away from you for eight, nine months already; how are you all doing, really? I have no knowledge whatsoever about your living conditions and such. . . . From now on I don't want you to spend any more money to buy me things to eat. Life here is acceptable, tolerable. From here on, our family's economic conditions will become even more difficult; you had better save money now to spend on yourselves later on. . . . I am very sorry that because of my sins, so much anguish and misfortune have come to you. At this time, you are all still young; you have not yet lived independently. . . . and your daddy cannot be with you. I'm sure that at this time other people probably will not

dare to be close to you; so you must be experiencing a time of the greatest isolation and difficulty. What should you do? How will you handle this situation? You must learn to take things philosophically and hold your heads up high, stand up straight and go on living your lives with dignity and honor. . . . Right now, all the schools are reopening classes and also carrying on the revolution in the schools. Anan, you must pay attention to your illness, and take the cure as well as rest. Wait till classes officially resume, and then decide what to do then. Have Benben's and Xilai's minor illnesses been cured? Don't just ignore them; they need some attention. Benben, you ought to try to go to a university. What middle school is young no. 7 attending? That needs to be resolved. My Little no. 5, Little Bei and Little no. 7, you must all listen to your elder brothers and sisters, and be obedient. . . . You must all help one another and each establish for yourself a correct, proletarian worldview, so you can blaze for yourselves a correct path of a revolutionary life. The more correct you are in the paths you take, the better lives you will lead, the more you will be able to console me and encourage me. . . . The pain I am suffering in my spine and my neck is getting a bit better. I haven't suffered from allergic sinusitis or caught the flu. In general, I feel that my body can stand this. . . . In regard to the masses' criticism of me, no matter how much and in what manner they criticize me or struggle against me, and whatever it may be that they say to me, I always listen patiently and attentively, and I think through these remarks carefully. . . . Naturally, whatever is not in conformity with the truth or with the facts, I still cannot admit, and whenever I have a chance to speak, I do so. . . . I am still of the same attitude, which is that if something is my own mistake, I will admit to it and I will gladly examine my own mistakes and make a self-criticism; but when it is not my mistake or if [the way something is described] is inconsistent with the facts, I will never, absolutely never, accept something or follow orders, blindly. . . . I am not a counter-revolutionary revisionist, and I am not a traitor. I must, and I will, refute that and make my rebuttal; that, however, is my own business. As for you, you should do only one thing, and that is obey the Party's orders.

But these sentiments and ideas of Bo Yibo's rubbed those who had the "mania for persecution" the wrong way. They then extended their persecuting hands to Bo Yibo's wife, Hu Ming, and to his children.

One day, after a brutal interrogation, the Case Group suddenly turned to Bo Yibo and told him, in bitingly sarcastic and cruel words: "I suppose you really would like to know about how your wife and

your children are doing, wouldn't you? Actually, I can tell you this—
your wife has committed suicide to escape punishment. And, of your
four children, three have already been rounded up. So even if you
didn't care about yourself or think on your own behalf, why don't you
give some thought to the children and consider their best interests—
after all, they have already lost their mother." The Case Group, taking
delight in someone else's misfortune and suffering, hoped to use this
leverage to soften up Bo Yibo and to force him to give up and admit he
was a traitor.

D. Making Rebellion

To the extent that it was a nationwide social movement, it is fair to say that China's Cultural Revolution remains poorly documented. There were no CNN crews present to cover the massacre of students in faraway Qinghai on 23 February 1967—when the PLA killed 169 and wounded 178 "masses" occupying the premises of a local newspaper.[1] The student leaders of Beijing's Red Guard movement were never once interviewed by the *Globe and Mail* or *Newsweek*. We still do not know exactly what happened in rural Wuxuan, Guangxi, in the summer of 1968, when incidents of ritualized cannibalism marked the climax of rallies to denounce and "thoroughly eliminate" the "class enemy."[2] The precious little that is known about the Cultural Revolution in, say, the major industrial center of Baoding, located less than a hundred miles southwest of Beijing, is hardly enough to sustain a slim working paper. Yet thousands died there in a brutal civil war that went on for years. As in the case of Mao Zedong's intentions, our extant record of "what really happened" in Chinese society between 1966 and 1969 provokes a wide range of questions but provides only sketchy answers.

A rare glimpse of the first weeks of "rebellion" in Shanghai is provided by an anonymous correspondent writing in the *Far Eastern Economic Review* (Document 23) in September 1966. This was after students on campuses all over China had first denounced their "petty bourgeois" teachers (Document 24), and the "revisionist authorities"— eventually to be associated with Liu Shaoqi and Deng Xiaoping—had attempted with the Party's traditional means of repression to silence the "troublemakers" (Document 25).

---

[1] Cf. Jin Chunming, Huang Yuchong, and Chang Huimin, eds., *"Wenge" shiqi guaishi guaiyu* (*Strange Things and Strange Words from the Time of the "Cultural Revolution"*) (Beijing: Qiushi chubanshe, 1989), p. 273. Four PLA soldiers were killed and twenty-six were wounded in the incident.

[2] Donald S. Sutton, "Consuming Counterrevolution: The Ritual and Culture of Cannibalism in Wuxuan, Guangxi, China, May to July 1968," *Comparative Studies in Society and History,* Vol. 37, No. 1, January 1995, pp. 136–72.

To the Red Guards, Mao was a God-like figure, and an ecstatic letter (Document 26) from a young teacher in Shanghai describes what it felt like to see him in person at a million-strong rally in Tiananmen Square. Not all Chinese, however, succumbed to mass hysteria, and a different, quite remarkable letter addressed to Mao himself (Document 27) bears testimony to this. Its nineteen-year-old author was sentenced to life in prison for questioning Mao's wisdom but was released in March 1979.

Ways of reforming China's political system were proposed by many rebels, and typically they would ask for "extensive democracy without precedent in human history" but under Mao's tutelage (Document 28). It was rare for someone to move beyond the limitations of the official discourse, to write as if freedom of thought and freedom of expression were realities—rather than proletarian privileges to be granted and withdrawn at will by Mao—and to engage critically with the notions espoused by someone like Lin Biao. For their attempt to do just that, the authors of Document 29 were, not surprisingly, arrested. Political criticism was more safely expressed in ironic terms (Document 30) and preferably directed not upwards but outwards (against one's "erring" peers) or at targets otherwise preapproved.

The Cultural Revolution was a violent movement, and the firsthand account (Document 31) of the savage beating suffered by the author of Document 26 at the hands of his students makes for gruesome reading. More violence, this time directed at foreigners, is the subject of an unsettling classified report to the Swedish Ministry of Foreign Affairs from the Swedish ambassador to China (Document 32).

As the Cultural Revolution wore on, the Red Guard "masses" became hopelessly divided into factions, each accusing the other of being "bogus" or otherwise less than genuinely "Leftist." In Document 33, a young Red Guard from a well-to-do (PLA?) cadre family privately admits that she "hates the guts" not just of the members of Beijing's most radical Red Guard organization—the so-called "Third HQ"—but also of their powerful backer Jiang Qing. By the summer of 1967, many young people had withdrawn from political activism altogether, and to the growing anxiety of the authorities, there was a sharp increase in petty crime and "hooliganism" (Document 34). When thousands of middle-school graduates were exiled to the countryside in 1968, their parents could do little else than pretend to be pleased and express their "warm support" for so drastic a measure to restore order (Document 35).

At one point, when literally the entire political establishment save for Mao's closest allies came under attack, the future of the children of the elite looked bleak indeed. The sons and daughters of Liu Shaoqi, Deng Xiaoping, et al. did not appear to stand much of a chance of ever "inheriting the rivers and mountains" (*zuo jiangshan*) their fathers had conquered. Yet, they refused to resign themselves to their fate and insisted that "In another twenty years, the world will belong to us!" As it happens, history is proving them right. Today, in 1996, the "prince-lings" (*taizidang*), who were in their teens when they wrote letters like Document 36, are calling the shots.

23
Rebels in Shanghai

Far Eastern Economic Review Correspondent

Source: *Far Eastern Economic Review,* 8 September 1966, pp. 443–45.

The second half of July and the first three weeks of August were extremely hot in Shanghai—but there were no school holidays this summer for those over sixteen. The students and the teachers stayed on, either living in or attending school every day in order to acquire the thinking of Mao Zedong and to conduct the Great Proletarian Cultural Revolution.

The initial stage of the revolution took place indoors: in colleges and schools, in industrial and commercial enterprises, and in various organizations. Students, workers, and other employees concentrated on criticizing and denouncing all those thought to be guilty of anti-Party leanings or unstable in their political thinking. Only after this stage were the student activities transferred outdoors to sweep over the whole city. Day after day, ever since 10 August, the sounds of drums, gongs, slogans, and songs have filled the air as columns of marchers have marched down the streets in unending processions, all heading toward the local headquarters of the Chinese Communist Party.

The first demonstration by students, workers and groups of residents was to greet the promulgation of the Sixteen-Point Resolution of the Central Committee on the Cultural Revolution.[1] The second was to greet the Communique of the Committee's Eleventh Plenary Session.[2] Then, third, people filled the streets to implement the decisions and to eradicate from the city all remnants of the bourgeois way of life, all traces of the former reactionary regimes, all vestiges of imperialism, feudalism, colonialism, and other objectionable isms.

Between 10 and 21 August the revolution was marked mainly by orderly processions, each group carrying the national flag, numerous portraits of Mao Zedong, red banners and paper flags with slogans, and

---

[1] Document 4.
[2] An English translation is in *Peking Review,* No. 34, 1966.

red-bound handbooks of Mao Zedong's sayings. One would shout a slogan, and the whole group would respond with "*Mao zhuxi wansui!*" ("Long live Chairman Mao!"), at the same time raising their right fists, their flags, or their books of sayings. Each group was preceded by large red posters expressing joy at having received the Sixteen-Point Resolution. After a couple of days, the processions grew in numbers and were reinforced with *yaogu* (kettle drums), gongs, cymbals, and other musical instruments, plus dancers. Enthusiasm appeared to grow as did the numbers of Mao Zedong's portraits. Now the posters praised the Central Committee's communique and pledged unlimited support.

At this stage, on 19 August, a huge meeting was held at the People's Square, Shanghai's counterpart of Tiananmen. A typhoon in the vicinity brought an end to the enervating heat with a moderate rainfall, but the rain failed to dampen the zeal of the demonstrators, who had prepared for a celebration and were accompanied by bands of musicians, dancers, and other entertainers. According to the press, nearly one million Shanghai residents took part in the day's processions, carrying portraits of Mao Zedong and banners, shouting slogans, and otherwise demonstrating their enthusiasm. Among the speakers from the central rostrum were the mayor of Shanghai, Cao Diqiu, and vice chairman of the Standing Committee of the National People's Congress, Guo Moruo, on a visit to Shanghai from Beijing. The meeting did not break up until well after midnight.

It was generally thought that this meeting would culminate the long period of processions and demonstrations and that at last the students and teachers would be allowed some rest and respite. Not so; to rest would be contrary to the revolutionary spirit. The processions continued the next day and the day after, ushering in a new phase, that of the Red Guards, who proudly styled themselves the "rebels," dedicated to the implementation of pledges.

On 22 August masses of college students and middle school pupils, some wearing red armbands, others simply with red strips of paper pinned to their chests, with the characters *hongweibing* (red guards) and *hongweibing zaofan* [sic] (red guard rebels) appeared everywhere. An immense number of posters appeared on the store windows and on buildings, demanding changes in the names of streets, shops, and enterprises.

From the outset the Red Guards had declared war on "teddy" boys and "flapper" girls, soon extending these words to include all those with any pretension to fashion or those who wore any individual, unusual clothes. Boys with tapered trousers, girls with slacks, boys wearing "rocket" (sharp-pointed) shoes—or even just leather shoes—and girls with stylish hairdos were the main targets. Here the Red Guards were outstripped in efficiency by throngs of children of anything between six and fifteen years of age, who, when spotting an objectionable garment or pair of shoes on anyone, were quick to gather around him or her and compel the offender to remove it there and then. Not a few girls and young ladies were escorted to the nearest barber shops to cut off their hairdos.

The Red Guards did not go inside enterprise buildings to speak to the managers or staff; they made their objections and their demands known by "large-character posters" put up on windows, doors, and the fronts of buildings. Such posters, once stuck up, could not be removed until those criticized expressed their willingness to comply with the demands in the form of big characters on red paper pasted up in a prominent position. Some especially objectionable places of business had their doors sealed by posters; such enterprises remained closed to customers (and frequently the operators themselves) until the demands of the Red Guards had been complied with.

Posters demanded the removal from window displays and from sale articles of such a type that would not be purchased by workers, peasants, or soldiers. Stores were ordered not to sell foreign merchandise, although this applied only to secondhand stores, the only ones to sell foreign goods, which are placed with them on consignment.

Fashionable tailors, beauty parlors, high-class barbers, western-style restaurants, and coffee shops were most severely criticized for having allowed their premises to become "beehives" of teddy boys and flappers. They were ordered to close until they had thoroughly reformed— so that in future they would serve only workers, peasants, and soldiers and would charge prices accordingly. Signboards along the city streets, advertising fashionable wear, silks, perfumes, and patent medicines were condemned and labeled: "Are these the articles that workers, peasants, and soldiers buy?" and "For whom are such articles made, for the proletariat or for capitalists?" All the signboards in town were subsequently repainted with political slogans.

The cry went up: "Eradicate from China all vestiges of imperialism, colonialism, feudalism, and reactionary regimes!" and a hunt was started throughout Shanghai for emblems of the past. Here, in the city where most of the large buildings and a great many other landmarks were associated with foreigners, and which was the headquarters of Chinese capitalism, objectionable vestiges were everywhere. Naturally, it was the Bund that was the first to receive attention. Here 80 percent of the buildings were built by foreigners—British, Japanese, French, and Russians. The architecture and decorations remained distinctively foreign. The Japanese, who occupied the International Settlement in December 1941, first began stripping the Bund, but they concentrated mostly on monuments, gates, plaques, radiators, boilers, and various fixtures made of brass and other metals so necessary for their war effort; their sense of national pride was not offended by the statuary of other materials that was allowed to remain.

The Cultural Revolution marked their end. Various student groups stuck posters on the buildings demanding the elimination of their objectionable names and features, which reminded people of Shanghai's inglorious past. It became the fashion to demand the names be changed of almost every store, street, and building—even though most of them had already had their original names changed into new revolutionary ones.

The most aristocratic building on the Bund is that which houses the Mayor's Office—the former premises of the Hongkong and Shanghai Bank. Besides its imposing appearance, it was famous for two brass lions that graced the granite pedestals on each side of the main entrance. The lions were reputed—among older residents—to bring luck to those who touched them, and many never failed to give them a pat whenever they passed by, while children enjoyed climbing on their backs. On 22 August 1966, the lions were removed—twenty-one years after they had been restored to their places. According to those who witnessed the scene, they were simply lifted up by workmen and loaded onto waiting lorries.

That day and the next, ladders were propped up all along the Bund; scaffolding was erected or bosun chairs swung down from roofs or upper windows to allow workmen and volunteers to chisel off old emblems. The former premises of the Mercantile Bank were stripped of a crest and a bas-relief showing junks and clipper boats, symbolizing trade with the East; the facade of the former Russo-Asiatic Bank featured heads of natives of various lands with which the bank was doing business, while two large Roman matrons dominated the entrance; the former Japanese banks were decorated with phoenixes and cherry flowers; the North China Daily News building had mythological scenes in bas-relief on its facade—and so on. All these were reminders of the past and had to be removed.

The Customs House building on the Bund is famous for its clock tower, erected by the imperialists, who controlled customs receipts and thus exploited the national economy of China. "We are determined to never again hear the devilish sound of the Customs clock, the legacy of the imperialist and colonial regimes; we request that the tune be changed to chime "The East Is Red," the posters demanded.

Among the names that became popular overnight for shops, streets, and buildings were: Red Guards, Anti-Revisionism, Anti-Imperialism, The East Is Red, Red Flag, Patriotic, and Worker-Peasant-Soldier. Hundreds of shops and buildings and dozens of streets were labeled with similar names; many buildings were renamed although they already boasted revolutionary names. Frequently, different groups of students suggested different names for the same building. It was proposed that Nanking Road should be changed to Five Continents Avenue (because of its international fame), Huaihai Road (formerly Avenue Joffre) to Anti-Revisionism Road (probably because it was formerly a Russian business center). The students proposed a new name for nearly every building on the Bund: the former Shell building, now Asia building, was tentatively renamed as Red Guard, the Customs building as Anti-Imperialism, the Peace Hotel as People's War Hotel, the former Sassoon's House as Five Continents, the Bank of China as People's Bank of China, while the Bund Garden, Garden Bridge, and Shanghai (formerly Broadway) mansions were redubbed Anti-Imperialism garden, bridge, and building, respectively. The former Soviet consulate, now rented by a Chinese organization, was of course called Anti-Revisionism building.

Most of the medium-size and small stores and industrial plants in Shanghai belong to the category of "joint public and private" concerns—and are so identified on the signboards and stationery. The former owners and their old staffs continue to work in those concerns and enjoy their former "high salaries," the owners also receiving interest on the estimated worth of the undertaking (interest also being received by former property owners who had transferred the property to the state). From the very first day of the Red Guards movement, "high salaries, interest on investments, and earnings from private practices of doctors and dentists" were severely attacked and demands made for their abolition. The character "private" was ordered to be removed from all signboards. Already doctors who carried on private practices have closed their offices. As for the problem of "high salaries and interest payments," the issue is to be decided by the government.

24
As I Watched Zhou Tianxing and Lu Wen Sweep the Floor

Liu Tianzhang

Source: Our translation of this big-character poster ("Guan Zhou Tianxing, Lu Wen saodi yougan") written by a Red Guard at the Beijing Aeronautical Institute, has been made from the booklet entitled *Hongweibing de hao bangyang—Liu Tianzhang* (*A Fine Red Guard Example—Liu Tianzhang*) (Beijing, 1967), p. 107, published by the Beijing Aeronautical Institute Revolutionary Committee and Red Flag Combat Team Political Department. In 1966, Zhou Tianxing was a deputy secretary of the Aeronautical Institute Party Committee, and Lu Wen was Zhou's wife.

I was delighted to see that ox-monster and snake-demon couple Zhou and Lu shorn of their old prestige, laboring under our surveillance. Such is the might of the proletarian dictatorship, the might of the popular masses.

Chairman Mao says: "I came to feel that compared with the workers and peasants the unremolded intellectuals were not clean and that, in the last analysis, the workers and peasants were the cleanest people, and, even though their hands were soiled and their feet smeared with cow-dung, they were really cleaner than the bourgeois and petty bourgeois intellectuals." Every month, the black gang elements Zhou "the Dog" Tianxing and Lu Wen take 300 to 500 yuan of the working people's money, and yet all they do is oppose the Party, oppose the people, and oppose Mao Zedong Thought. Everything they eat and wear comes from the people, but all they do is try to waylay and entrap the sons and daughters of the poor and lower-middle peasants, the workers, and the revolutionary cadres. They are a pair of vampires, neatly dressed and smelling of perfume all over, but with souls putrid and rotten to the core. If you threw them in the latrine, you'd end up soiling the latrine! Today we force them to perform some light physical labor to stir up their putrid and rotten souls and to destroy their petty bourgeois dreams! A joyous event like this one could only have taken place in today's Great Proletarian Cultural Revolution.

Long live the Great Proletarian Cultural Revolution!

Sweep away all ox-monsters and snake-demons!

Liu Tianzhang
Class 4141
6 August 1966

25
On Hunger Strike to Protest Illegal Political Persecution

Kuai Dafu

Source: The text of this protest note ("Jueshi kangyi feifa zhengzhi pohai") by a twenty-one-year-old student in the Chemistry Department is reproduced in Qinghua University Jinggangshan Red Guards Propaganda Team, ed., *Qinghua daxue dazibao xuan: Kuai Dafu tongzhi de dazibao* (*Selection of Big-Character Posters from Qinghua University: Big-Character Posters by Comrade Kuai Dafu*) (Beijing: Beijing renmin yinshuachang gonghui, n.d.), p. 39.

To the Qinghua University Work Team:

I am still a citizen of the People's Republic of China and I still enjoy the inviolable right of personal freedom!

But what now?

I step outside and you put me under surveillance!

I want to make a phone call and you will not let me!

Today I wanted to walk out the Xinzhai Gate and you would not let me!

I wanted to visit Qiangzhai and you would not let me! You even turned violent and there was bloodshed!

I wanted to go to the [Party] Center but you would not let me!

You want to break the law!? You want to blockade the Center?

No way! You will never succeed!

I now demand:

If you don't let me go to the Center tomorrow, I swear to die.

You can have someone tail me, but you have no right whatsoever to restrict my movement.

If you don't respond, I will begin a hunger strike at six A.M. on 5 July 1966 to protest this illegal political persecution!

Kuai Dafu
11 P.M., 4 July 1966

26
"I Saw Chairman Mao!!!"

Bei Guancheng

Source: This letter from a twenty-six-year-old teacher to his colleagues in the Jianguang Junior Middle School in Shanghai was published by the New Beijing University "Smile Mingling in Their Midst" Combat Team in *Jianguang zhongxue qingnian jiaoshi Bei Guancheng shi zemyang bei bisi de?—"Bei Guancheng shijian" diaocha baogao (How Was the Young Teacher Bei Guancheng from Jianguang Middle School Forced to Die?—Report of an Investigation into the "Bei Guancheng Incident")* (Shanghai, 1967), p. 6.

Comrades:

Let me tell you the great news, news greater than heaven. At five minutes past seven in the evening on the 15th of September 1966, I saw our most most most most dearly beloved leader Chairman Mao! Comrades, I have seen Chairman Mao! Today I am so happy my heart is about to burst. We're shouting "Long live Chairman Mao! Long live! Long live!" We're jumping! We're singing! After seeing the Red Sun in Our Hearts, I just ran around like crazy all over Beijing. I so much wanted to tell everyone the great news! I wanted everyone to join me in being happy, jumping, and shouting.

It was like this: Last night I knew that today Chairman Mao would receive the teachers and students who had come to Beijing, and so this afternoon I pleaded over and over again with the pickets to let me pass. I figured they never would, so I really did not make that much of an effort, and at first I did indeed have to remain on the outside. But by seven o'clock, the pickets finally let me pass. At that very moment, an ocean of people surged forward in the direction of the Tiananmen rostrum, and I also pushed like mad from the side to get in. Finally I managed to get to the visitor's stand, and by a stroke of luck just then Chairman Mao came over to the east side of the rostrum. I could see him ever so clearly, and he was so impressive. Comrades, how can I possibly describe to you what that moment was like? In any case, I together with everyone else just exploded in shouts of "Long live Chairman Mao!" Having seen Chairman Mao, I made a silent pledge to definitely become Chairman Mao's good pupil.

Comrades, join us in our joy and in our singing!

Greetings,

Bei Jr.

15 September 1966, under the midnight lamp

PS: Later I heard that Chairman Mao was coming forward for the second time when I saw him, after repeated pleas from the masses. In any case, what luck! How can I possibly go to sleep tonight! I have decided to make today my birthday. Today I started a new life!!!

27
"Dearest Chairman Mao: What Are You Doing?"

Wang Rongfen

Source: Yu Xiguang, ed., *Weibei weigan wangyouguo—"Wenhua dageming" shangshuji (Of Inferior Position but Concerned About the Fate of Their Country—Memorials from the "Great Cultural Revolution")* (Changsha: Hunan renmin chubanshe, 1989), p. 52.

Respected Chairman Mao Zedong:

Please, as a member of the Communist Party, think about it: What are you doing?

Please, with the Party in mind, think about it: What is the meaning of all that is happening before you?

Please, with the people of China in mind, think about it: In what direction are you taking China?

The Great Cultural Revolution is not a mass movement, but one man moving the masses with the barrel of a gun.

I solemnly declare: On this day, I withdraw from the Communist Youth League of China.

Respectfully,

Wang Rongfen
4th Grade 1st Class German Language Major
Department of East-European Languages
Beijing Foreign Languages Institute
24 September 1966

28

Proletarian Dictatorship and Proletarian Extensive Democracy

Tan Houlan

Source: Red Flag, No. 2, 1967, pp. 37–39. The twenty-six-year-old author is a cadre-turned-student at Beijing Teacher's University and leader of the "Mao Zedong Thought Red Guards, 'Jinggangshan' Combat Regiment." The article was most probably written by her ghostwriter and teacher in the Department of Chinese Language and Literature, Ms. Li Shaoming.

"Thousands of willows sway in the spring breeze; all the 600 million people of the divine country are Shun or Yao."[1]

In this thunderous and heroic Great Proletarian Cultural Revolution, millions of revolutionary masses in our great country have for the first time come to enjoy an extensive democracy without precedent in human history. The revolutionary people enjoy the democracy of free

---

[1]Lines quoted from Mao Zedong's poem "Saying Good-bye to the God of Disease (2)" (July 1958). "Shun" and "Yao" were semilegendary model emperors, said to have ruled China around 2200 B.C., praised by Confucianists for their exemplary virtue.

speech, of being able to organize demonstrations, of being able to put out their own publications, of being able to air their views freely, of being able to put up big-character posters, and of being able to exchange revolutionary experience. Looking back at the history of human civilization over several thousand years, in which dynasty or in which country was there ever such extensive democracy? None, absolutely none. The bourgeoisie and the counter-revolutionary revisionists sometimes also make noises about democracy and freedom, but their words are no more than sheer lies, meant to deceive. As far as the proletariat is concerned, they mean exploitation, oppression, and fascist dictatorship.

Our great leader Chairman Mao has the utmost faith in the masses, fully understands the desires of the popular masses, and greatly respects the revolutionary creativity of the popular masses. It was precisely our most respected leader Chairman Mao who first supported the revolutionary big-character posters, the revolutionary Red Guards, and the great exchange of revolutionary experience. Only a great Marxist-Leninist and ingenious proletarian revolutionary leader like Chairman Mao would be so bold and daring as to propose practicing extensive democracy under the conditions of proletarian dictatorship. The extensive democracy of the proletariat is a great innovation in the international Communist movement, and a major development of the theories of Marxism-Leninism by Chairman Mao.

Proletarian extensive democracy means for the popular masses to be their own masters. The issue of primary importance in extensive democracy is to mobilize and give free rein to the masses; to give the people the most extensive democratic rights; and to exercise dictatorship over all enemies of socialism.

With such extensive democracy, the broad masses can be aroused to the fullest extent to rebel against all forms of revisionism and all reactionaries, thus leaving the enemy no place to hide.

With such extensive democracy, we can fully bring into play the revolutionary spirit of the masses and fully arouse the activism of the masses for socialist revolution and socialist construction.

With such extensive democracy, we can create a social climate in which the common laborers may criticize the leading organs of the Party and government as well as the leaders of those organs.

With such extensive democracy, the masses in their millions will be able to supervise our Party and government leaders at all levels as well as our Party and government organs at all levels.

The development of proletarian extensive democracy is of great and far-reaching significance as far as the consolidation of the dictatorship of the proletariat and guarding against capitalist restoration is concerned.

The extensive democracy we have in mind is extensive democracy under the dictatorship of the proletariat. Proletarian dictatorship and proletarian extensive democracy constitute a unity of opposites. Without proletarian dictatorship, proletarian extensive democracy cannot be safeguarded. For the same reason, if there is no proletarian extensive democracy, proletarian dictatorship cannot be consolidated and may even degenerate into a bourgeois or fascist dictatorship. What makes it possible for our country to realize this extensive democracy is the fact that we have a consolidated dictatorship of the proletariat and the invincible People's Liberation Army. At a time when the struggle between the two classes and the two roads still goes on, departing from proletarian dictatorship will put us in no position to talk about proletarian extensive democracy. This is especially so in the midst of the present scrimmage between the proletariat and the bourgeoisie.

Proletarian dictatorship must closely integrate dictatorship over counter-revolutionaries with extensive democracy for the people. Proletarian dictatorship is powerful because it stands for the dictatorship of the working masses over the exploiters and the dictatorship of the majority over the minority, and also because it brings into being extensive democracy for the broad working people. There cannot be any proletarian dictatorship—or at least not any consolidated proletarian dictatorship—without the criticism, supervision, and active support of the broad masses. The more intense the class struggle, the greater the need for the proletariat to rely most resolutely and thoroughly on the broad masses of the people and to mobilize their revolutionary activism to triumph over the forces of reaction.

Of late, a small handful of Party-persons in power taking the capitalist road and an extremely small number of diehards clinging to the bourgeois reactionary line are not reconciled to their defeat. Working in collusion with ox-monsters and snake-demons out there in society, they launch frantic counter-attacks against the proletarian revolutionary line in an attempt to sabotage the Great Proletarian Cultural Revolution, sabotage proletarian extensive democracy, and sabotage the dictatorship of the proletariat. Under the guise of extensive democracy, they arbitrarily accuse the proletarian revolutionaries of all sorts of crimes and direct the spearhead of struggle at the Proletarian Headquarters. Unwilling to tolerate this, the broad revolutionary masses exercise dictatorship over the small handful of rotten eggs concerned.

This revolutionary measure has greatly strengthened the determination of the revolutionaries and dampened the arrogance of the reactionaries. The revolutionary masses jump with joy and applaud it. But a small handful of clowns are enraged. They are turning hysterical and viciously slander our revolutionary activities.

"You are sabotaging extensive democracy!" Because we exercise dictatorship over the clowns who bombard the Proletarian Headquarters, you call this sabotaging extensive democracy. It just goes to show that the democracy you have in mind is bourgeois democracy. Such "democracy," dear sirs, is indeed what we intend to sabotage.

Chairman Mao teaches us: "There is in the world only concrete freedom, concrete democracy, but no abstract freedom, abstract democracy. In the society of class struggle when the exploiting classes are free to exploit the working people, there is no democracy for the proletariat and the working people." In either case, A has to eliminate B. This is what has to happen and there can be no compromise. By eliminating bourgeois democracy to a greater extent and with greater thoroughness, proletarian democracy will greatly expand. As the bourgeoisie sees it, this means that in our country there is no democracy or that democracy is being sabotaged. Actually this is eradicating what is bourgeois and promoting what is proletarian, and the promotion of proletarian democracy means the eradication of bourgeois democracy.

"You are violating the freedom of speech!" Dear sirs, you are right. We mean to forbid the reactionaries from speaking and acting in an unruly way. Freedom is given only to the people and not to the reactionaries. Anybody among the people can say what he wants to say, write big-character posters against other persons, and put up such posters in whatever place he chooses. Just look at our factories, government organs, schools, rural villages, and city streets, and you will find big-character posters everywhere. Let us ask: In which country is there so high a degree of freedom and democracy?

"You have no faith in the masses!" This is complete nonsense! You small handful of counter-revolutionaries are definitely not the "masses," and we have no faith in you at all. We are dealing with you bad eggs in accordance with the demands of the broad revolutionary masses, and our actions are a manifestation of our great faith in the masses.

In refutation of that renegade Kautsky, Lenin said:

"With the attitude of a learned bookworm or the innocence of a ten-year-old girl, Kautsky asked: Since you have the support of the majority, why is dictatorship still necessary? Marx and Engels explained:

"—in order to break the resistance of the bourgeoisie.

"—in order to strike fear in the reactionaries.

"—in order to uphold the authority of the armed people to oppose the bourgeoisie.

"—in order to enable the proletariat to suppress their own enemies with brute force."

These teachings of Lenin were beyond the comprehension of that renegade Kautsky, and they are also beyond the comprehension of those clowns who accuse us of having "no faith in the masses." Only genuine revolutionaries can comprehend them.

Some muddle-headed individuals adopt a Philistine view toward the present life-and-death class struggle. They fail to see the class contradiction and the great battle between the two lines. They do not understand why we are so determined to repulse the frantic attack represented by this small counter-revolutionary adverse current. They say: "People are merely voicing some objections: Why do you have to take such dictatorial measures?" They see only the outward appearance of things and not their essence.

Among the people, when some comrades voice objections, we listen humbly to what they have to say, even though the words may be sharp and the argument heated. But those fellows with ulterior motives, who in the guise of criticism are actually attacking the proletarian headquarters, must be exposed. Otherwise, people may be taken in by them.

Chairman Mao has taught us that democracy is a means and not an end in itself. We use this means to reach our great goal of making a success of the Great Proletarian Cultural Revolution, of consolidating the dictatorship of the proletariat, and of promoting the socialist cause. Only by strengthening the dictatorship of the proletariat can we safeguard the extensive democracy of the proletariat. Those who want to bombard the Proletarian Headquarters and undermine the dictatorship of the proletariat in our country are having a pipe dream and will never succeed!

Right now, the Great Proletarian Cultural Revolution has entered a new phase. The proletarian revolutionaries must warmly respond to the great call of the Party and Chairman Mao and learn from the Shanghai revolutionaries. Let us unite all proletarian revolutionaries and tighten our grip on the destiny of the proletarian dictatorship, the destiny of the Great Proletarian Cultural Revolution and the destiny of the socialist economy. Let us fight to repulse the latest counter-attack of the bourgeois reactionary line and to gain new victories in the Great Cultural Revolution.

29
An Open Letter to Comrade Lin Biao

Yilin Dixi

Source: Yu Xiguang, ed., *Weibei weigan wangyouguo—"Wenhua dageming" shangshuji (Of Inferior Position but Concerned about the Fate of Their Country—Memorials from the "Great Cultural Revolution")* (Changsha: Hunan renmin chubanshe, 1989), pp. 75–81. This letter caused a major stir when first made public in the form of a big-character poster on the Qinghua University campus. Its pseudonymous authors are two students from the middle school attached to Beijing Agricultural University.

Dear Comrade Lin Biao:

These past few days, I have been reading a transcript of your speech at the Military Academy on 18 September [1966], and, to be frank, some of the key formulations in it are highly erroneous.[1]

You say: "The kind of attitude one maintains with respect to Mao Zedong Thought is a very important question. We must therefore grasp the question of attitude toward Chairman Mao and toward Mao Zedong Thought." "The writings of Marxism-Leninism are too numerous, one cannot read them all. Moreover, they are too far removed from us. In the classical works of Marxism-Leninism, we must devote 99 percent of our efforts to the study of the works of Mao Zedong." *"Chairman Mao stands much higher than Marx, Engels, Lenin, or Stalin.* There is no one in the world today who has reached the level of

---

[1]A full translation of Lin's speech under the title "Instruction on Raising the Study of Chairman Mao's Writings to a New Stage" is in Michael Y.M. Kau, ed., *The Lin Piao Affair: Power Politics and Military Coup* (White Plains, N.Y.: International Arts and Sciences Press, 1975), pp. 367–74.

Chairman Mao. Some people say that *Das Kapital* is the basis of all theories. In fact, it sets forth only the laws and problems of capitalist societies. In our country we have already overthrown capitalism; we are now setting forth the laws and problems of a socialist society." "A genius like Chairman Mao emerges only once in several hundred years in the world and in several thousand years in China." (Emphasis added.)

Dear Comrade Lin Biao, the formulation "Chairman Mao stands much higher than Marx, Engels, Lenin, or Stalin" is incorrect.

I recently looked at some of Stalin's writings on "the opposition" and came across the following passages dealing with Lenin's achievements in developing Marxism:

"Comrades, we must affirm that the truth of the possible victory of socialism in one country was first discovered by Lenin and not by anybody else. We must not obliterate the fact that this achievement was Lenin's. We must not fear the truth, but must dare to speak the truth, dare to openly declare that among the Marxists, Lenin was the first to raise in a new way the question of whether or not socialism can be victorious in one country and the first to resolve this question in the affirmative.

"*I do not mean to say that as a theorist Lenin was in a class above Engels or above Marx.* My words are meant only to illustrate two things:

"First, no matter how genial Engels and Marx were as thinkers, we must not demand of them that they, prior to the era of monopoly capitalism, should have been capable of predicting all the possibilities that were to appear in the class struggle and in the proletarian revolution in the era of developed monopoly capitalism some fifty years later.

"Second, as the genial student of Engels and Marx, it is by no means strange that Lenin should have been able to spot certain new possibilities in the proletarian revolution under the newly developing conditions of capitalism and as a consequence discover the truth that it is possible for socialism to emerge victorious in one country."[2] (Emphasis added.)

Stalin's attitude is correct, while Comrade Lin Biao's attitude is wrong. The formulation "Chairman Mao stands much higher than Marx, Engels, Lenin, or Stalin" is wrong—in theory as well as in practice. It will provide the revisionists across the world with an excuse for attacking the Chinese Communist Party. Chairman Mao would also definitely not agree!

---

[2]I have not succeeded in locating this passage in Stalin's selected works; the English text is thus a translation of Yilin Dixi's Chinese.

Just like you say: "The kind of attitude one maintains with respect to Mao Zedong Thought is a very important question. We must therefore grasp the question of attitude toward Chairman Mao and toward Mao Zedong Thought." It was over the question of what attitude to maintain toward Lenin and Leninism that Stalin split with Trotsky, Zinoviev, and Kamenev. Today, a major split over what attitude to maintain toward Chairman Mao and Mao Zedong Thought has already occurred and is continuing. In this major split, the tendency to underrate Chairman Mao and Mao Zedong Thought is—it is true—highly erroneous (it is untenable and should mainly be criticized); but the tendency to rate it higher than is warranted by historical development is equally untenable and easily leads one onto the wrong track. Comrade Lin Biao, the only correct attitude to have toward Chairman Mao and Mao Zedong Thought is that which Stalin had toward Lenin and Leninism. All other attitudes are wrong.

Next you say, "The writings of Marxism-Leninism are too numerous, one cannot read them all. Moreover, they are too far removed from us. In the classical works of Marxism-Leninism, we must devote 99 percent of our efforts to the study of the works of Mao Zedong." Given that you said this at the Military Academy, it is inappropriate regardless of whether your 99 percent refers to the time and effort to be spent on study as such, or whether it refers to the balance to be struck between the study of Chairman Mao's works on the one hand and the works of Marx, Engels, Lenin, and Stalin on the other.

First of all, "The writings are too numerous, one cannot read them all [and] they are too far removed from us" obviously cannot be used to justify the 99 percent.

Second, specialized theory is necessary and particularly necessary in view of China's present situation. Already twenty-four years ago, Chairman Mao made this profound critical observation:

"But our theoretical front is very much out of harmony with the rich content of the Chinese revolutionary movement, and a comparison of the two shows that the theoretical side is lagging far behind. Generally speaking, our theory cannot as yet keep pace with our revolutionary practice, let alone lead the way as it should. We have not yet raised our rich and varied practice to the proper theoretical plane. We have not yet examined all the problems of revolutionary practice—or even the important ones—and raised them to a theoretical plane. Just think, how many of us have created theories worthy of the name on China's economics, politics, military affairs, or culture, theories that can be regarded as scientific and comprehensive, and not crude and sketchy? Especially in the field of economic theory: Chinese capitalism has had a century of development since the Opium War, and yet not a single theoretical work has been produced that accords with the realities of China's economic development and is genuinely scientific. Can we say that in the study of China's economic problems, for instance, the theoretical level is already high? Can we say that our Party already has economic theorists worthy of the name? Certainly not."

This criticism, which Chairman Mao expressed twenty-four years ago, is even more to the point today, in the Great Cultural Revolution. The problem is even more pronounced at this time when we not only have to resolve domestic problems but international problems as well. Since the beginning of the Great Cultural Revolution, there are no longer any systematic and comprehensive (or even relatively systematic and comprehensive) books containing "theories worthy of the name" on China's and the world's economics, politics, military affairs, or culture to be seen on the shelves of our bookshops! In the past there were some thick tomes and specialized works on the shelves, but the Great Cultural Revolution has made it clear that if they weren't written by bastards who donned the robes of Marxism-Leninism Mao Zedong Thought in order to oppose Marxism-Leninism Mao Zedong Thought, then they were written by pedants and phrase mongers who had made it into but never managed to get out of the world of bookish learning.

Thanks to the role played by yourself, the Liberation Army has become a role-model in the study of Mao Zedong Thought and the entire country is learning from the Liberation Army. A countrywide movement to study the works of Chairman Mao is unfolding on an unprecedented scale, and we are entering a great era in which the broad masses of workers, peasants, and soldiers are generally and directly grasping theory! We have already long since reached the stage Chairman Mao had in mind when he said at the Yan'an Forum on Literature and Art [that popularization] "supplies the basis for the work of raising standards that we are now doing on a limited scale, and prepares the necessary conditions for us to raise standards in the future on a much broader scale." The question of raising standards has for natural reasons begun to stand out and what the revolutionary movement very much needs, now and in the near future, are large numbers of genuine theorists.

Third, given that large numbers of talented theorists are very much needed in the fields of economics, politics, military affairs, and culture, such theorists must, regardless of their specialization, have at least a *relatively* full and systematic understanding of Marxism-Leninism Mao Zedong Thought—of which the works of Chairman Mao constitute only a part, which makes the 99 percent comparison incorrect and not applicable to institutions of higher learning.

Fourth, although the works of Chairman Mao represent only a part of the classic works of Marxism-Leninism, it is Mao Zedong Thought that in the present era constitutes the most practically relevant Marxism-Leninism, the most supreme and most living Marxism-Leninism. Right now we are undoubtedly advancing along the great road of Mao Zedong Thought and using Mao Zedong Thought as our basic weapon. We are not denying this, but on the contrary affirming it. It is precisely at this point that we must show a thorough understanding of Mao Zedong Thought and have a clear sense of what makes it progressive. Consequently, we must have a fair understanding of how Marxism-Leninism has developed. Here, too, your reference to "99 percent" is off the mark as far as your target audience is concerned. Generally speaking, to devote the greater part of our energy and time to the study of Chairman Mao's works is correct.

Finally, you say, "Some people say that *Das Kapital* is the basis of all theories. In fact, it only sets forth the laws and problems of capitalist societies. In our country we have already overthrown capitalism; we are now setting forth the laws and problems of a socialist society." Against the background of what you have said earlier, this leaves one feeling as if the works of Marx are already out of date. Especially the point you make of denying that *Das Kapital* is still our theoretical basis. I have not yet read *Das Kapital,* but I know that it is Marx's principal work. By saying that the theory contained in it is no longer our theoretical basis, aren't you in fact saying that the basic tenets of Marxism are already out of date? Isn't this tantamount to entering the morass of new and old revisionism from the "left"? Your view appears to be that a Newton-to-Einstein–like leap separates Marxism-Leninism from Mao Zedong Thought. An essential qualitative leap! This is obviously wrong.

Dear Comrade Lin Biao, please explain these things.

Let me voice some criticism in passing. From the Tiananmen rostrum, you have already delivered six decisively important speeches to guide the Great Cultural Revolution. But we have not seen you involve yourself in person in the most important and quintessential part of the present movement—the student movement. Zhou Enlai, Tao Zhu, and Chen Boda, for instance, have all participated in our debates, read our big-character posters in person, and spoken to us at receptions. I doubt if your speeches are absolutely correct. Take your speech of 15 September, for instance, in which you far too early and excessively stressed the seriousness of the attack on the Proletarian Headquarters by "a handful of reactionary bourgeois elements, and those belonging to the five categories of landlords, rich-peasants, counter-revolutionaries, bad elements, and Rightists."[3] In fact, most of those who fervently "bombarded the headquarters" in the provinces and municipalities were students, and even among the initiators, a majority would deny that the "headquarters" being "bombarded" was indeed black. Many of them just wanted to drop a few bombs to see what might happen, or bombard one or two selected individuals or certain strongly conservative measures taken by the "headquarters." But you did not explain what to "bombard the headquarters" meant. Instead you stressed that "the leadership in our country is in the hands of the proletariat." You stressed the correct side of the dictatorship of the proletariat—that which needs no improvement. But you did not acutely perceive the problems that have become so prominent since the launching of the Great Cultural Revolution, e.g. the need to ameliorate (*gaishan*) the dictatorship of the proletariat and to improve (*gexin*) the socialist system. It is necessary to change the organizational form of our Party and government in a major way. The People's Republic of China with its people's democratic dictatorship set up seventeen years ago is already obsolete. A state apparatus suited to China's historical peculiarities and one unlike any other on this earth is very much needed. Will anything come out of the present destruction by light fire-power, shocks of limited magnitude, and blasts from low-temperature furnaces? It seems as if you do not really have a very deep understanding of Engels's famous saying "The Commune is no longer the state in its original sense." Chairman Mao has already mentioned the Commune a number of times, and you may already have been shocked out of your slumber, but still rubbing your eyes you may not have noticed that the machinery of officialdom is just about done for and that appearing across the horizon in

---

[3]Full text in Harold C. Hinton, ed., *The People's Republic of China 1949–1979: A Documentary Survey* (Wilmington: Scholarly Resources, 1980), p. 1586.

the east are the first brilliant rays of the Commune of the East (*Dongfang gongshe*) that will replace "China" (*"Zhongguo"*). Your speeches have not drawn attention to this aspect of the movement, but on the contrary have obstructed it and caused a backlash (albeit a minor one). On 24 September, Zhang Pinghua in his speech used this opportunity to brand a large portion of the masses counter-revolutionary.[4]

Dear Comrade Lin Biao, Chairman Mao's single closest comrade-in-arms and pupil, I wish that with respect to your six speeches you would be able to do what Chairman Mao does, which is to "let theory run up ahead of practice" [*sic*]. But to be honest, you disappoint me. Your six speeches ran to the back of practice. For instance, in your sixth speech, although you pointed out that "the good thing about exchanging revolutionary experiences on foot is that you can come into broad contact with the masses and all aspects of society and in this way gain an even deeper understanding of the class struggle in socialist society," you did not in what you said stress the "social investigation" that Chairman Mao engaged in during the summer and winter vacations when he was a student—the Mao Zedong–style "social investigation."[5] While in fact, on this point, already before you made your speech, the big-character posters at Qinghua University had expressed such hope for days.

I hope you will enter deeper into the movement; otherwise, it may not take long before you too "risk being shunted aside," given that the dialectic of history is merciless.

Dear Comrade Lin Biao, our deputy commander-in-chief and Chairman Mao's single closest comrade-in-arms and successor (very many central leaders put it like that, and the people in general already regard you as Chairman Mao's chosen successor), I hope you will possess the same high level of theory and practice as Chairman Mao and that you will be as correct and all-round as he is, because the Marxist-Leninist revolutionary undertaking that is being led by the leaders of the Chinese Communist Party is not just that of one country, China, but that of the entire Communist movement. On this path, the struggle will be

---

[4] I have been unable to locate a transcript of Zhang's speech at what one Red Guard source refers to as the "black ghostbuster mobilization rally" of 24 September 1966.

[5] An official translation of Lin's speech at the sixth Red Guard rally in Tiananmen Square (on 3 November 1966) is in *Survey of China Mainland Press,* No. 3817, 8 November 1966, pp. 5–7.

extraordinarily sharp, and there will always be the danger of an error the breadth of a single hair leading you a thousand miles astray. Chairman Mao has come up along this path, but if his successor cannot continue, the Chinese Party runs the risk of becoming a fascist party. I'll say it once more, the merciless dialectic [of history] may request that you "step aside."

Why am I saying this in public? In order to encourage the popular masses to make greater use of the "great freedom" you mention—of criticizing and supervising the work of the leadership and the leaders of the Party and the state at all levels.

Errors have to be criticized and that which fails to accord with Mao Zedong Thought must be pointed out. Or may one not criticize or disagree with you? (In their speeches, some leaders appear to be saying that one may not criticize or disagree with you. I don't think you would agree with those who act as if that is the case.)

Words of utter devotion, requesting only that you give them some thought. Should I have distorted the truth, please criticize and correct me.

Great Proletarian Cultural Revolutionary greetings!

Beijing Agricultural University Middle School student
Yilin Dixi
15 November 1966

30
It's OK to Touch Your Soul

"The File"

Source: This satirical essay ("Chuji ni de linghun mei cuo") first appeared in the Red Guard tabloid *Shoudu hongweibing* (*Capital Red Guard*) on 30 November 1966. Our translation is based on the text in *Wei Mao zhuxi er zhan: Sansi* Shoudu hongweibing *wenxuan* (*Fighting for Chairman Mao: Selections from the Third Headquarters' Capital Red Guard*) (Beijing, 1967), pp. 133–35. The pseudonymous Red Guard author is most likely a student or teacher at the Beijing Geological Institute.

Whether you really approve of the socialist revolution, or just pretend to, or even oppose the socialist revolution, will reveal itself in how you approach the Great Proletarian Cultural Revolution. This question is one that touches people to their very souls.[1]

Comrade, in the course of this Great Proletarian Cultural Revolution, we have already seen the filth in your soul. Now please, cleanse yourself! Touch your soul! That's right.

1. To "Protect" Is OK

"I'd rather be a Protector than assume the role of a 'counter-revolutionary'." To "protect" (*bao*) is safe; to "destroy" (*po*) is dangerous. A moment's carelessness, like destroying the wrong thing or opposing the wrong thing, and one is a counter-revolutionary and Rightist. My Party membership, my youth league membership, my promotion, my chances of becoming an official, my fame and gain, my future, my all, my everything. Ah, my God, it would all be lost! There is no way I can or dare destroy! I am going to protect, protect, protect the Party Committee, protect the work team, protect the Cultural Revolution Committee, protect a certain He, protect a certain Zou, and protect. . . . I shall remain a protector for the rest of my life.[2] Even if it turns out my protecting was wrong, it's no big deal. Why, it was simply a matter of understanding. One of deep feelings for the Party!

Right: protect is what I'm going to do from now on. "Unshakable in my determination" (*lei dabudong*) is what I'll be!

2. To "Obey" Is OK

Why, he is an "old revolutionary"! He represents the Party, the Party Center, and Chairman Mao. To do what he says cannot be wrong. If you don't do what he says, but merely affirm it in the abstract while negating it in practice, then that's opposition to the Party. To follow him is OK. If he struggles the masses, I'll compile dossiers on my fellow students. I'll hide behind his butt, shake my head now and then, waggle my tail now and then, like a puppy hoping

---

[1]Cf. the very first sentence of the "Sixteen Points": "The Great Proletarian Cultural Revolution now unfolding is a great revolution that touches people to their very souls. . . ." See Document 4.

[2]"A certain He" refers to He Changgong, the Party secretary of the Ministry of Geology; "A certain Zou" refers to Zou Jiayou, who headed the Cultural Revolution Work Team that entered the Beijing Geological Institute on 15 June 1966.

he'll throw me a bone. Who knows, if he's in a good mood, he may even feed me some soup. Of course, if he's wrong, it has nothing to do with me. My perception was unclear, I was fooled, though all I had done was simply listen to the voice of the "Party"!

3. To "Follow" Is OK

I am willing to follow the main current, so where everybody else goes that's where I'll go too. I "have faith in the masses" and "faith in the majority"! The more people, the greater our strength. Having joined the "majority faction," I don't have to worry and I don't have to be bothered. I won't starve and I won't suffer. Ah, how nice, how wonderful! When the majority faction emerges victorious, my contribution will naturally have been substantial. Go wrong? One cannot go wrong, definitely not. If by a chance in a million, I should have gone wrong, I still don't need to worry. So has everyone else, so my mistake will not amount to much.

Right, the "majority faction" is it for me; and I'll definitely follow the main current. I cannot go wrong!

4. To "Turn" Is OK

I turn with the wind. Sitting by my radio, I listen to the weather forecast. No matter how hot it is outside, if the forecast says "cold" I put on my fur coat. If I hear there is going to be a thunderstorm, I immediately retreat to my cozy nest to play my guitar or read a novel. Once the wind has died down and the seas are calm, I again become "brave" and announce my readiness to really go for it. In any case, you're not allowed to deny me the right to make revolution, right? So what about thunderstorms still to come? My strategy remains the same. It's an art called "flexibility and mobility"! To "trim one's sails" is OK.

5. To Be "Slick" Is OK

What I really like is playing the "slick and sly" double-dealer who speaks the language of men with men and the language of monsters with monsters. I get along with this faction, and yet my relations with that one are not bad either. I pick up a fishbone here, and grab a pork leg over there. What bothers me is that some people curse me and call me a fence-sitter who compromises, makes concessions, and tries to curry favors with everybody. In fact, that's where I am doing the right thing. I will always be right. And if not, then at least I am being "tactful" by stressing "unity"!

6. To "Flatter" Is OK

I am a master at flattery, I'm honey-tongued and I know all about how to suck up to people. If he has made mistakes, I'll cover them up. If he has flaws, I'll patch them up. I'll salute him and try to get him to appoint me to some post. My stand remains firm, even when promoted three ranks at a time. Meanwhile, you damned sons of bitches: Why are you laughing when you see us "old revolutionaries" make mistakes?

Some curse me and say I lick ass. I say asses are there to be licked. Why, "one divides into two," and praise should be the main thing![3] There is nothing wrong with a little flattery.

7. To "Touch Your Very Soul" Is OK

You have been talking all the time, but now it's time for me to say a few words. What is your soul? The character for "me" is written all over it, and the character for "self" is clearly in command. "Fame and gain"—that's your soul![4] In the Great Cultural Revolution, protecting this and protecting that—you've just been protecting yourself! In pointing this out, perhaps I am indeed "not stressing unity!" Perhaps I have indeed forgotten that "satire is not to be employed when describing contradictions among the people!" Perhaps even the accusation of "masses struggling the masses" will be thrown at me! So what? It does not matter. You've got so many "OKs," could I really be wrong for uttering just one sentence? That's really outrageous! So just touch your very soul—it's OK!

---

3. The author is alluding to a well-known remark by Mao: "Praise should be the main thing, and criticism should be supplementary." See "Remarks at the Spring Festival," in Stuart R. Schram, ed., *Mao Tse-tung Unrehearsed: Talks and Letters 1956–1971* (Harmondsworth: Penguin Books, 1974), p. 199.

4. Cf. the following remark in Lin Biao's speech, Document 2: "These are the people of communism. Their opposites are the people centered on 'self,' who are only interested in their own gain, fame, power, status, and with being in the limelight."

31
"As We Watched Them Beat Him . . ."

Eyewitnesses

Source: Extracts from big-character posters written by teachers and students in the Jianguang Junior Middle School and published in New Beijing University "Smile Mingling in Their Midst" Combat Team, ed. & publ. *Jianguang zhongxue qingnian jiaoshi Bei Guancheng shi zemyang bei bisi de?—"Bei Guancheng shijian" diaocha baogao* (*How Was the Young Teacher Bei Guancheng from Jianguang Middle School Forced to Die?—Report of an Investigation into the "Bei Guancheng Incident"*) (Shanghai, 1967), pp. 12–13. The person being beaten is the author of the letter translated as Document 26. He committed suicide right after the events described here, on the night of 2 October 1966.

[Original editor's comment:] These are extracts from big-character posters written by teachers and students who themselves either took part in or witnessed the violence. The extracts forcefully expose [School Party Secretary] Wang Xingguo as the instigator of these criminal acts of violence.

1. Fei Zhensheng (elderly staff worker):

I saw some twenty students surrounding Bei Guancheng on the terrace of Building No. 5. Three or four students were beating him up. And Bei himself? He did not utter a sound, but just let them go on beating him. A student by the name of XXX was most vicious and threw Bei to the concrete floor maybe five or six times. When Bei refused to get up by himself, they pulled him to his feet and hit and kicked him until once again he was lying on the floor. At one point he was lying face up when student XXX came forward and kicked him on the head. Once he managed to sit up, students XXX and XXX stepped forward to slap him in the face for about two minutes. They took turns, one taking over when the other had to rest, their slapping producing a sound like exploding firecrackers . . .

Later I watched through the window in Room 401 how Bei Guancheng was in a sort of frog-like position—his face pressed against the floor, his arms supporting him on the sides, and his behind up in the air. Only later did I find out that he had been enduring a form of punishment . . .

2. Chen Dongsheng (teacher) and Liu Xueqing (Red Guard):

At that point we heard the noise and excitement outside so we walked up to the window and looked in the direction of the North Sports Ground, where we saw a group of students dragging Bei Guancheng through a crowd that had gathered at the entrance of the main building. The students were violently beating and kicking Bei Guancheng. Finally they dragged him off to the ping-pong table (under the trees next to the North Sports Ground) and propped him up against it, his arms and legs already limp. Then some students ordered him to crawl onto the table, and they began hitting him in the face and on the head with their fists. From afar you could hear the noise and the "slam, bam, slam, bam" sound of him being beaten. Then the students ordered Bei Guancheng to lift his arms and lower his head and admit to being a counter-revolutionary, an ox-monster and a snake-demon. Then we saw one student kicking the legs out from under Bei Guancheng. At that point we could not bear to watch the violence any more, and so we walked away from the window.

3. Yin Honghai (Red Guard in the third grade):

I was also present when Bei Guancheng was beaten. That afternoon we returned from a meeting when we saw them dragging Bei Guancheng onto the terrace. I did not actually witness the violence on the terrace, but I saw it with my own eyes when they dragged him off to Room 401 to beat him up. I saw it when they told him to lift his arms up in the air and lower his head. Then later some people kicked his behind, others punched him on the back with their clenched fists, others twisted his arms, yelling over and over again: "You went to Beijing to establish counter-revolutionary contacts, didn't you?" By far the most vicious part was when they made him bend over and lean forward against the edge of the [concrete] ping-pong table and then pushed his head with full force against its edge. They did this not just once. Just as they were beating him, I saw Wang Xingguo coming out of Room 403. After she had taken a quick look at what was happening in Room 401, she walked off smiling with a triumphant look on her face. That's what I saw at the time. At the time, I too joined in the beating, which was wrong of me. I had been influenced by Wang Xingguo's bourgeois reactionary line.

4. Fu Xiaokang (Red Guard in the second grade, class 7):

Around 2:30 in the afternoon on 2 October, I and some of my

classmates including Ji Zhengliu were preparing to return home when a smiling Wang Xingguo came through the school gate and said, "Students, don't go away. Just now Wang Xiongxiang, Huang Longmin, and some others went to fetch Bei Guancheng." Since we are all rather mischievous students who don't mind a fight or beating up on somebody now and then, and since we had heard that some people had already beaten Bei Guancheng, we said right away in unison: "So we can beat him up too then?" Having said that, we got some bamboo sticks and other weapons to thrash him with and got all fired up. Wang Xingguo saw all of this but did nothing to stop us. On the contrary, she was laughing loudly. From what we were able to tell at the time, Wang Xingguo was highly supportive of our "revolutionary action."

It is only now that we have seen through Wang Xingguo's vile personality, how she provoked us into beating Bei Guancheng. Wang Xingguo is Bei Guancheng's executioner. She must take the blame for what happened. We were duped.

5. Chen Yong (Red Guard in the first grade, class 1):

Under the leadership of the Party branch headed by Wang Xingguo, I carried out the bourgeois reactionary line of the Shanghai municipal party committee and branded the revolutionary masses "counter-revolutionaries," "fake Leftists," "genuine Rightists," "demanders" (*shenshoupai*), etc. Under the circumstances, many students were hoodwinked, and I am one of them.

I am a worker's son. I have boundless love for the Party and for Chairman Mao.

The Red Guard organization at our school had barely been established when I joined. But because it was controlled and dominated by Wang Xingguo, it ended up doing many things in contravention of the "Sixteen Points." Our language teacher, Bei Guancheng, developed a bad attitude after some Red Guards had ransacked his home. He went to Beijing to tell on Wang Xingguo, the powerholder in our school. As a result, he was branded a "counter-revolutionary." After teacher Bei left for Beijing, everybody was gossiping, saying that he had "absconded to Beijing to avoid punishment for his crimes," etc.

At the time, we were all really furious. On 29 September, when teacher Bei came back from Beijing, my classmate X X X and I went to look for him. We told him, "The Cultural Revolution Committee is looking for you!" He said, "I have already spoken to Zhang Li on the

Cultural Revolution Committee and made my attitude clear." Soon after that, Bei Guancheng was dragged off by us to the roof of Building No. 5 to be given a beating. I said we should not beat him, but student X X X said that teacher X X X (leader of the Red Guards and a member of the Cultural Revolution Committee) had said: "You just go ahead and beat him up. Even if you kill him, you won't be held responsible." Words like that actually gave us the courage, ordering us to go and beat him, which is what we did next. In the course of the beating, student X X X tried to force Bei Guancheng to commit suicide by jumping off the roof, but I pleaded with him, "What if he commits suicide and drags you with him? You'd die too." Because I said that, students X X X and X X X no longer tried to force him to commit suicide by jumping off the roof. Then later quite a few students who had attended a city district Red Guard Company meeting returned to beat him up. I pleaded with X X X not to let teacher Bei return home, as I was convinced if allowed to return home, he would commit suicide. That is all I witnessed, and as for what happened later I don't know. Nobody came forward to try and stop the beating. That's what happened.

There is a mountain of hard evidence, and Wang Xingguo will not escape responsibility for her crimes!

Bei Guancheng was a revolutionary comrade and not a counter-revolutionary!

It was Wang Xingguo who hounded Bei Guancheng to death!

32
Chinese Molestation of Diplomats

Lennart Petri

Source: This is a translation of "Kinesiska övergrepp mot diplomater," a note to the Swedish Ministry for Foreign Affairs from the Swedish ambassador to China, Lennart Petri. The original note is in the Ministry Archives (File HP 1 XK: Ink UD 5/6 1967, 204).

Peking, 29 May 1967

Colleague,

From mid-July to New Year's Eve 1966 the Dutch chargé d'affaires in Beijing was imprisoned in his embassy, and Dutch wives and children were for one month refused exit visas. In January 1967 a screaming crowd armed with loudspeakers started a siege of the Soviet embassy that lasted for weeks. Soviet diplomats were at times not allowed to come out. On one occasion, Soviet embassy staff about to purchase tickets for wives returning home were detained for sixteen hours in their vehicles, etc., etc. The "Friendship Store," exclusively for foreigners, as well as hotels and restaurants in the city would according to insulting notices no longer serve Soviet citizens. At the railway station and elsewhere in town, there were posters in a variety of languages that read "Hang Kosygin; smash Brezhnev's head," etc.

The ambassadors from the eastern bloc were detained for hours in their cars by the crowds—in the presence of the police—when they attempted to visit the Soviet embassy. In some cases, their tires were deflated. Soviet wives and children about to return home were subjected to insults and threats that absolutely terrified the children. Many lower-ranking East European embassy staff have been molested. The French trade counselor was forced to stand for seven hours, and his wife more than five hours, in the street in freezing cold surrounded by a furious crowd ten meters from the French embassy without the police intervening except to prevent physical assaults. For a few days and nights, the French and Yugoslavian embassies were surrounded by thousands of demonstrators with loudspeaker vans that made such a noise it was at times difficult to make oneself heard in the offices of this mission even when the windows were shut.

The Indonesian chargé d'affaires, who was declared persona non grata after the Chinese chargé d'affaires in Djakarta had met the same fate, was molested and insulted at the airport when departing.

Now it is the British embassy's turn to be subject to retaliatory measures motivated by the disturbances in Hong Kong. Its office in Shanghai (which does not have the right to call itself a consulate)[1] was stormed on 16 May by a crowd of people who, in the presence of first secretary Hewitt, his wife and three children, spent three hours destroying all their personal possessions. When Hewitt and another British first secretary were about to leave Shanghai, they were kicked and

---

[1]The official Chinese designation of the British mission in Shanghai was "Office of the British chargé d'affaires looking after the affairs of British nationals in Shanghai."

beaten and their clothes were torn and smeared with glue.[2] The Hewitt family has not yet been allowed to leave China. One million people demonstrated outside the British embassy on 15–17 May, and there have been sporadic demonstrations since then. The garden walls facing the street are covered with posters, most of them in Chinese but some in English that read, "Blood debts must be repaid in blood," "Crush British Imperialism," "Hang Wilson," etc.

Demonstrations, mainly involving noise—terror in the form of shouting and loudspeaker vans, have in recent days also been held outside the Mongolian embassy, and as is already the case with the Soviet, Yugoslavian, French, Indonesian, and British embassies, here too the garden walls have been covered with hostile posters. These last few days, an Indian embassy secretary was detained for six hours and a Bulgarian for two hours at the police station, where they had been taken by the "masses" after having purchased tabloids in the streets.

Under present conditions here in Beijing, any embassy may suddenly become the target of the organized fury of the "revolutionary rebels." It is therefore crucial that we receive instant notice of any possible incidents involving China occurring in Stockholm. In the event of such an incident, our Chinese servants will immediately be ordered to go on strike, and it is not that easy to manage the household, without prior warning, in for instance the mission residence with its coke-burning Chinese stove. The temptation to create incidents is almost certainly great among Chinese diplomats stationed abroad, in particular among the young ones, who believe that in this way they will become heroes, "Chairman Mao's good diplomatic fighters."

The mood within the diplomatic corps in Beijing is not exactly friendly toward the regime, despite the appreciation many of us have of the many good sides of the Chinese people. A constantly recurring topic of conversation among the foreign staff, regardless of race and nationality, is the likelihood of being transferred out of here soon. The mood among the wives who remain (about half went home in the spring) is affected by such in themselves innocent things like the little Chinese children playing on "Anti-Revisionism Street," the street that leads up to the Soviet embassy, shaking their fists in imitation of their

---

[2]A copy of the British note, dated 24 May 1967, protesting this gross violation of diplomatic immunity is in the archives of the Swedish Ministry for Foreign Affairs (File HP 1 XK: Ink UD 5/6 1967, 208).

elders and shouting "beat, beat" or "beat to death, beat to death" even when the car of a single child-loving non-Chinese woman drives past. This spring there has all the same been only one suicide within the diplomatic corps. In addition, one East German diplomat suddenly passed away due to, we are informed, the mental pressures we all endure. "It is hard to have to earn one's living as an ambassador in Beijing," one of the European ambassadors sighed the other day.

So far there have been no incidents involving the staff of our mission, but that must be regarded as coincidental. As an example of what we all have to be prepared for—and by now have come to regard as quite normal—I shall mention the following:

On 17 May, on the eve of the departure of most chiefs of mission on a journey [arranged for them by the Chinese], the British chargé d'affaires requested my participation (I am the senior West European chief of mission) in informing the acting doyen of the diplomatic corps, the ambassador of the United Arab Republic, about the infringements upon British embassy office and staff in Shanghai. This in view of the absence of diplomatic relations between Great Britain and the Arab Republic. When I left the British chargé d'affaires' residence at about eight P.M.—he was himself not allowed to leave the premises— to walk over to the Egyptian embassy nearby (no cars are allowed to approach the British embassy), I was for a few minutes stopped by the crowds blocking the gates. Above my head a doll was suspended, presumably in effigy of chargé d'affaires Hopson. The words "Burn the wily Anglo-Saxon" were written on it. On the wall of the embassy next to me I read, in half-meter-high letters, "Hang Wilson." The crowd made such a noise I had to shout directly into the ears of the policemen or soldiers standing by the gate to tell them who I was. I signaled to the policemen to make way for me through the crowd, but before that happened a few minutes passed. Meanwhile, the crowds were shouting furiously and shaking clenched fists. The Chinese closest to me, students, extended their fists as if to hit me but stopped short by half a centimeter from touching my face. If the intention of the crowd had been to tear me to pieces (something that I fortunately imagined was not the case), it would hardly have behaved very differently. A few square decimeters of my suit was smeared with glue—one demonstrator had a glue-brush in his hand—but the glue was of such poor quality it washed out quite easily upon my return home. When I finally, with the help of the police, succeeded in getting past the crowd, the worst of the shouting died down and the loudspeakers again began to dominate. The scattered Chinese demonstrators at the rear of the crowd took no particular interest in my person; they were, after all, not within sight of the agitators, the leaders of the crowd.

I have not submitted a protest, as such a move would only be met with accusations of my having provoked the Chinese people. The incident furthermore took place shortly after I had received the insolent Chinese note about Taiwan's participation in the Swedish Fair in Gothenburg. The Chinese Foreign Ministry is not interested in—perhaps not even capable of—doing anything to promote respect for the accepted rules of diplomatic immunity. I want to delay my protest until something more serious happens involving the staff of our mission. In the present climate here, that may be at any moment.

Yours sincerely,

Lennart Petri

33
"Dear Parents, . . . Don't Worry About Me!"

United Action Committee Red Guard

Source: Red Guard Congress New Beijing University Middle School "Jinggangshan" Regiment Headquarters, ed., *Dazibao xuan* (*Selected Big-Character Posters*) (Beijing, 1967), p. 11.

Dear parents:

A white terror is spreading across the city of Beijing. The Third HQ is picking up people at random, and large numbers of innocent school-mates and people who don't agree with the Third HQ have been thrown in jail.[1] The Public Security Bureau is also taking people into custody. We've set up a Joint Action Committee made up mostly of old Red Guards from before 18 August. The masses maintain that the

---

[1]The "third HQ" was a rebel Red Guard umbrella organization with close links to the Central Cultural Revolution Group. Its leading members included Kuai Dafu, the author of Document 25, and Tan Houlan, the author of Document 28.

Joint Action Committee is a counter-revolutionary organization, and anyone who wears the committee's armband in public is likely to be picked up at any time. If I'm not in Tianjin by the 28th, I may very well have been taken into custody by the Public Security Bureau.

When it was set up, the public aim of the Joint Action Committee was to fight the Third HQ, but "the drinker's heart is not in the cup," and actually our intention has been to fight the Central Cultural Revolution Group. I really hate Jiang Qing's guts. She's done things that make me genuinely dissatisfied and that I just cannot understand. Now Jiang Qing and Chen Boda have attacked Tao Zhu by name, and in Beijing people are starting to bombard Tao Zhu. Tao ranks number four [in the CCP], and at this point they still haven't been able to pin anything on him. There are ominous signs suggesting that number three, Premier Zhou, may also be dragged out. If Jiang Qing starts fighting the premier, we're going to call her to account and ask what on earth she is up to. The Cultural Revolution Group has been supporting the Third HQ all along; it has put an equal sign between itself and the Third HQ by saying that if the Third HQ collapses, then the Cultural Revolution Group will collapse too. They manipulate a group of confused members of the masses to protect them, but because the Joint Action Committee is made up mainly of revolutionary cadres' sons and daughters, all of whom have a lot of brains, they aren't able to manipulate us.

Our ideological level is fairly high, and we are politically sensitive. We saw clearly that there were major discrepancies between the speeches of the four vice chairmen of the Central Military Commission and those made by the Cultural Revolution Group.[2] Therefore, in society there has now emerged a group of members of the masses like ourselves who follow the Military Commission. The Military Commission puts particular stress on the class line and the mark left by the class one belongs to, while the Cultural Revolution Group stresses how everybody's equal and how the impact of one's

---

[2]The "speeches of the four vice chairmen" refers to the speeches by Ye Jianying, He Long, Chen Yi, and Xu Xiangqian at two controversial mass rallies on 13 and 29 November 1966. Transcripts are in *Douzheng shenghuo bianjibu*, ed., *Wuchanjieji wenhua dageming ziliao huibian* (*Collected Materials on the Great Proletarian Cultural Revolution*) (Beijing: Hebei Beijing shifan xueyuan, 1967), pp. 359–68, 464–71.

family is limited. . . . Recently I heard Ye Jianying's self-criticism.[3] When the speeches of the Military Commission led the masses to fight against the masses, the Cultural Revolution Group ought to have produced a self-criticism, since the fault was really theirs. But the Cultural Revolution Group just doesn't dare to assume responsibility, and instead they caused trouble for Marshal Ye by making him produce a self-criticism. Later I heard that Lin Biao was really angry, because Marshal Ye's speech had been gone over by the Military Commission prior to delivery. Jiang Qing's level is just too low. The errors she makes now are, to put it lightly, those of someone whose bourgeois ideology has not yet been successfully transformed. She still does not understand proletarian things. To put it strongly, one must suspect her of harboring wild ambitions. I don't want to talk about the details in a letter like this. We are planning a rally to bombard the Ministry of Public Security on the 10th, to bake Xie Fuzhi and to drag out his backstage boss, because there's a link between Xie Fuzhi and Jiang Qing.[4]

Now there are slogans in the streets bombarding Commander Chen [Yi] and Ye Jianying. And now the Cultural Revolution Group has thrown out Tao Zhu, Wang Renzhong, Liu Zhijian, and Zhou Rongxin. Jiang Qing claims they're all two-faced double dealers and says they've done bad things behind her back. I doubt if what's happening is not actually that the Cultural Revolution Group is just putting the blame for all its errors on them, while protecting itself. There's too much going on, I don't feel like writing about it. Last night we went to the Ministry of Public Security where we were surrounded and given the honorific label of "counter-revolutionaries" before finally being released and allowed to return to school on foot. Today a number of boys were picked up, all because of us, while others went to the Ministry to ask for our release. In Beijing right now, the overall direction of the Great Cultural Revolution is not right, the Cultural Revolution Group is quite incompetent. I'll try to make it back home once the rally we've planned for the 7th [*sic*] is over.

---

[3]This refers to Ye Jianying's self-critical speech at a PLA rally in Beijing on 31 December. A transcript is in Hebei Beijing Teacher's College *Douzheng shenghuo bianjibu,* pp. 628–30.

[4]On 10 January 1967, the United Action Committee convened a mass meeting in the Beijing Exhibition Hall to "bombard" the Ministry of Public Security. For more information on this and other activities of a similar nature by the committee, see Red Guard Shanghai Headquarters, ed. & publ., *Zalan "Liandong"* (*Smash "United Action"*) (Shanghai, 1967).

Mom and Dad, don't worry about me. Nothing is going to happen to me. I'm not naive, and I'm not someone who's got no brains or who blindly follows and is taken advantage of by others. I really am quite capable of observing and analyzing problems by myself. Recently I haven't been keen on returning home, because I don't want to waste my time, but would rather "face the world and brave the storm" in the Great Cultural Revolution. I am a person with aspirations, and I want to achieve something, except now the situation is forcing me to leave—to follow the "supreme stratagem!"[5] Don't show this letter to X X X.

Don't worry about me, and get a lot of rest. I deeply believe and do not doubt that the Chairman is on our side.

Your daughter
7 January [1967], evening

---

[5]This refers to the last of the traditional Chinese "Thirty-Six Stratagems" for coping with most of life's problems, be they big or small. It reads: "The supreme stratagem is to walk off."

34
After-School Activities of Middle School and Elementary School Students

Heilongjiang Provincial Revolutionary Committee

Source: This report was originally circulated nationwide by the CCP Center on 6 June 1967, in Central Document *Zhongfa* [1967] 179. Our translation is of the text reproduced in CCP Central Committee General Office and State Council General Office Joint Cultural Revolution Reception Office, ed., *Wuchanjieji wenhua dageming youguan wenjian huiji* (*Collection of Documents Concerning the Great Proletarian Cultural Revolution*), 5 vols. (Beijing, 1967–68), Vol. 3, pp. 47–57.

In April, we visited Harbin's Majiagou district, the Wenchang Elementary School, and the Residents' Committee of the employees of the original provincial government to investigate the after-school activities of middle school and elementary school students. We now report our findings:

After Chairman Mao and the Party Center called upon middle schools and elementary schools to resume classes and make revolution, the broad masses of revolutionary teachers and students in Harbin's middle schools and elementary schools gradually returned to school to resume classes on the one hand and to make revolution on the other. In the course of this historically unprecedented Great Proletarian Cultural Revolution, the students in middle schools and elementary schools have all received a profound education and training, and developed a revolutionary spirit of daring to think, daring to speak, daring to act, daring to charge, and daring to rebel. Their spiritual outlook has changed tremendously. But, just as Chairman Mao teaches us: "The class struggle is by no means over." The class enemy will not accept defeat, and he tries in a thousand and one ways to win the younger generation away from us. At present, due to the influence of bourgeois ideology and entrapment by bad people, a number of unhealthy tendencies have developed among the young. Their main forms of expression are:

1. Picking people's pockets and other acts of theft. Some students, inspired and spurred on by thieves and hooligans, regularly visit crowded department stores, bus stops, cultural and recreational sites, etc., to pick pockets and steal. Others engage in destructive activities such as cutting off electrical wiring, stealing roof tiles, and stripping off machine parts. Particular attention should be paid to the fact that some students not only do not regard such acts of theft as something to be ashamed of but on the contrary regard them as something to brag about. They say: "So you steal something and end up spending a week in jail. So what?" As a result, it is difficult to come to grips with the problem.

2. Serious damage to public property. Some students not only damage chairs and desks and fail to take good care of public property in their schools, but even willfully destroy public property outside school. There are some fifty street lights in the vicinity of the Residents' Committee of the employees of the original provincial government. Forty-five of them have been shattered by students using slingshots. Sometimes new light bulbs have no sooner been installed before they have again been broken. In some residential quarters, children cut off the fuse wires almost every day, and in some corridors there is not a single light switch that still works. Electrical wiring has been exposed,

and the likelihood of someone getting a shock is extremely great. Quite a few windows in some office buildings have been broken by the students, and with their slingshots they have broken almost all of the glass window panes stored in the Residential Buildings Repair Shop.

3. Some have been tainted with the bad habits of hooligans. Some wear their hats askew and use foul language, assail and insult girl students, and mimic the behavior of Teddy Boys. Some form gangs, call each other "sworn brothers," adopt their own "brotherhood codes," and copy all kinds of feudal rituals. Some even swear "oaths" in which they guarantee not to divulge their activities to outsiders and promise never to let a "sworn brother" down, meaning that if one of them is in trouble, the others will all come to his rescue. After ganging up like this, some students have begun hanging out in the streets bullying younger students, blocking the road, and threatening teachers and local cadres who criticize them. At night, some of them knock on the doors and windows of the homes of those whom they don't like, all in the hope of frightening them.

4. Emergence of gangs and gang fights. Some students form gangs, elect leaders, and provoke fights. Some students carry knives, clubs, leather belts, or other weapons and hide in dark corners in public parks and elsewhere. When the opportunity arises, they lure others into fights. Some have been wounded and some—on occasions when things really got out of hand—have even been killed. This is a very big problem. Nobody is allowed to criticize them, and those who do risk all kinds of reprisals. For instance, when the students dislike someone, they come together outside his home in the evening. One of them shines a flashlight at the windows and the others shoot stones with their slingshots, smashing the window panes. Some students who in the past would brag about whose father was the biggest official are now bragging about whose father belongs to what faction. They bully those whose father is a member of the conservative faction, or whose father is not a member of any faction at all.

The causes of the problems listed here are, in our view, as follows:

First, the sharp and complicated class struggle in society finds its reflection in the minds of the young, and some students are unable to distinguish between proletarian great democracy and bourgeois liberalization (*ziyouhua*). They develop a form of extremist democratic (*jiduan minzhuhua*) sentiment in which everything revolves around the will of the individual and wherein—all in the name of "making rebellion" and "opposing slavishness"—one acts altogether as one pleases. Consequently, nobody listens to what teachers and local cadres say, and some teachers and local cadres are even made to suffer for speaking up against the bad behavior of the students.

Second, the parents of some students dote on their children and neglect their proper education. Some parents indulge their children, fail to discipline them, spoil them rotten, and will not in the least accept the criticisms of others. The children of some leading cadres in particular are doted upon at home and nobody dares to discipline them. In the dormitories where the employees of the original provincial government live, most of the trouble is caused by the sons and daughters of certain leading cadres. They are invariably the leaders of the children and are impossible to control. They are domineering and act like overlords. For instance, one of the sons of Gao X stole and drove off with the motorcycle belonging to the messenger of the Government Office. Afterwards, Gao X not only did not educate his son to make him see the error of his ways, but on the contrary spurred him on by calling him "really courageous." And then there are the three children of Wang XXX, who seriously beat and hurt a neighbor's child. Wang XXX not only failed to discipline his children, but even went so far as to quarrel with and curse the parents of the child who had been hurt.

Third, the teachers neglect their educational duties and in some cases do not even discipline the most flagrant cases of misbehavior and error. They do not actively encourage the students to mend their ways, but just let things be. At the same time, the hours that the students and the elementary school students in particular actually spend in class are far too few. Some students have only one or two hours of classes a day. They have no homework at all, and when classes are over there is nobody there to encourage them to study on their own. Most of them spend most of their time just playing.

On the basis of the problems and their causes as identified above, we turned to the relevant departments for advice. The consensus was that active measures should be adopted to deal with the situation, e.g. strengthening class education and communist moral education aimed at elementary and middle school students. They are at an important stage in their lives when they develop physically as well as mentally. The young represent a battleground over which the bourgeoisie is engaged in combat with the proletariat, and if the proletariat does not occupy this battleground, the bourgeoisie will. The quality of our education of the young has a direct impact on what kinds of successors to the revolution we shall end up fostering. It is just as Chairman Mao has taught us: "an extremely important life-and-death question that will determine the fate of our Party and of our state, and with respect to our proletarian revolutionary undertaking a matter of fundamental import- ance for centuries, millennia, and ten thousand years to come." Conse- quently, we make the following proposals:

1. The launching of a movement in middle schools and elementary schools to propagate the living study and living application of Chair- man Mao's works, e.g. to read Chairman Mao's works, obey Chairman Mao's words, act according to Chairman Mao's instructions, and be- come Chairman Mao's good children. To destroy the notion of "self" on a massive scale while promoting the idea of the "public" on an equally massive scale; to destroy the four olds, establish the four news; to establish the absolute authority of Mao Zedong Thought on a mas- sive scale; and to arm the broad masses of young people with Mao Zedong Thought.

2. Cadres, staff, and parents must assume their responsibility and look upon the fostering of their sons and daughters as a common political task to be carried out properly through constant education with the help of Mao Zedong Thought. Those who instigate their chil- dren to do bad things should be criticized and educated, and in serious cases be subjected to disciplinary action.

3. The People's Liberation Army enjoys high prestige among the young, and we propose that the army aid the schools and local authori- ties in strengthening young people's class education, in teaching them the "Three Main Rules of Discipline and Eight Points for Attention," in teaching them to cherish public property, and in teaching them to unite with their fellow students and to learn new and proper socialist habits.

4. All elementary schools are to actively organize the students into Little Red Soldier (*Hongxiaobing*) groups and regularly engage them in meaningful collective activities. The time during which the students are studying at school should be suitably extended and should nor- mally not be less than four hours of classes each day.

5. Prefectural, municipal, and county-level Revolutionary Commit- tees, as well as the organizations of the revolutionary masses in the various departments, factories, mines, enterprises, and schools, should appoint a special person and set up a special unit to take charge of the

task of educating the young and to help schools and residential areas to organize the education of the young outside school hours, so as to truly foster the young to become all-round developed communist new men with a proletarian political consciousness.

Heilongjiang Provincial Revolutionary Committee
Political Commission Culture and Education Group
13 April 1967

35
I Support My Child in Taking the Revolutionary Road

Qu Guishan

Source: Survey of China Mainland Magazines, No. 654, 12 May 1969. This letter from an employee in the East Is Red Garment Factory in Beijing originally appeared in *Beijing ribao* (*Beijing Daily*) on 21 July 1968.

My son, Qu Che, is a senior middle school graduate from the No. 25 Middle School in Peking. In October last year when ten graduates, including my son, decided to go to Inner Mongolia to set up their homes, I gave them my full support without saying anything. I thought, Chairman Mao had long ago pointed out: "How should we judge whether a youth is a revolutionary? How can we tell? There can be only one criterion, namely, whether or not he is willing to integrate himself with the broad masses of workers and peasants and does so in practice. If he is willing to do so and actually does so, he is a revolutionary; otherwise, he is a nonrevolutionary or a counter-revolutionary."

What an impressive teaching of Chairman Mao! The road my son is taking is a road pointed out by Chairman Mao, a revolutionary road, a road for the prevention of revisionism. Being the father, I naturally gave him 100 percent support.

Going to Inner Mongolia to work, one must expect some hardship. And it is precisely because my son is willing to go to a place of hardship that I feel particularly happy. Chairman Mao said: "A good comrade is one who goes to the most difficult place." What attitude one takes toward hardship is an important indication of whether one is loyal to Chairman Mao and whether one works for "public interest" or "self-interest." Fear of hardship is a bad bourgeois idea of hankering after comfort and leisure. That our children are willing to go to a difficult place proves that they are obedient to Chairman Mao, and therefore we as parents should support them. Failure to support them would ruin not only the children but also ourselves. Our children would become more selfish and could easily turn revisionist.

Yes, Inner Mongolia is far away from home, and we cannot keep our children by our side to look after us. But then I thought that in the old society the laboring people could hardly make a living even by selling their sons and daughters. Could they keep their children by their side to look after them? The road our children are taking—to integrate themselves with the workers and peasants—is a bright road. By taking this road, they will ensure that the color of the red mountains and rivers will not change and that millions upon millions of the laboring people will not return to the cannibalistic old society. There is no reason at all why we should stop [our children] from going.

The several months of practical training Qu Che has received in Inner Mongolia shows that he is taking the right road. Inner Mongolia is just like a place described by Chairman Mao, "a place where great possibilities are provided." The land is so large and so fertile, but so sparsely populated, that there is really a need for many young people to go there to make revolution and engage in construction work. The training and education our children receive in the sharp and complicated class struggle will be much better than those they would receive in the cities. Today's young people have been reared in peaceful and happy circumstances, and keeping them in the cities and by our side and not letting them go to the difficult places to train themselves, to the place where class struggle is sharp and complicated, would be against Chairman Mao's teaching concerning the cultivation of successors to the proletarian revolution. Every time I write to Qu Che, I say: You must travel along this road indicated by Chairman Mao to the end, be an ordinary herdsman all your life, and not give up halfway.

Recently, large groups of middle school graduates have again zealously headed for the countryside and flocked to the frontier regions to build their homes there. With so many youngsters in our country who are loyal to Chairman Mao, China's Khrushchev will never be able to succeed in his plot to restore capitalism!

36
"In Another Twenty Years, the World Will Belong to Us!"

Beijing No. 101 Middle School Red Guard

Source: Red Guard Congress New Beijing University Middle School "Jinggangshan" Regiment Headquarters, ed., *Dazibao xuan (Selected Big-Character Posters)* (Beijing, 1967), p. 22.

To the fucking bastards of the Beijing University Middle School "Jinggangshan" Regiment:

Today you may be jumping for joy, but just you wait! One day you crazy donkey-heads and sons of bitches had better watch out! In another twenty years, the world will belong to us sons of cadres and you will be out of the way! Today you have struggled against our people, but you shall have to pay for this blood debt. So don't you fuckers get merry too early.

You may be real activists or fake activists, but no matter what, you will not get to shoulder the heavy burden of revolutionary responsibility. The world is ours, the nation is ours, society is ours.[1] Sons of bitches, try to find a way out of this one!

On 13 April, you went so far as to trample on the "Sixteen Points" and physically molest our two revolutionary comrades Peng Xiaomeng and Gong Xiaoji. You could hardly be more reckless!

Peng Xiaomeng, Gong Xiaoji, and Niu Wanping are good sons [*sic*] of cadres, and their main orientation has been correct from the beginning.[2] If you try to convene another meeting like the one on 13 April, we old Red Guards won't be polite anymore!

---

[1]This sentence is quoted from part III of Mao Zedong's "The Great Union of the Popular Masses." See translation in Stuart R. Schram, ed., *Mao's Road to Power: Revolutionary Writings 1912–1949*, Vol. 1: The Pre-Marxist Period 1912–1920 (Armonk, NY: M.E. Sharpe, 1992), p. 386.

[2]Peng, Gong, and Niu were three famous early Red Guard leaders. The author is here paraphrasing the "Sixteen Points," in which the Central Committee had described the "main revolutionary orientation" of the first Red Guards as "correct from the beginning."

Down with the "red" landlords!
Down with the "revolutionary" capitalists!
No sons of bitches may shake the sky!
Resolutely repulse the reckless attacks of all sons of bitches!
Power to the sons of cadres!
The world (*tianxia*) is ours!

Beijing No. 101 Middle School
Your father—the old Red Guard

Mao Zedong and Lin Biao—the CCP Chairman and his "Closest Comrade-in-Arms."

The "Revolutionary Masses."

Mao Zedong with Red Guard leader Song Binbin on the
Tiananmen Rostrum, 18 August 1966.

"We want to see Chairman Mao!!!"

Lin Biao

Jiang Qing

Premier Zhou Enlai

With official endorsement, Red Guards change the name of the street in front of the Soviet Embassy to "Anti-Revisionist Street."

Distributing Red Guard tabloids in Shanghai.

Reading big-character posters denouncing Vice-Minister of Culture Shi Ximin.

"Down with the old anti-communist reactionary!"—Students at Beijing University attacking History Professor Jian Bozan.

Beijing city officials Zhang Wensong and Peng Peiyun kneeling in the "airplane" position.

Peng Peiyun and Lu Ping, president of Beijing University, at a Beijing University mass rally.

"Down with Confucius!!!" The sacking of the Confucius temple in Qufu, Shandong.

The exhumed remains of one of Confucius' descendants.

Celebrating the publication of Chairman Mao's latest directive.

After the "Wuchan Incident": Captured members of the conservative "Million Heroes" faction in July 1967.

Painting slogans:
"Chen Yi can go to . . . "

"On 7 and 9 June 1967, a group of 'foreign experts' [entered] the office compound accompanied by the police [and] broke windows, hit members of the staff, hauled down the Union Jack and destroyed it and on the first occasion they tore up two portraits of the Queen." From the British ambassador's account of a confrontation between foreigners in Beijing provoked by the eruption of the Arab-Israeli War.

Middle school students are sent to the countryside upon graduation.

Studying the Little Red Book before going to the fields.

Hard, hard labor.

The wreck of a downed
U.S. Air Force drone.

Hydrogen bomb test.

Two members of the R.O.C.
Air Force on Taiwan defect to
the mainland in May 1968,
"inspired and influenced by
the tremendous victories of
the Cultural Revolution."

PLA soldiers preparing to "support the revolutionary Left" in Inner Mongolia. Note the framed portraits of Mao on their chests.

Celebrating the establishment of Revolutionary Committees in all of China's provinces "except Taiwan!"

Relaxing with a good book?

Building
socialism.

In the wake of the Twelfth Plenum in 1968, a campaign to denounce Liu Shaoqi is launched.

Workers against Liu Shaoqi.

Khrushchev, Liu Shaoqi, and Deng Xiaoping "singing the same old revisionist tune."

A scene from the Revolutionary
Ballet "Red Detachment
of Women."

"Young Mao Zedong goes to
Anyuan," a revolutionary oil
painting from 1968.

"That's a great badge
you've got there. . . ."

Mao badges.

Replicas of Mangoes presented
by Mao to representatives of
China's working class.

The dead Liu Shaoqi in November 1969—"China's Khrushchev."

The dead Lin Biao in September 1971—"double-dealer and conspirator."

Mao Zedong and Hua Guofeng at the Ninth Party Congress, in 1969. Hua succeed Mao as CCP Chairman in 1976.

E. Revolutionary Culture

What is culture? Postmodern anthropologists have characterized it as a "mysterious residual category" to which "what we cannot understand is respectfully assigned."[1] Jiang Qing claimed in 1966 that it encompassed a wide range of phenomena, some of which were abstract and intangible—like notions of loyalty and integrity—and some of which were highly concrete, like stage plays, novels, paintings, opera, ballet, and poetry. In the course of the Cultural Revolution, she said, the linguistic forms or words (*ci*) that came with the existing culture would not necessarily have to be discarded, but their content (*neirong*) had to be radically transformed. Hence "workers, peasants, and soldiers, under the leadership of the Communist Party" were called upon to *critically* inherit rather than totally negate the present.

One of many cultural phenomena thus defined and "critically inherited" at the beginning of the Cultural Revolution was religion. Indirectly acknowledged with irony by the author of Document 37—an Australian language teacher in Shanghai—the persistence of a quasireligious discourse is quite pronounced in an official collection of "Revolutionary Aphorisms" praising Mao Zedong (Document 38) and in a Central Committee member's discourse on "how to be stupid for the collective, stupid for the people, and stupid for socialism" (Document 39).

With respect to material culture, official ideology was probably less important than the personal tastes of selected leaders. The aesthetic sensibilities of someone like Jiang Qing or Yao Wenyuan largely defined what was and what was not genuinely "proletarian art" (Document 40). Mao's off-the-cuff remarks about not appreciating "potted flowers" (Document 41) were cited in support of a major reshaping of Beijing's public gardens. And, on a somewhat different note, his express appreciation of the Red Guard press was hailed, by the publishers

---

[1]George E. Marcus and Michael M. J. Fischer, *Anthropology as Cultural Critique: An Experimental Moment in the Human Sciences* (Chicago: University of Chicago Press, 1986), p. 39.

of one tabloid, as definite proof of such publications being, indeed, "great things" (Document 42).

The onslaught on culture that for whatever ideological or aesthetic reasons was regarded as "feudal, capitalist, or revisionist" was brutal. Some of the most remarkable aspects of the Cultural Revolution in this respect find expression in a manifesto from hairdressers in Guangzhou (Document 43) and a long list of things to be "done away with" (Document 44). A desire to create "revolutionary" alternatives to that which was about to be destroyed is expressed in two texts on festivals, the first (Document 45) about the Spring Festival (the Chinese traditional New Year) and the second (Document 46) about a proposed "Cultural Revolution Holiday" to be celebrated on 18 August, the date on which, in 1966, Mao first reviewed the Red Guards in Beijing.

This section ends with two generic texts—one (Document 47) in praise of one of Jiang Qing's revolutionary operas, "The Red Lantern," and the other (Document 48) denouncing a program in classical studies at China's foremost seat of higher learning. They are included because they are perfectly predictable, uninspired, unconvincing, and ugly and as such may just possibly help explain why the *Cultural* Revolution failed to "win the hearts and minds of the Chinese people."

37
"Truckload of Big Buddhas . . . Smiling"

Neale Hunter

Source: In Transit: The Gary Snyder Issue (Eugene, Ore.: Toad Press, 1969), pp. 26–28. The author taught English at a university in Shanghai during the Cultural Revolution.

The Great Proletarian
Cultural Revolution I

Changan Boulevard   Peking
truckload of big buddhas and bodhisattvas
all with their eyes down
smiling

riding up top
schoolkids in red armbands with flags
shout long live this
                    and that

the golden passengers sit real still
meditating on China burning buddhas
China setting fire on fire

The Great Proletarian
Cultural Revolution II

monastery of the White Horse
                              Loyang
little old abbot with new roof
                 new robes
                 rice in the bowl
                        great life
after the easy bit
       the set speech
plugs into the Partyman next to him
and will take questions

August 1966
thirteen centuries since Hsuan Tsang left for the west
muttering in sanskrit about books

> yogatcharya
> buddha bhumi etc

> hetuvidya
> mahavibhasa etc
>> ask him says someone
>> why he meditates

without warning the bonze unplugs
> is solo

Daruma in a cave across the river
face to the blank wall nine years
>> I want to know he says
>> who does my deeds

silence
>> the four interpreters
>> ransack their liberated minds

turns out they can't conceive
what this old man means

38
Revolutionary Aphorisms

Anonymous

Source: Chinese Literature, No. 9, 1966, pp. 142–46.

[Original editor's note:] Aphorisms form an integral part of Chinese folk literature. The people compose them whenever they want to state a general truth derived from their own experience of life. The following is a selection of new aphorisms widely circulated among the men of the Chinese People's Liberation Army.

Chairman Mao's works shed a golden light,
Like the red sun, forever bright.

Chairman Mao's works are the sun,
It shines on the Four Seas and high they surge.

All-powerful, the works of Mao Zedong;
The Five Continents reel, racked with storm.

Relying on mere physical strength is of little worth,
But relying on Mao Zedong's thought we can make a new
    heaven and earth.

All rivers in the world flow to the sea,
All truths are found in the works of Mao Zedong.

Past counting, the stars in the sky;
Past measuring, the water in the sea;
Past telling, the might of Mao Zedong's thought.

Each word in Chairman Mao's works
Is a battle-drum,
Each sentence is the truth.

Bullets and shells
Are no match
For the spiritual atom bomb of Mao Zedong's thought.

A revolutionary staunch and true
Reads Chairman Mao his whole life through.

Dearer than rain or dew to the parched crops
Are Chairman Mao's works to our troops.

Of all rules to remember, the first, best one
Is to practice the teachings of Mao Zedong.

However busy we may be,
We must never forget to study Chairman Mao's works
And apply them creatively.

Difficulties by thousands may hedge us around,
But with Chairman Mao's thought a solution is found.

Learn from Chairman Mao to keep a firm class stand,
Or you may betray the Party in the end.

If you don't study Chairman Mao
You will be blind;
If you do
A red sun will light your mind.

Fish cannot live without water;
Without studying the works of Chairman Mao
Soldiers cannot be true revolutionaries.

Study Chairman Mao's writings well
And you will know right from wrong, you will see plain;
Take the road of communism
And you will stand firm, come tempest or pelting rain.

Study Mao Zedong's works well
And no trials will daunt you, however overwhelming;
His works will light up your mind
And speed communism's coming.

A soldier will fight like a hero
Only if on the thought of Mao Zedong he relies;
But armed with Mao Zedong's thought
He can cross seas of fire, climb hills of knives.

Without the sun, the moon can shed no light;
Without rain or dew, a crop dies;
Soldiers who don't study Chairman Mao's works and put
     them into practice
Will lose their way—even with open eyes.

Keep Chairman Mao's thought in mind
And no hardships can cause you dismay,
No setbacks can make you give way.

A man armed with the thought of Mao Zedong
Has a backbone stronger than iron,
A will firmer than steel.

Heads may fall
Blood may flow;
But never let go
Of the thought of Mao Zedong.

A key in daily use
Sparkles with light,
Just as fresh-springing fountains
Are always clear and bright;
And men who study the works of Chairman Mao
Are full of drive and fight.

The eagle that soars through the sky must have strong wings;
The soldier who wants to take long views must rely on the thought of
        Mao Zedong.

Read Chairman Mao's works every day,
You'll not lose your way but see clear;
Read Chairman Mao's works every day,
And you'll have drive to spare;
Read Chairman Mao's works every day
And you'll overcome hardships of every kind;
Read Chairman Mao's works every day
And nothing can poison your mind.

To solve a problem, read Chairman Mao's works;
When fresh problems crop up, read Chairman Mao's works.

You must hit the right spot when you're beating a drum,
You must pluck the right strings when you're playing a lute;
And to study Chairman Mao's works well
You must put what you've learned into practice.

Mao Zedong's thought is a telescope for a revolutionary
To see clearly what lies thousands of miles away.

Mao Zedong's thought is a microscope for a revolutionary,
All germs, all pests enabling him to see.

No matter how black a crow's wings,
They cannot shut out the bright sun;
No matter how vicious the lies of bourgeois "authorities,"
They cannot harm the great thought of Mao Zedong.

A fierce dog fears a stick,
A fierce wolf fears the hunter's gun,
The enemy fears most the thought of Mao Zedong.

39
Why Do Some People Call Me Foolish?

Lü Yulan

Source: "Weishenmo youren shuo wo 'sha,' zemyang kandai 'jing' he 'sha'?," a lecture by CCP Central Committee member and nationally famous labor hero Lü Yulan. Our source for this document is an untitled pamphlet picked up by the editor in 1981 in a candy shop in Guanxian, Sichuan, where the proprietor was preparing to shred it and use it to package his produce. Translated by Anna Andersson.

Different Standpoints, Different Understandings of "Stupidity"

Some people say I'm a great big fool, that I'm simple-minded, that I don't understand the meaning of "happiness," that I don't know how to "live" and always act like an idiot.

So am I stupid then?

I don't know how to enrich myself at public expense, I don't know how to take advantage of a situation to benefit myself, and I'm not good at scheming or calculating. So, if that's what you call being stupid, well, then I am indeed stupid.

But I do my best for the Party, for my country, and for the collective, and I work wholeheartedly for them as best as I can. If you call that stupid, well, then I disagree.

"Stupid" or not—it all depends on what you think really counts!

"You don't have any brains at all!" Well, I say, it depends on what you mean by brains. A head full of "self" is an individualist's brain, whereas only a head full of "public" is a communist brain.

If your standpoint is different, you will have a different way of reckoning. What you think is reasonable will be different from what he thinks. So how can you two understand each other? You sleep on the *kang*[1] and say it's warm; he sits on the bench and says it's cold. You don't share a common language. You say I'm too stupid, but I think I have my own kind of intelligence.

Chairman Mao says: "Reason comes in different sizes, and big reason takes precedence over small reason." Why do we live and for whom? These are the root questions from which everything grows. If the roots are different, the flowers that grow look different.

If your standpoint is different, your outlook will be different. As far as I am concerned, selfish people are the most ignorant and foolish of all. If you are selfish, then you will also be prejudiced. It's only when you're unselfish that you will be fair and truthful.

Different Times, Different Criteria of "Stupidity"

If you use stupidity as a criterion when discussing right and wrong, or if you use it to judge people, then stupidity has a class character.

Old poor peasants often tell me that in the old society, the ruling classes treated people any old way they liked and would say to poor people that they were stupid and therefore deserved to be poor, while the rich were clever and therefore deserved to be rich. In those days, poor people were looked down upon and couldn't argue back; those who weren't dull were regarded as dull anyway, and those who weren't stupid were regarded as stupid all the same.

In the old society, the real slaves and true idiots were those who only exerted themselves on behalf of the ruling class.

But as the social system and the times have changed, so have the criteria for cleverness and stupidity.

Some people have returned their land and cattle to the collective but have kept their thoughts to themselves. Their bodies ride on the socialist cart, but in their minds "self" still rules supreme. If you tell them

---

[1]A heatable brick bed, common in the countryside in northern China.

you wish to "serve the people," they don't believe you; and once you really serve the people, they call you a fool.

When you arm your brain with Mao Zedong Thought, the "public" will be what's most important and the "self" will have to step back. The people who are "clever at little things" will become fewer, while the "big fools" will grow in number. In our society, those who "don't work for the public will be cursed by heaven." The word "self" will become as repugnant as the word "thief."

Stupid for the Collective, Stupid for the People, Stupid for Socialism

Selfless people are mocked and called stupid by those who enrich themselves at public expense.

"You call me 'stupid,' well, then I am 'stupid'!"

But the meaning of the first "stupid" and the second "stupid" are completely different.

"I am stupid for the collective, I am stupid for the people, and I am stupid for socialism"—there you have the meaning of the second stupid.

"I would rather be a big fool all my life, than egoistic and clever for a single day." Leading the masses, we have started a big discussion about cleverness and stupidity in the course of which we criticize "clever and egoistic people" and praise "big fools." The word "clever" stinks, while the word "stupid" has a sweet and lovely fragrance. Now everybody is fighting to become the revolutionary fool.

Some people, who do not deserve to be called "fools," are so anxious about this they begin to cry, and some people who hear others calling them "clever" consider this to be the worst form of abuse. . . .

"Public Versus Public"—Not "Private Versus Private"

In 1962, my uncle intended to privately deep-fry [and sell] wheat cakes without permission. I took his cooking pot away. He said: "We are one family." I said: "The closer you are, the stricter you have to be." It wasn't that I turned on a friend, but simply that I was thinking how a member of the Communist Party must care only about class feelings and not about private emotions. I couldn't simply "make things easier for the people close to me." If I would have let him deep-fry the cakes in private, then I would have harmed the national interest. If I would have let him earn a private income and engage in capitalism, I would not have acted in the best interest of the masses.

There are old sayings that go: "Friendship is precious" and "You don't argue with friends." We can't bother with rubbish like that. You can't first set up a sign with the word "public" on it and then take advantage of the power of your office and act according to your feelings. You must act according to principles, according to rules and regulations.

Not only must you avoid turning public matters into private, you must also keep the public good in mind at all times. Only when the public spirit guides us can we claim to be totally unselfish.

When I'm sick, my comrades take good care of me. I think this is an expression of their class feeling for me. What they do is political work. When I thank them, I don't necessarily return their favors in a private way. I work diligently instead and do the best I can. I repay them through my accomplishments at work and not by "giving a horse in return for an ox." You should return a public good by doing good deeds for the public, and not return a personal favor with a personal favor.

People Good to Me May Actually Be Harming Me

Usually, when people say something nice to you, it seems as if they're good to you. Actually, they may be harming you, intentionally or not. "You don't have to be afraid of an angry Lord Guan, only of a smooth-lipped bodhisattva." In some cases, when people are good to you, they're not really good—you have to make a class analysis of it. In 1962, a man gave me some sesame seed cakes and vermicelli: His was a so-called "good deed," but what he really wanted was for me to do something wrong. He wanted me to help him in a certain matter. I told him: "The more things you give me, the more difficult it will be for me to handle this matter. I refuse to do something that is contrary to policy, even if you give me a mountain of gold."

"To fall for somebody's tricks and be fooled by his sweet talk." In the villages, if you rely on the power of your office to collect gifts from the villagers—giving and receiving, back and forth—then you will soon have given your revolutionary stand away as well. People don't give gifts for nothing. They think that for each gift they give you they will receive ten in return. Therefore, those who accept gifts will really come to grief. The class enemy really likes giving gifts, so we should be doubly on our guard against such behavior.

When I listen to people, there is one thing I know: No matter if people say nice things or bad things about me, I must always look to their intentions. The "goodness" of something doesn't depend on if it is good only to me, but if it is good for the collective, good for socialism.

Private Emotions Cannot Explain Class Feelings

My mother fell ill. As soon as she was a little bit better, I went off to attend a meeting. There were those who said that I didn't show proper piety (*xiao*) to my mother.

These last few years, whenever I have had problems at work or in my struggle against capitalist forces, I have not once cried in front of my parents even though at times I have been very upset. When I met people from the Party Committee, however, tears began to flow. Some people don't understand this kind of feeling. I don't understand such people: In my opinion, one's parents are never as close as the Party, and there is no greater goodness than that of socialism.

In daily life, some people base their understanding of public feelings on private emotions.

For instance, they say: "You really have a good job!" What do they mean by good? That it gives you a good reputation or a good income? That it is easy and not tiring? Or that you can make a great contribution to the revolution? What meaning do they give this word "good"? The way I see it, all kinds of work are good. We all work for the revolution, we only have to worry about performing our tasks well or not. When we love the kind of work we are engaged in, it is not because we are personally interested in it, but simply because it is revolutionary work. If it is not revolutionary work, we don't love it, no matter what kind of work it is.

And another example: "You're really good at working, you are a master at everything you do." When we try to excel at work, it is in order to make a greater contribution to the revolution and not in order to be given some fancy title. When we make up our minds to do something, it mustn't be in order to win fame or wealth. When we work energetically, it mustn't be in order to win fame or fortune: We must be determined to carry out the great task of revolution, to work for the people, and to work energetically for revolution.

Class Viewpoints in Everyday Work

We used to think that the reason some people had different ways of thinking was because they were intelligent and good-tempered. If we make a careful analysis, we find that a person's consciousness or thoughts have nothing to do with his temperament. People of the same class are all the same, no matter if they're impatient or not.

People with different family backgrounds have their thoughts branded differently according to class. The fact that many members of society are unable to live a harmonious family life may seem to be due to a problem with their disposition. In fact, it is just like with Li Shuangshuang and Sun Xiwang—a battle between two kinds of thought.[2]

---

[2]Li and Sun are the central characters in the popular novel *Li Shuangshuang,* in which Li represents the progressive and Sun the conservative "kind of thought."

40
Reforming the Fine Arts

Jiang Qing

Source: This transcript ("Tan meishu gaige") of a tape-recorded meeting of Jiang Qing, Yao Wenyuan, and Chen Boda with members of the Zhejiang Provincial Revolutionary Committee on 19 May 1968 is included in *Jiang Qing tongzhi lun wenhua yishu (Comrade Jiang Qing on Culture and the Fine Arts),* published by students in the Chinese Language Department of Hangzhou University in July 1968 (pp. 69–73). Our translation is slightly abridged.

I don't like Pan Tianshou's paintings. They are so gloomy. Those bald eagles he paints are really ugly. Gloomy and hideous. (Wenyuan: The fact that they are so gloomy has to do with him being a special agent. Those bald eagles Pan Tianshou likes to paint are embodiments of special agents.)

A few years ago, how come there were so many paintings by Pan Tianshou around? Why did you here in Hangzhou praise him so much? I remember there was even an exhibit of his in Beijing, and the prices were really high. There was Fu Baoshi as well. Xu Beihong should be affirmed, artistically he should be affirmed. He made foreign things serve China and the old serve the new, and he was quite sophisticated. Xu Beihong's gallery should not be closed down. Qi Baishi is an old miser, a real scoundrel! Tan Zhenlin's wife is also an old miser. (Wenyuan: Huang Zhou is a very nasty person.) . . .

Now as for paintings, they must serve the workers, peasants, and soldiers. The workers, peasants, and soldiers should occupy that battle front. The central ideological theme of what is painted must be quite clear, the composition must be quite simple, and the central theme must be pronounced. At present, the general appearance of your paintings is far too scattered, too messy. (Refers to the paintings shown on this occasion.)

We must popularize; popularization is our basis. But we must also, on the basis of popularization, raise our level. We must have works of art on a higher level. The fine arts must produce a few model works. If there are no works on a higher level, people will curse us and say what we do is all as plain as boiled water, in which case we shall not be able to stand our ground. We will be chased off the stage. . . .

Just painting portraits is not enough. There must be greater variety. But in the past, all those bright and colorful paintings just did not take as their subject the workers, peasants, and soldiers, nor did they serve the workers, peasants, and soldiers. You must train talented artists from among the workers, peasants, and soldiers, as well as serve the workers, peasants, and soldiers. The Academy of Fine Arts need not necessarily produce specialists. It is very good of you to organize amateur training classes for talented workers, peasants, and soldiers. There are many talented workers, peasants, and soldiers. Initially, we had planned to experiment in the same way in all of the arts schools, not just in fine arts, but in music, opera, and ballet as well, but it just did not work. Right now we still don't have the capacity. Right now we're concentrating our energies on grasping politics, and there is no time for us to carry out experiments in the arts schools. At lower levels, they cannot figure things out. The forces in your schools seem to be quite concentrated, so you could be quite bold! Merge some departments, and send them down to the countryside and down to the factories. Turn them into comprehensive arts schools, or at least conduct some trials! Move out into the world of practice! We have not set any restrictions. You can report your achievements to us. We'll allow you to keep a few extra backbone elements and a few extra graduates for the sake of educational reform.

(While being briefed about the deep roots that Zhou Yang, Cai Ruohong, Hua Junwu, Jiang Feng, Mo Pu, and other black-line representatives of the 1930s bourgeoisie had in the Academy of Fine Arts:) And there's the 1920s, the 1940s, the 1950s, all the way up to the 1960s as well. Centuries of the bourgeoisie, and millennia of feudalism, have made an impact. But it's nothing to be afraid of. Take opera reform: Didn't the eight model operas, as soon as they were out, just overwhelm and devastate them?

(While being briefed about the fact that large numbers of provinces and municipalities all have their own fine arts institutes, arts and crafts schools, opera and music academies:) What's the point of having that many in every province? It's a big mess and they're just turning out little "lords." There is a teacher in the Central Academy of Fine Arts who uses oil to paint traditional New Year's paintings in the Dunhuang style. Totally divorced from reality! New Year's paintings, picture-story books, and wood-block prints all have a future, and their role might even be bigger. Painting for the stage is very important. Now they move huge trees onto the stage in some places! They're not utilizing stage lighting properly. Oil paintings, as an art form, need to be reformed. Models still need to be painted. But to rely solely on models won't do. You also have to learn how to draw from memory. Some people don't know how to paint without a model.

(While speaking of arts and crafts:) The students in the Central Academy of Arts and Crafts are complaining and want to go down to the countryside. Why not select a few factories and mines for them to go to? I once talked with Comrade Ke Qingshi about how to arrange for arts and crafts to enter the factories. We have a fine tradition of artistic design in our country, a national tradition of printing on cotton and satin and silk. As long as you don't draw dragons and phoenixes and that kind of stuff, all you have to do is adjust the design a little and you shall have something very pretty, very elegant, and tasteful. Nowadays the designers keep printing puppies and kittens on our cotton in imitation of Western designs; as a result, nobody likes to wear it, and it cannot compete on the international market either. We even lose money on some of the pottery made for export at Jingdezhen.

You have to be particularly cautious when painting the leadership, or you shall suffer defeat. Paintings of the Chairman must not be produced in a rough and slipshod way. (Criticism voiced by Comrade Jiang Qing while looking at, and basically approving of, the painting *Our Seas Turn Into Mulberry Fields* produced at the Central Academy of Fine Arts:) Still, too much detail creates problems too. The background is too complex. [In this painting] the Chairman's lower cheek-bones look uncomfortable, and his right hand is not very well painted either. The person should stand out, and the background must not be too complex. (Comrade Jiang Qing went on to look at an oil painting of Chairman Mao shaking hands with Comrade Hoxha.) There is an unfortunate trend in what you do, which is not to give prominence to the person and to clutter up the background. You don't appear serious. There are problems with everything from the ideological theme to the actual composition. Recently, I saw an excellent oil painting of Chairman Mao going to Anyuan that really succeeded in depicting the Chairman's air.

Once the issue of the political stand has been resolved, you still have to resolve the issue of craftsmanship. Essential techniques still have to be taught.

What about the future of sculpture? The Center has issued repeated injunctions against the production of giant sculptures of the Chairman, because when they're that big, it is difficult to achieve a good semblance. Just to make a mess of it won't do. If things go wrong, there may even be international repercussions.

The Zhejiang Bureau of Culture has been spreading an awful lot of rumors about me, claiming it was I who asked for *Fourth Son Calls on His Mother* to be performed. The old Central Propaganda Department and the old Ministry of Culture, as well as the old East-China Bureau, Peng Zhen, and Wang Fang, all spread rumors about me. *Fourth Son Calls on His Mother* was already being performed prior to my arrival. When I criticized it, they stopped, but once I had left, they began performing it again. I read reports in the paper, and in fact in 1961 I did not even visit Hangzhou. It's all calumny and slander. Women impersonating men is a strange sixties phenomenon. I'm thoroughly disgusted with it! The Yue Opera *Militant Youth* is one big poisonous weed. The novel itself is already bad. Once the Youth & Vigor Yue Opera Troupe came to Huairentang to perform, and I thought this time for sure the performers would be men! But no, it was once more women impersonating men, and they were really ugly! The more I saw, the angrier I got, and I considered walking out. There was another play too that really upset me when I saw it, about a drunkard and a madwoman, implying that our new society is one of drunkards and madwomen. The story was set in Zhejiang, and therefore Zhejiang had produced this new historical play. Its name was *Drunken Verdict*. It is truly extraordinary that you here in Zhejiang should be performing old plays and ghost plays to such an extent. You even have ossified corpses turning into ghosts and emerging from coffins. I certainly do not watch performances like that. I read about them in the paper. And then there is *The Mother in the Nunnery,* which was performed everywhere in different opera forms. (Wenyuan: At the time it was euphemistically renamed *Lineage Property Salvaged.*)

(While being briefed on Hu Qiaomu's activities in Hangzhou:) Hu Qiaomu together with Chen Bing had them perform *Xin Wenbing.* (Wenyuan: Hu Qiaomu has visited Hangzhou a number of times.) Every time I criticized him, he just would not listen. . . . All of that was done by Zhou Yang and those people in order to prepare public opinion for a restoration of capitalism. (Chen Boda: Right! Right! It's all in preparation for a restoration.)

(While speaking of reforming opera forms:) There is a problem with Zhejiang in that all of its old opera forms are problematic. The Shaoxing full ensemble has a solid martial arts foundation. Can the model operas be transplanted? Are there any old opera forms that can be utilized? First, one must determine what's right and what's wrong, and then act differently depending on the circumstances. (Wenyuan: A little while ago Comrade Jiang Qing said that the eight model operas can be transplanted, [but] that transplanting is a very arduous task involving many changes.)

The Yue Opera has to be reformed. The Yue Opera is bourgeois. In the past, people with money in Shanghai would have girls come to perform a selection of favorites for money. The music of the Yue Opera is very low spirited. The opera form has to be reformed, and new plays have to be written. There should be men and women performing together, and the music has to be reformed. Right now, the octave range of the performers is too narrow.

Zhejiang is where Chiang Kai-shek used to have his old lair. (When briefed about the crimes of the number one capitalist roader in Zhejiang, Jiang Hua, and how he had said, "I prefer capitalism that lets me eat my fill over socialism that leaves me starving," Jiang Qing remarked angrily:) Before Liberation, did your families have enough to eat? There is no such thing as socialism that lets you starve; only capitalism lets you starve!

One is allowed to make mistakes when making revolution. You must not be afraid of making mistakes and should engage in reform while engaged in practical work. (Wenyuan: The Revolutionary Committee should talk about drawing up a concrete plan.) There will be a disaster unless the schools are reformed. This applies to universities, middle schools, elementary schools, and arts schools, as well as all artistic and cultural institutions.

41
Gardens and Parks Must Serve the Workers, Peasants, and Soldiers

Gardening Revolution Editorial

Source: "Yuanlin bixu wei gongnongbing fuwu." This editorial, celebrating the third anniversary of Mao Zedong's instructions concerning the "revolutionization of flower gardens," appeared in Vol. 2 of *Yuanlin geming*, 1967, a publication edited by the Capital Gardens Denounce Revisionism Liaison Station.

Three years have passed since our great leader Chairman Mao issued, in July 1964, his important instructions concerning the revolutionization of flower gardens. These important instructions of Chairman Mao took into consideration the long-term strategic policy of opposing and preventing revisionism and of "preparing for war, avoiding shortages, and doing everything for the people," and laid down the basic direction for the greening (*lühua*) of gardens and parks. The publication of these instructions had an extremely far-reaching impact upon garden and park work. Today, in the high tide of the all-out attack we have launched against the biggest handful of Party-persons in power taking the capitalist road, and in our battle to destroy the counter-revolutionary revisionist black line in the garden and park system, our renewed study of these important instructions and our celebration of the third anniversary of their publication are events of immense immediate significance.

Chairman Mao teaches us: "The question of whom to serve is a fundamental question and one of principle." The basic question of direction contained in Chairman Mao's July instructions about the greening of gardens and parks is that of whom gardens and parks ultimately should serve. For the past seventeen years, this has been the focal point of the struggle between the two classes, the struggle between the two roads, and the struggle between the two lines in garden and park circles.

Gardens and parks are living environments created (as art forms) by people of definite classes in accordance with their own ideals, interests, habits, and customs. Consequently, gardens and parks have pronounced class characteristics. Those gardens in existence today that were created already in the old society were created by and as expressions of the likes and desires of the exploiting classes. They are permeated by the ideology and culture of the exploiting classes and reflect the hopes and demands of the exploiting classes. This is particularly true of some of the classic gardens and parks created expressly for the feudal court, e.g. the Yuhua Garden in the Forbidden City, the Summer Palace, and the Temple of Heaven. After Liberation, the greater part of these old things so full of the ideological forms of the exploiting classes were basically preserved as they were. Some were thrown open to the public in their original form and with their original contents. The greater part of their old staffs, who had served the exploiting classes in the past, were retained. These bourgeois so-called "cultural figures" were never properly remolded and some of them even managed to grab hold of key positions in government departments managing gardens and parks. At the same time, once the working masses under the leadership of the proletariat had taken political power away from the exploiting classes, it was not yet possible to escape completely the influence of old ideology and old culture shaped by the exploiting classes over an extended period of time. Hence, it became inevitable that counter-revolutionary revisionists would extend their black hands into the departments managing gardens and parks with the aim of restoring capitalism. Was it not precisely with this sinister aim in mind that the biggest Party-person in power taking the capitalist road, Liu Shaoqi, came to Taoranting Gardens in 1959 to peddle his black wares?!

While enjoying himself in Taoranting Gardens, Liu Shaoqi publicly opposed giving prominence to proletarian politics in public gardens. He did his utmost to propagate capitalist and revisionist forms of recreation and advocated capitalist forms of management. He preached the doctrine of "returning to the ancients" by insisting that gardens and parks should serve the exploiting classes and his own attempts to restore capitalism. Liu Shaoqi's visit to Taoranting Gardens led to an intensified capitalist restoration in all of Beijing's public gardens.

A mass of evidence shows that the representatives of the bourgeoisie who wormed themselves into the Party are not only reactionary politically but also invariably lead corrupt and decadent lives. In order to satisfy their craving for food, drink, and entertainment they demand that gardens and parks provide them with spaces where they may indulge. Hence gardens and parks are made to serve the needs of a handful of members of the privileged strata. The counter-revolutionary revisionist element Peng Zhen put the big capitalist Yue Songsheng in charge of the departments managing gardens and parks and furthermore informed him, "Just keep on managing them in whatever way you found appropriate in the past." This big careerist and big schemer even organized "Petöfi Circles"[1] in quite a number of public gardens. Didn't the shocking counter-revolutionary "Changguanlou" incident[2] take place precisely in the Beijing Zoological Gardens in 1961?

But, no matter how frenzied the activities of the biggest handful of Party-persons in power taking the capitalist road may be, they are still not able to escape the splendid rays of invincible Mao Zedong Thought. In 1963, in his instructions concerning literature and art, Chairman Mao pointed out: "In many departments, very little has been achieved so far in socialist transformation. The 'dead' still dominate in many departments." "Isn't it absurd that many Communists are enthusiastic about promoting feudal and capitalist art but not socialist art?" Weren't these words also a sharp criticism of the situation in garden and park circles at the time? In July 1964, in his instructions concerning the revolutionization of flower gardens, Chairman Mao again di-

---

[1]The label "Petöfi Circles" refers to informal debating clubs. The original Petöfi Circle, named after a 19th-century poet, was formed in Hungary in March 1956 and its members strongly criticized the crimes of the Rákosi regime and contributed to the ferment that exploded in the Hungarian revolt.

[2]The so-called "Changguanlou" incident refers to a series of meetings, held in a building by this name in western Beijing, in the winter of 1961, at which senior members of the Beijing Municipal Party Committee produced a highly critical evaluation of the Great Leap Forward.

rected severe criticism against the trend—promoted by the counter-revolutionary revisionist clique on the old Beijing Municipal Party Committee—of growing potted flowers and plants in "astronomical numbers." Hitting the nail on the head, he pointed out: "Decorating with potted flowers is something left over from the old society. It's what the feudal class of local senior officials, the bourgeoisie, pampered sons of wealthy or influential families, and people who carry birds around in cages enjoy doing. The only people who have time to grow flowers and arrange flowers are the ones who have nothing better to do once they've eaten their fill. More than a decade has passed since Liberation, yet not only has the number of potted plants not decreased, but on the contrary, it has gone up. Now is the time to make some changes!" At the same time, he also—bearing the fundamental interests of the broad laboring people in mind—set forth some basic demands as far as the greening of gardens and parks is concerned. He pointed out: "In our courtyards we should from now on plant more trees, more fruit trees, or even some grain, vegetables, and oil-bearing crops. Step by step, we should transform the Sun Yat-sen and Xiangshan Gardens in Beijing by planting some fruit trees and oil-bearing crops. In this way, the gardens will not only be nice to look at but be of some benefit as well. They should be of some good to coming generations." Proceeding from the fundamental interests of the proletariat, Chairman Mao made a profound analysis of the demands raised by different classes with respect to the greening of gardens and parks and pointed out clearly that gardens and parks are not meant to serve the exploiting classes but to serve the workers, peasants, and soldiers, and to serve proletarian politics. Chairman Mao demanded that in our work we should see to it that gardens and parks are "not only nice to look at but of some benefit as well," and that they "be of some good to coming generations." How profound, indeed, is the meaning of these words![3]

In accordance with the basic spirit of Chairman Mao's instructions, our work of turning gardens and parks ever greener must proceed in accordance with the great long-term strategic policy of preparing for war, avoiding shortages, and doing everything for the people. Step by

---

[3]The full text of Mao's 1964 "instructions" can be found in the Red Guard collection of his works entitled *Xuexi ziliao 1962–1967* (*Study Documents 1962–1967*) (Beijing: Beijing University, n.d. [1967]), p. 124.

step, we must change the face of nature in our country and achieve a universal greening as well as the integration of greening and production. The forms of recreation provided in our gardens and parks, the variety of plants, and other gardening issues must all, in every respect, give prominence to the propagation of Mao Zedong Thought; make the masses never forget class struggle; constantly get rid of what is bourgeois and foster what is proletarian; destroy "self" and establish "public"; and aim at making gardens and parks forever serve the needs in struggle and fundamental interests of the workers, peasants, and soldiers, as well as forever serve the consolidation of the dictatorship of the proletariat.

Chairman Mao's wise instructions have been tremendously inspiring to the proletarian revolutionaries in our gardens and parks system. They were a devastating blow to the counter-revolutionary revisionist elements, and for this very reason a tiny handful of counter-revolutionary revisionist elements have remained very much afraid of them becoming known to the broad masses. They have utilized a thousand and one devices to have them suppressed, to oppose them, and to distort their meaning. Theirs has truly been a case of "an ant trying to topple a giant tree—ridiculously overrating one's own strength!" In this historically unprecedented Great Proletarian Cultural Revolution, the tiny handful of counter-revolutionary revisionist elements were finally dragged out. They must be overthrown altogether and never be allowed to stage a comeback.

"In June our soldiers of heaven fight against evil and rot; they have a huge rope to tie up the whale or fabulous cockatrice."[4] At present the situation in the Great Proletarian Cultural Revolution in the gardens and parks sector is excellent throughout. Guided by Chairman Mao's brilliant work "On the Correct Handling of Contradictions Among the People," the section of the front occupied by the Great Alliance with proletarian revolutionaries at its core is expanding daily, and a new high tide of great exposure, great denunciation, and great struggle aimed at the counter-revolutionary revisionist black line headed by Liu Shaoqi is surging forward. Under these circumstances, it is inevitable that a major task faced by the proletarian revolutionaries in the gardens and parks sector will be to resolve the matter of basic direction for the greening of gardens and parks by looking back at the basic reality of

---

[4]Lines quoted from Mao Zedong's poem "Dingzhou to Changsha" (July 1930).

the struggle between the two classes, between the two roads, and between the two lines in the gardens and parks sector during the past seventeen years and by further studying and applying in a living way Chairman Mao's "Talks at the Yan'an Forum on Literature and Art" and his 1964 instructions concerning the revolutionization of flower gardens.

In the lofty spirit of the proletariat, let us advance in the direction pointed out by our great leader Chairman Mao in his instructions, hold high the great red banner of Mao Zedong Thought, and blaze a new trail by creating socialist gardens and parks that will serve as front positions of education illuminated by the splendid rays of Mao Zedong Thought!

42
Red Guard Tabloids Are Great Things!

Nankai University "Weidong" Red Guards

Source: The History of the Great Proletarian Cultural Revolution at Nankai University Writing Group of the Red Guard Congress Nankai University "Weidong" Red Guards, ed., *Tianfan difu kai er kang—Ji Nankai daxue wuchanjieji wenhua dageming (Heaven and Earth Are Moved with Emotion—Record of the Great Proletarian Cultural Revolution at Nankai University)* (Tianjin: Nankai daxue "Weidong" hongweibing zongbu zhengzhibu, 1968), pp. 163–65.

Chairman Mao—the reddest, reddest, red sun in our hearts—said after having read the article "Dare to Employ Revolutionary Cadres" written by our *Weidong* editorial board commentator that the "Weidong Red Guards at Nankai University in Tianjin have written a good article in which they raise a new question. These Red Guard tabloids are great things." This shows Chairman Mao's tremendous concern for the Red Guards. It is a tremendous inspiration to us all and constitutes tremendous support and praise for the Red Guard tabloids. Chairman Mao's words will forever encourage us to march forward!

The *Weidong* tabloid does indeed deserve praise!

The Weidong fighters, wielding their pens like knives, like rifles, and poised as if to command the wind and the clouds, launched an all-out exposé, all-out denunciation, and all-out settling of accounts with the heinous crimes and filthy counter-revolutionary revisionist trash of the Liu-Deng black headquarters. Theirs is truly a case of "Strokes powerful and vigorous, sweeping away a thousand mighty armies; pens pointed and sharp, piercing the sky like swords never turning blunt." The *Weidong* tabloid as well as the *Weidong* magazine have made outstanding contributions to revolutionary great criticism.

Pioneering work is always difficult. In those early days, the only thing the handful of Weidong fighters had at their disposal was an empty room, a few tables and chairs, and a few discarded stencil-cutting tools. None of them had any experience of running a newspaper, nor had they ever watched a paper being printed. Despite one difficulty after the other, the Weidong fighters never lost heart. Over and over again, to spur themselves on, they would study the quotation: "Be resolute, fear no sacrifice, and surmount every difficulty to win victory." A tiny handful of Party-persons in power taking the capitalist road stirred up hoodwinked representatives of the masses to steal, loot, and smash up the premises. Disaster struck as the printing plant was raided and the printing and typesetting equipment was smashed to pieces. The floor was littered with bits and pieces of lead type. The Weidong fighters set out to repair the machinery and to cast new type. As they did not know how, they humbly invited the workers to be their teachers. They learned the art of typesetting and layout from the skilled workers.

On 13 February 1967, the very first issue of *Weidong* reached the broad masses of readers. Each page, every sentence, and every character represented the sweat and labor of the Weidong fighters. Having firmly captured yet another segment of the front along which to propagate Mao Zedong Thought, how could the proletarian revolutionaries of Nankai University not be ecstatic with delight and wild with joy?

When Chairman Mao motions forward, the Red Guards surge ahead. The *Weidong* tabloid and magazine have in the past year firmly adhered to the main orientation of struggle. In the course of the bloody battle waged against Liu, Deng, Tao [Zhu], and their ilk, *Weidong* has published serious and profound denunciations of the Liu-Deng black headquarters as well as complete, systematic, and accurate investigation reports, and by so doing has won the attention and respect of proletarian revolutionaries all over China.

Incomplete statistics show that more than 1.5 million characters, in published articles exceeding four hundred characters in length, have been devoted just to investigation reports concerning the crimes of Liu, Deng, and Tao.

Up to now, no less than 140 issues of the *Weidong* tabloid have been published (not including extra issues, special issues, conference issues, joint issues, etc.), averaging one every two days. Twenty-five issues of the *Weidong* magazine have also been published.

Chairman Mao takes a great interest in the Red Guard press, as do proletarian revolutionaries all over China. So far, no less than forty-nine articles totaling 1.67 million characters submitted by the *Weidong* editorial board have appeared in the *People's Daily*, *Wenhui Daily*, *Liberation Daily*, *Liberation Army Art and Literature*, and elsewhere (this figure does not include reprints). Articles published in the *People's Daily* include "What the Soviet Revisionists Are Peddling Is Bogus Communist Contraband," "Firmly Grasp the Class Struggle in the Ideological Sphere," "Zhou Yang's Wolfish Nature as Reflected in the Hai Rui Play *The Colorful Sedan Chair*," "Dare to Employ Revolutionary Cadres," "Step Forward Boldly and Begin Working Enthusiastically," "Thousand Times as Important, Ten Thousand Times as Important, Great Denunciation Is *the* Most Important," "Rely on the Working Class to Protect the Dictatorship of the Proletariat," "Expose the Reactionary Essence of the 'Theater of National Defense'," "Sholokhov's Conscience," "Smash China's Petöfi Circle, the 'Loafer's Hall'," and "The Soviet Revisionist Renegades' Lament."

From the Zhoushan islands in the east to the Tianshan mountains on the border of the Gobi desert; from the snow-covered frozen lands of Heilongjiang to the Hainan island of eternal springtime, the enthusiastic readers and subscribers of *Weidong* are everywhere. Every day, the editorial board receives countless bundles of ebullient readers' letters and submissions, inspiring the Weidong fighters to raise high the great red banner of Mao Zedong Thought, do a good job of managing the Red Guard press, fiercely denounce Liu, Deng, and Tao, and render new contributions to the Great Proletarian Cultural Revolution.

43
Vigorously and Speedily Eradicate Bizarre Bourgeois Hair Styles

Revolutionary Workers of the Hairdressing Trade
in Guangzhou

Source: Survey of China Mainland Press, No. 3776, 8 September 1966. Originally published in *Yangcheng wanbao* (*Yangcheng Evening News*), 27 August 1966.

Holding high the great red banner of Mao Zedong Thought and displaying vigorous revolutionary spirit, young revolutionary fighters in Guangzhou have been busy putting up revolutionary big-character posters in the streets to attack the old ideas, culture, customs, and habits of all exploiting classes, in a determined effort to build Guangzhou into a city extraordinarily proletarian and extraordinarily revolutionary in character.

This revolutionary rebel spirit displayed by these young fighters is indeed splendid, for it has greatly boosted the morale of revolutionary people and provided us with profound inspiration and enlightenment. We want to learn from these young fighters and their revolutionary rebel spirit by launching a proletarian revolutionary rebellion in the hairdressing trade of the city. The following proposals are put forward by us before all revolutionary workers of the hairdressing trade in Guangzhou:

1. All revolutionary workers of the hairdressing trade should ardently and resolutely support the revolutionary actions of the young revolutionary fighters and the revolutionary masses. We should warmly welcome their criticisms and ardently support big-character posters that speak out against us. We should provide the young revolutionary fighters and the revolutionary masses beforehand with necessary facilities such as tables, benches, brush pens, ink, paper, and paste so they can write big-character posters and paste them up on the walls.

2. All revolutionary workers of the hairdressing trade should promptly take action and make revolution alongside the young revolutionary fighters and the revolutionary masses in a highly militant spirit.

They should tidy things up and make corrections where necessary. They should demolish all old ideas, culture, customs, and habits and establish new culture, new customs, and new habits. With regard to bizarre bourgeois hairstyles, they should vigorously and speedily eradicate them. But with respect to new proletarian hairdos, they should energetically and promptly promote them.

3. All revolutionary workers of the hairdressing trade should take prompt action by smashing all shop signs tinged with feudal, capitalist, and revisionist ideas. They should replace old signs with new ones fraught with revolutionary significance so our shops will forever shine with revolutionary brilliance!

4. All revolutionary workers in hairdressing salons should first and foremost make self-revolution in a determined manner, whether concerning what they have in mind, what they wear, or their own hairstyles. They should vigorously rebel against all those bizarre and fantastic things that do not conform to Mao Zedong Thought. They should forgo the "cowboy" hairstyle and shed their "cowboy" outfits. They should uphold revolutionary ideas, go in for revolutionary hairstyles, and put on revolutionary clothes.

5. We refuse to serve those customers who insist on "cowboy" or "bun-like" hairstyles! We boycott all customers who are dressed like "cowboys" or "cowgirls"!

6. We welcome customers who want to change their bizarre hairdos. We may even attend to them on a priority basis so that their bizarre hairstyles and newfangled ideas may be changed as soon as possible!

7. We should give prominence to politics and put Mao Zedong Thought in the lead. We should place the great red banner of Mao Zedong Thought in our shop windows, in this way turning them into a front for propagating Mao Zedong's ideas.

8. We should seriously and creatively learn and apply Chairman Mao's writings, remold our thinking, and transform ourselves into both hairdressing personnel and propagandists for spreading Mao Zedong Thought.

9. We should vehemently open fire on all outmoded practices of commercial enterprises and all things that do not conform to the superstructure of the socialist economic base.

10. We should seriously learn, master, and apply the "Sixteen Points" and use them to unify our understanding and action—in this

way carrying through the Great Proletarian Cultural Revolution to the end.

Cheng Yulian, barber, Nanyi Hairdressing Salon
Chen Shu, barber, Mufan Hairdressing Salon
Huang Songjun, barber, Guojian Hairdressing Salon

44
One Hundred Items for Destroying the Old and Establishing the New

Beijing No. 26 Middle School Red Guards

Source: Chinese Sociology and Anthropology: A Journal of Translations, Vol. 2, No. 3–4, Spring–Summer 1970, pp. 215–26. Revised translation by Douglas Merwin.

The onrushing tide of the Great Proletarian Cultural Revolution is just now crashing down on the remnant strength of the bourgeoisie with the might of a thunderbolt, washing the old ideology, the old culture, the old customs, and the old habits of the bourgeoisie down the stream. Chairman Mao tells us: "In the last analysis, all the truths of Marxism can be summed up in one sentence. 'To rebel is justified.'" The present Great Proletarian Cultural Revolution must overthrow the old ideology, the old culture, the old customs, and the old habits; to rebel all out against the bourgeoisie is to completely smash the bourgeoisie, to establish the proletariat on a grand scale, to make the radiance of great Mao Zedong Thought illuminate the entire capital, the entire nation, the entire world. Armed with great Mao Zedong Thought we are the most militant troops, the mortal enemy of the "four olds"; we are the destroyers of the old world; we are the creators of the new world. We must raise high the great red banner of Mao Zedong Thought, open savage fire on the "four olds," smash to bits imperialist, revisionist, and bourgeois goods and all things not in accord with Chairman Mao's thought. We must thoroughly clear the books of the utterly illogical capitalist system. We must make great Mao Zedong Thought shine out over the whole world; we must make our great fatherland revolutionary, militant, and radiant with Mao Zedong Thought; we must make a brand-new China appear in the world.

* * *

1. Under the charge of residential committees, every street must set up a quotation plaque; every household must have on its walls a picture of the Chairman plus quotations by Chairman Mao.

2. More quotations by Chairman Mao must be put up in the parks. Ticket takers on buses and conductors on trains should make the propagation of Mao Zedong Thought and the reading of Chairman Mao's quotations their primary task.

3. The management bureaus of publishing enterprises must mainly print Chairman Mao's works, and most of the sales of New China bookstores must make the radiance of Mao Zedong Thought shine in every corner of the whole country.

4. Printing companies must print quotations by the Chairman in large numbers; they must be sold in every bookstore until there is a copy of the *Quotations from Chairman Mao* in the hands of everyone in the whole country.

5. With a copy of the *Quotations from Chairman Mao* in the hands of everyone, each must carry it with him, constantly study it, and do everything in accord with it.

6. Fine art publishing companies must print large batches of stock quotations by the Chairman. Especially on anniversary occasions, they must sell great quantities of quotations and revolutionary couplets enough to satisfy the needs of the people.

7. Plaques of quotations by the Chairman must be hung on all available bicycles and pedicabs; pictures of the Chairman must be hung and Chairman Mao's sayings painted on motor vehicles and trains.

8. The relevant departments must manufacture bicycle and pedicab quotation plaques on a scale large enough to meet the needs of the people.

9. Newly manufactured products such as bicycles, motor vehicles, trains, airplanes, etc., must uniformly bear quotation plaques. This procedure must be increased, not decreased.

10. Neighborhood work must put Mao Zedong Thought in first

place, must set up small groups for the study of Chairman Mao's works, and must revolutionize housewives.

11. Every school and every unit must set up highest directive propaganda teams so that everyone can hear at any time the repeated instructions of the Chairman.

12. Broadcasting units must be set up in every park and at every major intersection, and, under the organizational responsibility of such organs as the Red Guards, propagate Mao Zedong Thought and current international and national events.

13. The old national anthem absolutely must be reformed by the workers, peasants, and soldiers into a eulogy to the Party and Chairman Mao; this big poisonous weed of Tian Han must be rooted out.

14. Neighborhood residential committees must put up several newspaper display cases so that everyone can take an interest in major national and world events.

15. From now on every newspaper must put Mao Zedong Thought in first place. Editorials must be few and to the point, and there must be more good articles dealing with the living study and living application of the Chairman's works by the workers, peasants, and soldiers.

16. Letters and stamps must never have bourgeois things printed on them (such as cats, dogs, or other artistic things). Politics must be predominant. A quotation by Chairman Mao or a militant utterance by a hero must be printed on every envelope.

17. When members of companies celebrate brigade days, they are not permitted to visit parks. They must strengthen their class education and their education in Mao Zedong Thought.

18. Hereafter on the national day, everyone must carry a copy of the Chairman's quotations and a bouquet, and the bouquets must be arranged in slogans.

19. Shop windows cannot be dominated by displays of scents and perfumes. They must be decorated with simplicity and dignity and must put Mao Zedong Thought first.

20. Theaters must have a strong political atmosphere. Before the movie starts, quotations from Chairman Mao must be shown. Don't let the bourgeoisie rule our stages. Cut the superfluous hooligan scenes, and reduce the price of tickets on behalf of the workers, peasants, and soldiers.

21. Literary and art workers must energetically model in clay heroic images of workers, peasants, and soldiers engaged in living study

and living application of Chairman Mao's works. Their works must be pervaded by the one red line of Mao Zedong Thought.

22. All professional literary and art teams must gradually be transformed into Mao Zedong Thought propaganda teams like the *Ulanmuqi* [cultural team] and the "Sea-Borne Cultural Workers' Company"; they must be highly proletarianized, highly militant, and highly ideologized.

23. Our nation has already been established for seventeen years. But those who drank the blood of the people and oppressed the people before the Liberation, those bourgeois bastards, are still collecting fixed interest and interest from stocks and living the lives of parasites. We warn you: Immediately desist from collecting fixed interest and interest from stocks; you are only allowed to honestly reform your bastardly ideology—you are not permitted to exploit the people.

24. You landowners who still rode on the people's heads and drank the people's blood after the Liberation, we order you bastards to hurry up and turn over all your private holdings to the state. In a socialist state we absolutely cannot allow you vampires to exist.

25. In a proletarian society, private enterprise cannot be allowed to exist. We propose to take all firms using joint state and private management and change them to state management and change joint state and private management enterprises into state-owned enterprises.

26. Our socialist society absolutely cannot allow any hoodlums or juvenile delinquents to exist. We order you right this minute to get rid of your blue jeans, shave off your slick hairdos, take off your rocket shoes, and quit your black organizations. Peking is the heart of world revolution. It is not the big world you squatted on before the Liberation. We warn you: You are not allowed to go on recklessly doing your evil deeds—if you do, you will be responsible for the consequences.

27. All who are in service trades are not permitted to serve the bourgeoisie. Clothing stores are firmly prohibited from making tight pants, Hong Kong–style suits, weird women's outfits, and grotesque men's suits. All revolutionary comrades in service trades must strictly adhere to this.

28. All daily necessities (perfume, snowflake cream, etc.) that do not serve the broad worker, peasant, and soldier masses must be prohibited from sale right away. Merchandise trademark designs must be radically changed.

29. Photography studios must serve the broad worker, peasant, sol-

dier masses and must abolish the taking of profile photos and all kinds of grotesque pictures. Display windows should be arranged with large, simple photos of workers, peasants, and soldiers.

30. Stop producing poker cards, military chess, and all other such things that advertise bourgeois ideology.

31. Trading stores cannot sell secondhand clothes, Western clothes, or any other ridiculous things the bourgeoisie love to see.

32. Laundries must cease washing pants, stockings, and handkerchiefs for those bourgeois wives, misses, and young gentlemen and completely crush their stuck-up airs. Do not yield to their senseless demands; you should greatly enhance the pride of the proletariat and utterly destroy bourgeois pomp.

33. Public baths must consistently desist from serving those bourgeois sons of bitches. Don't give them massage baths, footrubs, backrubs; don't let them bow our heads again, or abuse and ride roughshod over us.

34. Bookstores for classical books must this minute stop doing business. Children's bookstores must immediately destroy all pornographic children's books, and all bookstores and libraries must be internally purified and must clear away all poisonous weeds; do not permit these goods of the bourgeois ideology to be poured into our youth ever again.

35. All the landlords, rich-peasants, counter-revolutionaries, hooligans, Rightists, and other members of the bourgeois class are not permitted to collect pornographic books and decadent records. Whoever violates this rule will, when discovered, be treated as guilty of attempting to restore the old order, and his collections will be destroyed.

36. Children must sing revolutionary songs. Those rotten tunes of the cat and dog variety must never again waft in the air of our socialist state. In this great socialist state of ours, absolutely no one is allowed to play games of chance.

37. The bastards of the bourgeoisie are not allowed to hire governesses. Whoever dares to violate or resist this rule and thus continues to ride on the heads of the laboring people will be severely punished.

38. All service industries must turn their faces toward the workers, peasants, and soldiers. They must bear a class nature; they cannot produce anything for the service of the bourgeoisie.

39. Every hospital must turn its face toward the workers, peasants, and soldiers. They must reform the old system and abolish the registration system.

40. Peddlers who make little toys to deceive and, in a disguised form, poison children, we order you to stop business right away. Not the least consideration will be shown toward those who violate this order. In addition, we order toy shops immediately to stop selling small toys such as watches, etc., that advertise bourgeois ideology.

41. Every industrial enterprise must abolish the bourgeois bonus award system. In this great socialist nation of ours, the broad worker, peasant, soldier masses, armed with the great Mao Zedong Thought, have no need for material incentives.

42. Heads of families are not allowed to educate their children with bourgeois ideology. The feudal family-head system will be abolished. No more beating or scolding of children will be tolerated. If the child is not of one's own begetting, no mistreatment is allowed. Children will be consistently educated in Mao Zedong Thought.

43. Cricket raising and cricket fights will no longer be permitted. The raising of fish, cats, and dogs and other such bourgeois habits shall not exist in the midst of the Chinese people. Whoever breaks this rule will be responsible for the consequences.

44. You old bastards of the bourgeoisie who receive high salaries, listen well: Before Liberation you rode on the heads of the people, sometimes severe, sometimes lenient. Now you still receive salaries many times more than ten times higher than those of the workers. You are thus drinking the blood of the people—you are guilty. Starting in September, you are ordered to lower your high salaries to the level of those of the workers. Landlords, rich-peasants, counter-revolutionaries, hooligans, and Rightists who have deposits in banks are not allowed to take even a penny for themselves. Whoever breaks this rule is responsible for the consequences—there will not be the least politeness.

45. Scoundrels of the bourgeoisie are not allowed to wander around or visit parks at will. The monthly tickets of those who have bought them to visit parks or ride in cars as a way to enjoy their leisure will be destroyed. They cannot indulge in wild fancies.

46. Except for the old, the weak, the sick, and the crippled who may ride in pedicabs, the bastards of the bourgeoisie are forbidden to ride in pedicabs. Whoever violates this rule will be handled with severity. The number of pedicab workers must be reduced, and suitable arrangements for good jobs will be made.

47. Landlords, rich-peasants, counter-revolutionaries, hooligans, Rightists, and capitalists, when they go out, must wear plaques as

monsters and freaks under the supervision of the masses. Whoever violates this rule will be dealt with severely.

48. All monsters and freaks and puppets of the "Black Gang" are forbidden to receive salaries without the approval of the masses. We want to lower the salaries of these old bastards. The scoundrels will get only enough to keep them alive.

49. Restaurants can no longer be places where the bastards of the bourgeoisie go to eat, drink, and enjoy themselves. Service personnel are not allowed to respond to their senseless demands and prepare for them delicacies from the mountains and seas. The finger guessing game cannot be played in restaurants. No service may be rendered these bastards.

50. Factories must not give pensions to landlords, rich-peasants, counter-revolutionaries, hooligans, and Rightists. Their payments and benefits will all be abolished, and they will be required to labor under the supervision of the masses.

51. The bastards of the bourgeoisie are not permitted to occupy a large number of houses, the [minimum] limit being three persons to one room. The surplus rooms shall be turned over to the Housing Bureau for management, lest we take action.

52. All those of the five categories of landlords, rich-peasants, counter-revolutionaries, hooligans, and Rightists who are jobless shall go back to their native place to engage in production.

53. Social youth who loaf around, we order you: Register immediately at the employment office and go to the frontier territories to participate in labor and production.

54. From now on, police stations are not allowed to find jobs in the cities for those who don't adhere to the state assignments. Let them go to the frontier territories.

55. Old bastards of the bourgeoisie, we order you instantly to hand over to the government all the money you took by exploitation before Liberation. You vampires are no longer allowed to squander at will.

56. Wrestling areas throughout the country will be disbanded, and the wrestlers will go to police stations to register for participation in labor. You can no longer poison the people.

57. We order magicians throughout the country who depend on deceiving the people for a living: Stop your business immediately; go to police stations to register!

58. All circus and theater programs must be changed. They must

put on meaningful things. Actors are not allowed to dress up in strange fashions, because we don't need those filthy things.

59. We order all those young rabbits who have not joined pedicab associations and are driving black pedicabs (i.e., those who go out during the night to train or bus stations, large streets, and small alleys to look for customers and who unnecessarily pass through large streets and small alleys to stretch the mere two *li* of the original distance to five in order to charge twice as much) to immediately stop engaging in this kind of criminal business and to submit themselves to the bureaus of public safety.

60. All those athletic activities that don't correspond with practical significance will be appropriately reduced. Physical education for national defense, such as swimming, mountain climbing, shooting, etc., will be greatly developed so that gradually every youth or adult over fifteen years of age will have a range of enemy-killing abilities. All the people are soldiers, always prepared to annihilate the invading enemy.

61. Those who repair shoes on large streets and small alleys, we order you to stop doing business at once. Under the responsible organs, organize yourselves into shoe-repair associations. The price for shoe repairs must be reduced.

62. Nobody may address letters to "Sir" so and so. The whole range of feudal practices must be abolished and new customs advocated.

63. The limousines, television sets, and motorcycles in households of "five category-elements" and "Black Gang"[1] elements shall all be confiscated. Television sets will be turned over to residential committees, who will then give them to the families of the workers, peasants, and soldiers to watch.

64. From now on, no newspapers are allowed to give excessive payments for writing articles. This hole of black wind shall be stopped up.

65. The family-head system shall be destroyed, and children may make suggestions to grownups.

66. Hospitals must not charge in advance for emergency treatment (excepting "five category-elements"). Complicated treatment must be abolished. Specific reforms will be left for the medical workers to

---

[1]"Five category-elements" refers to landlords, rich-peasants, counter-revolutionaries, hooligans, and Rightists. See above, proposal no. 52. "Black Gang" elements were cadres denounced for a variety of political crimes in the summer of 1966.

decide. The old and Western frameworks shall be smashed, and everything will serve the people.

67. All the monsters and freaks (old bureaucrats, landlords, capitalists, hooligans, etc.) are prohibited from teaching the traditional military skills, boxing, and internal hygiene in parks or other places.

68. All broadcasts of literary and art performances and movies shall immediately eliminate the names of authors, actors, conductors, etc. This road to individual fame and profit will thus be blocked.

69. We order those under thirty-five to quit drinking and smoking immediately. Bad habits of this sort absolutely may not be cultivated.

70. Telling dirty jokes, uttering profanities, and doing vulgar things are strictly forbidden. Violators will be severely dealt with. The bad habits of using nicknames, job titles, etc., are strictly forbidden. Everyone shall be called comrade (with the exception of the "five black categories").

71. Advanced elements of the workers, peasants, and soldiers are responsible for being street activists. Bourgeois elements will not be allowed to usurp their roles.

72. From now on, postmen will not deliver letters upstairs or into compounds. Letter boxes will be prepared inside multistored buildings. For large compounds, a special man will be found to take on the responsibility. The labor of postmen comrades will be reduced.

73. Resplendent wedding ceremonies are forbidden. There must be no extravagance or squandering. New customs and new habits can be advocated.

74. The wearing of feudal things such as bracelets, earrings, and longevity chains is forbidden.

75. We recommend for the consideration of the responsible organs that the interest system in banking be abolished and the people be allowed to save self-consciously on the basis of patriotism and assistance to socialist construction.

76. We suggest that from now on no admission will be charged to any critical movies and that they be seen by organized groups. There will be no tickets sold to individuals. All elements of the "five black categories" will not be allowed to see these movies.

77. Things left over from the old society, such as buying snacks or fruits while visiting friends or relatives, will all be abolished. We hope that the worker, peasant, soldier masses will support this movement.

78. Except for urgent and crucial matters, taxis will not be hired. The bastards of the bourgeoisie will not be allowed to ride in these taxis.

79. The responsible organs must do their best to find ways to establish public toilets in the various alleys so as to reduce the heavy work of the sanitation workers.

80. The state must vigorously develop the motor-transportation industry in order to reduce the heavy labor of the cart-pulling workers.

81. From now on, the Changtian Amusement Park will not open during Chinese New Year. We must take account of economics, and we must take account of politics.

82. From now on, all universities, high schools, and vocational schools will be run as communist schools with part-time work and part-time study and part-time farming and part-time study.

83. We students must respond to Chairman Mao's appeal. Students must also learn from the workers, the peasants, and the soldiers, and each year during their vacations they must go to factories, farms, and military camps to train themselves.

84. We are determined to demand reform in the vacation system. Vacations shall be taken during the busy season for the peasants so that we can go to the villages to help in agricultural production.

85. Sofas, couches, etc., may not be produced in great quantities.

86. Expensive articles such as gold pens, etc., shall not be produced in great quantities (except for export) because they do not serve the broad worker, peasant, soldier masses.

87. No manufactured goods in shops may be called by their Western names. Meaningful Chinese names must be used.

88. We appeal to all League members to take off and throw away their League emblems. Get rid of this poisonous weed.

89. When prescribing medicine, doctors must destroy the Western framework of writing in English and clearly explain the type of medicine prescribed. Their signatures have to be legible.

90. We are determined that the youth vanguard corps cannot be allowed to turn into an all-people's corps. Otherwise, it would lose its significance as a vanguard.

91. Schools must use Mao's works as textbooks and educate the youth in Mao Zedong Thought.

92. All schools must have physical training and participation in labor in a primary position and strengthen military training.

93. Schools must destroy the feudal teacher-student etiquette and establish an equal relationship between teacher and student.

94. Starting this year, normal colleges, normal schools, and schools

for training primary school teachers must absorb the sons and daughters of the "five red elements" into their schools.

95. Those who have names with feudal bourgeois overtones will voluntarily go to police stations to change their names.

96. No fences or small houses are allowed to be built inside or outside a garden. The growth of such selfish thoughts must not be encouraged.

97. Abolish the system of the sale of annual tickets for parks. If the workers, peasants, and soldiers need to rest, all tickets will be distributed to them by factories and agencies.

98. We suggest that the state consider a universal increase in wages of the workers and a decrease in wages for the authorities of the bourgeoisie.

99. "Black Gang" elements shall be fined according to their criminal acts.

100. Advocate simplified characters. From now on, all newspapers and other publications will use simplified characters in their headlines.

The Maoism School (originally No. 26 Middle School) Red Guards
[August 1966]

45
"Revolutionize the Spring Festival"

Shanghai Workers Revolutionary Rebel General Headquarters et al.

Source: The source for the text of this proposal is a collection compiled and printed in the 1980s by the Committee for the Historical Documentation of the Shanghai Labor Movement. We have deleted from our translation the names of the thirty-four cosignatory organizations.

Chairman Mao's Teachings:

"We are not merely good at destroying an old world, but will also be good at building a new world."

"Practice frugality while making revolution."

PROPOSAL

The Great Proletarian Cultural Revolution has already entered a new stage. Proletarian revolutionary rebels are in the midst of achieving great unity and with the force of a thunderbolt they are embarking upon an all-round struggle to seize power from the small handful of Party-persons in power taking the capitalist road. The revolutionary situation is excellent and getting better. How should we approach the upcoming 1967 Spring Festival in the midst of this Great Proletarian Cultural Revolutionary high tide? We—the revolutionary rebels—reply without any hesitation: by making it a target of revolution!

The Spring Festival is one of the spiritual shackles forced upon the working people for millennia by the exploiting classes. In the old society, the Spring Festival was heaven for the rich and hell for the poor. Our ancestors sacrificed blood and sweat, yet for generations got no more than the "freedom" to labor like oxen, like horses. During the seventeen years that have passed since Liberation, a small handful of Party-persons in power taking the capitalist road have utilized the forces of old social conventions represented by the Spring Festival to praise the bourgeois lifestyle of eating, drinking, amusing oneself, and having fun, and to faithfully work in the service of the exploiting classes. They utilize the Spring Festival to engage in feudal superstitious activities on a massive scale, to beseech the gods and sacrifice to ancestors, to promote hypocritical etiquette, to invite guests and present gifts, to get drunk, gamble, and eat and drink excessively, and in this way to turn the Spring Festival into a marketplace for the unchecked spread of the "four olds." The working people remain subject to spiritual enslavement by the ideology of the exploiting classes. Chairman Mao leads us in carrying out a Great Cultural Revolution involving the destruction of the "four olds" on a massive scale and the establishment of the "four news" on an equally massive scale. This has made the working people demand a thorough liberation, necessitating the destruction of the old world, the cleaning away of its filth and mire, and the thorough transformation of the spiritual outlook of our entire society. Can we still put up with a Spring Festival that is so heavily tainted with the hues of feudalism, capitalism, and revisionism? No we cannot! Absolutely not! We must act in accordance with Chairman Mao's teachings and promote the revolutionization of people's thinking in the course of the Great Cultural Revolution. We must make the Spring Festival a target of revolution!

To make the Spring Festival a target of revolution is to make the "four olds" a target of revolution, which is also to make economism a target of revolution.[1] It is a revolutionary measure that revolutionary rebels are compelled to adopt, given the situation at present in the Great Proletarian Cultural Revolution. Not so long ago, the revolutionary rebels repulsed the new counteroffensive of the bourgeois reactionary line by exposing the sinister plot in which the class enemy resorted to economism. But, we must also realize that the class enemy will not perish of himself. The small handful of Party-persons in power taking the capitalist road and the tiny handful of stubborn elements who persist in the bourgeois reactionary line will not step off the historical stage out of their own free will. We must note that the devious tricks of economism are still being acted out and that the sinister ghost of economism is still hanging around. All revolutionary masses and all revolutionary organizations should heighten their vigilance one hundredfold and guard against the enemy's latest sinister plot. This latest plot concocted by a bunch of reactionary scoundrels is to use the Spring Festival to unite the reactionary elements in society and the forces of old conventions in an attempt to stage a comeback, to whip up once more the sinister wind of economism, to deceive the masses, to damage production, to damage and interrupt transport and communication, to damage finance and banking, and to damage market supplies—all with the aim of obstructing the Great Proletarian Cultural Revolution and of staging a new counteroffensive against the revolutionary rebels. We must absolutely not let the enemy succeed in his sinister plot. Our policy is diametrically opposed, and we shall fight for every inch of land. The revolutionary rebels "with power and courage to spare must pursue the tottering foe and not ape Xiang Yu the conqueror seeking idle fame";[2] we must avail ourselves of the opportunity presented by the excellent situation of the Great Proletarian Cultural Revolution and make the Spring Festival and economism targets of revolution on a massive scale, thoroughly smash the new counteroffensive of the bourgeois reactionary line, and carry the Great Proletarian Cultural Revolution through to the end!

---

[1]"Economism" (*jingjizhuyi*) is here employed by the authors to refer to attempts to "buy off" the poorer segments of the Shanghai working class by giving them salary increases, end-of-the-year bonuses, etc.

[2]Lines quoted from Mao Zedong's poem "The People's Liberation Army Occupies Nanjing" (April 1949).

To this aim, we—a number of revolutionary mass organizations—jointly put forward the following proposals:

1. Hold high the great red banner of Mao Zedong Thought and extensively propagate Mao Zedong Thought.

Mao Zedong Thought is the great pinnacle of Marxism-Leninism in the present era and a powerful ideological weapon to be used in the transformation of the objective world and the subjective world. Every revolutionary rebel organization should extensively organize the study and propaganda of Mao Zedong Thought—by linking it to the situation in the Great Cultural Revolutionary struggle at present—to destroy "self" and establish the public, destroy the old and establish the new, and promote the revolutionization of people's thinking. A variety of forms can be utilized, such as the convention of rallies to discuss experiences gained in studying Chairman Mao's works; singing revolutionary songs; performing revolutionary rebel operas [*sic*]; organizing theater troupes to perform for the workers, peasants, and soldiers in the factories, rural areas, train stations, harbor, and residential areas, etc. In this way, Mao Zedong Thought will come to occupy every sector of the battle front.

2. Pay attention to affairs of state and carry the Great Proletarian Cultural Revolution through to the end!

Every revolutionary rebel organization should give play to the revolutionary spirit of "seizing every minute,"[3] and on no account slacken in the present struggle against the bourgeois reactionary line. Sum up experiences from the most recent phase of the Great Cultural Revolution. We must strengthen revolutionary great alliances, follow up a victory with hot pursuit, vigorously pursue and fiercely maul, and continue to develop and deepen the all-round struggle to seize power.

3. "Grasp revolution, promote production."

Resolutely implement Chairman Mao's great call to "Grasp revolution, promote production." Revolutionary comrades in all production units should remain at their production posts during the Spring Festival;

---

[3]The expression quoted here is from Mao Zedong's poem "Reply to Guo Moruo" (9 January 1963).

revolutionary comrades on the commercial front should serve the broad workers, peasants, and soldiers heart and soul. The State Council notification about not taking days off during the 1967 Spring Festival, distributed nationwide on the 29th, is to be resolutely implemented.[4]

4. "Practice frugality while making revolution."

Act in accordance with the spirit of Chairman Mao's instruction "Practice frugality while making revolution." Revolutionary rebels must always persist in hard work and plain living while making revolution—strike down economism; staunchly oppose ostentation, extravagance, and luxury; oppose excessive eating and drinking and inviting guests and presenting gifts; practice strict economy; and vie with each another in saving money in the bank.

5. Destroy the "Four Olds" and establish the "Four News."

Revolutionary rebels should be models when it comes to destroying the "four olds" and establishing the "four news." They should establish Mao Zedong Thought on a massive scale while thoroughly eradicating every remnant of feudalism and capitalism. In the rural areas, the broad poor and lower-middle peasants should together with the revolutionary rebels extensively propagate the destruction of the old and establishment of the new, and firmly ban feudal superstitious practices and practices such as gambling, etc.

6. Heighten revolutionary vigilance and be strictly on guard against enemy disturbances and sabotage.

Strengthen public security work and be strictly on guard against enemies taking the opportunity to sabotage production and to sabotage the Great Cultural Revolution. The small handful of Party-persons in power taking the capitalist road as well as the ox-monsters and snake-demons out there in society must be kept under strictest surveillance. They are only allowed to behave themselves, not to speak and act

---

[4]The text of this notification appeared in the *People's Daily* on 30 January 1967.

irresponsibly. Anyone who violates these rules should immediately be dealt with severely! The broad revolutionary masses are to self-consciously respect and maintain order in traffic, maintain social order, and aid the departments concerned in strengthening market controls and in clamping down on profiteering and other illegal activities.

7. We hope that revolutionary rebel organizations in all sectors will formulate concrete proposals and measures according to the prevailing concrete circumstances, as well as engage in extensive propaganda.

Proposing units:

Shanghai Workers Revolutionary Rebel General Headquarters

. . . .

30 January 1967

46
"Let Us Celebrate a 'Proletarian Cultural Revolution Holiday' "

Beijing No. 1 Middle School Red Guards

Source: This is a translation of a crudely stenciled proposal on yellow paper picked up by a Swedish diplomat in the streets of Beijing in late August 1966. A copy of this document is reproduced in *Red Guard Publications* (Washington, D.C.: Center for Chinese Research Materials, 1975), Vol. 19, p. 6100.

PROPOSAL

First of all, we propose turning this great day of "August 18th" into a "Proletarian Cultural Revolution Holiday" during which, in years to come, there will be gatherings and parades to commemorate and celebrate.

The Great Proletarian Cultural Revolution aims at destroying on a massive scale all old ideas, old culture, old customs, and old habits; it aims at reforming all superstructures not suited to the socialist economic base.

We think that a number of our present "holidays" such as the Spring

Festival, Mid-Autumn Festival, Dragon Boat Festival, etc., have a very strong feudal flavor, a widespread baneful influence, and a bad impact. In our new socialist China, we must absolutely not allow this remnant poison of the feudal landlord class and its emperors, monarchs, generals, and ministers to spread wantonly and unchecked. We propose observing only holidays that have a political content, such as the "May 1st" International Labor Day, the "March 8th" International Women's Day, the "June 4th" Day of Youth, the "June 1st" International Children's Day, the anniversary of the founding of our Party on "July 1st," the "August 1st" Army Day, and the "October 1st" National Day. All those filthy feudal "holidays" are to be abolished. We will continue to observe the "Qing Ming" Festival by sweeping the graves of revolutionary martyrs—not by visiting the graves of our ancestors.

Long live the Great Proletarian Cultural Revolution!
Long live the great Chinese Communist Party!
Long live our great leader Chairman Mao! Long live! Long live!
Long live the great Mao Zedong Thought!
Long live the revolutionary spirit of rebellion!
Smash the old world, build a new world!

"Resistance University" No. 1 Middle School
Red Flag Combat Group

Beijing, 22 August 1966

47
On "The Red Lantern"

Workers and PLA Men

Source: Chinese Literature, No. 2, 1969, pp. 99–104.

[Original editor's introduction:] *The Red Lantern* is a revolutionary modern Beijing opera depicting the heroic struggles of the Chinese working class. It has been warmly acclaimed by the workers, peasants, and soldiers and all revolutionaries. They have praised it highly in articles and discussions. The heroic characters in the opera have captured their hearts. We print below a few comments by workers and PLA men.

Gao Zhen'en (railway worker): In *The Red Lantern* there is this dialogue between Communist Li Yuhe, a railway worker, and Hatoyama, Japanese military police chief, after Li has been arrested:

Hatoyama: Actually, the highest creed can be summed up in two words.

Li: And what are they?

Hatoyama: For me.

Li: For you eh?

Hatoyama: No. Every man for himself.

Hatoyama goes on to say: "Anyone who doesn't look out for his own interests will be destroyed by the gods. It's an absolute rule of life."

This "for me" philosophy is the bourgeois world outlook, pure and simple. It is the "highest creed" and "absolute rule of life" of all exploiting classes. How do we workers feel about it? Just as Li Yuhe says: "It's as reasonable as trying to puff up the fire through a rolling pin."

The world outlook of the working class is fundamentally different from the world outlook of the bourgeoisie. They believe in "for me," that "anyone who doesn't look out for himself will be destroyed by the gods." We believe in acting for the public good, in "utter devotion to others without any thought of self."

Liu Yuhe is a hero of the working class. His every word and deed shines with the glory of our world outlook. For the sake of the revolution, he is ready to "step into the place of the fallen and press on," to relentlessly struggle against the enemy. For the sake of the revolution, he is not afraid of "wearing out the floor of a jail cell," he is willing to endure "being ground to powder." In other words, he is entirely for the public good, he has an "utter devotion to others without any thought of self."

There is a direct confrontation between the two world outlooks in the scene "Hatoyama Is Defied." Li fights Hatoyama measure for measure, refusing to give an inch. With his noble proletarian world outlook, he trenchantly exposes and repudiates the ugly world outlook of the bourgeoisie.

Li Kunlu (railway worker): *The Red Lantern* portrays the heroic figure of railway worker Li Yuhe to perfection.

Li is absolutely loyal to the revolution. Hatoyama tries both hard and soft tactics against him in their struggle, but Li fully displays the lofty revolutionary morality of a Communist. His every thought and deed for the revolution, Li battles courageously and willingly gives his life.

He is a fearless revolutionary. In the prison he says to his mother: "I have always been as tough as steel." Nothing daunts him. He fears neither arrest nor torture, nor imprisonment, nor death. He is full of revolutionary optimism, right up to the moment of his execution. "The storm will pass, flowers will bloom," he says. "A new China will glow like the rising sun."

In his face-to-face struggle with the enemy, besides showing an implacable revolutionary will, Li also thoroughly demonstrates the wisdom of the working class. He cleverly conceals the secret code in the scene "A Narrow Escape at the Gruel Stand." His witty defiance of Hatoyama at the "feast" causes the enemy military police chief to groan: "My eyes are dim, my head's ready to burst. My blood pressure's up, my hands are icy."

Renegade, traitor and scab Liu Shaoqi preached a marketplace philosophy of "take a small loss for the sake of big gains," and a traitor's philosophy of "cherish yourself." The splendid image of Li Yuhe is a striking repudiation of both these creeds.

Revolutionary modern Peking opera *The Red Lantern* is praised by us railway workers because it warmly commends the morality, courage, and wisdom of our working class. All railway workers, whether veterans or new hands, learn a good lesson from it. The veterans grow stronger in their revolutionary resolve, they feel younger. The opera makes them determined to live out their remaining years as revolutionaries, boundlessly loyal to Chairman Mao and to carry the revolution through to the end.

The young fellow's reaction is that they must learn from the older generation of revolutionaries, do a good job of taking over the revolutionary cause, never forget their origins, and go forever with Chairman Mao to wage revolution.

Yuan Xiyu, Zeng Zhian, and Cai Binyuan (soldiers): In *The Red Lantern* young heroine Li Tiemei is a fine daughter of the working class. The storms of class struggle temper her into a determined far-sighted girl, loyal and staunch. She is completely devoted to the revolutionary cause of the working class and to the proletarian revolutionary line of Chairman Mao.

Seventeen-year-old Tiemei is bold and fearless on the execution grounds. When the enemy demand that she reveal where the secret code is hidden, she retorts with angry finality: "I don't know." After cruelly torturing and murdering her father and grandmother, they let her go, hoping that they can trail her to the secret code.

But the girl is like forged steel. She sings: "No tears I show, to my heart they go, to irrigate flowers of blazing fire." The more savagely the enemy behave, the more courageous and determined she becomes. "Flames of rage leap a thousand leagues high, to consume this reign of filthy darkness," she tells herself. Utterly defiant of the enemy, she sings: "Arrest me, release me, I'm well prepared. I fear not the whip and lash, I fear not lock and chains. I won't give you the code even if you grind me to powder."

Tiemei is like a thriving green pine atop a high mountain. Her thorough-going proletarian revolutionary spirit is a great encouragement and education to us young soldiers.

"Whatever the sapling thus the fruit, whatever the seed thus the grain." Tiemei's noble character is derived from the great thought of Mao Zedong, it is a result of the education she received from her revolutionary elders. Grandma tells the revolutionary history of their family to make her remember in the depths of her soul "the debt of blood and tears" that the enemy owes. This plants the seeds of fierce class and national hatred in the girl's heart. She and her father and grandmother fight shoulder to shoulder against the enemy. Their fearless proletarian revolutionary spirit is an inspiration to the girl. Her class stand grows firm, she knows what to love and what to hate. She takes a broad view, she becomes brave and staunch.

Tiemei puts it well: "Pa leaves me his moral qualities; I'll stand as steady as a rock. Pa leaves me his wisdom; I'll be clear-sighted and never deceived. Pa leaves me his courage; I'll dare to contend with the most savage beasts." In this daughter of the working class we see how the glorious fighting tradition of the proletariat exercises a powerful influence over the younger generation.

Our great leader Chairman Mao teaches us: "The revolution cannot succeed without the modern industrial working class, because it is the leader of the Chinese revolution and is the most revolutionary class." Under the leadership of Chairman Mao and the Chinese Communist Party, the Chinese working class has waged brave and stubborn battles and performed great deeds. The glorious tradition that the working class bequeaths to us is our most precious revolutionary wealth. It is indeed as Tiemei sings: "Pa, neither a thousand carts nor ten thousand boats could contain all the wealth you leave me."

We revolutionary soldiers promise to be like Tiemei, inheriting and extending the glorious traditions of the working class. We shall carry out the bequests of our martyrs and, holding high the red lantern of revolution, temper ourselves in revolutionary storms to be worthy successors to the proletarian revolutionary cause.

Xu Yongji (assistant head of an army cavalry station): Recently, I saw the model revolutionary Beijing opera *The Red Lantern,* produced under the personal supervision of our dear and respected Comrade Jiang Qing. That glowing red lantern, so featured in the opera, has been shining before my eyes and illuminating my heart ever since.

Tiemei's grandmother tells the girl: "We've had the lantern for thirty years. It has been lighting the road for us poor people, for us workers, all that time. Neither wind nor rain can put it out. . . . Your grandfather before you had it. Now it's in the hands of your father. . . . The red lantern is our family's most precious heirloom."

This is no ordinary red lantern. It symbolizes the spirit of carrying the revolution through to the end possessed by China's working class, which is armed with Mao Zedong's thought. Chairman Mao teaches us: "It is only the working class that is most far-sighted, most selfless and most thoroughly revolutionary."

The veteran worker who taught Li Yuhe his job, holding the lantern, waged revolution until he nobly laid down his life for the proletarian revolutionary cause. Li took the lantern from his hand and "wiped off the blood, buried the dead, and went again into battle." Tiemei took the lantern from the hand of her father, Li. "Determined, eyes gleaming," she vowed: "I won't leave the battlefield before all the savages are destroyed." Just as the red lantern is passed on from generation to generation, so the noble revolutionary character and fine revolutionary traditions of the working class extend and grow from one generation to the next.

Under the wise leadership of Chairman Mao and the Communist Party, thousands of people like Li Yuhe and his daughter stepped into breaches in the ranks, fought bravely, and finally defeated the enemy, liberating all China. On Tiananmen the red flag dances in the east wind and red lanterns cast their beams far. In the course of the socialist revolution and socialist construction, the working class—the class that leads the revolution—has made earth-shaking achievements.

Today, guided by Chairman Mao's latest brilliant directive: "The working class must exercise leadership in everything," and striving for complete victory in the Cultural Revolution, our great working class has militantly, and with proletarian fearlessness, brought into full play its spirit of carrying the revolution through to the end. It is striding on to the political stage of struggle, criticism, and transformation in all aspects of the superstructure. What a magnificent scene!

Let us hold high the red lantern of revolution and victoriously advance!

48
Unveiling the Dark Side of the Chinese Department's Program in Classical Studies

Students in the Department of Language and Literature
at Beijing University

Source: Chinese Sociology and Anthropology: A Journal of Translations, Vol. 2, No. 1–2, Fall–Winter 1969/70, pp. 77–88. Revised translation by H. Y. Cheng.

Liu Shaoqi, the biggest Party-person in power taking the capitalist road, has always been fighting against Chairman Mao on the educational front and stubbornly promoted the counter-revolutionary revisionist educational line in order to train successors to the bourgeoisie. To achieve their evil aims, the bourgeoisie used all possible ways and means to weaken and poison our youth in an attempt to convert us into tame instruments for the restoration of capitalism.

The Classical Literature Professional Program in the Department of Chinese Language and Literature in Beijing University is really a "black shop," especially set up to poison our youth by a handful of counter-revolutionary revisionists from the former Central Propaganda Department, the former Ministry of Culture, and the former Beijing Municipal Party Committee, under the direction of Liu Shaoqi.

1. How the Professional Program in Classical Literature Was Established

From 1959 to 1962, because of a succession of severe natural calamities and the treachery of the modern Soviet revisionists, our country suffered temporary economic difficulties. Domestically, class enemies began to make trouble. With the cooperation of the right opportunists in our Party, they started a fierce attack on our Party. Under these circumstances, and with the secret plots of counter-revolutionary revisionists Qi Yanming, Deng Tuo, Lu Ping, Wu Han, Jian Bozan, the "black shop" of the Professional Program in Classical Literature had a grand opening.

Liu Shaoqi once said: "We Party members, Youth League members, and revolutionary intellectuals should study hard and devote ourselves to the study of how to utilize and manage specialized skills and scientific knowledge. Those who are qualified should turn themselves into red experts." Counter-revolutionaries such as Qi Yanming and other reactionary academic "authorities" faithfully carried out Liu Shaoqi's "black directives." Qi Yanming personally came to Beijing University three times to make propaganda. Wei Jiangong of the Department of Chinese Language and Literature, Jian Bozan of the Department of History, and Feng Youlan of the Department of Philosophy met secretly several times. They announced everywhere: "We must permit those students who have done their work well to become experts in certain fields." "We must set our standards higher, so that when they are finished they are able to do research work." Their ugly purpose was clear. They established this professional program for the sole purpose of training us to become anti-Party "experts" like Wu Han and Jian Bozan.

Counter-revolutionary revisionist Lu Ping personally issued the "business license" for the establishment of this professional program and signed the "contract" with Qi Yanming. The manager of China Book Publishers (*Zhonghua shuju*), Jin Canran, told Beijing University students, "You go ahead. We at China Book Publishers will take as many as there are." It was clearly written on our "contract" that "the main consideration for the courses given, the number of new students each year, and the job allocation of graduates shall be the demand of party A (that is, China Book Publishers)." Lu Ping, in a letter to Wei Jiangong on 27 April 1962, jubilantly wrote, "I have seen the draft contract; the entire way it is to be done is beneficial to both parties." The so-called "benefit to both parties" actually meant training successors to the bourgeoisie for them and serving their bourgeois educational system. That is the reason Lu Ping happily agreed to and signed the contract.

After carefully planning, they picked Wei Jiangong, who had been scorned by Mr. Lu Xun as a reactionary bourgeois academic lord, as the director of the Professional Program in Classical Literature. The black shop was thus even more formally opened for business.

How obnoxious those monsters and devils were at that time! Wu Han hastened to boastfully write his "In Celebration of the Admission of Students into the Professional Program in Classical Literature at Beijing University." Jian Bozan simultaneously released his article "From the Professional Program in Classical Literature at Beijing University to the Problem of the Organization of Classical Books," boasting that the establishment of the Professional Program in Classical Literature was a "big happy event" and that this professional industry was a "heavy industry"; thus he made a big effort for continual propaganda on behalf of this "heavy industry."

2. Monsters and Freaks Spreading Poison

Chairman Mao said, "The most important problem for a military academy is the choice of its president." Who, after all, held power in yesterday's Professional Program in Classical Literature? One was the counter-revolutionary revisionist Cheng Xiance, who was Lu Ping's loyal running dog; one was the reactionary academic lord Wang Li; and another was the feudal remnant Wei Jiangong. This group of monsters and freaks controlled our program. They worked hard on peaceful transformation and the restoration of capitalism.

Liu Shaoqi said long ago: "You must study with quiet minds." "Listen not to what happens outside; read only the books of the sages. You may ask what is happening in the outside world, but don't be interrupted by it." "Students should bury their heads in books; they should engage themselves in theoretical studies." People like Lu Ping and Cheng Xiance faithfully carried out Liu Shaoqi's black directives. As soon as we entered Beijing University, they had bourgeois "professors" and "experts" open fire on us. In class, Wei Jiangong propagated Liu Shaoqi's "theory of the fusion of public and private." He said, "We study not only for the society but also for the individual." At the same time, he encouraged all of us to dig into the classics. And he wanted us all "to travel the road to scholarship." He also said, "The library is the temple of knowledge. You cannot go into the temple and return empty-handed." One "professor" deliberately publicized the notion of "studying and seeking fame with the religious vigor of a Sichuan monk visiting Guanyin in the South Sea." Cheng Xiance tempted us to become famous and scholarly by saying: "All of you must work hard. After graduation, you will be promoted to lecturers in three years, to assistant professors in five years." The traitor and Trotskyite, Wang Xiaoyu, who lectured on *The Analects,* boasted fearlessly, "I will change your personality after you study *The Analects.*" How insane and how venomous they are! They openly resisted Chairman Mao, and they tried hard to sidetrack us into doing evil by designing for us a "white expert" road of personal struggle for fame and profit.

In order to train successors to the bourgeoisie, they brought a large number of feudal dregs and bourgeois intellectuals to control our program.

Since 1959, when the program was established, we have had about thirty people from the school and outside giving us lectures. Among the thirty or so lecturers, there were anti-Party pioneers such as Wu Han; feudal "comprador" scholars such as the infamous author of *Studies on the Dream of the Red Chamber,* Yu Pingbo; bourgeois reactionaries like Gu Jiegang, who had been scorned by Lu Xun; reactionary "academic lords" like Feng Youlan and Wei Jiangong; member of the Qing dynasty royal family, Qi Gong; the traitor and Trotskyite Wang Xiaoyu; and the big Rightists Sun Yunbin and Wang Zhongmin. These so-called "experts" tightly controlled our program, vigorously selling such "black merchandise" as feudalism, capitalism, and revisionism and committing one evil act after another.

We have studied in the Professional Program in Classical Literature for five years and taken a total of twenty-five courses. Only five courses can be considered contemporary, and even three of those were superficial courses on politics (Party History, Political Economy, and Philosophy). Indeed, these courses were loaded with revisionist goods. Courses on the classical period accounted for 80 percent of the total. They once planned to force such poisonous feudal materials as *The Analects, Mencius, The Book of Odes, The Book of History, A Commentary on the Spring and Autumn Annals, The Book of Rites,* and *The*

Huai Nan Zi into students' minds without the slightest critical judgment. To their dismay, we finished only five of these because of the shortage of time. Regarding the heritage of our ancient culture, Chairman Mao teaches us: "We must respect our own history and never cut it apart. But this kind of respect is to give history a specific scientific value; it is also to respect the development of the dialectics of history. However, this does not mean we praise the historical past and denounce the present; in no way do we applaud feudal poison. For our proletarian masses and young students, the main point is not to guide them to look backward, but to lead them to look forward." Despite these teachings, a handful of Party-persons in power taking the capitalist road and the reactionary academic "authorities" have continued to disobey Chairman Mao's directive and used feudalistic, reactionary thinking to poison the young.

Take Wei Jiangong's *Philology, Phonetics, and Etymology* for example; four-fifths of the contents of his lectures were collected from the black goods of Qian Xuantong and Luo Changpei, who were scholars of the feudal class and the bourgeoisie. The entire contents are idealistic and get blacker and blacker. He once foolishly asked: "Why is the character for 'jade' written with a dot? Why doesn't the character for 'ten' have a hook? Why does the character for 'seven' have a hook? To understand all of this is to have great learning." This is ridiculous! What kind of "great learning" is this! Workers, peasants, and soldiers do not need these things! We, the revolutionary youth, will never play such word games.

The two courses "*Mencius*" and "*The Analects* of Confucius" were taught by Wang Xiaoyu, who is a traitor and a Trotskyite. Lu Ping's "Black Gang" treated this reactionary fellow like an honored guest. They made sure he was driven around in a limousine and treated him very attentively. Wang malevolently attacked the thought of Mao Zedong in the classroom: he maligned our most beloved leader, Chairman Mao. He openly made the ridiculous remarks: "Chairman Mao's phrase: 'To get rid of the old and bring out the new,' has the same meaning as what Confucius meant by: 'To know something new, review the old.'" "Chairman Mao's phrase: 'To integrate theory with practice,' has the same meaning as Confucius' phrase: 'Learning without thought is labor lost; thought without learning is useless.'" Lu Ping's "Black Gang" claimed that such an old rotten egg as this had "outstanding opinions" and allowed him to lecture for two years.

The "Bibliographic Editions and Exercises" class was first started by ultra-Rightist Wang Zhongmin. These lectures were based on a murderer, Zhang Zhitong, who suppressed peasant uprisings during the Qing dynasty and wrote *Questions and Answers in Bibliography.* Wang Zhongmin, a reactionary "authority," upheld his worthless book *Appendix to Questions and Answers on Bibliography,* and lectured on it for half a year. He shamelessly said, "After learning it, you can answer your friends' questions concerning the classics and recommend some titles." What a purposeless, muddle-headed fellow!

Lu Dingyi, Qi Yanming, Lu Ping, and their backstage manager, Liu Shaoqi, were, like all the rest of the reactionaries, scared to death of the bright and boundless thought of Mao Zedong. They listed works from as early as the Warring States period and as late as the May 4th Movement, including hundreds of classics of this period as our "required readings," yet not a single copy of the classics of Marxism-Leninism or a copy of Chairman Mao's works were on the list. They put the study of Chairman Mao's works outside of all regular classes in school. We are students of the Department of Chinese Language and Literature who have now spent five years in college, but we have yet to really systematically learn Mao Zedong's thought on literature and art; nor have we had systematic lectures on Chairman Mao's writings. They openly remarked: "Chairman Mao's works are studied for the purpose of quoting when writing essays; copying what others have used is sufficient and guarantees you will commit no errors." How vicious! Chairman Mao's works are the supreme directives in all our endeavors; whoever dares object to learning the works of Chairman Mao will be thrown down and his bones smashed to pieces!

All of this is the result of Liu Shaoqi's promotion of the counter-revolutionary, revisionist educational line! This small handful of counter-revolutionary revisionists has raised bourgeois academic "authorities" to great heights, allowing them to spread venom and poison among young students; thus, numerous youths have gradually become prisoners of the bourgeoisie. The black hearts of people like Liu Shaoqi are more venomous than a poisonous snake's.

3. The Cruel Suppression of Our Struggle

Wherever there is counter-revolutionary suppression, there is a revolutionary reaction. Wherever there is bourgeois restoration, there is a proletarian revolutionary struggle against restoration. No matter how great Liu Shaoqi's dark influence is, he can never cast a shadow over the brilliance of Mao Zedong Thought. The struggle of our fellow students in the program was never once interrupted. But Lu Ping's "Black Gang," with the support of the biggest Party-person in power taking the capitalist road, was madly suppressing our counter-attack. We boundlessly love Mao Zedong Thought; we boundlessly worship it; and we boundlessly believe in it. We can never tolerate the slander against our great leader by Wang Xiaoyu, the counter-revolutionary scholar. In 1963, we resolutely demanded the removal of Wang Xiaoyu, but Lu Ping's "Black Gang" immediately sent people to carry out the work of persuasion as soon as they heard the message. They said, "Mr. Wang's lectures can only be understood gradually. He puts a great deal of study into his subject, and his opinions are independently derived. Fellow students should give him an honest hearing." They shamelessly introduced us to the ideas they obtained from their study of "Mr. Wang," suppressing our revolutionary struggle under the banner of concern for youth. Later, in 1964, after undergoing the resolute struggle of their fellow students, they no longer dared allow Wang Xiaoyu to poison us.

Wei Jiangong's *Philology, Phonetics, and Etymology* was lectured on as if it were the word of God. No one understood it. When a number of students offered suggestions to him, he had temper tantrums. He scorned us when we were in class and threatened us with examinations. Whatever you asked him, that is what he examined you on; he was really irrational. Once, a fellow student in our class told him that his lectures were unsystematic. After hearing this, Wei Jiangong jumped around like a thunderbolt, yelling, "You say that mine is unacceptable; show me yours." He was indeed an absolute scoundrel. When Lu Ping's "Black Gang" heard about Wei Jiangong's tantrums, they hurriedly sent their dogs to threaten our fellow student, saying, "Wei Jiangong is a philologist second to none, within our country or abroad. Can you find someone else like him right now? If you cannot, then listen to him. If you don't understand him, you should learn to adapt to him; stick with him!" He is such a reactionary bourgeois "academic authority." Even so, the Lu Ping "Black Gang" proposed that he be promoted to "vice president" of our university in 1962. The Lu Ping "Black Gang" 's use of both force and persuasion on us was indeed carried to the extreme.

By 1964 we had already realized that the leadership of the Professional Program in Classical Literature was not in the hands of the proletariat, but rather in the hands of bourgeois reactionary "authorities." The direction of the program was not the direction of proletarian socialism, but rather the direction of bourgeois capitalism. We united several members of our class, League cadre brothers, and prepared some relevant materials to submit to the graduating class, the class of 1959, in an attempt to expose the class struggle and open fire on bourgeois "authorities." After the Lu Ping gang heard of it, they hurried to suppress it. They began by despicably using methods of sowing dissension and discord to undermine the united action among several of our classes; then they exerted tremendous pressure on us by saying, "Don't rebel against the policy of the Party," and, "Wei Jiangong is a high-level person of the united front." They would not permit us to start a revolution, to rebel. As for Wei Jiangong, the reactionary academic "lord," they allowed him to boast during the ceremony, "The Professional Program in Classical Literature started from nothing"; "It really represents the spirit of Daqing."[1] He spoke so extravagantly and without any sense of shame.

Facts clearly prove that the Party-persons in power taking the capitalist road, led by Liu Shaoqi, worked hand in hand with the reactionary "authorities" for the insane promotion of the counter-revolutionary, revisionist educational line and to surround the revolutionaries. Liu Shaoqi was indeed the head of the devils who poisoned the young on the educational front line.

4. The Evil Bonds of the Counter-revolutionary Revisionist Line

Liu Shaoqi repeatedly demanded that we "produce talents" and "put out experts." Let us examine what kind of "talents" were produced under the rule of his revisionist educational line.

Over the past seven years, although most of our fellow students were willing to follow Chairman Mao and engage in revolution, not a few of them were poisoned by feudalism and revisionism. In some people there still existed serious bourgeois individualist thinking. They

---

[1]The reference is to the Daqing oil fields, which the Party media said at the time had "started from nothing, yet achieved tremendous successes."

followed in the footsteps of bourgeois "professors" and devoted them-selves to their vocations without paying attention to politics. Even more seriously, some of them had even become reactionary students!

In the class of 1959, there was a student who had been brought up by the Party and who was originally a superior League cadre. After entering the Professional Program in Classical Literature, he changed day by day into a man without spirit. He alternated between "expert" and "scholar," devoting himself all day only to his vocation without paying any attention to politics. He even said that he would devote his "whole life and youth" and "total energy and time" to "a few lines of notes." When he got a fee for publication, he would forget his original nature in self-indulgence, get drunk, and beat up other people. What a serious case of "peaceful evolution" this was.

Another fellow student in the class of 1960 was of working-class family background. In his freshman and sophomore years, he still made political progress. But when he entered his fourth year, he told the Party branch, "The fourth year is a time for putting out good grades. I'll consider joining the Party later." In order to seek fame and profit, even the son of a worker abandoned his own political existence.

There was another youth in the class of 1959 who became very depressed and sick of life because of his failure to obtain "fame and profit." A youth of just a little over twenty years of age wrote his own epitaph—"I am dying slowly because of my inability to achieve fame."

These sad facts tell us that the Professional Program in Classical Literature of the Department of Chinese was a huge dyeworks. The reds went in and came out black. Lu Dingyi, Qi Yanming, Deng Tuo, Lu Ping, and their backstage boss, Liu Shaoqi, should be condemned to death for their promotion of the counter-revolutionary, revisionist educational line.

5. No Retreat Without Total Victory

Something suddenly happened. On 7 May 1966, Chairman Mao issued a great call to us. Chairman Mao said: "This holds good for students too. While their main task is to study, they should in addition to their studies learn other things, that is, industrial work, farming, and military affairs. They should also criticize the bourgeoisie. The school term should be shortened, education should be revolutionized, and the domi-nation of our schools by bourgeois intellectuals should not be allowed to continue."[2] Chairman Mao's directive pointed out the direction to us and illuminated our route. The Great Cultural Revolution, initiated and led by Chairman Mao, thoroughly crushed the plots and fantasies of a handful of people headed by Liu Shaoqi. It was the Party and Chairman Mao who saved the students in the Professional Program in Classical Literature. It was the Party and Chairman Mao who caused our fellow students in the Professional Program in Classical Literature to turn a new leaf. "The school term should be shortened, education should be revolutionized." This revolution will remain a part of our Great Proletarian Revolutionary cause for many hundreds and thousands of years to come. We, the entire student body of the fifth year (second) class declare to the Party that: We shall definitely raise high the great red banner of Mao Zedong Thought, thoroughly criticize the counter-revolutionary, revisionist educational line of Liu and Deng, and thoroughly smash the old educational system! We shall definitely extend the spirit of daring to think, daring to speak, daring to make revolution, and daring to rebel. We shall fight for a proletarian, socialist, and revolutionary educational system that raises high the great red banner of Mao Zedong Thought. We shall never retreat without total victory!

[2]"Letter to Comrade Lin Biao," translated in *Current Background,* No. 891, 8 October 1969, pp. 56–57.

F. The Economy

With a determination similar to that of the Western political scientist who *insists* that capitalism and "better times" invariably pave the way for democracy, so Mao Zedong had declared on the eve of the Great Leap Forward that skillful manipulation of the political levers of communism would create, without fail, an economy double-digiting toward relative comfort for all (*xiao kang*). In the Cultural Revolution he was quoted as saying: "Magnificent ideological and political flowers will inevitably bear bountiful economic fruit—such development is entirely in accordance with the laws."[1] The trick, according to the Chairman, was not to "grasp" (*zhua*) the economy directly, but to "promote" (*cu*) it through the intermediary of a radical revolution of the superstructure.

Once that revolution got under way, the substance of Mao's mediated development of the economy found its expression in unusual ways. When Red Guards first confiscated from "bourgeois" households in Beijing and Shanghai—and handed over to the state—more than five million U.S. dollars, this was described by Kang Sheng as a major event in the "class struggle in the economic realm."[2] Document 49 hints at what happened to the money and how, involuntarily, the "class enemy" ended up strengthening the hard currency reserves of the PRC.

The new Revolutionary Committees came down hard on all forms of market-related economic activities (Document 50). There was to be no competition, and the forces of "capitalist restoration" were to be quelled by force, once and for all. Then—so the theory had it—increasingly rapid economic development would follow with law-bound

---

[1] See below, Document 52. The remark originally appeared in a *People's Daily* editorial entitled "To Oppose Waste and Conservatism Is the Central Task of the Rectification Movement at Present," published on 18 February 1958.

[2] "Kang Sheng tongzhi zai Urumqi jiejian Xinjiang daxue geming shisheng shi de jianghua" (Comrade Kang Sheng's Speech at a Meeting in Urumqi with Teachers and Students from Xinjiang University) (15 November 1966), in Joint Editorial Group, ed., *Shouzhang jianghua xuanbian* (*Selected Speeches by the Leadership*) (N.p., 1967), p. 36.

certainty. In the end, the only means whereby an illusion of change for the better could be created were by saving and "practicing frugality." A warehouse inventory in Shanghai (Document 51) reveals the extent to which considerable savings were indeed possible yet says nothing about whether they were ever achieved. A remarkable report from the PLA General Logistics Department (Document 52) was no doubt originally meant to depict an army that took "thrift" very seriously, yet in retrospect it merely underscores the validity of recent observations that during the Cultural Revolution "there were serious shortages, . . . the utilization of equipment was in disarray, resource management was lax, and upkeep was seriously neglected."[3]

Official statistics (Document 53) released in the early 1980s paint a bleak picture of China's economy as a whole during the Cultural Revolution, defined here as the decade from 1966 to 1976. The years 1966–69 were disastrous, with a major decline in clear evidence on virtually every economic "front." Hereafter, Western economists maintain, ever higher levels of investment and energy input were used with decreasing efficiency. By the time Mao went to call on Karl Marx, China's economic development had all but stagnated completely.

---

[3]Li Ke and Hao Shengzhang, *"Wenhua dageming" zhong de renmin jiefangjun* (*The People's Liberation Army in the "Great Cultural Revolution"*) (Beijing: Zhonggong dangshi ziliao chubanshe, 1989), p. 282.

49

On How to Handle Foreign Currency, Foreign Currency Receipts, and Foreign Currency Securities Confiscated by Red Guards

State Council and People's Bank of China

Source: State Council Document *Guofawen* [1968] 23, dated 17 January 1968, entitled "Guowuyuan pizhuan 'Zhongguo renmin yinhang guanyu hongweibing chachao de waibi, waibi piaoju he waibi youjia zhengjian chuli wenti de baogao'." Our translation is of the full text as reprinted on 2 March 1968 in No. 58 of *Dou Pi Gai* (*Struggle Criticize Transform*), a daily bulletin edited by the Revolutionary Committee of the Beijing Institute of Politics and Law.

To all provincial, municipal, and autonomous regional Revolutionary Committees (including preparatory groups) and Military Control Commissions; all military regions and districts:

We are now distributing to you a report from the People's Bank of China entitled "On How to Handle Foreign Currency, Foreign Currency Receipts, and Foreign Currency Securities Confiscated by Red Guards." The State Council agrees with the proposals made by the People's Bank of China in this matter and hopes that you will study and implement the proposals.

[Original] appendix: *Report from the People's Bank of China on How to Handle Foreign Currency, Foreign Currency Receipts, and Foreign Currency Securities Confiscated by Red Guards*

To the State Council:

In the course of the Great Proletarian Cultural Revolution, the little Red Guard generals and revolutionary organizations of the masses have confiscated no small amount of foreign currencies, foreign currency receipts, and foreign currency securities. Some have already been deposited in banks, while others remain in the possession of various work units. Given the absence of a clear policy and the fact that the [political] status of the persons [whose possessions have been] confiscated still has to be confirmed, how to ultimately handle this matter has in most cases not been decided upon. In order not to further delay the utilization of these foreign exchange funds (*waihui zijin*) for China's socialist construction and in order not to incur any financial losses from [their possible] devaluation, we propose that the foreign currencies, foreign currency receipts, and foreign currency securities be sold and in this way transformed into utilizable (*kedong*) foreign exchange. Once the foreign exchange has been properly received it should, for domestic purposes, be converted into RMB according to the listed exchange rate and be retained by the banks. Once the [political] status of the persons from whom it has been confiscated has been confirmed, a decision will be made whether to expropriate or return it.

Practical procedures:

1. All of the foreign currencies, foreign currency receipts, and foreign currency securities already deposited in banks should be transferred abroad without delay. Once cashed or sold off, the [foreign exchange] should be converted into RMB and frozen, pending any further decision.

2. All of the foreign currencies, foreign currency receipts, and foreign currency securities still in the possession of work units should be collected by the banks and handled as under point 1 above.

3. Funds that, in accordance with the policy regulations of the Center, should be expropriated according to law are to be handed over in RMB to the state financial departments. Funds that, in accordance with the policies of the Center, should be returned [to the owner] are to be given back in RMB after having been unfrozen and once the proper formalities have been completed.

We ask that the above proposal, if deemed feasible, be sent out for implementation to all provincial, municipal, and autonomous regional Revolutionary Committees (including preparatory groups), Military Control Commissions, Military Regions and Districts.

People's Bank of China
20 January 1968

50
Public Notice on Cracking Down on Speculation and Strengthening Market Controls

Shanghai Municipal Revolutionary Committee

Source: This notice ("Guanyu daji touji daoba jiaqiang shichang guanli de tonggao") was circulated nationwide for reference purposes by the State Council and Central Military Commission on 18 August 1967. Our translation is based on the text reprinted in CCP Central Committee General Office and State Council General Office Joint Cultural Revolution Reception Office, ed., *Wuchanjieji wenhua dageming youguan wenjian huiji* (*Collection of Documents Concerning the Great Proletarian Cultural Revolution*), 5 vols. (Beijing, 1967–68), Vol. 3, pp. 282–88.

In its resolution "Fight to Strengthen the Dictatorship of the Proletariat" of 2 June 1967, the Shanghai Municipal Revolutionary Committee pointed out that "the unfolding of revolutionary big criticism should furthermore be integrated with a crackdown on capitalist forces active in society today, as well as with the struggle between the two roads." In order to strengthen the dictatorship of the proletariat, protect socialist construction, and guarantee the successful unfolding of the Great Proletarian Cultural Revolution, we must resolutely crack down on a variety of wicked trends set in motion by capitalist forces in urban and rural areas, including the practices of economism, independent [economic] operations (*dan'gan*), and speculation. In view of this, we issue the following notification:

1. Firmly crack down on speculation. The following kinds of activities by landlord, rich-peasant, counter-revolutionary, hooligan, Rightist elements, law-breaking bourgeois elements, and speculators all constitute criminal acts of sabotage against the socialist economy and the dictatorship of the proletariat and must be punished according to law: reselling goods and materials covered by the state purchase and marketing monopoly; reselling industrial and agricultural means of production; reselling gold, silver, industrial products, and ration coupons; rushing to purchase and forcing up the prices of [scarce commodities]; trafficking in goods over long distances; trading in nonexistent goods (*maikong maikong*); privately contracting con-

struction work; privately setting up workshops; employing and exploiting people; smuggling and bribing; and engaging in any and all other forms of speculation.

All those who come clean on their own initiative, who wash their hands and stay clean, may be dealt with leniently.

2. Illegal trade in industrial products and ration coupons is strictly forbidden. Places where such illegal exchange and illegal trade take place are to be shut down without exception.

3. Unlicensed traders and unlicensed craftsmen must suspend operations. No unlicensed traders or unlicensed craftsmen are allowed to operate in this municipality. Persons from other provinces or cities who have come to and reside in this municipality without the proper documentation and who engage in trades or crafts should promptly return to wherever they come from and participate in industrial or agricultural productive labor there. They are not permitted to continue their activities in this municipality.

4. Licensed individual traders and craftsmen operating in this municipality should fully respect the policies and laws of the state and accept socialist transformation. They should not without authorization expand the scope of their economic activities or put up unauthorized stalls. They may not engage in such law-breaking activities as labeling second-rate merchandise first-rate, raising retail prices, or refusing to pay state taxes.

5. Strengthen control over trade at rural markets. The sale at rural markets of state unified purchase goods and materials such as grain, cotton, oils, tobacco, hemp, etc., is strictly forbidden. It is strictly forbidden for traders to interfere with market operations or to speculate. To give up farming for the sake of trading is not permitted, nor is operating as an itinerant salesman in streets and lanes. Price controls are to be strengthened, and there must be no bargaining or driving up of prices.

6. Cooperative shops and handicraft cooperatives must consciously respect the policies and laws of the state and accept socialist transformation.

Enterprises run by People's Communes and production teams and production and service organizations run by [urban] neighborhoods must adhere to the socialist direction. They must not compete with the state for raw materials or markets. They are not permitted to engage in irresponsible cooperation or sabotage the national plan. Even less permissible is it for them to engage in speculation.

7. The following kinds of people must all be dealt with seriously: Those who resist control, those who act in a provocative way deliberately, those who counter-attack to settle scores, and those who violently retaliate against, besiege, beat up, or kidnap market management cadres or revolutionary masses. Leading elements, backstage manipulators, and assailants must be punished according to the law by political and legal departments.

8. Public security departments and political and legal departments must cooperate with the Industry and Commerce Administration in resolutely cracking down on speculation. Post and telecommunications departments and transport departments as well as bus stations and train stations and harbors are to give prominence to proletarian politics, heighten vigilance, and keep things under control. Banks and tax departments are to strengthen their supervision of financial activities and taxation. The various commercial departments are to stand firm in their control of the socialist front and cooperate in order to control the marketplace.

9. The Industry and Commerce Administration is an arm of the dictatorship of the proletariat that protects the socialist economy and upholds the socialist market order (*shehuizhuyi shichang zhixu*). Market management cadres must hold high the great red banner of Mao Zedong Thought, study and apply Chairman Mao's works in a living way, give prominence to proletarian politics, stand fast at their posts, and correctly implement and carry out the long-term and short-term policies of the Party. They must keep close links with the revolutionary masses and the organizations of the proletarian revolutionaries and wage a resolute struggle against capitalist forces.

10. Work units, organizations of the broad revolutionary masses and proletarian revolutionaries, revolutionary little Red Guard generals, the revolutionary masses, and revolutionary cadres throughout the municipality should all extensively propagate Mao Zedong Thought, propagate the long-term and short-term policies of the Party, and actively cooperate with the Industry and Commerce Administration in controlling and informing against acts of speculation, in shutting down unregistered businesses, in waging a resolute struggle against capitalist forces in society, and in strengthening the dictatorship of the proletariat.

(This notification may be reprinted and posted in public.)

51
Warehouse Inventory Work in Shanghai—A Survey

Municipal Warehouse Inventory Group

Source: This is a translation of "Guanyu Shanghai shi qingcang gongzuo qingkuang de jieshao" as published by the Chinese Academy of Sciences Revolutionary Committee Warehouse Inventory Office in *Yao jieyue nao geming* (*Practice Thrift While Making Revolution*) (Beijing, 1969), pp. 9–10.

1. Warehouse Inventory Work in the Past: Situation and Problems

In 1966, we carried out a triple checkup [of equipment, materials, and floating funds (*liudong zijin*) in enterprises and institutions[1]], and in August this year we also made an inventory of warehouses. In the past, when making warehouse inventories, we employed the same old methods, i.e. mobilizing a handful of people from above to check the records and to produce some figures. It was all very much done in quiet isolation, and the results were neither penetrating nor particularly thorough. Once the figures had been sent to the commodity departments, they would form the basis for comprehensive balancing and overall redistribution, but not many problems were solved. At lower levels, there was always plenty of criticism. The situation was one of overstocked items continuing to fill the warehouses and scarce items remaining in short supply. The masses say: "Warehouse inventory work like that is just a lot of scholasticism." During this year's warehouse inventory in August, many units at lower levels did nothing. Although the commodity departments took limited action, they too were less than committed. In the opinion of the municipal leadership, in this way, work will never really take off. As production reaches and sur-

---

[1]Cf. Central Document *Zhongfa* [1966] 48: "CCP Center and State Council Circular with Comment Containing a Report from the State Planning Commission on Opposing Waste, Practicing Frugality, Embarking upon a 'Triple Checkup,' and Retrieving Scrap Metal" dated 16 January 1966 and summarized in Ma Qibin et al., eds., *Zhongguo gongchandang zhizheng sishi nian 1949–1989* (*The CCP Forty Years in Power, 1949–1989*) (Beijing: Zhonggong dangshi chubanshe, 1989), p. 267.

passes the level of 1966, the commodity contradiction will only get worse and worse and may one day even impede production. Consequently, in mid-September, preparations got under way for a new warehouse inventory.

2. Summarizing the Experiences Gained
This Time Around

a. Putting Chairman Mao's latest directive into practice
and having the working class lead the work of carrying
out warehouse inventories.

Once Chairman Mao's latest directive "The working class must exercise leadership in everything" had been published, the leading members of the municipal Party Committee ordered Workers' Mao Zedong Thought Propaganda Teams to be dispatched to the commodity departments to make warehouse inventories. This time around, the warehouse inventory was formally launched on 7 October. Responsibility for inventory work in industry was put in the hands of the municipal departments in charge of the various industrial sectors. The municipal [Revolutionary Committee] itself has taken direct charge of four key units: the East China Commodity Bureau, the Shanghai Municipal Commodity Bureau (means of production), the Foreign Trade Bureau, and the Bureau of Commerce (means of subsistence). A team of some 120 persons was organized and led by the Industry and Communications Group and Finance and Trade Group of the municipal Revolutionary Committee. The team mainly consists of members of Workers' Mao Zedong Thought Propaganda Teams (half of the membership). In addition, production workers were transferred from their jobs (to make up one-quarter of the membership), as were cadres with the various bureaus and commodity departments, in order to make it a "three-in-one" combination. All in all, about three-fourths of the members of this team are either from workers' propaganda teams or factory workers, and this fully expresses the leadership of the working class. Cadres take part only to give advice (*qi canmou zuoyong*). The team is divided into numerous small groups, each led by a comrade from and acting in the name of the Workers' Propaganda Teams (when entering the higher and lower levels of each sector). The might of the working class has made a big impact on warehouse inventory work. Workers do not abide by conventions: They are utterly unselfish, possess a strong fighting spirit, and are good at interacting with the masses. In the municipality of Shanghai, the commodity departments constitute "old, major, and complex" problems. In the past, they always insisted that their statistics were classified, that their work was special, and that therefore they should not be interfered with. This time around, some members of the East China Commodity Bureau Revolutionary Committee were extremely resentful toward the Workers' Propaganda Team sent down from the [municipal] Revolutionary Committee and failed to respect the worker comrades, citing the fact that the statistics were classified as a pretext and refusing to provide information. The members of the Workers' Propaganda Team relied on the broad revolutionary masses—the basic-level revolutionary masses in particular—of the unit in question and launched a tit-for-tat struggle against the minority on the Bureau Revolutionary Committee. The worker comrades said: "You say the information is secret: secret from whom? We intend to stir up this hornet's nest of yours. We're not going to let you keep these things secret." With the support of the broad masses, they overcame the quiet isolation that had characterized warehouse inventory work in the past and set a vigorous and dynamic movement in motion.

b. One has to implement the class line and launch a large-scale mass movement, starting from below and using the lower levels to set the higher levels in motion.

First of all, one has to get a firm grip on the mobilization of the basic-level masses by engaging them in person-to-person contacts. Once the mass movement is under way at the basic level, it should be used to set the higher levels in motion. Having entered the basic-level work units, the small groups of the Workers' Propaganda Team should rely on the broad revolutionary rebel masses to grasp, first of all, propaganda and mobilization work. They should make extensive propaganda directed at the masses and by way of mobilization rallies and various kinds of informal meetings propagate Mao Zedong Thought among the broad revolutionary masses, and make the masses realize the political meaning of warehouse inventory work by discussing the excellent situation in revolution and production. Once the masses have come to an ideological realization and have been mobilized, warehouse inventory work becomes a self-conscious act on the part of each individual member of the revolutionary masses (*meige geming qunzhong*). Their enthusiasm and creativity fully mobilized, warehouse inventory work gets under way on a wide and penetrating scale. They vie with each other in exposing problems, explaining the situation, providing documentation, and checking records the mass way. In this way, a vigorous and dynamic warehouse inventory mass movement takes shape at the basic level. While doing a good job of mobilizing the masses at the basic level, the Workers' Propaganda Teams also grasp the ideological guidance and arousal of the leading members of higher-level Revolutionary Committees (Bureaus or Corporations). In this way, the mobilized basic-level masses give an impetus to work at higher levels. The various levels come together in a high tide of overall mobilization. The results achieved in this way by the East China Commodity Bureau are outstanding. The "old, major, and complex" problems are finally being dealt with, and warehouse inventory work is proceeding in a way that is both penetrating and thorough. Many problems have been attacked. There has been a thorough investigation of the situation with respect to overstocking and waste of state capital and funds. For instance: There is extensive overstocking of machinery and electrical equipment, to the extent that overstocked items—including scrapped and obsolete items—occupy one-fifth of the total reserve. There is imported steel, paid for with foreign currency, that was purchased in tons but is being used only by the kilo. As a result, it is overstocked in amounts close to ten thousand tons. There is one kind of imported steel the overstocking of which is so enormous that, at current consumption figures, supplies are likely to last for a thousand years. The worker comrades ask in anger: "Why have they imported too much of this stuff and wasted our country's foreign exchange?" Some commodities have been overstocked for more than ten years and have already rotted and gone to waste. One piece of equipment originally cost 380,000 yuan; now it can at best be sold as scrap for 1,200 yuan. The worker comrades working in the warehouse also say in anger: "We have cars here who were unmarried girls when they came in, but who will have become old women before they leave." The big mass movement has not only led to a thorough inventory of the warehouses and the utilization of previously underutilized commodities; it has also permitted the utilization of previously underutilized storage space. In the past, many work units under the Shanghai municipality complained about a lack of storage space and asked for the government to provide additional warehouses. In the course of the present storage inventory, it was discovered that quite a few warehouses were excessively specialized and characterized by "selfish departmentalism." There was a considerable amount of empty storage space and the actual utilization rate was only 20–25 percent.

Our experience shows that: As long as one begins by mobilizing the basic-level masses and does a good job of the movement at the basic level, warehouse inventory work can be carried out quite thoroughly and in depth. On the other hand, as illustrated by what happened in the Foreign Trade Bureau, if one does not begin at the basic level but starts at the top—the Bureau and Corporation—then warehouse inventory work will not make good progress and remains unsatisfactory to this day.

c. Integrating warehouse inventory work and revolutionary great criticism.

Quite a few worker comrades, including some with the Workers' Propaganda Team, originally thought that warehouse inventory work was only an economic task that did not involve class struggle. Some comrades with the Workers' Propaganda Team maintained: We are out to grasp the class struggle, so why let us do economic work? In the course of this warehouse inventory, huge problems were discovered, and they drove home the point that the struggle between the two lines in commodity work is sharp and complicated: Warehouse inventory work is not merely a matter of sorting out commodities, but more important a profound class education. Quite a few comrades exposed and denounced the revisionist system of checks, blocks, and pigeonholing carried out by Liu, Deng, and Bo [Yibo] in the commodity sector. This revisionist system led to the freezing of commodities and the disengagement of the commodity departments from the production departments. Against the background of what they witnessed, some production workers insisted on being told: "Why do you insist on hoarding these things? Don't you know how badly they are needed in the production sector?" The commodity departments know only about storing things; they don't know how to keep them in good repair. Nobody asks how long things are being stored. In some cases they are simply left to rot and deteriorate. The masses say angrily: We must absolutely smash this revisionist system to pieces. We must launch a revolutionary great criticism on the basis of this warehouse inventory and thoroughly denounce and eradicate the pernicious influence of the revisionist system of checks, blocks, and pigeonholing carried out by Liu, Deng, and Bo.

23 October 1968

52
Situation Report (1968) on Thrift Within the Armed Forces

PLA General Logistics Department

Source: This report ("1968 nian quanjun shixing jieyue de qingkuang baogao") was ratified by Mao Zedong and Lin Biao and circulated throughout the national military, government, and party bureaucracies as Central Document *Zhongfa* [1968] 9 on 14 February 1969. Our translation is based on the text reprinted in Hubei Provincial Revolutionary Committee, ed., *Wuchanjieji wenhua dageming wenjian huibian* (*Collected Documents from the Great Proletarian Cultural Revolution*) (Wuhan, 1969), Vol. 3, pp. 1242–52.

In 1968, the entire army implemented our great leader Chairman Mao's great directive "Practice frugality while making revolution." Our attempts to economize have been very successful. According to initial calculations, the size of the administrative costs (e.g., money spent on miscellaneous office items, water and electricity, heating, business travel, and barracks maintenance) saved by the army as a whole amounted to more than n hundred million yuan (corresponding to 30 percent of the army's total administrative costs). The army also saved more than n hundred million *jin* of grain and recycled large amounts of old equipment, hereby saving goods and matériel in huge quantities. Army units have begun to repair equipment themselves, hereby further cutting down significantly on expenditures. The combined value of the expenditures, goods, and materials saved in this way amounts to roughly 296.15 million yuan RMB.

In 1968, the Great Proletarian Cultural Revolution gave a new impetus to our attempts to economize, which in turn led to the emergence of new phenomena. In our economizing, we gave prominence to proletarian politics and took class struggle as the key link. Everyone is of the opinion that to be hard working and thrifty and to practice frugality are important integral parts of the implementation of Chairman Mao's proletarian revolutionary line. This may be summed up in three aspects: First, a matter of awareness. It is by no means the case that leading organs at all levels, or even the companies themselves, do not have any money or that the system is literally strangling them to death. On the contrary, what has happened is that Party Committees at all levels have reduced the extent of their departmental selfishness and adopted more of an overall point of view. Expenditures have been cut as a result of this increased awareness. Second, the mass aspect. In order to do any and all work well, the masses have to be mobilized and relied upon. Once the political awareness of the masses has been raised, their sense of responsibility will increase; and once they have a good working style, everyone will be sure to "practice frugality while making revolution." Third, consistency between higher and lower levels. In the past, the supply system was characterized by many irrational rules and regulations, and the contradiction between higher and lower levels was very pronounced. The system was not only not able to guarantee that frugality was practiced; on the contrary, it even encouraged waste. After 1965, the long-term policy of pure "control" (*guan*) was changed to "the Party Committee manages household affairs [*dangjia*], and the army as a whole handles logistics." Quite a few irrational rules and regulations in the financial system were altered as a consequence. As far as administrative costs are concerned, a system of responsibility (*baogan banfa*) has been introduced. This has led to a mobilization of initiative throughout the army and the "great" public (*gong*) has now become united with the "small" public.

The army-wide drive to economize is rich in content. Below, we merely account for some of its key points.

1. Cutting down on expenditure. Observing Chairman Mao's teaching "Every copper coin we save can be used in the war effort, for our revolutionary cause, and for the sake of economic construction" and the relevant regulations of the Center concerning the need to curtail expenditure, all army units remain hard working and thrifty, make careful calculations, maintain strict budgets, and strive to spend less while doing more, or even doing well and doing better without spend-

ing more. While still guaranteeing war preparedness and supplies, the army as a whole has succeeded in cutting down administrative costs by *n* hundred million yuan. It has frozen funds totaling *n* hundred million yuan. All army units are firmly implementing policy, and after the Center issued its "Urgent Notification" on 18 February 1968 about further practicing thrift while making revolution, they promptly adopted a variety of effective measures, hereby cutting down on administrative costs by 30 percent.[1]

2. Saving on goods and matériel. All army units have conscientiously implemented Chairman Mao's directive about how "in everything we do, we should follow the principle of frugality," and have aggressively utilized latent potential in every area. This past year, they have saved extensively on goods and matériel.

a. They have saved 330,000 tons of coal. In order to reduce the amount of coal spent on heating, steam-carried heat has been extensively converted to water-carried heat. Coal-burning methods have been much improved, and the coal energy-utilization factor has been raised from about 40 or 50 percent to about 70 or 80 percent. A number of army units employ makeshift heating stoves or heating walls [*sic*] and in this way have been able to reduce the average amount of coal spent on heating one square meter of floor space from two *liang* to about one *liang*. Units of the railway corps based at higher elevations where the temperature remains low have made extensive use of makeshift air channels from brick kitchen stoves to chimneys for heating purposes. By not setting up [separate] heating stoves, they are able to save on coal and firewood. Room temperatures remain even, and the rooms stay cleaner. The successful reduction of the amount of coal spent on cooking is even more remarkable. An absolute majority of units have already reduced it from a daily one *jin* per person to about five or six *liang*. Army

---

[1]The reference is to CCP Central Document *Zhongfa* [1968] 31: "Zhonggong Zhongyang, Guowuyuan, Zhongyang junwei, Zhongyang wenge guanyu jinyibu jieyue nao geming, jianjue jieyue kaizhi de jinji tongzhi" (Urgent Notification of the CCP Center, State Council, Central Military Commission, and Central Cultural Revolution Group on Further Practicing Thrift While Making Revolution and Firmly Curtailing Expenditure), in Chinese People's Liberation Army Nanjing Unit No. 825, ed., *Wuchanjieji wenhua dageming wenjian huibian* (*Collected Documents from the Great Proletarian Cultural Revolution*) (N.p., 1969), pp. 382–87.

units have made a variety of improvements to their kitchen stoves and have been successful not only in saving more and more coal, but also in reducing the time spent preparing meals. In the past, it took on average two hours to prepare a meal; now, thanks to the improved stoves, it normally takes only an hour or so.

b. They have saved *n* hundred million *jin* of grain, which corresponds to 4.83 percent of the total amount of grain used by the army. All army units have conscientiously implemented Chairman Mao's teaching: "We must keep a very firm grip on the issue of saving grain. Supplies must be rationed, and while people should be allowed to eat more when busy, they must also eat less when idle." Many [grain-growing] production corps have harvested bumper crops, yet have not forgotten that elsewhere other units may have suffered crop failures. They still practice frugality and remain firmly in control of four crucial links (e.g., procurement, transport, management, and use) so as to prevent losses and waste. A majority of army units in the Guangzhou, Shenyang, Ji'nan, and Nanjing military regions have saved about 9 to 12 percent on standard grain rations.

c. They have saved more than 7,100 tons of steel, 57,000 cubic meters of timber, and 30,000 tons of cement, and have recycled more than 8,000 tons of scrap metal. The railway corps has substituted angle steel and fibre board for reinforcing bars when constructing activity buildings (*huodong fangwu*) and has in this way been able to save more than 1,170 tons of steel. Engineering units constructing fortifications in the Guangzhou Military Region are now excavating and roofing simultaneously and are in this way able to save some 60 percent of the timber previously used for reinforcement purposes, as well as reduce construction time. Air force units constructing airports in . . . add plasticity pellets to the cement they use and have in this way been able to save some 6,880 tons of cement.

d. According to incomplete statistics provided by eleven different units, the army has saved more than 6,000 tons of oil. The use of vehicles has become subject to better planning. When two corps in the Guangzhou Military Region traded places, thanks to careful planning and careful dispatching, the use of vehicles was kept down by some 20,000 instances equal to more than 12 million vehicle miles. Regiment XXX in the Beijing Military Region came up with a number of ways to reduce the distances that its vehicles run empty and has now been able to achieve a 60 to 70 percent utilization rate of returning vehicles. When training new drivers, the military now generally follows the practice of "training while transporting" and has in this way been able to reduce the amount of gasoline necessary to train one driver from 254 kilo to some 50 kilo. After one month of training, new drivers are capable of executing tasks singlehandedly. By improving the techniques used to operate construction machinery, the army has been able to save oil. Regiment XXX in the Beijing Military Region was able to bring down the average amount of oil used to excavate to a depth of one meter from 26.7 kilo in 1967 to 12.8 kilo in 1968.

e. Remarkable results have been achieved in recovering and recycling old supplies. The combined savings achieved this past year by recycling old and discarded bedding and clothing and by issuing fewer new items totaled 23,400 million yuan. Recovered items include 8 million *jin* of cotton cloth and 160,000 *jin* of cotton. Some 2.7 million old and discarded items of bedding and clothing have been mended by the various army units. An additional 2.78 million items of bedding, clothing, etc., have been either recycled or converted. The number of new athletic shoes and cotton-lined shoes issued has gone down by some 1.09 million pairs, and the number of new unlined garments issued has gone down by 42,000. Throughout the Shenyang Military Region, the practice of employing foamed plastic rather than cotton cloth to clean firearms has been popularized, and in this way it has been possible to save some 240,000 meters of cotton cloth. The army as a whole has been able to recover from old epaulets and old cap insignia some 6,972 *liang* of gold and 64 tons of brass.

3. Cutting down on repair and maintenance costs. Very many army units have adopted the revolutionary spirit of daring to think, daring to act, and daring to be creative. They repair and maintain their equipment themselves, and now arms and vehicles stay with the division, or on the island, even while major service is being performed. This past year, army units themselves performed major and medium service on 6,200 vehicles, or about 33.2 percent of the total number of vehicles in need of service. In this way they were able to save 1,200 yuan per vehicle in repair costs. Also, the nonuse time of a vehicle being serviced was reduced from forty to ten days. According to the statistics from *n* military regions, army units have themselves performed major and medium service on *n* thousand cannons, *n*-ten thousand firearms,

and *n* thousand pieces of optical equipment. In the Shenyang Military Region, cannons no longer leave the division while major service is being performed. Last year, none of the *n* thousand cannons in need of service were sent back to the plant, but were serviced by the army units themselves. The repair and maintenance crews based in the . . . fortification sector broke with superstition and carried out bold reforms and have in the past year serviced twenty-two cannons themselves. In the past, it took six months from the time cannons were sent off to the plant for service to the time they returned, and each service cost 6,000 yuan. Now the cannons are serviced in ten days, and each service costs only 500 yuan. The army has promoted self-service and self-repair on a broad scale and in this way not only saved large amounts of money and manpower but, more important, strengthened war preparedness and solved even more effectively the problem of [cannons actually] "functioning and hitting the target."

4. Cutting down on engineering costs. Defense engineering works and basic construction projects depend on meticulous design and meticulous construction. One furthermore has to use one's own hands, adopt measures suited to local conditions, and draw on local resources. While guaranteeing quality, the army has reduced building costs and equipment expenditure as much as possible and in this way succeeded in saving some 2.274 million yuan in construction and barracks maintenance costs. The new barracks constructed last year on average cost between 30 and 35 yuan per square meter of floor space, which is between 5 and 10 percent less than in 1967. The supply of ordinary building materials not subject to unified state distribution (e.g., bricks, tiles, lime) has been resolved by the army units themselves. An absolute majority of army units construct ordinary barracks and garages by themselves. Army units in the Shenyang, Ji'nan, Guangzhou, Wuhan, Lanzhou, and Xinjiang military regions, as well as a majority of navy and air force units have, according to incomplete statistics, built and repaired 800,000 square meters of barracks and storehouses themselves. Two regiments with the South China Fleet swiftly resolved their housing problem by going into the mountains to cut firewood and timber and by constructing more than 20,000 square meters of thatched shacks themselves without spending hardly any money at all.

5. Coming up with new ways of saving. Army units everywhere have been innovative and have come up with many new ways of saving. In addition to widespread technical innovative activities such

as self-maintenance, self-manufacture, and self-construction, factories everywhere have set off a high tide of technical innovation and technical revolution. According to statistics provided by eighteen factories, through technical innovation and improved equipment, the degree of mechanization and automation has been increased by the equivalent of a labor force of 2,040 persons. Some 1,035 technical innovations were recorded in factories serving the needs of the army last year. Production processes in quite a few bedding factories have already been interlinked (*liandonghua*) or semi-automated, and this has resulted in an n-fold increase in productivity. In one bedding factory, production processes have now been automated and semi-automated by 40 percent, and work efficiency in the production of cotton-padded clothes is more than twice as high as it used to be. In one optical instrument factory, a mass movement of technical innovation and technical revolution resulted in the successful design and test-manufacture of China's first . . . multipurpose distance measuring device with an n magnification factor and capable of measuring distances to targets within an n-thousand-meter range. The . . . chemical factory has manufactured China's first combined automatic high-frequency heat-joiner, which allows for a fourfold increase in efficiency when producing [plastic] covers for the "Treasured Red Books."

Chairman Mao's profound teachings tell us that "Magnificent ideological and political flowers will inevitably bear bountiful economic fruit—such development is entirely in accordance with the laws." The achievements of the entire army through hard work and thrift are the bountiful fruits of the living study and living application of Mao Zedong Thought and strengthened ideological revolutionization in the course of the Great Proletarian Cultural Revolution by the broad officers and men. It is a great victory for Chairman Mao's proletarian revolutionary line. Guided by all the latest directives issued by Chairman Mao, an army-wide movement to economize is surging ahead. Recently Chairman Mao personally ratified the circulation of the Beijing Military Region Party Committee's "Report on the Implementation of Our Great Leader Chairman Mao's Great Directive 'Practice Thrift While Making Revolution'," hereby greatly encouraging and greatly motivating the broad officers and men of the entire army.[2] The military regions and various service arms all express their determina-

---

[2]We have not been able to locate a copy of this report.

tion to add to their achievements, overcome shortcomings, and do an even better job of economizing, and to repay with new and outstanding achievements our great leader Chairman Mao's profound concern.

In the army, signs of waste are still quite widespread and in some cases quite serious. In view of this, we must definitely strive to do a good job of adding to our achievements and overcoming shortcomings and errors.

From now on, we must hold the great red banner of Mao Zedong Thought even higher, give prominence to proletarian politics, and execute our professional tasks well. We must excel in being economical and strive, in everything we do, to be diligent and conscientious, hard working and thrifty, and industrious and ingenious.

> The General Logistics Department of the
> Chinese People's Liberation Army
> 3 January 1969

53
Concerning the Speed of Economic Development during the Ten Years of Domestic Turmoil

State Statistical Bureau

Source: This is a translation of "Dui shinian neiluan shiqi jingji fazhan sudu de yixie fenxi," a document produced "for reference purposes" by the State Statistical Bureau and published in CCP Central Secretariat Research Office Economy Group, ed., *Jingji wenti yanjiu ziliao* (*Research Materials on Economic Problems*) (1983–1984) (Beijing: Zhongguo caizheng jingji chubanshe, 1986), pp. 217–20.

Untold damage was done to the national economy during the ten years of domestic turmoil, and yet the speed of development remained fairly high. How is this possible? Do the statistics reflect what actually happened? Our tentative analysis of this problem is as follows:

1. The development of industry and agriculture during this period was actually not very rapid.

During the ten-year period from 1967 to 1976, the gross output value of industry and agriculture grew by an annual average of 7.1 percent, which is less than the annual average of 8.5 percent recorded during the fourteen-year period from 1953 to 1966. The growth rate of industry was only 8.4 percent, which is less than the annual average of 12.9 percent of the earlier period. The net annual average growth rate of the gross output value of industry was 7.2 percent, which is far less than the 13.6 percent of the earlier period.

2. There is tremendous annual fluctuation.

As a result of the nationwide violence instigated by Lin Biao and the "Gang of Four," quite a few enterprises suspended work and/or production, and this led to an annual decrease in the combined gross output value of industry and agriculture in 1967 and 1968 by 9.6 percent and 4.2 percent respectively. In 1974–76, the anti-Lin anti-Confucius movement and so-called "Movement to beat back the Right-deviationist wind to reverse correct verdicts" launched by the "Gang of Four" reduced the annual average growth rate of the combined gross output value of industry and agriculture to less than 2 percent. This is to say that during four of the ten years, the economy stagnated or even retrogressed. If we look at the years when growth was relatively rapid, we find that the 23.8 percent figure for 1969 in fact constitutes a recovery from the decline in the gross output value of industry and agriculture over the preceding two years. The 25.7 percent growth in 1970 and the 12.2 percent growth in 1971 reflect mainly the massive investment in construction along the "Big Third Front," which resulted in a growth in heavy industry. The 11.9 percent growth in 1975 came about as a result of comrade Deng Xiaoping's leadership of the work of the Center, where he put a priority on economic rectification and saw to it that order was restored in production. The fluctuation in production throughout the period basically reflects the changing political and economic situation at the time.

3. The energy sector quickly took off and helped support the development of industry.

During the ten years, rapid development of oil extraction capabilities resulted in an annual average growth rate of 9.2 percent in the production of nonrenewable energy (including an annual average growth rate of 18.1 percent in crude oil production). This was more than the 8.4

percent annual average growth rate of the gross output value of industry during the same period.

The developing oil industry not only generated a relatively abundant energy supply for economic development, but in itself also provided the petrochemical industry with raw material. This, in turn, had quite a big impact upon the speed at which the gross output value of industry increased. By 1976, the gross output value of the oil industry had reached 20.1 billion yuan, or a level 2.8 times that of 1966. If we add to this the gross output value of the petrochemical industry, then the rate of increase becomes even greater. For instance, in 1966, the amount of crude oil processed in Shanghai municipality had been 1.154 million tons; by 1976, this amount had grown to 4.472 million tons. This led to an 8.8–fold increase in the output of ethylene and a 1.6–fold increase in the output of chemical fibres. The development of the petrochemical industry also provided the light industry and textile industry sectors with plenty of raw materials, which allowed the gross output value of the Shanghai textile industry to grow by 46 percent even though the supply of cotton did not increase.

4. "Speed" during this period was in pursuit of empty glory and resulted in many real disasters.

First of all, a high rate of accumulation was pursued at the expense of people's livelihood. The average accumulation rate during these ten years was 30.3 percent, compared to 27 percent during the previous fourteen years. During the earlier period, some 69 percent of the total had consisted of productive accumulation (*shengchanxing jilei*); during these ten years, that figure was as high as 77 percent. The grand total of productive accumulation over the ten-year period was 458.8 billion yuan, or 45.88 billion yuan/year, which is more than twice the 21.7 billion yuan/year average of the previous fourteen years. Since accumulation was achieved at the expense of consumption, and productive accumulation was achieved at the expense of nonproductive accumulation, the urban and rural standard of living (*xiaofei shuiping*) grew by an annual average of only 1.9 percent. The real wage level of state-owned enterprise employees went down by 6.5 percent between 1966 and 1976. In sectors like culture, education, public health, urban facilities, residential housing, employment, etc., there were countless outstanding accounts and the problems were simply allowed to pile up unresolved.

Second, the economy developed in an irrational fashion, causing serious imbalances. During those ten years, great efforts were made to develop the heavy industrial sector and steel production in particular. The proportion contributed by heavy industry to the combined gross output value of industry and agriculture went up from 32.7 percent in 1966 to 38.9 percent in 1976. Within heavy industry itself, "the head was heavy while the feet were light." The excavation industry grew by an annual average of 7.2 percent; the raw material industry grew by an annual average of 7.8 percent; and the manufacturing industry grew by an annual average of 11.6 percent. The excavation industry engaged in the "plundering" of resources and in the oil sector, the reserve and production ratio went down from 73.4 in 1966 to 15.6 in 1976. The period of profitable output of coal in mines under unified central planning decreased from 8.7 to 6.8 months. Agriculture developed slowly, and the proportion it contributed to the combined gross output value of industry and agriculture decreased from 35.9 percent in 1966 to 30.4 percent in 1976. In agriculture, the focus remained almost exclusively one of grain, at the expense of cash crops and economic diversification. Production of cotton, peanuts, sesame, etc., all declined to varying extents.

Third, there was a notable decline in economic efficiency. During these ten years, the average per capita income increased by a mere 1.9 percent annually, which was far less than the 5.4 percent annual average of the earlier fourteen years. One hundred yuan of productive accumulation generated only 18 yuan of national income, which was 61 percent less than the 46 yuan average of the earlier fourteen years. The fixed-asset payment utilization rate was on average 59.8 percent, far less than the 76.9 percent of the earlier fourteen years. Huge numbers of projects never got more than halfway done. By the end of 1976, engineering projects under construction absorbed 71.6 billion yuan of investments. Whereas each ton of energy spent generated 782 yuan of national income in 1966, that figure had declined by more than a third to 507 yuan by 1976. Between 1966 and 1976, the amount of profits and taxes handed over by state-owned industrial enterprises constituting independent accounting units declined from 34.5 yuan to 19.3 yuan for each 100 yuan of capital. The intactness of equipment in large numbers of enterprises declined.

5. Statistical figures from this period must be taken with "a grain of salt," since statistics work at lower levels was sabotaged, enterprise management was chaotic, and quality control was not stringent.

Guided by "Leftist" ideology, some industrial enterprises, for example, set out merely to raise output value without taking quality or product ranges into consideration. As a result, they produced products that were poor in quality, high in price, and for which there was no market. Very many "support agriculture" products soon turned out to be "undermine agriculture" products. Having remained overstocked in the warehouses for years, they could in the end only be scrapped or otherwise sold at a loss. The total financial loss incurred in this way amounted to approximately 20 billion yuan, or approximately 40 billion yuan if expressed in terms of gross output value of industry. These scrapped products were accumulated over a ten-year period and included some from before the decade of turmoil as well as imported products. The true state of affairs with respect to products of poor quality that have already found some use in production or construction is hard to estimate and also difficult to account for.

The above shows that during the ten years of domestic turmoil, our country's economy took the road of high accumulation, low consumption, and diminishing returns. While it may appear as if the speed of development was not slow, the after-effects were and remain very serious. Although the quality of the statistics from this period is far from good, the above figures nonetheless approximate reality and do reflect, on the whole, the changing political and economic trends at the time.

G. Mutual Perceptions:
Chinese and Western

Why is it that Westerners and Chinese alike tend to regard the perception of themselves by the other as skewed and distorted, while at the same time insisting that their own picture of the other is essentially accurate? Western attempts to explain the supposed inability of the Chinese to perceive us the way we "really are" tend to fall back on the notion of culture, as in Lucian W. Pye's claim about China's America watchers (some of whom he calls "certifiable crackpots" prone to "weird fantasies") that "their culture blocks real understanding of the culture of those who are for them still only 'foreigners'."[1] Chinese writers, on their part, prefer to point at class-determined ideology as the key reason for *our* supposed inability to understand *them*. So, for example, Chen Boda, in an editorial he wrote for the *People's Daily* at the beginning of the Cultural Revolution, insisted that Western "China experts" (*Zhongguo tong*) "will forever remain incapable of producing timely and accurate assessments of the events occurring in China" because their "wild flights of fancy (*husi luanxiang*) run counter to the development of history."[2]

The three texts included in this section are meant to illustrate—to the extent that it is possible—the degree to which *mutual* perceptions were skewed during the Cultural Revolution. Pye and Chen are equally wrong in suggesting that it's only the "other" that has such a distorted picture of "us," while "we"—be it by virtue of our superior political science or thanks to our mastery of Marxism-Leninism Mao Zedong Thought—are somehow able to perceive and understand "them" with essential accuracy. Because, even though the fantastic element in the diatribe against "reactionary, decadent, and vicious . . . imperialist cul-

---

[1] Lucian W. Pye, review of David Shambaugh, *Beautiful Imperialist: China Perceives America, 1972–1990,* in *The China Quarterly,* No. 129, March 1992, pp. 229–31.

[2] "Hengsao yiqie niugui sheshen" (Sweep Away All Monsters and Freaks), *People's Daily,* 1 June 1966.

ture" (Document 54) and the description of the "decaying and moribund capitalist system" (Document 55) no doubt appeared more striking to a Western reader, there is little reason to believe that some of the remarks made in front of the U.S. Senate Committee on Foreign Relations (Document 56) would not have stood out as equally wild flights of fancy to a Chinese audience two and a half decades ago. Hence, regardless of whether one chooses to explain the differences in terms of culture or history, it is probably safe to admit that at the time we may very well have misunderstood "them" as much as they misunderstood "us."

54
Salesmen of Reactionary Western Culture

Hong Xinda and Nan Xuelin

Source: Chinese Literature, No. 11, 1968, pp. 104–10.

The so-called "Western culture" is nothing but imperialist culture, which is most reactionary, decadent, and vicious. With the imperialist system heading for total collapse, its culture, like the sun setting beyond the Western hills, resembles a dying person who is sinking fast. Since Khrushchev and his successors came to power, they have gone all out to carry out "cultural cooperation" with U.S. imperialism and thrown the door wide open to "Western culture," which has thus found a new market in the Soviet Union. Amid the fanfare of their all-round reactionary collaboration, a new sinister deal was made between the Soviet Union and the United States not long ago—the Soviet-U.S. cultural exchange agreement for 1968–1969 signed in Moscow . . .

Let us see how "productive" Soviet-U.S. "cultural cooperation" is at present . . .

Disguised as "cultural cooperation," degenerate Western music, commercialized jazz, has become the rage in the Soviet revisionist musical, dancing, and theatrical world. The rock 'n' roll, the twist and other similar vulgar dances are executed more madly than before. The Soviet revisionist renegade clique has not only spent big sums of money to invite large numbers of night club jazz bands from the West to perform in different parts of the Soviet Union, it has also sent its own musicians to take part in "international contests" so as to learn from Western jazz bands. As a result, various weird-named American and British jazz bands have performed in the Soviet Union. Last 12 December, the Soviet revisionist Central Television Station started a monthly series of lectures on "Jazz Music, Yesterday and Today" in its fourth program. In these lectures, American commercialized jazz was unctuously described as the "real music" and the "sacred music" and was lauded as helping to "understand the world." Seven disgusting "jazz music festivals" have been held in Moscow and six other Soviet cities this year to give such vulgar music a big boost. And as before, the Soviet revisionist clique has given the green light to performances of many vulgar American plays on the Soviet stage.

As a result of Soviet-U.S. "cultural cooperation," Soviet revisionist screens have been turned into an instrument for publicizing "Western culture." As it did previously, the Soviet revisionist clique has spared no efforts to lavish praise on American films through its newspapers and magazines, and it has printed many books to publicize these reactionary American films. Moreover, in January this year, the Soviet revisionist Central Television Station began obsequiously introducing American film stars to its viewers. The Soviet revisionists, in effect, have handed over a large part of the Soviet screen to Hollywood. S.K. Romanovsky, chairman of the Soviet Committee for Cultural Relations with Foreign Countries, admitted that often "there are several hundred copies of American films being shown in our country." Even this cannot satisfy the Soviet revisionist clique. The new "cultural agreement" explicitly provides for "the widest possible distribution" of American films.

Under the signboard of "cultural cooperation," the Soviet revisionist clique has thrown the door wide open to Voice of America, an instrument of U.S. imperialism for opposing communism, China, the people, and revolution. The notorious V.O.A., as former U.S. President Kennedy said, is an "arm" of the U.S. government. But the Soviet revisionist clique loves it as dearly as flies love muck. As far back as soon after the Twentieth Congress of the C.P.S.U., the revisionist clique intermittently stopped jamming V.O.A. broadcasts to the Soviet Union. Later, an agreement was reached between the Soviet Union and the United States under which the former formally and completely stopped jamming and provided facilities for V.O.A. transcription programs to be broadcast in the Soviet Union. After Brezhnev and Kosygin came to power, they gave V.O.A. the go-ahead signal, allowing it to be heard all over the country. With great exultation, the U.S. press said that in content, form, and technique, the Soviet revisionist radio and television programs had been "radically reformed" after the fashion of the West.

Soviet revisionism's television is the same as the radio. Last year the Soviet revisionist clique racked its brains making a television newsreel called "Chronicle of Half Century" in the name of "celebrating" the fiftieth anniversary of the October Revolution and "reviewing" the history of the Soviet Union over the past half century. On the one hand, the newsreel frantically attacks China; on the other hand, it nauseatingly advocates "Soviet-U.S. friendship" to curry favor with its master. A good number of shots of Soviet revisionists embracing and kissing Americans were produced to show Soviet-U.S. "friendship" and "cooperation." Even the coming to power and the death of the U.S. imperialist chief Kennedy was shamelessly brought into the "chronicle" as a "big event" in the Soviet Union. The commentary flatters Kennedy as a "clear-headed" and "practical" man and sadly "mourns" his death.

It is also under the camouflage of Soviet-U.S. "cultural cooperation" that the decadent way of life of the Western bourgeoisie penetrates the Soviet Union everywhere. Not long ago, a so-called "Soviet fashion design show" was held in Washington. On display were "outstanding fashions" by Soviet revisionism's "top contemporary designers," including so-called "space age" fashions and "revolutionized" clothing designed by "the Soviet Union's best-known avant-garde designer," who copied the cowboy pants and miniskirts of the West. The marked trends of "Westernization" in the fashion show won praise and applause from their U.S. master, who cheered it as "inspiring." The Soviet revisionists also put on dog shows in Moscow similar to those in New York and London and went so far as to make this thing fashionable. All this is absolutely the height of rottenness.

To speed up the "Westernization" of the Soviet Union, the Soviet revisionist clique is becoming more and more open in utilizing "international tourism" to attract by all possible means "tourists" of all descriptions from the Western capitalist countries, allowing them to spread the dissipated Western way of life in the Soviet Union. The Soviet revisionists recently announced that more than one hundred cities in all fifteen union republics will be opened to large numbers of pleasure-seeking foreign bourgeois gentlemen and ladies coming to the Soviet Union. In addition, the Soviet revisionists are developing "cultural cooperation" with U.S. imperialism in a big way so as to surrender completely to the latter and bring on a wholesale "Westernization" of the Soviet Union through such channels as setting up "night clubs," free "distribution" of the U.S. magazine *America,* holding rotating U.S. exhibitions, introduction of American experience, exchanging students, commendation of scholars, sponsoring pen clubs, and reprinting articles of the reactionary U.S. press, etc. . . .

Why is Soviet-U.S. "cultural cooperation" carried out so unscrupulously and so feverishly in this period? The U.S. magazine *Newsweek* in its 15 July 1968 issue admits outright that Soviet revisionism and U.S. imperialism "have often found themselves undergoing many of the same internal and external stresses and strains in the rapidly changing world of the 1960s." What are these "internal and external stresses and strains"? First of all, in this period, under the leadership of our great leader Chairman Mao himself, China has victoriously unfolded the Great Proletarian Cultural Revolution, which has tremendous influence on the whole world and deals a heavy blow to imperialism, revisionism, and reaction. The radiance of Mao Zedong's thought lights up the road for liberation of the world's revolutionary people. The news of victories from the hills of the Truong Son Range, the war drums on the equator, the red flags fluttering in the Pu Pan Mountains, the roar of the raging tide along the Mississippi River, and the revolutionary storm in West Europe and North America . . . all these converged into an irresistible revolutionary torrent that is rapidly breaching the dam of global Soviet-U.S. counter-revolutionary collaboration. The drastically deepening political and economic crises in imperialist countries headed by the United States have become an incurable disease. Modern revisionism with the Soviet revisionist clique as its center, which is daily disintegrating, is in a shaky state. Such an excellent revolutionary situation naturally means "stresses and strains" for U.S. imperialism and the Soviet revisionist clique. It is in these days that they have to depend on each other to bolster up their tottering bourgeois dictatorships and use decadent "Western culture" as a talisman in a vain effort to prevent the surging tide of the world revolution and save themselves from being drowned in it.

55
A Great Storm

People's Daily Editorial

Source: This official translation of the *People's Daily* editorial of 27 May 1968 appeared in *Chinese News Bulletin,* No. 5, issued by the Embassy of the People's Republic of China to Sweden on 30 May 1968.

A quotation from Chairman Mao:

> The proletariat and working people of Europe, North America, and Oceania are experiencing a new awakening.

The great storm of revolutionary mass movement that is rising in France and Europe and in North America has continued to develop rapidly in the past few days with the momentum of an avalanche. Ten million French workers have gone on strike and have occupied half of the country's industrial and mining enterprises. With the support of the workers, the Paris students have heroically fought against the reactionary troops and police and have stirred up a new roaring wave of struggle. As the workers' struggle gains in depth, the peasant movement is also developing swiftly. This tidal wave of the struggle of the masses of the people is spreading to more and more capitalist countries. It is a tremendous mass struggle that broke out in the heartland of the capitalist world and that knows no parallel in several decades. It is pounding at the decaying and moribund capitalist system with tremendous force.

The enormous strength of the masses of the people has showed itself with remarkable clarity in this storm. The revolutionary actions taken by the French workers and students and the broad masses of the people in general, which can move mountains and drain the seas, have once again demonstrated to us how correct is the truth pointed out by Chairman Mao that "imperialism and all reactionaries are paper tigers."

Thus, just struggles of the people of France and of other European and North American countries have had enormous repercussions all over the world. They have won wide sympathy and support from the revolutionary peoples of the various countries of the world. The continuous massive demonstrations that have been held in different places in China in the last few days and in which army men and civilians totaling 20 million took part are an expression of the resolute support of the 700 million Chinese people for the revolutionary struggles of the European and North American peoples.

Our great teacher Chairman Mao has pointed out that "the proletariat and working people of Europe, North America, and Oceania are experiencing a new awakening." The vigorous growth of the current revolutionary mass movement in Europe and North America is a sign of this new awakening of the proletariat and broad masses of the people in these countries.

Exactly like all the old-run renegades and opportunists, the Soviet revisionist renegade clique and the French revisionist renegade group are playing a most shameless role in this great storm. As soon as the mass movement rose, they sordidly vilified all revolutionary actions that broke their revisionist restrictions as acts of "adventurism" and so on and so forth. When the revolutionary mass movement swept aside their calumnies like rubbish and quickly became a conflagration, they hurriedly ganged up with the monopoly capitalist class and are trying to betray and stamp out the revolution as soon as possible, in order to gain a few crumbs for themselves. We shall wait and see what further wretched performances this bunch of miserable clowns will act out on the stage of history.

In this storm, daring to despise the laws and bayonets of the reactionary ruling clique and having no fear of its suppression, the revolutionary masses of Europe and North America are persevering in their heroic struggle and have displayed a vigorous revolutionary spirit.

In this storm, the people of various strata have put forth various concrete demands and militant slogans. They are clearly directing the general spearhead of their struggle at the evil rule of the monopoly capitalist class and the entire capitalist system. This indicates that the masses of Europe and North America have raised the level of their struggle to a new height.

In this storm, the young students have played a vanguard role and are more and more uniting with the workers' movement. The mutual support and inspiration of the student movement and the workers' movement has given a powerful impetus to the further upsurge of the entire people's movement.

In this storm, the broad masses of the European and North American students and workers have broken out of the general forms for struggle in the mass movements of the past and have begun to take a series of violent actions full of fighting spirit, thus creating completely new experiences in struggle for the revolutionary mass movement of the capitalist countries.

Chairman Mao has taught us: "Imperialism has prepared the conditions for its own doom. These conditions are the awakening of the great masses of the people in the colonies and semicolonies and in the imperialist countries themselves."

Today, we have entered a great new era of world revolution. The national liberation movements in Asia, Africa, and Latin America have dealt heavy blows at imperialism headed by the United States, accelerated the development of the political and economic crises of the imperialist countries, and intensified the class contradictions in these countries. The broad masses of the working class and the oppressed people have expressed their ever more bitter grievances against the reactionary rule of the monopoly capitalist class and the existing social system and have increased their resistance. The new high tide of the revolutionary mass movements in Europe and North America is precisely a striking expression of the daily deepening and intensifying internal conflicts in the capitalist world.

The extensive dissemination of Mao Zedong's thought throughout the world has promoted the development in depth of the contemporary world revolution. The tremendous victory of China's Great Proletarian Cultural Revolution has inspired in the people the revolutionary will of daring to struggle and daring to win victory. People can see in the vigorously developing revolutionary mass movement in Europe and North America the daily increasing impact of China's Great Proletarian Cultural Revolution on the broad masses of the people in these regions.

Elucidating his thesis eleven years ago that the east wind is prevailing over the west wind, Chairman Mao said, "The imperialist camp has a population of only about four hundred million, and besides, it is divided internally. There will be 'earthquakes' there."

Europe and North America are the historic lairs of the imperialists. U.S.-led imperialism has always regarded these regions as its solid base areas, where it exercises the strictest control; and the modern revisionists with the Soviet revisionists as their center, including the renegades, scabs, and counter-revolutionary pawns of different shades and hues, are all doing their utmost to help the imperialists stabilize their reactionary rule in these regions. Like a violent earthquake, the rapid development of the people's mass movement in Europe and North America today has shattered the fond dreams of the international monopoly capitalist class. There is no longer any paradise for imperialism.

Wherever there is the dark rule of the imperialists and reactionaries, the people who make up more than 90 percent of the population will rise up to make revolution. The development of the revolutionary struggle of the working class and the broad masses of the people in Europe and North America is inevitable. Neither the monopoly capitalist class, nor the social democrats, nor the modern revisionists can check it. In Europe and North America, it is definitely not the monopoly capitalist class but the broad masses of the people in these regions who are really powerful. The prospects of the revolution in these countries are very bright.

The people throughout the world rejoice over the big storm of the mass movement in Europe and North America. Armed with Mao Zedong's thought, the 700 million Chinese people stand firmly on the side of the revolutionary people of Europe and North America. We believe that in their burning struggle, the working class, the peasants, progressive youth, and all revolutionary masses will continuously temper themselves, raise their political consciousness, strengthen their unity, and expand their own forces. We believe that provided the working class and the broad masses of the people of Europe and North America unite with the revolutionary people of the whole world and persevere in courageous and sustained battle, the system of capitalism and imperialism will surely be buried.

56
"Is China Almost Like a Dead Society?"

United States Senate Committee on Foreign Relations

Source: Excerpts from *China and the United States: Today and Yesterday,* a transcript of hearings before the Committee on Foreign Relations, United States Senate, 92nd Congress, 2nd Session, on "China Today and the Course of Sino-U.S. Relations over the Past Few Decades" (Washington: U.S. Government Printing Office, 1972), pp. 45–57. The chairman is Senator J.W. Fulbright, and witnesses are John S. Service and Raymond P. Ludden, two former Foreign Service officers and members of the American "Dixie Mission" to the CCP headquarters in Yan'an in 1945, and Warren I. Cohen, professor of diplomatic history at Michigan State University.

Are Present Conditions in China Threatening?

THE CHAIRMAN: Do any of you feel that present conditions in China, which you have reported, constitute a threat to the United States? They are very different. Granted it is a different approach from our own.

Do any of you feel this is something we should be deeply concerned about? I would like you and also Mr. Service particularly, to answer. Do you feel what is going on in China is a threatening thing and that we ought to be deeply concerned about it?

MR. SERVICE: I don't believe it threatens the United States. No. I don't believe China is a threat to the United States.

THE CHAIRMAN: Is it a threat to its neighbors?

MR. SERVICE: Not in any military sense.

THE CHAIRMAN: We have been told within the last ten years, in the early days of the Johnson administration and I think in the Kennedy administration, that one of the principal justifications for our involvement in Vietnam, was that China was a threat, that they were an aggressive community and they were threatening us, and in some extreme. If we didn't stop them in Vietnam they would be in San Diego and San Francisco. This was said by members of the administration. You are familiar with that?

MR. SERVICE: But I do not believe it.

THE CHAIRMAN: It seems absurd to me in the light of recent developments. Yet it was said by responsible men, was it not?

MR. SERVICE: It was. But when I say China is not a threat, as Premier Zhou said to me in discussing the whole business of support of wars of liberation and so on, he said, "No people can win their freedom"—liberation, as he calls it—"except by their own efforts. However, ideas know no boundaries. We can't stop the people following our example." To some extent you can make this a threat to some other countries: the ideas of a people's war, the example of China may give other people the same ideas, and if they do the Chinese will give them sympathy and to some degree support. But in a military sense I don't think China has designs on any of the countries around her.

THE CHAIRMAN: When I read your piece in the *Times* a thought did occur to me if you are telling the truth. I mean I know you tell the truth as you see it. There is also the possibility that you—or I or anyone else, since we all see things from a different point of view—may have exaggerated certain aspects of it, such as the civility of the people. And the lack of crime, the lack of necessity for policemen to control everyone by force, the use of persuasion as a means of relationships between the government and the people, in a sense does threaten the continuation and certain aspects of our own society, doesn't it?

MR. SERVICE: It is an attractive example, certainly.

THE CHAIRMAN: That is a threat, isn't it? What can be more threatening than to present a picture of a society which to at least some people has certain elements of considerable superiority? One of the great issues in the last election in 1968 was law and order. Law and order was a thing that the candidates said they were going to bring us, particularly Mr. Wallace. If the Chinese society, even though it is considered a Communist society, has achieved some of the greatest aspirations of this country, it is a threat, isn't it? Is that what you mean by a threat?

MR. SERVICE: Yes.

SENATOR COOPER: Will the Chairman yield for a question?

THE CHAIRMAN: Let him answer. Then, of course, I will yield. I want him and any of you to answer, and then I will yield. Of course, I would like an answer to the question.

MR. SERVICE: It is hard to consider it as a real threat.

THE CHAIRMAN: Why not?

MR. SERVICE: It is hard to know how the Chinese example can be imported into the United States, because the Chinese success depends upon to a large extent—one can't measure this—on the long history and the social organization, social history of the Chinese people. And it is not really very exportable. The Chinese people had to learn to live in—

THE CHAIRMAN: You just said ideas were exportable. You just made the case. Mr. Zhou said ideas don't stop at international lines.

MR. SERVICE: Then we were moving a little further to applying them to the United States and as to the sort of possible success, and I don't see unless—

THE CHAIRMAN: You are saying law and order isn't possible in the United States? Is that what you are saying?

MR. SERVICE: The Chinese success depends upon the character and history of the Chinese people that makes them willing to accept a certain amount of regimentation, control, and effective, I mean, very, very persuasive persuasion. It is as though we would have to go into a very, very fervent evangelistic sort of religion.

THE CHAIRMAN: Is law and order possible anywhere without discipline?

MR. SERVICE: If we have a new era of puritanism, this would be comparable to China, but I don't see how the Chinese experience is going to have very much applicability to the United States. When I am talking about the threat, I am thinking about some of the countries of Southeast Asia, which are going to be certainly much more attracted, much more direct, closer. They are oriental societies. Their societies are not so different from China, and the example of success in China, and what happened to the Chinese people, is going to have some effect in other countries of Southeast Asia.

THE CHAIRMAN: I can't think of any greater threat than to set an example which other people wish to emulate. I think this is very subversive of our views here. If it is true that it is an exemplary society, it seems to me it is much more attractive than one armed to the teeth.

SENATOR COOPER: May I ask my question now?

THE CHAIRMAN: Yes.

Killing and Destruction during the Cultural Revolution

SENATOR COOPER: We have all read more about China in recent months, but I think we read a good deal during the Cultural Revolution, too.

Is it a fact that Mao called upon the students, and that they did kill, destroy. I don't know how many, maybe thousands of those that Mao thought were opposed to him? Is that part of the example?

MR. SERVICE: It is part of the religious fervor that characterizes the process at one stage. Mao felt the Party was on the wrong track; it was under the control of people who were following policies which he thought were going to lead toward the creation of new elites, bureaucracy, and a new class which he equated with a revival of capitalism and so on. To overthrow the Party he called in the enthusiastic young youth. They got very fired up, and they did commit a lot of excesses; there is absolutely no question about it. This is one of the reasons I was so surprised to go back to China only a few years afterward and find the atmosphere of civil life rather relaxed and so on. I thought there would be more holdovers, more vestiges of that struggle still apparent.

We don't know how many people were killed. A good many people were killed. Finally, of course, the students got out of hand. Some of them got too radical, too Leftist. They took too seriously some of the gospel they had heard, and eventually they had to be set down.

The same sort of strife went on in the factories between workers willing to follow Mao's line of more or less equal pay, reduced emphasis on special benefits, and Liu's (Liu Shaoqi) line of differential pay, prerogatives for specialists, and so on, and there was fighting. In Sichuan, where I went, and where other foreigners had not been, you still see marks on the buildings of active warfare that went on between these groups. Everyone that I talked to, though, said that the groups that were engaged in this sort of fighting were relatively small numbers of the whole population; the main population was not seriously affected.

No one really knows how much violence there was in the Cultural Revolution. There was a good deal. . . .

Absolute Power as Best Way Questioned

SENATOR CASE: Mao today seems in direct contrast to our conception that nobody should have absolute power. I think I find it difficult to be as serene about Mao as you said Mao is about the world or about his successors. It is not evident from human experience that absolute power is to be trusted as the best way.

MR. SERVICE: I think we have got to really look a little more at the history of the Party and the history of the regime. He has not been the absolute man in command all the time.

SENATOR CASE: It is a committee.

MR. SERVICE: His policies have been opposed, and, of course, this is one of the reasons why he got rid of some of them.

He did stage a revolution, shall we say, in the Cultural Revolution, but he had to do it, partly, there had been strong opposition to him in the Party and in the country, and the country was not going in the direction he thought it should go. But the Great Leap, which he apparently promoted in 1958, was a failure, and the policies which were followed in the years after that were very conservative policies. He stepped down as president, and he hasn't always been the sole dictator as much as we commonly think.

Traditional Concept of Mandate from Heaven

THE CHAIRMAN: May I suggest that historically this isn't so unusual in China. After all, it is the oldest organized community, I guess, in the world, of any consequence. This concept of the mandate of heaven has been the traditional way for an awfully long period of time.

He [Mao] isn't departing from the tradition of China; he is carrying it out in a little different way. Do they still not consider he is probably the successor to his predecessor? They haven't had an election, as they didn't before. They have never believed in elections, have they?

MR. SERVICE: He has inherited some of the mantle of the old emperor. But the communist methods of control, of course, are far more persuasive and far more complete and thorough than anything that was known under the empire.

SENATOR CASE: It really was a bunch of warlords.

MR. SERVICE: The government was far above and the people were interfered with very little; so it didn't affect the complete life, every aspect of personal life, the way the government now does.

But I still think there is some validity in the idea that Mao is there, and the Party has been successful, because it by and large has served the interests and the livelihood of the people as a whole. They support the Party because life in China is far better for the great majority of people than they have ever had before. Never having known democracy and never having voted, never having experienced these things, they don't resent the lack of them; they don't know about them. Democracy has never been applied in China.

THE CHAIRMAN: I know it hasn't. But what I suggested a moment ago was that the way you describe the conditions doesn't certainly indicate any great inferiority to a lot of the so-called democratic countries that exist in the world today. I can think of a number about whom it would be difficult to say what you have said about China.

MR. SERVICE: Well, everyone has, shall we say, a guaranteed income; everyone has a job; everyone can get medical care. There are things like that. People don't choose their jobs; they don't move around. There are things that we treasure very highly which are not present in China.

Lack of Intellectual Ferment

SENATOR CASE: There is no intellectual commitment or activity. In many ways it is a very simple, primitive civilization. There isn't any intellectual ferment; is that not a correct statement? We would find it intolerable, wouldn't we?

MR. SERVICE: Yes, we would. There is very little intellectual ferment that one sees. I think that the literature and so on has to follow the doctrine that it must serve the revolution, must serve the people, and, as a result, it is not the type of art that we treasure, generally speaking.

There are not any great novelists. At least they are not getting published in China. We don't know of any great intellectual ferment going on . . .

Problem of Pollution and Quality of Food

THE CHAIRMAN: Is pollution a serious problem there as it is here?

MR. SERVICE: Not yet, because their industry is much less than ours. There are not as many pollutants, but they will certainly have a pollution problem if they don't do something about it, and they are doing something now.

THE CHAIRMAN: Was the food good?

MR. SERVICE: Very good. You must remember, on the whole, on the pollution problem, that night soil, manure, is carefully used and saved; they don't have a sewage problem.

THE CHAIRMAN: Would you call that recycling? That is a traditional practice?

MR. SERVICE: That is correct.

THE CHAIRMAN: For centuries.

SENATOR CASE: We are going to do the same. There is no doubt about it.

Comparative Intellectual Ferment in Calcutta and China

THE CHAIRMAN: On this question of intellectual ferment, what I had in mind was not comparing it to the freedom of expression which we find in Greenwich Village, but, say, a city like Calcutta. Is there a great intellectual ferment, do you think, in a democratic city like Calcutta?

MR. SERVICE: There are all sorts of political parties that are very active.

SENATOR CASE: Are there many newspapers and magazines?

MR. SERVICE: There are various views expressed. In China generally only one view is expressed. There is no forum for opposition.

THE CHAIRMAN: Only one view about everything, or just about politics?

MR. SERVICE: Well, yes, if you want to get down to purely technical matters, industrial techniques or something like that. When it comes down to anything that can be related to politics, and that can be defined pretty broadly, then you don't get the dissent in the public realm. You may have arguments; apparently, that has been permitted in higher circles, also, of the Party.

THE CHAIRMAN: Then I would have to revise the way I interpreted the significance of your article, the one about China's army being very unstarchy. In the description of the attitude toward the army, for example, you say that, "Interviewing high school seniors, one finds that to serve with the People's Liberation Army is the most popular career goal. One serious girl, though, hopes to 'benefit mankind' by making a great scientific discovery." That is a quote from your recent article.

All of this seems very favorable until, however, the thought injected by the Senator from New Jersey that this is all very well, but this finally amounts to a sterile unimaginative community in which there is no dissent, no initiative, no innovative ideas. It is almost like a dead society.

Is it a better impression that one should draw from your article that there is nothing going on that is promising and new and vigorous and innovative ideas as to the improvement of society than what I did? Would that now be the way you have turned it around?

MR. SERVICE: Well—

THE CHAIRMAN: I am trying to get to the bottom of this. My first reaction is, having met some of our most critical problems, such as the violence in the streets, and law and order, and even the minimum of health provisions, food, many of the problems that we are trying to struggle with, welfare—the most troublesome problem, I suppose, immediately facing this Congress is the welfare bill, H.R. 1. Everybody has a different view, and everybody is upset about it.

You leave the impression they have gone far toward solving these basic problems, truly, at a lower level. Now I get the impression they have done all of this, but it is almost like a dead city. There is no life left in this community which bids fair to revive the glorious art of the Chinese, for which they are famous. The ideas of invention, all of the things we are told about, all the way from gunpowder, God forbid, and printing of papers and all of these things—and leave the impression now that that is all over. It is just a monolithic dictatorship in which nobody has any idea except Mao.

MR. SERVICE: I think you have to define the areas of dissent. I don't think there is very much political dissent, and most of the policy argument goes on within the ranks of the Party; it is not public.

There is a great deal of effort to stir up initiative on inventions, on industrial improvements. The Cultural Revolution has gone just mad on appealing to the innate creativeness of the people, and every factory will tell you all of the improvements.

SENATOR CASE: The mechanical arts?

MR. SERVICE: Yes, sir. And there are letters to the paper disagreeing with the way things are carried out, criticizing the government for failure to do this and that, but in the public discussions, the public press, you don't get a great deal of discussion of political matter. I think obviously there has been discussion within the Party because they have had the Party shifting course at various times, but this is not regarded as something that is to be taken up in the press. There are no conflicting parties, each with his own paper, and so on.

So you get a certain drabness and sameness in what you hear from people and what you read. Even the art is not completely dead, though it all must serve a purpose, a useful purpose, to support the revolution. It may be quite beautiful art, and the old traditional arts are continuing in things like porcelains, and so on. But even there the tendency during the Cultural Revolution has been to introduce more political themes. Since the Cultural Revolution, I think we see a moving back more toward traditional themes because they are beautiful. So I don't think we should say it is a completely dead society; it is not that, I think.

SENATOR COOPER: It is a controlled society?

MR. SERVICE: Very much.

Price Chinese Are Paying for Law and Order

MR. COHEN. I think this relates back to your earlier question about the danger of the Chinese model for us. Is it a subversive idea? I think what has to be kept in mind is that this Chinese model is not an attractive one to us in this sense; it is not a danger to our society; it is not attractive to large numbers of people. The price that the Chinese are paying for law and order is a price that we would not want to pay. We have a society which has by and large enjoyed a large degree of order, which is now declining, but we have not yet reached the point at which we would be willing to sacrifice the intellectual freedom, the privacy, the individualism, which we prize so much in our own society.

But when you transform it to the Chinese scene, it is a completely different thing. What is the price the Chinese are paying for this? A few intellectuals enjoyed this kind of freedom in the past, but we are talking about a society in which the overwhelming majority of the people, 95, perhaps 99 percent of the people, have given up the right to starve, the right to throw their daughters in the canal, these kinds of rights, and it is a price which they, I think, for the most part are willingly going to pay. It is not a price I would be prepared to pay. It is not the kind of society I would want my child to live in, but I think it is a society which the Chinese people have been willing to accept because of the alternatives they have known and the alternatives which were available at this time.

Future World Prospect

SENATOR CASE: What do you think of the world prospect when we are going to have great masses of humanity under the control of this kind of a system? What kind of a future do you look for?

MR. COHEN: I don't foresee a need for these societies to come into conflict. I don't think that it is essential, inevitable, that ideological differences in society will create conflict, that their society, because it is organized in one way, will necessarily conflict with our society. I think the national interests tend to be very much the same, regardless of the ideological considerations involved.

I do not think that a Chinese government which was democratic would have very much different attitudes toward its boundaries, toward its neighbors than the Chinese government that exists today.

In terms of its relations for us, I think the manner in which a society is organized is less important.

MR. SERVICE: May I thank the professor for saying what I have been trying in a stumbling way to say.

Controlled and Directed Ferment in China

SENATOR CASE: Mr. Ludden has been awfully quiet. I wonder if you may have a word or two on these matters. What do you think about them?

MR. LUDDEN: I certainly can't believe that China is a dead society. That I can't choke down. There are all sorts of ferment there, I believe, but I think it is a controlled ferment, it is a directed ferment.

The revolution did not start with the Communists. The revolution goes back many years. It certainly goes back to 1911, and you might say it goes back to the Taiping Rebellion in the middle 1850s. There was an old French historian, I think it was Cordier, who made the remark at one time that the Manchus, when they conquered China, that was in 1644, they were great until they forsook the saddle for the couch. And I think that at the time of the Cultural Revolution Mao was afraid that his people who had come up from the caves and the ditches were forsaking the saddle for the couch, that they were getting soft, they weren't carrying on the revolution with the old punch that it should have, and I think that is what the revolution was, one of these ups and downs in the development of a Chinese body politic, if you wish to call it that, and I think those will go on, and I don't see any reason why it shouldn't occur at some time in the future.

Possibility of Future Cultural Revolution

SENATOR CASE: You mean a cultural revolution?

MR. LUDDEN: Yes. I think the Chinese are a very dynamic people. Next time it might come from the army. This time the army had to be called in to save the day when the Cultural Revolution got out of hand; wouldn't you say that?

MR. SERVICE: That is right.

SENATOR CASE: Where are you going to get the corrective to an army if it goes on the rampage?

MR. LUDDEN: Well, I have a great deal of faith in the innate common sense of the Chinese, who do not wish to destroy themselves. That may be wishful thinking on my part.

SENATOR CASE: I have no opinion of that.

MR. LUDDEN: I don't believe they have any intention of destroying themselves.

THE CHAIRMAN: Their history would support you. They have been around a long time.

MR. LUDDEN: They have been around a long time.

THE CHAIRMAN: I don't recall they have done anything quite as fully as they have done in the last ten years—maybe they have, I don't know their history well enough, I confess I don't know their history well enough—against their own interest.

MR. LUDDEN: One of the great cries from the time of Sun Yat-sen, you could read it on the wall of every official establishment: "The revolution has not been completed." The revolution is still not completed in terms of the Chinese. They wish to establish a society which is compatible to their desires, and I don't think we can stop it. Maybe we shouldn't try to stop it.

THE CHAIRMAN: Why would we want to?

MR. LUDDEN: I don't know.

SENATOR CASE: I don't know anybody who wants to. I am trying to find out where we are going.

THE CHAIRMAN: I don't see why we should want to. As a matter of fact, it could well be that they could teach the world a good deal. They have in the past, haven't they?

MR. LUDDEN: Yes, and still I think it is a very dynamic society. I haven't been there since 1949. I just don't know.

Reestablishment of Normal Relations with China

THE CHAIRMAN: None of you can see any reason, I assume, against our doing everything reasonable to reestablish normal relations with China. I assume you all feel that, don't you?

MR. SERVICE: Yes.

MR. LUDDEN: Yes.

MR. COHEN: Yes.

THE CHAIRMAN: And it is likely to be mutually beneficial?

MR. LUDDEN: Certainly.

Part III

After the Event

H. The Trouble with History:
Official Verdicts

To the leaders of the Chinese Communist Party, the Cultural Revolution remains a singularly sensitive issue. While in actuality they may by now have succeeded in undoing most of what Mao Zedong, on his deathbed, called a "lifetime achievement" (Document 57), the specter (once the "revolutionary spirit") of rebellion, sanctioned by the Great Leader, and directed squarely at the Party *apparat* still haunts them. The erosion of the political authority of the CCP as a result of the Cultural Revolution has been devastating and permanent.

The legitimizing myth of the Communist Party as an agent of progressive historical forces and surrogate of truth was shattered by what happened in and after 1966.[1] Official history has since been reemplotted to account for the rehabilitation of Liu Shaoqi (Document 58)—the unfortunate figure who became Mao's ninth metonymic representation of reaction (Lin Biao, of course, becoming the tenth and last). A Central Committee resolution has been passed in which the story of the Cultural Revolution is narrated as the "error of a great revolutionary," compounded by the "counter-revolutionary crimes" of Lin Biao, Jiang Qing, et al. (Document 59). Yet the CCP has all but given up the search for rhetorical devices powerful enough to turn what happened into something capable of legitimizing the present regime. The Party's history is tacitly acknowledged to be in a mess—hence Deng Xiaoping's injunction to historians to be "crude rather than finicky" (*yicu bu yixi*) when dealing with it.[2]

In practical terms, the reversal of Mao's verdict on the Cultural Revolution involved the reexamination of countless so-called "unjust, false, and mistaken" cases. Translated here are the guidelines (Docu-

---

[1]See David E. Apter and Tony Saich, *Revolutionary Discourse in Mao's Republic* (Cambridge, Mass.: Harvard University Press, 1994).

[2]Cf. Qu Jiang, "Jixu 'wenhua dageming' yixi bu yicu" (When Narrating the "Great Cultural Revolution" One Should Be Finicky Rather than Crude), *Sichuan Difangzhi Tongxun* (*Sichuan Local History Newsletter*), No. 1, 1987, pp. 7–9.

ment 60) for weeding Public Security Bureau dossiers dealing with just such cases. As victims big and small were exonerated, the fates of those who had once been heroic perpetrators took some bizarre twists. Quite a few civilian "rebels" who had been designated martyrs, in view of the circumstances surrounding their deaths, were posthumously deprived of their martyr status by the Ministry of Civil Affairs (Document 61). PLA officers and men, on the other hand, were allowed to retain their martyr status—even when they had died supporting the "wrong" faction—since all they had done, according to the regulations, was simply "carry out orders" (Document 62).

Attempts by outsiders (e.g., historians *not* working directly for the Politburo) to write the history of the Cultural Revolution is still subject to draconian censorship. The final text in this section (Document 63) is a set of censor's regulations, the promulgation of which was prompted by the application for a publication permit, in 1984, by the editors of a *Dictionary of the Cultural Revolution*. The *Dictionary* still has not seen the light of day.

57
"Seal the Coffin and Pass the Final Verdict"

Mao Zedong

Source: This is a record of remarks Mao is alleged to have made in conversation with Wang Hongwen, Zhang Chunqiao, Jiang Qing, Hua Guofeng, Wu De, and Wang Hairong on 15 June (possibly 13 January) 1976. Our translation collates the transcript reprinted in Wang Nianyi, *Da dongluan de niandai* (*Years of Great Turmoil*) (Zhengzhou: Henan renmin chubanshe, 1988), pp. 600–601, and the handwritten excerpt included in a collection of documents donated in 1989 to the Fairbank Center for East Asian Research Library, Harvard University, by an anonymous member of the Chinese Academy of Sciences.

It's rare for a man to live to the age of seventy, and now I am already past eighty. When one has reached the end, one cannot help but think about one's funeral arrangements. There is a Chinese saying, "Seal the coffin and pass the final verdict." Although the lid is not yet on my coffin, the moment is drawing near, and I think the final judgment can already be passed. I've done two things in my lifetime. One was battle all those years against Chiang Kai-shek and in the end chase him off to that little island. In the War of Resistance, I asked the Japanese to return to their ancestral home. Battling back and forth, I finally battled my way into the Forbidden City. Only a tiny number of people would argue with me about this. At most, some would say I should have reclaimed that island a long time ago. The other thing, as you know, was to launch the Great Cultural Revolution. Here I don't have many supporters, and I have quite a few opponents. The Great Cultural Revolution is something that has not yet been concluded. Thus I am passing the task on to the next generation. I may not be able to pass it on peacefully, in which case I may have to pass it on in turmoil. What will happen to the next generation if it all fails? There may be a foul wind and a rain of blood. How will you cope? Heaven only knows!

58
Concerning Open Propaganda About the Redressing of the Unjust Case of Comrade Liu Shaoqi

CCP Central Propaganda Department

Source: This is the text of "Guanyu pingfan Liu Shaoqi tongzhi yuanan de gongkai xuanchuan," originally published in *Xuanchuan dongtai (Propaganda Trends)*, the organ of the Central Propaganda Department, on 25 February 1980. Our translation is based on the reprint in *Xuanchuan dongtai xuanbian 1980 (Selections from Propaganda Trends 1980)* (Beijing: Zhongguo shehui kexue chubanshe, 1981), pp. 52–54.

A formal resolution to redress the unjust case of Comrade Liu Shaoqi will be made by the Fifth Plenum of the Eleventh Central Committee and will be announced in its communique.[1] This is an event of major domestic and international political impact, and we must absolutely do a good job of dealing with it in our open propaganda.

1. Until the communique of the Fifth Plenum has been made public, newspapers and magazines should refrain from attempting to be the first to publish news, articles, photographs, or other materials about comrade Shaoqi's rehabilitation.

2. Eventually, a series of articles, based on the Center's resolution to rehabilitate and the relevant historical reinvestigation materials (not to be openly published), will be put together and published in a uniform fashion. They will illustrate how comrade Shaoqi's alleged "arrest and defection" in Changsha, his alleged "treacherous activities" in Wuhan and Lushan, and his alleged "arrest and defection" in Shenyang, etc., are all totally unfounded frame-ups. The three great crimes imposed on him, of "renegade, hidden traitor, and scab," will be thoroughly overturned.

---

[1] Cf. "Communique of the Fifth Plenary Session of the 11th Central Committee of the Communist Party of China," *Beijing Review,* No. 10, 10 March 1980, pp. 7–10.

3. A series of articles must be put together to clarify what's right and wrong about some of the major issues touched upon in past erroneous criticism, such as the so-called "Liu Shaoqi's counter-revolutionary revisionist line" and the "black cultivation," etc. Once the communique has been made public, these should be published one after the other. We must make full use of this opportunity to further propagate the development of the Party's ideological line of seeking the truth from facts.

4. Articles in memory of comrade Shaoqi may be published prior to and after his memorial service. We should emphasize quality, not quantity. The stories they present should conform to the contents of the rehabilitation resolution and the memorial address, and they should emphasize the revolutionary achievements of comrade Shaoqi and not describe in great detail the circumstances of how he was persecuted. Be careful not to counterpose comrade Liu Shaoqi and Chairman Mao. As far as the reasons that this major unjust case came about, you may follow the contents of the resolution and not dissect things in too much detail, although nor should you simply refer it all to Lin Biao and the "Gang of Four."

5. Appropriate arrangements must be made. Overall plans must be made for the arrangement of propaganda concerning all aspects of the Fifth Plenum, from the rehabilitation of comrade Shaoqi to the revision of the Party statutes and the adoption of the norms for the political life inside the Party.

6. Important articles about the rehabilitation of comrade Shaoqi and important commemorative articles to be published by central propaganda units must be submitted for censorship to the Central Propaganda Department; propaganda units in the provinces, municipalities, and autonomous regions should send their articles to the standing committees of the provincial, municipal, and autonomous regional Party Committees for censorship.

7. The propaganda sections of the Party Committees at the various levels and press units should pay attention to the timely gathering of responses to the rehabilitation and pass them on to higher levels.

59
The Cultural Revolution—Excerpt from "Resolution on Certain Questions in the History of Our Party Since the Founding of the People's Republic of China"

CCP Central Committee

Source: Beijing Review, No. 27, 1981, pp. 20–26. The resolution was passed by the Sixth Plenum of the Eleventh CCP Central Committee on 27 June 1981.

The "cultural revolution," which lasted from May 1966 to October 1976, was responsible for the most severe setback and the heaviest losses suffered by the Party, the state, and the people since the founding of the People's Republic. It was initiated and led by Comrade Mao Zedong. His principal theses were that many representatives of the bourgeoisie and counter-revolutionary revisionists had sneaked into the Party, the government, the army, and cultural circles, and leadership in a fairly large majority of organizations and departments was no longer in the hands of Marxists and the people; that Party-persons in power taking the capitalist road had formed a bourgeois headquarters inside the Central Committee, which pursued a revisionist political and organizational line and had agents in all provinces, municipalities, and autonomous regions, as well as in all central departments; that since the forms of struggle adopted in the past had not been able to solve this problem, the power usurped by the capitalist roaders could be recaptured only by carrying out a great cultural revolution, by openly and fully mobilizing the broad masses from the bottom up to expose these sinister phenomena; and that the "cultural revolution" was in fact a great political revolution in which one class would overthrow another, a revolution that would have to be waged time and again. The theses appeared mainly in the 16 May Circular, which served as the programmatic document of the "cultural revolution," and in the political report to the Ninth National Congress of the Party in April 1969. They were incorporated into a general theory—the "theory of continued revolution under the dictatorship of the proletariat"—which then took on a specific meaning. These erroneous "Left" theses, upon which Comrade

Mao Zedong based himself in initiating the "cultural revolution," were obviously inconsistent with the system of Mao Zedong Thought, which is the integration of the universal principles of Marxism-Leninism with the concrete practice of the Chinese revolution. These theses must be thoroughly distinguished from Mao Zedong Thought. As for Lin Biao, Jiang Qing, and others who were placed in important positions by Comrade Mao Zedong, the matter is of an entirely different nature. They rigged up two counter-revolutionary cliques in an attempt to seize supreme power and, taking advantage of Comrade Mao Zedong's errors, committed many crimes behind his back, bringing disaster to the country and the people. As their counter-revolutionary crimes have been fully exposed, this resolution will not go into them at any length.

The history of the "cultural revolution" has proved that Comrade Mao Zedong's principal theses for initiating this revolution conformed neither to Marxism-Leninism nor to Chinese reality. They represented an entirely erroneous appraisal of the prevailing class relations and political situation in the Party and state.

1. The "cultural revolution" was defined as a struggle against the revisionist line or the capitalist road. There were no grounds at all for this definition. It led to the confusing of right and wrong on a series of important theories and policies. Many things denounced as revisionist or capitalist during the "cultural revolution" were actually Marxist and socialist principles, many of which had been set forth or supported by Comrade Mao Zedong himself. The "cultural revolution" negated many of the correct principles, policies, and achievements of the seventeen years after the founding of the People's Republic. In fact, it negated much of the work of the Central Committee of the Party and the People's Government, including Comrade Mao Zedong's own contribution. It negated the arduous struggles the entire people had conducted in socialist construction.

2. The confusing of right and wrong inevitably led to confusing the people with the enemy. The "capitalist roaders" overthrown in the "cultural revolution" were leading cadres of Party and government organizations at all levels, who formed the core force of the socialist cause. The so-called bourgeois headquarters inside the Party headed by Liu Shaoqi and Deng Xiaoping simply did not exist. Irrefutable facts have proved that labeling Comrade Liu Shaoqi a "renegade, hidden traitor, and scab" was nothing but a frame-up by Lin Biao, Jiang Qing, and their followers. The political conclusion concerning Comrade Liu

Shaoqi drawn by the Twelfth Plenary Session of the Eighth Central Committee of the Party and the disciplinary measure it meted out to him were both utterly wrong. The criticism of the so-called reactionary academic authorities in the "cultural revolution" during which many capable and accomplished intellectuals were attacked and persecuted also badly muddled up the distinction between the people and the enemy.

3. Nominally, the "cultural revolution" was conducted by directly relying on the masses. In fact, it was divorced both from the Party organizations and from the masses. After the movement started, Party organizations at different levels were attacked and became partially or wholly paralyzed, the Party's leading cadres at various levels were subjected to criticism and struggle, inner-Party life came to a standstill, and many activists and large numbers of the basic masses whom the Party has long relied on were rejected. At the beginning of the "cultural revolution," the vast majority of participants in the movement acted out of their faith in Comrade Mao Zedong and the Party. Except for a handful of extremists, however, they did not approve of launching ruthless struggles against leading Party cadres at all levels. With the lapse of time, following their own circuitous paths, they eventually attained a heightened political consciousness and consequently began to adopt a skeptical or wait-and-see attitude toward the "cultural revolution," or even resisted and opposed it. Many people were assailed either more or less severely for this very reason. Such a state of affairs could not but provide openings to be exploited by opportunists, careerists, and conspirators, not a few of whom were escalated to high or even key positions.

4. Practice has shown that the "cultural revolution" did not in fact constitute a revolution or social progress in any sense, nor could it possibly have done so. It was we and not the enemy at all who were thrown into disorder by the "cultural revolution." Therefore, from beginning to end, it did not turn "great disorder under heaven" into "great order under heaven," nor could it conceivably have done so. After the state power in the form of the people's democratic dictatorship was established in China, and especially after socialist transformation was basically completed and the exploiters were eliminated as classes, the socialist revolution represented a fundamental break with the past in both content and method, though its tasks remained to be completed. Of course, it was essential to take proper account of certain undesirable

phenomena that undoubtedly existed in Party and state organisms and to remove them by correct measures in conformity with the Constitution, the laws, and the Party Constitution. But on no account should the theories and methods of the "cultural revolution" have been applied. Under socialist conditions, there is no economic or political basis for carrying out a great political revolution in which "one class overthrows another." It decidedly could not come up with any constructive program but could only bring grave disorder, damage, and retrogression in its train. History has shown that the "cultural revolution" initiated by a leader laboring under a misapprehension and capitalized on by counter-revolutionary cliques, led to domestic turmoil and brought catastrophe to the Party, the state, and the whole people . . .

Chief responsibility for the grave "Left" error of the "cultural revolution," an error comprehensive in magnitude and protracted in duration, does indeed lie with Comrade Mao Zedong. But after all it was the error of a great proletarian revolutionary. Comrade Mao Zedong paid constant attention to overcoming shortcomings in the life of the Party and state. In his later years, however, far from making a correct analysis of many problems, he confused right and wrong and the people with the enemy during the "cultural revolution." While making serious mistakes, he repeatedly urged the whole Party to study the works of Marx, Engels, and Lenin conscientiously and imagined that his theory and practice were Marxist and that they were essential for the consolidation of the dictatorship of the proletariat. Herein lies his tragedy. While persisting in the comprehensive error of the "cultural revolution," he checked and rectified some of its specific mistakes, protected some leading Party cadres and non-Party public figures and enabled some leading cadres to return to important leading posts. He led the struggle to smash the counter-revolutionary Lin Biao clique. He made major criticisms and exposures of Jiang Qing, Zhang Chunqiao, and others, frustrating their sinister ambition to seize supreme leadership. All this was crucial to the subsequent and relatively painless overthrow of the "Gang of Four" by our Party. In his later years, he still remained alert to safeguarding the security of our country, stood up to the pressure of the social imperialists, pursued a correct foreign policy, firmly supported the just struggle of all peoples, outlined the correct strategy of the three worlds, and advanced the important principle that China would never seek hegemony. During the "cultural revolution" our Party was not destroyed but maintained its unity. The State Council and the People's Liberation Army were still able to do much of their essential work. The Fourth National People's Congress, which was attended by deputies from all nationalities and all walks of life, was convened, and it determined the composition of the State Council with comrades Zhou Enlai and Deng Xiaoping as the core of its leadership. The foundation of China's socialist system remained intact, and it was possible to continue socialist economic construction. Our country remained united and exerted a significant influence on international affairs. All these important facts are inseparable from the great role played by Comrade Mao Zedong. For these reasons, and particularly for his vital contributions to the cause of the revolution over the years, the Chinese people have always regarded Comrade Mao Zedong as their respected and beloved great leader and teacher.

The struggle waged by the Party and the people against "Left" errors and against the counter-revolutionary Lin Biao and Jiang Qing cliques during the "cultural revolution" was arduous and full of twists and turns, and it never ceased. Rigorous tests throughout the "cultural revolution" have proved that standing on the correct side in the struggle were the overwhelming majority of members of the Eighth Central Committee of the Party and the members it elected to its Political Bureau, Standing Committee, and Secretariat. Most of our Party cadres, whether they were wrongly dismissed or remained at their posts, whether they were rehabilitated early or late, are loyal to the Party and people and steadfast in their belief in the cause of socialism and communism. Most of the intellectuals, model workers, patriotic democrats, patriotic overseas Chinese and cadres, and masses of all strata and all nationalities who had been wronged and persecuted did not waver in their love for the motherland and in their support for the Party and socialism. Party and state leaders such as Comrades Liu Shaoqi, Peng Dehuai, He Long, and Tao Zhu and all other Party and non-Party comrades who were persecuted to death in the "cultural revolution" will live forever in the memories of the Chinese people. It was through the joint struggles waged by the entire Party and the masses of workers, peasants, PLA officers and men, intellectuals, educated youth, and cadres that the havoc wrought by the "cultural revolution" was somewhat mitigated. Some progress was made in our economy despite tremendous losses. Grain output increased relatively steadily. Significant achievements were scored in industry, communications, and capital construction and in science and technology. New railways were built, and the Changjiang River Bridge at Nanjing was completed; a number of large enterprises using advanced technology went into operation; hydrogen bomb tests were successfully undertaken and manmade satellites successfully launched and retrieved; and new hybrid strains of long-grained rice were developed and popularized. Despite the domestic turmoil, the People's Liberation Army bravely defended the security of the motherland. And new prospects were opened up in the sphere of foreign affairs. Needless to say, none of these successes can be attributed in any way to the "cultural revolution," without which we would have scored far greater achievements for our cause. Although we suffered from sabotage by the counter-revolutionary Lin Biao and Jiang Qing cliques during the "cultural revolution," we won out over them in the end. The Party, the people's political power, the people's army, and Chinese society on the whole remained unchanged in nature. Once again history has proved that our people are a great people and that our Party and socialist system have enormous vitality.

In addition to the above-mentioned immediate cause of Comrade Mao Zedong's mistake in leadership, there are complex social and historical causes underlying the "cultural revolution," which dragged on for as long as a decade. The main causes are as follows:

1. The history of the socialist movement is not long, and that of the socialist countries is even shorter. Some of the laws governing the development of socialist society are relatively clear, but many more remain to be explored. Our Party had long existed in circumstances of war and fierce class struggle. It was not fully prepared, either ideologically or in terms of scientific study, for the swift advent of the newborn socialist society and for socialist construction on a national scale. The scientific works of Marx, Engels, Lenin, and Stalin are our guide to action but can in no way provide ready-made answers to the problems we may encounter in our socialist cause. Even after the basic completion of socialist transformation, given the guiding ideology, we were liable, owing to the historical circumstances in which our Party grew, to continue to regard issues unrelated to class struggle as its manifestations when observing and

handling new contradictions and problems that cropped up in the political, economic, cultural, and other spheres in the course of the development of socialist society. And when confronted with actual class struggle under the new conditions, we habitually fell back on the familiar methods and experiences of the large-scale, turbulent mass struggle of the past, which should no longer have been mechanically followed. As a result, we substantially broadened the scope of class struggle. Moreover, this subjective thinking and practice divorced from reality seemed to have a "theoretical basis" in the writings of Marx, Engels, Lenin, and Stalin because certain ideas and arguments set forth in them were misunderstood or dogmatically interpreted. For instance, it was thought that equal right, which reflects the exchange of equal amounts of labor and is applicable to the distribution of the means of consumption in socialist society, or "bourgeois right" as it was designated by Marx, should be restricted and criticized, and so the principle of "to each according to his work" and that of material interest should be restricted and criticized; that small production would continue to engender capitalism and the bourgeoisie daily and hourly on a large scale even after the basic completion of socialist transformation, and so a series of "Left" economic policies and policies on class struggle in urban and rural areas were formulated; and that all ideological differences inside the Party were reflections of class struggle in society, and so frequent and acute inner-Party struggles were conducted. All this led us to regard the error in magnifying class struggle as an act in defense of the purity of Marxism. Furthermore, Soviet leaders started a polemic between China and the Soviet Union and turned the arguments between the two parties on matters of principle into a conflict between the two nations, bringing enormous pressure to bear upon China politically, economically, and militarily. So we were forced to wage a just struggle against the big-nation chauvinism of the Soviet Union. In these circumstances, a campaign to prevent and combat revisionism inside the country was launched, which spread the error of broadening the scope of class struggle in the Party, so that normal differences among comrades inside the Party came to be regarded as manifestations of the revisionist line or of the struggle between the two lines. This resulted in growing tension in inner-Party relations. Thus it became difficult for the Party to resist certain "Left" views put forward by Comrade Mao

Zedong and others, and the development of these views led to the outbreak of the protracted "cultural revolution."

2. Comrade Mao Zedong's prestige reached a peak and he began to get arrogant at the very time when the Party was confronted with the new task of shifting the focus of its work to socialist construction, a task for which the utmost caution was required. He gradually divorced himself from practice and from the masses, acted more and more arbitrarily and subjectively, and increasingly put himself above the Central Committee of the Party. The result was a steady weakening and even undermining of the principle of collective leadership and democratic centralism in the political life of the Party and the country. This state of affairs took shape only gradually, and the Central Committee of the Party should be held partly responsible. From the Marxist viewpoint, this complex phenomenon was the product of given historical conditions. Blaming this on only one person or on only a handful of people will not provide a deep lesson for the whole Party or enable it to find practical ways to change the situation. In the Communist movement, leaders play quite an important role. This has been borne out by history time and again and leaves no room for doubt. However, certain grievous deviations, which occurred in the history of the international Communist movement owing to the failure to handle the relationship between the Party and its leader correctly, had an adverse effect on our Party, too. Feudalism in China has had a very long history. Our Party fought in the firmest and most thoroughgoing way against it, and particularly against the feudal system of land ownership and the landlords and local tyrants, and fostered a fine tradition of democracy in the antifeudal struggle. But it remains difficult to eliminate the evil ideological and political influence of centuries of feudal autocracy. And for various historical reasons, we failed to institutionalize and legalize inner-Party democracy and democracy in the political and social life of the country; or we drew up the relevant laws, but they lacked due authority. This meant that conditions were present for the over-concentration of Party power in individuals and for the development of arbitrary individual rule and the personality cult in the Party. Thus, it was hard for the Party and state to prevent the initiation of the "cultural revolution" or check its development.

60

On the Appropriate Handling of Materials Related to Unjust, False, and Mistaken Cases Dating from the Great Cultural Revolution Movement

Ministry of Public Security

> *Source:* This notification ("Guanyu tuoshan chuli wenhua dageming yundong zhong yuan, jia, cuo an cailiao wenti de tongzhi") was issued on 21 July 1980. Our translation is based on the text reproduced in the Ministry of Public Security Policy and Law Research Office, ed., *Zhifa shouce (Law Implementation Handbook)*, Vol. 2 (Beijing: Qunzhong chubanshe, 1982), pp. 255–56.

To Provincial, Municipal, and Autonomous Regional Bureaus of Public Security:

Recently, a number of localities have inquired about how they should process materials forming part of the unjust, false, and mistaken cases dating from the Great Cultural Revolution movement. After having investigated the matter and in order to do a proper and good job of it in accordance with the spirit of the relevant regulations issued by the Center and State Council and in conformity with the actual situation in public security organs, we herewith notify you as follows:

1. Materials forming part of those cases processed by public security organs in the course of the Great Cultural Revolution movement that upon reexamination have been overturned as unjust, false, or mistaken are to be dealt with in one of the following ways depending on the circumstances:

a. The following materials are to be preserved and to be stored in the archives together with the concerned party's appeal documents, the conclusion announcing his rehabilitation, and investigation reports and testimony documenting the same: the basis in writing for the launching of the original case [investigation] and the [original] leadership's comments [on it]; technical appraisals; reports documenting important successful detective work; reports on major breakthroughs; requests, permissions, and decisions to detain and arrest people; detention, arrest, and search warrants; search records; lists of confiscated and handled items; conclusive reports; indictments; verdicts; release notifications; illness and death reports; and reports containing requests for instructions as well as decisions to subject the concerned party to reeducation through labor, surveillance, or the affixation of a [political] label.

b. The following materials may, after having been signed for, be returned to the concerned party: self-examinations and accounts, exposures and denunciations produced under duress by the person subject to investigation; letters, manuscripts, documents, photographs, and diaries belonging to the person under investigation and not related to the rehabilitation.

c. Remaining miscellaneous materials may in principle be destroyed after having been weeded, itemized, and recorded and after permission has been obtained from the leadership.

2. Clerical material and cadre investigation materials from the Great Cultural Revolution movement, the contents of which bear upon unjust, false, and mistaken cases, should be disposed of in accordance with the "Opinion of the State Archives Bureau Concerning the Disposal of Clerical Materials Dating from the Great Cultural Revolution Movement the Contents of Which Bear Upon Unjust, False, and Mistaken Cases" as circulated with a comment by the CCP Center and State Council on 3 November 1979 and the "Notification in the Matter of the Disposal of Cadre Investigation Materials Dating from the Great Cultural Revolution Movement" issued by the CCP Central Organization Department on 30 November 1979.[1]

3. Original dossier material concerning cases dating from before the Great Cultural Revolution movement that now upon reexamination have been overturned need not be disposed of separately but may be preserved in the original case dossier together with the conclusion announcing the rehabilitation after reexamination and other relevant material.

You are asked to abide by and implement the above notification in accordance with the concrete circumstances in your locality.

---

[1] CCP Central Document *Zhongfa* [1979] 81: "Zhonggong Zhongyang, Guowuyuan pizhuan Guojia dang'anju guanyu chuli wenhua dageming yundong zhong xingcheng de hanyou yuan, jia, cuo an neirong de wenshu cailiao de yijian," in State Archives Bureau, ed., *Dang'an gongzuo wenjian huiji* (*Collected Documents on Archival Work*), Vol. 1 (Beijing: Dang'an chubanshe, 1985), pp. 52–54; CCP Central Organization Department Document *Tong zi* [1979] 54: "Zhonggong Zhongyang zuzhibu guanyu chuli wenhua dageming yundong zhong ganbu shencha cailiao wenti de tongzhi," in China People's Bank Personnel Section, ed., *Renshi gongzuo wenjian xuanbian* (*Selected Documents on Personnel Work*) (Beijing: Zhongguo jinrong chubanshe, 1985), pp. 869–74.

61
Civilian's Martyr Status Revoked . . .

Ministry of Civil Affairs and Civil Affairs Bureau of
Jiangsu Province

Source: Translation based on reprint in *Xiangzhang shouce* (*Township Magistrate's Handbook*) (Beijing: Falü chubanshe, 1989), pp. 693–94.

Ministry of Civil Affairs
Preferential Treatment
Document [1984] No. 4

To the Civil Affairs Bureau of Jiangsu Province:

Your document Su Civ. Pref. [84] 2 has been received and processed. The two persons in Nanjing who died while putting up a big-character poster—one from falling down, the other from being stabbed with a knife—do not fulfill the requirements for martyrs specified in the *Regulations Governing the Commendation of Revolutionary Martyrs* and should therefore not be issued with [new] martyr's certificates.
Ministry of Civil Affairs
15 February 1984

[Original] appendix: *Request for Instructions from the Civil Affairs Bureau of Jiangsu Province*

Jiangsu Civil Affairs Bureau
Preferential Treatment
Document [1984] No. 2

To the Ministry of Civil Affairs:

The Civil Affairs Bureau of Nanjing municipality recently reported to us the case of two residents of that city who died during the "Cultural Revolution" in 1967 while putting up a big-character poster—one from falling down, the other being stabbed with a knife—and who at the time were formally recognized as martyrs by the then Jiangsu Province Military Control Commission. The commission presented each family with a *Commemorative Certificate Issued to the Honored Families of Those Who Gave Their Lives While on Duty,* and the families have to this day enjoyed the preferential treatment accorded descendants of revolutionary martyrs. In the course of our ongoing work of replacing and reissuing martyr's certificates, we have so far dealt with this matter by postponing the issue of [new] certificates, but the relatives keep pressuring us and demanding that such certificates be issued. According to the *Regulations Governing the Commendation of Revolutionary Martyrs,* the men do not qualify as martyrs, and we find ourselves unable to issue [new] certificates. But, since the case touches upon matters of policy, we still do not quite know how to handle it and therefore request special instructions and look forward to your reply.

Civil Affairs Bureau of Jiangsu Province
30 January 1984

62
... and Soldiers' Martyr Status Reaffirmed

Ministry of Civil Affairs and Civil Affairs Bureau of Guangxi Zhuang Autonomous Region

Source: Translation based on reprint in *Xiangzhang shouce* (*Township Magistrate's Handbook*) (Beijing: Falü chubanshe, 1989), pp. 713–14.

Ministry of Civil Affairs
Preferential Treatment
Document [1984] No. 55

To the Civil Affairs Bureau of the Guangxi Zhuang Autonomous Region:

Your request for instructions Gui Civ. Pref. [84] 100 has been received and processed. After having consulted with the General Political Department in the matter of whether members of the Chinese

People's Liberation Army who laid down their lives in the "Cultural Revolution" are to continue to receive recognition as martyrs or not, we in principle agree to your proposal, i.e. that revolutionary army men who received formal recognition as martyrs for having laid down their lives while acting on orders should generally still be recognized as revolutionary martyrs and [their families should] be issued with [new] *Revolutionary Martyr's Certificates* on which should be written words to the effect that "Comrade X X X laid down his life on such-and-such a date while carrying out orders in the X X region."

The matter of those rare individuals who clearly fail to satisfy the criteria for martyrs yet were mistakenly recognized as such on a *Certificate Issued to the Families of Heroic Revolutionary Army Men* should be rectified in accordance with the principle of seeking truth from facts, and the families concerned should be consulted and presented with a proper explanation.

In response, with greetings.

Ministry of Civil Affairs
20 December 1984

[Original] appendix: *Request for Instructions from the Civil Affairs Bureau of the Guangxi Zhuang Autonomous Region*

Guangxi Civil Affairs Bureau
Preferential Treatment
Document [1984] No. 100

To the Ministry of Civil Affairs:

This year our region has supplemented and replaced previously issued *Revolutionary Martyr's Certificates*. Some municipalities and counties noted that the armed forces had already posthumously recognized as martyrs those who served with the Chinese People's Liberation Army and who died in the course of "supporting the Left" or while executing orders like the "3 July Proclamation."[1] At present, as we

---

[1] The text referred to as the "3 July Proclamation" is Central Document *Zhongfa* [1968] 103, translated as "An Order to Stop Fighting in Guangxi," in Harold C. Hinton, ed., *The People's Republic of China 1949–1979: A Documentary Survey* (Wilmington: Scholarly Resources, 1980), pp. 2118–19.

deepen our study of the policy concerning the need to thoroughly negate the "Great Cultural Revolution," we must fully realize that it was equally wrong to be a member of either faction and that the army's support of the Left was in fact the support of factions, etc. Only in this way shall we be able to successfully eradicate factionalism and strengthen our Party spirit. Consequently, we ask whether or not the above-mentioned dead should still be referred to as martyrs. If not, should their martyr's status be revoked by the armed forces or by the local civilian authorities? If they are still to be recognized as martyrs, how should the circumstances surrounding their heroic death be described? We have already written a report to the regional People's Government on this matter and made the following proposal: Persons serving with the People's Liberation Army who laid down their lives while acting on orders and who have already received recognition as martyrs should continue to receive such recognition, and [their families] should be issued with [new] martyr's certificates. The circumstances surrounding their heroic deaths should be described as "Comrade X X X laid down his life on such-and-such a date while carrying out orders in the X X region" or "Comrade X X X laid down his life on such-and-such a date while carrying out orders in Nanning."

The Guangxi Military District agrees with our views as expressed here, and the "Small Group in Charge of the Resolution of Outstanding Matters" of the Regional Party Committee Rectification Office states: We agree with the views expressed by the Civil Affairs Office, yet in view of the possibility of similar problems existing in other parts of the country, we propose that it approach the Ministry of Civil Affairs for instructions.

We now specifically ask the Ministry to provide us with instructions. Please comment and respond.

Civil Affairs Bureau of Guangxi Zhuang Autonomous Region
5 September 1984

63

Regulations Governing the Publication of Books about the "Great Cultural Revolution"

CCP Central Propaganda Department and State Press and Publications Administration

Source: This is a translation of "Guanyu chuban 'wenhua dageming' tushu wenti de ruogan guiding" reprinted in PRC State Press and Publications Administration Policy Laws and Regulations Section, ed., *Zhonghua renmin gongheguo xianxing xinwen chuban fagui huibian (1949–1990) (Operative Press and Publishing Laws and Regulations of the People's Republic of China, 1949–1990)* (Beijing: Renmin chubanshe, 1991), pp. 231–32.

Recently, some publishing houses have published a number of books specifically researching and presenting the history, people, and events of the "Cultural Revolution"; other publishing houses are in the midst of planning the publication of books of this kind; and some publishing houses have, for the sole purpose of making a profit, already put out so-called Cultural Revolutionary "anecdotes," "secrets," and "behind-the-scenes accounts" to attract a readership. This has had a negative impact in society. Most recently, a leading comrade with the Center pointed out with respect to the publication of books dealing with the "Cultural Revolution" that in view of the Center's consistent spirit of uniting as one, looking forward, and dealing with historical matters in a sweeping rather than in a finicky way; and in view of comrade Deng Xiaoping's instructions about the need at present to strengthen the Party's concentrated and unified leadership and to make full use of its dominant political position, there is really no need to consider the publication of a *Dictionary of the Cultural Revolution,* since a work of that kind in all likelihood would be controversial and lead to the re-opening of old controversies. To disregard the *Notification* [in this matter] issued earlier by the Central Propaganda Department, to present the department with a *fait accompli,* and in this way force the Center to give permission to publish, is unacceptable.[1] [We] reaffirm the regulations laid down by the Center in the past and stress

---

[1] We have not been able to locate a copy of the Central Propaganda Department notification referred to here.

the detrimental effect that the publication of books of this kind may have. Consequently, in the foreseeable future we will not even consider applications [for permission] to publish a *Dictionary of the Cultural Revolution.*

In connection herewith, we issue the following regulations to govern the publication of books about the "Great Cultural Revolution":

1. From now on and for quite some time, publishing firms should not plan the publication of dictionaries or other handbooks about the "Great Cultural Revolution." Unless special permission to publish has been granted by the Central Propaganda Department and State Press and Publications Administration, any such titles already under way (or already printed) should be withdrawn and a report stating the circumstances should be submitted to the Central Propaganda Department and State Press and Publications Administration.

2. Under normal circumstances, one should not plan to publish titles specifically researching the "Great Cultural Revolution" or specifically telling the history of the "Great Cultural Revolution." Separate permission to publish works on selected topics of definite value should be sought by local publishing firms from provincial (autonomous regional, municipal) Propaganda Departments and by central publishing firms from the superior ministry (commission) under which they belong. These [superior bodies] should in turn carry out a rigorous investigation and produce a written report stating their reasons and apply for final permission to publish from the State Press and Publications Administration and the Central Propaganda Department.

3. Recently quite a number of recollections, memoirs, reportage literature, etc., dealing with the "Great Cultural Revolution" have been published, and in principle one should not plan to put out any more. The publication of works that have as their theme the so-called "unofficial history" and "secret story" of Lin Biao and the "Gang of Four," and works in which there is a lot of chasing of the wind and clutching of shadows—hearsay—willful fabrication and distortion of the facts, should cease. Separate permission to publish seriously and conscientiously written recollections with a definite value may be sought by local publishing firms from provincial (autonomous regional, municipal) Propaganda Departments and by central publishing firms from the superior ministry (commission) under which they belong. Only when final permission has been granted may one arrange for publication. These recollections must be factually accurate, not violate the spirit of the Center's "Resolution on

Certain Questions in the History of Our Party since the Founding of the People's Republic of China," not cite at will historical materials not formally declassified by the Center, and not touch upon the moral character of leading Party and government individuals.[2]

4. The above-mentioned kinds of books about the "Great Cultural Revolution," the publication of which is permitted, may at present be produced and published only by the various People's Publishing Houses and the relevant central social science publishing houses. No other publishing firms should arrange to publish such books, either in cooperation with or on behalf of others.

5. The distribution of the above-mentioned kinds of books should be handled exclusively by the Xinhua Book Stores and may not be handled by private or collective book traders.

6. Translations of foreign works concerning the "Cultural Revolution" are also to be dealt with according to the above principles.

7. Upon receipt of this notification, publishing firms in the process of printing or arranging for the publication of books about the "Cultural Revolution" without having been given prior permission from the Central Propaganda Department or the State Press and Publications Administration should, without exception, momentarily suspend the printing and distribution of such books. Meanwhile, they should present to the Central Propaganda Department and State Press and Publications Administration a report on the topics [of the books] and the current situation with respect to their publication, and await further instructions.

8. These regulations are to be enforced from the day they are received. Those who violate these regulations are, depending on the seriousness of the violation, to be punished either by confiscation of profits, by fines, and/or by holding the leadership responsible. Punishments are to be decided upon by the press and publications bureaus of the provinces, autonomous regions, or municipalities, or—when necessary—the State Press and Publications Administration.

9. Past regulations contravening the above are no longer to be enforced.

10 December 1984

---

[2]See Document 59 above.

I. Ordinary People Remember

Feng Jicai, the writer who took down the first story below—about a man whose lifelong suffering forces him to ask if the Cultural Revolution had not actually been under way for 2,000 years—insists, "We Chinese (*women de minzu*) forget far too easily."[1] Perhaps Feng is right, though in all likelihood the Chinese *minzu* is no better and no worse at forgetting than people in general.

In China today, a tiny active contingent of oral historians is recording the memories of those who spent the better part of their lives living the Communist revolution, and the Cultural Revolution in particular. The belief shared by many of these aspiring Studs Terkels is that "one records the experiences of ordinary people because the essential reality of life is only found in the reality of the common grassroots."[2] Li Hui, a journalist with the *People's Daily* who has published the anthology *Bloodstained Innocence—The Cultural Revolution in the Hearts of the Young* (Documents 65–69), maintains optimistically, "As long as our recollections are not wiped out, history not only will not be wiped out, but may even appear ever more vivid."[3]

Did the Cultural Revolution really have a meaning? If so, what was it? That is the question asked by many ordinary (and some not so ordinary) people. The relatives of members and supporters of the "15 August" faction killed in Chongqing are still grieving for their dead (Document 70)—buried in what is possibly the only remaining Red Guard cemetery in all of China—and asking, "Why?" Philosopher Zhang Zhiyang tries to come to terms with the Cultural Revolution by unburdening himself, not of a story that claims to be "real" in the usual sense (Document 71), but through introspective association that is both ironic and absurd. His aim is not to communicate historical knowledge

---

[1]Feng Jicai, preface to *Yibaige ren de shinian* (*One Hundred People's Decade*) (Nanjing: Jiangsu wenyi chubanshe, 1991), p. 2.

[2]Ibid., p. 4.

[3]Li Hui, afterword to Li Hui and Gao Lilun, eds., *Dixue de tongxin—Haizi xinzhong de wenge* (*Bloodstained Innocence—The Cultural Revolution in the Hearts of the Young*) (Beijing: Zhongguo shaonian ertong chubanshe, 1989), p. 318.

but to give his readers a sense of what it felt like to be imprisoned for crimes not committed.

The final text in this reader was never meant to tell us about the past but contains an important historical message all the same.[4] It throws a rare flicker of light upon the psychology of the perpetrators—the men who operated the Cultural Revolutionary state machinery. It is a remarkable letter from Wang Li—once a member of the Central Cultural Revolution Group—to the leading members of the Politburo, in which Wang is asking to be readmitted to the Party. "Perhaps," he suggests, "I can be of some use to the Party if I am allowed to . . . denounce myself by summing up the bitter negative experiences in which I took part." Although the CCP had kept him imprisoned without a trial for fifteen years and during that period did its best to drive him insane with mind-altering drugs, Wang still has no higher wish than to rejoin the Party and to die as a member of the "organization."

---

[4]Jan Vansina, *Oral Tradition as History* (Madison: University of Wisconsin Press, 1985), p. 91.

64
The "Cultural Revolution" Has Been Under Way for Two Thousand Years

Anonymous, as told to Feng Jicai

Source: " 'Wenge' jinxingle liangqian nian" as translated by Xiaoxia Gong and published in *Chinese Sociology and Anthropology: A Journal of Translations*, Vol. 26, No. 1, Fall 1993, pp. 92–103. Originally published in Feng Jicai, *Yibai-ge ren de shinian (One Hundred People's Decade)* (Nanjing: Jiangsu wenyi chubanshe, 1991), pp. 272–86.

You want someone to write about his or her experience during the ten-year Cultural Revolution, but I would rather tell you about my fifty years. Probably you think I stray too far from the subject. But, don't fear, my Cultural Revolution began fifty years ago.

After learning of my suffering over these fifty years, you will definitely conclude that the Cultural Revolution did not begin in 1966. How about a hundred years ago? No. The Cultural Revolution as I understand it has a two-thousand-year history in China!

I will tell you my story and my reasons as well.

I could not figure this out for decades. I joined the revolution several decades ago and was mistreated as a counter-revolutionary for dozens of years. I could not understand why I was not able to leave the ranks of the "enemy." In 1968 I was detained in a small room near a river, after being beaten by a rebel organization. The sound of the rushing water reminded me of the river in my hometown, where I grew up. When I participated in the Anti-Japanese War there, I crossed the river many times. It was so long ago. . . . Revolution, revolution, and again revolution; enemy, enemy, and again enemy. I participated in the revolution, but I am its enemy. The pain after the beating gradually left my body, not disappearing, but concentrating in my heart. . . . I do not know how, but suddenly it all became clear.

There were two lineages in our village, Wang and Li. I am a Li. From the very beginning, the two lineages fought each other without stopping. I can recall three battles. People were badly wounded. My distant uncle "Cripple Li" was crippled during one of them. No one could tell how and why the hatred began. When I was a kid in my split-bottomed pants, my grandma told me that someone in the Wang family gained a *Juren* degree in the Qing dynasty. A *Juren* then was unbeatable in such a village. Usually, *Juren* Wang opened his arms when walking down the road with a stick in his hand. If any Li touched him, he would beat them.

Village head was a key position. Whoever took it would be able to control the other side. The Wang lineage had more people and always occupied that position, both under the Japanese and the Communist Party. From this fact you can learn how history influences present-day realities. If you want to find out the root of the Cultural Revolution, this is the longest and deepest one. But how did this occur to me at the time?

Our village was an old liberated area; after the Marco Polo Bridge incident, it became the famous Central Hebei Anti-Japanese revolutionary base area. The masses were enthusiastic. I was then fourteen, studying in elementary school. I had the most genuine faith in the Communist Party, tending to believe whatever they said. When the Eighth Route Army came in, I was too excited to fall asleep. If a soldier looked at me only for a little while, I would be delighted. I liked reading and writing and was a capable public speaker. My school selected me to be head of the Children's League. Every evening, I went from house to house, propagating anti-Japanese slogans and communist theories. The adults were enthusiastic, and so was I. During that period, a no-smoking and no-drinking campaign was launched in the base area. Wall posters in each village called for no smoking and no drinking and criticized the cadres first. Our village head was fond of smoking, drinking, and gambling. I wrote a short piece criticizing him with good intentions: "Someone asks the others not to smoke, while he smokes one pack after another; someone asks the others not to drink, while he drinks a great deal. What should we call this?"

Is that soft and childlike? Don't forget I was only a fourteen-year-old boy. Before I could post it to the wall, I lost it on my way to school. It was picked up by a public security worker in the village whose name was Wang. He submitted it to the village head. Then the village head accused me of being a spy. The village head said that he represented the Party. Whoever opposed him was actually opposing the Party. Who would oppose the Party? Of course, the nationalist spies. Right! The public security worker suggested that I be buried alive. The district authorities heard about this. A cook working in the district office belonged to our Li lineage. He came to see the head of the district and asked for a pardon for me. I was only a child without any clear ideas, he explained. The district leaders stopped the execution. Anyway, the village still pushed their case against me, accusing me internally of being suspected as a "spy." The first page in my dossier said "spy suspect." From then on, I bore such an allegation for the rest of my miserable life.

You might think it strange that they determined to put a fourteen-year-old kid into the ranks of the enemy for a few simple sentences, since they did not have any previous conflict with me. It was simple. They could not allow a Li to gain the honor of being head of the Children's League. I was therefore purged. Politics turned nasty under such cultural conditions. I had a distant uncle who studied at a normal school before the Anti-Japanese War. He was educated and well respected in the village. When the Communists came, he was too cautious to contact them. The village cadres in the Wang lineage accused him of being a Nationalist. He had seniority in the lineage, and, accordingly, the whole Li lineage was put under suspicion and could not raise their heads. In order to escape from this situation, my elder brother married the daughter of a county cadre and left the village. Nor could I stay. After I graduated from lower primary school, I went to another county for upper primary school. I thought I had left these difficulties behind. I never expected that I left with a political stain I was not able to get rid of.

Having graduated from upper primary school, I was assigned to teach in a village when I was sixteen. I had no knowledge that my dossier followed me like the shadow of a devil. The villagers appreciated my work. I felt great and wished to join the Party and to sacrifice myself for the revolution. I asked the village head if there was any Party branch in the village to which I could apply for Party membership. He teased me. First I thought they were treating me as a child and did not consider my application seriously. Later, I discovered that I was to be switched from one village to another constantly, as if I had some disease and should be kept away from the others. In 1942 the Japanese invaders launched their "1 May Mopping-Up" campaign. People were dispersed to various places for hiding. The county authorities found hiding places for everyone except me. Therefore, I went back to hide in my home village. During that period, someone wrote down a reactionary slogan in the snow. Without even investigating, those Wang cadres put the allegation against me in my dossier, further confirming that I was a "spy suspect." However, I was not informed about all this. I felt that the revolution only drove me away, never allowing me to join it. Still, I was faithful to the revolution and considered myself a part of it. I did not want to stay in the occupied area without doing anything and was determined to join the Eighth Route Army. Fortunately, in the most dangerous time of the "Mopping-Up," the Wang cadres went into hiding, and a Li—the one who worked as a cook in the district office and saved my life when I was going to be buried alive—was named village head. He wrote me a letter of recommendation. I hid the letter in my shoe and found the Eighth Route Army after great difficulties. I barely escaped from the clutches of the Japanese ten times along the way. . . . I was so excited when I saw our own army, just like seeing my own mother.

In the beginning I was a secretary in the Political Department, the Eighth Branch of the Central Hebei Military District. This period was a short spring in my life, full of trust, care, and friendship. Once when I had a fever, my comrades took turns caring for me day and night. . . . When my comrades put their hands on my head, tears dropped from my eyes. This was the first time I felt revolutionary friendship. It was better than mother love! I liked writing and often wrote to *Central Hebei Herald* and *Battle Front.* I sent out various writings, including short stories, poems, plays, and interviews. I am not saying my writings were good, but they reflected my true feelings. During the period, I met Sun Li, Yuan Qianli, and Wang Lin [several famous communist writers—Ed.]. They considered me to be a worker-peasant writer and gave me special training. The Political Department often sent me to work as a correspondent at the front. *Battle Front* published my reports every day for a while. My name appeared frequently in newspapers, and I became somewhat famous. I wanted to pursue a higher goal and again applied for Party membership. My leaders in the department were happy for me.

In fact, I made another mistake. My dossier did not follow me to the army at the time. After I applied for Party membership, the department sent people to investigate me in my village, and my files came. Dark clouds hung over my head once again. Not only was my application no longer mentioned, but journalistic work at the front was suspended— the army was attacking Po Town and Qing County at the time, and journalists were desperately needed in the field. One day, the director of the department entered my room with his hands behind his back and said, "Now we are in a very crucial conflict with our enemies. Some enemy agents are looking to recruit help, particularly among you political officers." "How can that be?" I asked with surprise. He was staring me in the face, observing my response. It was lucky I had no idea that they were suspicious of me at the time, and that this was a surprise examination. If I knew they suspected me, I would not be able to look natural even if I were not a spy. In that case, I would definitely have been seen as a spy and arrested. Later I learned that Central Hebei and Shandong were two experimental areas for Kang Sheng's Anti–Secret Agent Campaign. Whoever was put under suspicion would be arrested immediately. It was lucky my director was a cadre who had experienced the Long March, the Yan'an Rectification, the Rescue Campaign, and the Anti-"AB" Clique Campaign. He knew that many good people were wrongly accused. Having seen my faithful face, he left the room quietly. I was secretly put under control. All my activities and utterances were put in my files. Not until I was put under investigation by a military court in 1949 did I understand how great was the danger I faced. Nevertheless, I sensed that the light of trust had faded from the eyes of my comrades. I could question no one, appeal nowhere. If I defended myself, the situation would be even worse. Gradually, I became very sensitive. Though they were suspicious of me, I was skeptical of them, too, not knowing true or false in their attitudes toward me. To be suspicious made me feel bad. I was nervous and overreacting. My insomnia started then. My short and enjoyable spring was thus gone.

One year later, I was hospitalized in the Peace Hospital of the Central Hebei Military District with tuberculosis. I felt fine when I entered the hospital—I mean in the political sense rather than my physical health. Soon people were obviously keeping their distance from me. No one would even play chess with me. On my way back home during the Spring Festival, a soldier who was once my student walked together with me without saying anything. When we parted, he said to me hesitantly, "You are a good man. I have something to tell you. Please don't mention it to the others." My sincere promise moved him, and he said, "Remember your colleague Teacher Zhang? He was a spy and committed suicide."

I was shocked and said, "How could he be? His father was killed by a Japanese bombing raid. He was loyal to the revolution and had good moral spirit. Once he even put up a wall poster criticizing a village cadre, about whom no one dared speak a word, for his adultery and graft!"

My soldier student said, "It was said that the village cadres called him a 'spy suspect' for that very reason. He was expelled from the school and later worked in a military medicine plant. When the 'Eliminating Secret Agents' campaign began, the military checked his files and found that he was a 'spy suspect.' He was hung up and beaten. Not being able to bear it, he hung himself. It is said that your name is in his dossier, indicating you cooperated with him in his spy activities."

I asked, "What activity?" I was stunned.

He said he had no idea.

I was shocked and eventually recalled one fact. Teacher Zhang came to borrow my ink when writing his poster. The next day, the security personnel of the village suddenly came to borrow my ink. I was thrown into confusion. Why did he borrow ink from me? It seemed that they now had their evidence. How frightening!

The soldier student again asked, "One month ago, someone from the office of the Military District talked with you. Is that right?"

I said, "Yes. That was a special agent. He was nice, asking questions about my family, my personal history, and my health. So what?"

He said, "He was not a special agent! He was from the security office of the Military District! Now our army is having an internal campaign to eliminate spies. Your name was discovered in the old files of the Teacher Zhang spy case. That day, that man intended to arrest you in the hospital. But after chatting with you for a while, he felt that you did not look like a spy. I was working for hospital security when I heard this. I worried about you. You could have been arrested at any moment!"

That was during the winter. The weather was not very cold, but I shivered and my teeth chattered. After momentary panic, I feared nothing. I had wanted to grab that devil off my back for such a long time and see what it was. I wanted to cut myself open in front of the Party organization and let them examine me cell by cell, and to see once and for all if I was an enemy or a true revolutionary! After thinking this, I became confused. I had no way to prove myself! I was held by a huge iron hand and manipulated independent of my will.

Soon the Liberation War began. I went to Baiyangdian region with the army. The newspaper *Battle Front* was there. They needed help, and I happened to be a frequent author for the paper. The manager told me that he would like to transfer me to their paper and asked me to get an official introduction letter from the personnel department. I was delighted. However, I again ran into trouble when requesting the letter. I was not transferred to the newspaper but instead to the "Party rectification center" of the Military-Administrative Cadre School. Not everyone in the center was a Party member, but each of us was called to solve his own problem. I was simple-minded, thinking that the problem would be solved through questions and answers, like what one would see in plays. Unexpectedly, the problematic people there were ordered to attack one another. When you were attacked, your materials would be shown to the others, and vice versa. Everyone wanted to put on a good performance and treated the others badly. One night I stood guard with another young man. I asked him: "Can you tell me, what are their doubts about me? I feel mistreated. I never betray the revolution. Why am I always treated as an enemy?"

He was an honest young man from the countryside. Believing me to be sincere, he asked, "Did you write down a reactionary slogan in the snow of your home village during the '1 May Mopping-Up'? And did you say to a security cadre when you were working in the Political Department that you wished for a Nationalist air raid? . . . Also, did you write to your wife, telling her that the Fu Zuoyi Army would attack the Hejian Area? They wondered how you could know the enemy's maneuver ahead of time." In addition to this, he told me many other allegations.

I was in a panic, thinking I had no way to overturn such allegations. All these were based partly on fact but were terribly twisted, in some cases to the opposite of what was true. Take, for example, the air raid. When I was on a business trip with a security cadre, he asked me, "Li, you are a writer. How do you get all this material for your stories that we cannot even get?" At that moment, nationalist airplanes were flying overhead. I used it as an example and said, "Look, the enemy planes are flying. This is not news, there's no need to write about it. However, if they drop bombs on the village in front of us, it should be reported." I was talking about the value of news, but this was twisted to indicate that I wished for an enemy air raid and this was put into my dossier! Another example: News of an anticipated attack of the Fu Zuoyi Army was sent down by the military authorities, asking us to prepare for battle. How could this put me under suspicion for getting news from the enemy ahead of time? The more threatening fact was that my letter to my wife was checked! If I were a true enemy, how could I leave so much evidence against myself! During the Cultural Revolution, a rebel told me: Did you know how big your dossier is? More than a whole cart! Why did they put so much energy into putting me under surveillance, control, and investigation? Me, who was absolutely loyal to the revolution? I couldn't understand and became obstinate. The next day, the director of the rectification team again talked with me and oppressed me. I could bear it no more and ran out to the river to throw myself in, but was stopped. The director was furious. He held a struggle session in the school at once. The next day, I was escorted by force to the military court of the zone as an "active agent." In court, they forced me to submit evidence to prove that I was a spy. I told them that the only thing I could prove was that I was a revolutionary. They should submit tangible evidence if they accused me of being a spy. After this, I was handcuffed. This was the first time I wore such a thing, and in our own ranks! Forty-seven days after my being handcuffed, the whole country was liberated. I was delighted when I heard the news. But looking at the handcuffs I wore and the iron bars on the window, I felt sorry. Whenever I remembered that I greeted Liberation in handcuffs, I became sad, as if I had very dark shadows deep in my heart.

My experiences over the decades educated me: If someone praises you, it is useless and it will not be put in your dossier; but if someone said you had problems, even if this was only a suspicion, it would in most cases be put in your file. Anything put in your dossier is difficult to get out. It follows you your whole life. Dare you say that you are an honest and clean person in your dossier? The person hiding inside the thick cover of your dossier might be another one with dirty spots all over his body. At key moments, people would judge you from this picture and accordingly determine how to treat you.

The military court sent out investigators on horseback to the villages, schools, and army units where I once worked. No one could submit sufficient evidence to prove me a spy. Fortunately, the cadres in my home village had been changed. The new ones, even the Wangs, had no direct conflict with me and did not add new testimony against me. The military court released me. The conclusion to my case was: "Should be examined in his work. A good performance will prove no problem, while a bad one will lend credence to the charge." With such an ambiguous allegation, I entered New China.

For the first few years after the Liberation, I worked for several units and was not promoted because of my unresolved historical problem. I did not care about promotion very much. I was working hard, not to gain achievements but to avoid errors.

In 1955, I led an editing section in a publishing house in B City, with the ambiguous title of "person in charge." I worked very hard. Suddenly, the Elimination of Counter-Revolutionaries Campaign was launched. The old accusation was brought up again. I was attacked and interrogated, experiencing another political storm. However, though I had a hard time, this time my case was closed. My unit sent four or five people to the whole country, to Yunnan, Guizhou, and Sichuan, even to Inner Mongolia and Xinjiang. They questioned each of my acquaintances. Thanks to the Party Committee of Anping County: they said to them, "We checked the whole country during the Suppression of Counter-Revolutionaries Campaign and developed a list of names of all the spies in the county. He was not on it!" These words saved me. The allegation was refuted. The conclusion of the case was: "After investigation, the allegation of 'spy suspect' is overturned."

Since 1939, the year I joined the Children's League, I had been an enemy. Not until 1956 was I admitted as one of the people. No one but me cared about my suffering over these seventeen years. In the rally announcing the dismissal of my "spy suspect" charge, standing on the stage, I trembled constantly. Back at home, I did not celebrate with wine or burst into tears. No, I could no longer recognize myself. It was as if I had just risen from the dead.

Forgive me if I say something that sounds superstitious. I believe in fate.

What is fate? It is some invisible spirit that surrounds you. You have no control over it, while it influences you powerfully.

To me, good luck is always like a bird, which hangs over my head for but a short while. This is a trait of my fate, a typical characteristic of my life history.

The general Party branch secretary in our unit would have liked to promote one of his own men, but my capability and position stood out at the top. He put pressure on me. Meanwhile, a new publishing house was going to be set up in T City, and the one in charge happened to be my old leader. I asked for a transfer. It was no problem for me to change jobs this time. For the first time in my life, I went to work in a new place with a clean dossier. I felt such great relief. However, only a month after my transfer, the Rectification Campaign began. This was 1957.

Without warning, I received a letter from my former work unit in B City, signed by the Party branch of the editing section where I worked. They invited me back to help them in rectification. I could not turn down the request from the organization and went back to talk for two hours in a meeting. I complained about my mistreatment during the Elimination of Counter-Revolutionaries Campaign and made some criticisms of our general Party branch secretary. The guy sat right there with a darkened expression, saying nothing. How could I know that this two-hour speech would bring me misery for the next twenty years, just like what had happened before!

Not long after I gave the speech and came back to T City, the Anti-Rightist Campaign was brought down on our heads. This time, my former unit asked me back and announced that the general Party branch had named me as a Rightist. The Party branch of my editing section was accused of being an "anti-Party branch." Among some fifty editors, twenty-five were accused of being Rightists. Their crime, "bombarding the Party," occurred when they raised their voices in criticism of the general Party branch secretary.

Later I learned that the branch secretary and the general branch secretary had a personal conflict. The former took the chance of rectification to get rid of the latter. Because I was mistreated in the Elimination of Counter-Revolutionaries Campaign, he was using me as his weapon. The Anti-Rightist Campaign turned the tide, and I was thus sacrificed. Did it not resemble the conflict between the Wangs and the Lis in my home village? . . .

Looking back now, I should never have felt relieved when I went to T City so joyfully after the favorable verdict of the 1956 campaign. In fact, the shadows of my fate already hung over me, except I didn't know it. The former allegation was only "spy suspect," and now it was changed to convicted Rightist. Without even a decent interval, I was changed from one kind of enemy to another, like changing a name tag.

Now let us go back to the original topic, the Cultural Revolution.

I should blame myself for my misfortune during the Cultural Revolution. I was an old Rightist, a "dead tiger," and would always be a secondary target in anyone's struggle session. I was only used for setting the stage, I was not the main target of the struggle. In the first stage of the campaign, the Party secretary persecuted the manager. I

worked well with the manager when the publishing house was established. Accordingly, I became living proof that the manager "promoted
Rightists." The purpose of attacking me was to attack the manager.
Later, when the Oppose the Bourgeois Reactionary Line Campaign
began, the manager's faction fought back and persecuted the Party
secretary. In that case, I was neither attacked nor promoted. I stood
aside. When the Cleansing of the Class Ranks Campaign began, the
faction of the Party secretary rose up again and attacked the manager. I
never joined the manager's faction and therefore was of secondary
importance. During the period, those "bad people" were classified into
two kinds: one being detained in the "cowshed," the other allowed to
go home every night. I belonged to the second and was comfortably
ignored.

   In the publishing house, one female editor had once been outstanding in her line of work. Her ex-husband served as an officer in the
Nationalist army, and this earned her a "spy" label for political reasons. While having done nothing, she became the main target. The
purpose was also to add more evidence in the allegations against the
manager, showing the kind of bad people he protected. I should have
stood clear whenever I saw the word "spy." But one day I crossed the
yard on my way home just as she was sweeping the floor. Noticing no
one around, she put a piece of paper in my hand. I took it home and
read it. She begged me to give the note to her son-in-law. In the note,
she asked him to tell her brother to submit to the special investigation
team of the unit her manuscripts of the posters he wrote in the early
stages of the Cultural Revolution. I thought she might be afraid of
affecting her relatives and so informed her son-in-law with sympathy.
Unexpectedly, she confessed about the note under torture. I was affected and accused of being an active counter-revolutionary who delivered messages for a spy. I was detained in the cowshed, tortured
brutally every day. My arms still feel the pain to this day. They forced
me to confess that I saw a radio transmitter and code book in her
house. The female editor could not bear the torture and hung herself
with a bed sheet. Though she died, they still forced me to testify to
having seen a transmitter in her house. I thought it so strange that they
had to convert nonsense into fact. One day, they demanded that I admit
I was a "spy who slipped through the net" during the Elimination of
Counter-Revolutionaries Campaign: the female editor and I formed a
spy group, with the manager as our head. I suddenly understood. The

reason they persecuted us so hard was to target the manager. In like fashion, when the manager's faction had earlier attacked the Party secretary, they induced a non-Party member to announce the revocation of the secretary's Party membership. The spy allegation, to which I had bid farewell ten years before, once again fell down on my head, throwing me back into historical limbo. Once again I had become an object to be sacrificed in the struggle between two factions! For the third time! . . .

How can our nation ever end this continuing cycle?

65
Childhood without Toys

Yang Yan

Source: "Meiyou wanju de tongnian." In Li Hui and Gao Lilin, eds., *Dixue de tongxin—Haizi xinzhong de wenge (Bloodstained Innocence—The Cultural Revolution in the Hearts of the Young)* (Beijing: Zhongguo shaonian ertong chubanshe, 1989), pp. 88–89. The author of this recollection is now a librarian in the middle school attached to the Central Academy of Fine Arts, Beijing. Translated by Bengt Pettersson.

I was born in 1964. Although I was the second oldest child in my family, my mother, father, grandmother, grandmother's sister, and—I almost forgot—my great grandmother, who was still living at the time, all loved me dearly. Even my sister, who was four years older than I, knew this. She used to say: "Everyone likes that little black rascal!" My grandmother couldn't stand the word "black" and used to say, "What do you mean by 'black'? Don't you use such foul language!"

Despite the fact that so many people liked me, I never had any toys during my childhood. I remember my father once bought me a doll in a green military uniform, wearing a Red Guard armband. In its pocket it had a tiny copy of *Quotations from Chairman Mao* and on its military cap was a five-pointed star. The mere sight of the "doll" made me all excited. I lifted her, removed her little cap and the *Quotations*. Then I started playing with her. My grandmother happened to enter the room the very moment I dropped the doll on the floor. She picked her up right away, carefully brushed off her "green uniform," and put her cap on properly. With eyes wide open, I watched my grandmother's movements, believing that she would give the doll back to me. Instead, she unexpectedly put it in the corner next to the picture of Chairman Mao, a place we children weren't allowed to go near. I remember crying loudly for a while and also my father being criticized because of this: "How could you buy it for the child to play with? If it gets dirty or broken, then what do we do?"

From then on my only company were "songs of praise" and [slogans wishing Chairman Mao] "long life" and [expressing the hope that Lin Biao would remain] "forever healthy." Once when my aunt returned from the Production and Construction Corps [in Heilongjiang], to recuperate from an illness, she taught me to perform the "Loyalty Dance." Nobody ever told me any beautiful children's stories, but my grandmother often took me along to "recall-suffering meetings." I never understood what they were all about, but still I did not dare to make any noise. I only did what my grandmother did: When she cried, I cried, and when she shouted slogans, I shouted slogans, too.

Believe me, I really did have a childhood without any toys. But now I have a big doll given to me by my parents on my tenth birthday. Are they spoiling me? When visitors ask this question, I answer just like my mother and father: "It is in memory of a childhood without toys."

66
Burning Books

Liu Yan

Source: "Fenshu." In Li Hui and Gao Lilin, eds., *Dixue de tongxin—Haizi xinzhong de wenge* (*Bloodstained Innocence—The Cultural Revolution in the Hearts of the Young*) (Beijing: Zhongguo shaonian ertong chubanshe, 1989), pp. 171–72. The author now works in the Qianmen Hospital, Beijing. Translated by Björn Kjellgren.

Except for those books whose covers featured Chairman Mao's portrait, almost all of the books in the library were removed and carried out to the center of the sports ground by the "Black Gang."[1] Forcing

---

[1]This was the label affixed to "reactionary academic authorities" and other "bourgeois" elements in schools all over China during the first months of the Cultural Revolution.

them to do this were my classmates—Red Guards brandishing leather belts with brass buckles. The Red Guards insisted that these books had spread feudalist, capitalist, and revisionist ideas and that therefore they had to be burned.

I still have sharp and vivid memories of two Red Guards forcing our school's Party branch secretary, comrade Lin Jin, to carry the books to the sports ground. It is as if it all happened only yesterday. She had no choice but to carry her heavy load, and she appeared almost totally unaware of the surrounding mob, shouting and lashing out at her with their belts. She just kept shaking her head. . . .

Finally the books—by now a small mountain—were set on fire by the Red Guards. The books that they had only recently fought over, borrowed, and read were consumed by the raging fire of the Great Proletarian Cultural Revolution. Excited and passionate slogans accompanied the thick smoke rising up into the sky. Perhaps the Red Guards felt that the act of merely burning books was not "revolutionary" enough. In any case, using their belts, they prodded the "Black Gang" to the edge of the fire and made them stand there with heads lowered, bodies bent forward, to be "tried in the raging flames of the Great Cultural Revolution."

Among the members of the "Black Gang" I spotted my language teacher, Yu Changjiang, silently weeping. Her tears provoked the Red Guards to give her a few extra lashings, and the belts left ugly scars on her skin.

At the time, I was myself a daughter of the "Black Gang," and of course the Red Guards would not allow me to fight with them. So I could only watch in silence.

The August sun was mercilessly hot. As the "Black Gang" stood by the fire, they soon developed blisters on their faces and forearms. In front of them the raging fire—behind them the brass-buckled leather belts of the Red Guards. Some of the older members of the "Black Gang" fell to the ground, unable to take it anymore. The Red Guards pulled them to their feet and kept up the merciless regimen of leather belts and thunderous slogan shouting. Again I spotted Secretary Lin, caught between the strong sun and the blistering flames, still shaking her head . . .

What I had witnessed was the Beijing No. 11 Middle School Red Guard book fire, which caused a major stir all over the city. Last spring, as I visited the book fair at the Museum of History, unable to control my thoughts, I recalled the scenes of the burning books. I clasped my books to my chest, my eyes full of tears. I imagined seeing Secretary Lin, carrying her books, sadly shaking her head. One day I shall return to the library of my old school to see how many books are left.

67
Comrade Wu Han, I Apologize!

Zhang Yidong

Source: "Wu Han tongzhi, xiang nin daoqian!" In Li Hui and Gao Lilin, eds., *Dixue de tongxin—Haizi xinzhong de wenge* (*Bloodstained Innocence—The Cultural Revolution in the Hearts of the Young*) (Beijing: Zhongguo shaonian ertong chubanshe, 1989), pp. 1–4. Translated by Håkan Friberg.

It all took place in June 1966. I was fifteen years old and a third-grader in the Beijing No. 1 Middle School for Girls. At that time, the whole country was criticizing [Wu Han's play], *Hai Rui Dismissed from Office.* In the papers we read article upon article criticizing the play, and though at first we were only mildly curious, as we read on, the case quickly had us totally absorbed. Newspapers and the printed word—these were sacred things! The more we read, the more enraged we became. We even stopped going to classes, day in and day out doing nothing but paying attention to affairs of state.[1]

How could we stand idly by, doing nothing, if so many years after Liberation there were still people in the capital who attacked our Great Leader by innuendo?

One afternoon, at the end of June, while in the midst of a discussion in one of our classrooms, we suddenly noticed the students in the "Long to Be Red" schoolyard surging toward the gates, shouting "To Wu Han's home!" and "Let's go struggle against Wu Han!" Our hearts burning with rage, we too followed the crowd as it charged through the school gates and ran along Nanchang Avenue to the entrance of Wu Han's home at the north end of the street.

---

[1]The author is alluding to Mao Zedong's famous remark of August 1966, quoted in Document 2: "You should pay attention to affairs of state and carry the Great Proletarian Cultural Revolution through to the end."

The place was packed with students. The air was filled with the sound of slogans being shouted and fists pounding the gates. It seemed as if the crowd was about to raze Wu Han's home to the ground. A girl was standing on the steps shouting at the top of her lungs "Down with Wu Han!" and "Whoever opposes our Great Leader should have his dog's head smashed to a pulp!" Sounds of pounding, kicking, and banging on the door blended with loud excited shouts to form a chaotic din.

At this time, a little girl living next door led me and another student into her back yard, where we climbed a tall tree and onto the top of the wall surrounding Wu Han's home. We jumped down and started scuffling with the bodyguards. I don't know who opened the gates, but suddenly the frenzied crowd came pouring in.

In an instant, the north room was packed with students. Wu Han was sitting on a couch by the window. A person who was most likely his secretary sat next to him, desperately trying to protect him. The students were throwing books around and spitting. It seemed as if the slogans and invectives shouted were going to lift the roof of the building.

I had been pushed into a position next to Wu Han. Looking at his kind, benevolent eyes, I thought that they didn't look anything like the triangular jackass eyes of a scoundrel, and though I tried not to, I couldn't help feeling sympathy for him. However, I immediately recalled that he had opposed our Great Leader, and, putting on a stern face, I asked him, "Why did you oppose our Great Leader?" He hurriedly shook his drooping head, saying over and over again, "I didn't oppose our Great Leader." As the spittle on his bald forehead slid down into his face, I felt sorry for him.

Shortly thereafter, our school president and Party secretary arrived. They led the students in a criticism meeting in the courtyard, shouted a few slogans and left, leaving me and some other students behind to write slogans. As I was holding a slogan-covered strip of paper in my hand—not knowing quite where to paste it—a student outside the window knocked on the glass and patted his forehead with his hand, suggesting I paste it onto Wu Han's forehead. At first I didn't have the heart to do that, but, again recalling that we had to be firm in our class stand, I pulled the tea table in front of him out of the way with an air of indignation and pasted the slogan in the designated place.

Later, after the smashing of the "Gang of Four," I happened to read in an article that Wu Han and his wife had died under tragic circumstances in the Cultural Revolution.[2] A feeling of sudden discomfort filled my heart. How could we not bear responsibility for the tragic fate of Wu Han's family? Twenty years have passed, and still, every time I come to think of this incident, I feel remorse. Having now at long last confessed my great wrongdoing, I silently ask for forgiveness, hoping that in his heavenly abode, the martyred spirit of comrade Wu Han will have found solace.

---

[2]The circumstances surrounding the deaths of Wu Han and his wife, Yuan Zhen, in 1969 (Wu died in prison; Yuan died from abuse and medical neglect after being released from a labor correction team) will be dealt with in a forthcoming book by Wu's American biographer, Mary G. Mazur.

68
Go on Red! Stop on Green!

Yu Xiaoming

Source: "Quxiao hongdeng de zhenglun." In Li Hui and Gao Lilin, eds., *Dixue de tongxin—Haizi xinzhong de wenge* (*Bloodstained Innocence—The Cultural Revolution in the Hearts of the Young*) (Beijing: Zhongguo shaonian ertong chubanshe, 1989), pp. 293–95. The author now works for the State Commission of Science, Technology, and Industry for National Defense. Translated by Bengt Pettersson.

Many absurd dramas in history have been acted out in an atmosphere of extreme seriousness. As a result, absurdities have sometimes acquired an aura of mystique. To prevent absurdities from turning into disasters is a serious task. At the same time, absurdity is sometimes the only form in which the serious can act itself out.

The latter half of 1966 was truly a time of madness. Red Guards were running about "smashing the four olds," swearing to completely upset the status quo. At the time, some Red Guards discovered that there was a problem with the traffic lights: red, the color of revolution, meant stop and hence served to "obstruct the progress of revolution"! They pointed out that this was nothing less than blasphemy. It was an error that had to be corrected: red should mean "go"! The red light ought to illuminate the progress of revolution.

If a demand like this one were to have been accepted, it would have created chaos in our country's traffic control system and caused any number of accidents. At that time, who dared to go against the trend and turn down this absurd and ignorant demand raised by the Red Guards in the name of revolution? Fortunately Premier Zhou was able to prevent a disaster by engaging the Red Guards in a rather humorous discussion.[1]

One day in September, I and many other self-appointed "most revolutionary" Red Guards presented Premier Zhou with many "most utmost revolutionary proposals" at a meeting in a small hall in the Working People's Palace. We all sat on the floor. When someone brought up the matter of the traffic lights, Premier Zhou said: "I already heard about this suggestion a few days ago, and I really envy your excellent revolutionary spirit. I went to ask my driver and some other comrades, and they told me that the distinguishing feature of the red light is that no matter if it is day or night, clear or foggy, it can be seen from afar. The green and yellow lights are not like that, and under certain conditions they are not very visible. It is precisely for this reason that, all over the world, the red light is used as a stop sign: to ensure the safety of drivers by reducing the risk of a collision." Having said this, the premier paused briefly. He went on: "Can we agree on the following, that the red light is the light of revolution that guarantees the safety of all revolutionary activities?" We answered in unison: "Agreed!" Premier Zhou went on: "So it is OK for me to say that continued use of red as a stop sign is meant to guarantee the safety of

---

[1] We have been unable to locate a contemporary transcript of this "humorous discussion." On 10 September 1966, Zhou told a gathering of Red Guards: "The students at the No. 15 Middle School for Girls asked for the red and green lights to be changed. I looked into this matter together with Comrade Xie Fuzhi, and first we thought of testing it. Then we asked a few drivers, and they said it wouldn't work because the red light is really striking and if you change its color to green, in daylight you will not see anything and there would easily be accidents. I said this to the girls at the No. 15 Middle School, and they accepted it and agreed not to insist on the change." See "Zhou Enlai tongzhi zai shoudu hongweibing zuotanhui shang de jianghua" (Comrade Zhou Enlai's speech at an informal gathering of Red Guards in the capital), in *Wuchanjieji wenhua dageming cankao ziliao* (*Great Proletarian Cultural Revolution Reference Materials*) (Beijing: Zhongguo qiche gongye gongsi, 1967), p. 154.

revolutionary activities?" We Red Guards shouted back: "OK!" With an understanding laugh, Premier Zhou waved his hand and said: "We are in agreement." The Red Guards raised their arms high in the air, as if they had just passed a resolution affecting the world revolution. They laughed and expressed their approval.

I was sitting only a few meters from Premier Zhou when all of this happened, and I can still recall his relaxed posture and smiling face. Twenty years later, the memory has not yet faded. However, with the passage of time I have gradually come to realize that it takes true wisdom to tell the sound of a wise laugh from that of an ignorant laugh.

69
All Because of *On Practice*

Zhao Yiming

Source: "Du *Shijian lun* de fengbo." In Li Hui and Gao Lilin, eds., *Dixue de tongxin—Haizi xinzhong de wenge* (*Bloodstained Innocence—The Cultural Revolution in the Hearts of the Young*) (Beijing: Zhongguo shaonian ertong chubanshe, 1989), pp. 52–55. The author is now a cadre in the PLA Air Force. Translated by Björn Kjellgren.

If I were to tell you that during the Cultural Revolution one could not even read [Chairman Mao's] *On Practice,* perhaps you would not believe me. But this is something I actually experienced myself.

In March 1968 I left my home near Fudan University in Shanghai to join the army. The only books to be found in our company barracks were [Mao's] *Little Red Treasures* (even the books on weaponry had been locked away because their authors were "old revisionists"). Now—being someone who had grown up on books—I found it impossible to change my habit of constantly reading. Without books I would have suffocated. So the only thing left for me to do was to go over the *Selected Works of Chairman Mao* from cover to cover. One Sunday, just as I was reading *On Practice,* old Shen Aihua came over for a "heart-to-heart conversation." He asked me if I understood *On Practice.* I said: "Yes, more or less." He lowered his voice and whispered to me: "People are talking about you. You shouldn't go on reading those things." I did not understand what he was getting at and said: "Why? *On Practice* was written by Chairman Mao!" He then told me in earnest: "*On Contradiction* and *On Practice* are for the leadership to read. For us ordinary soldiers, reading the 'Three Constantly Read Articles' is enough. If you don't stop what you're doing, it may affect your advancement!" Unfortunately, at the time I failed to appreciate his good intention.

Not long after that, I learned my lesson the hard way. In January 1969 our company launched a "party reconsolidation movement."[1] Since I had been targeted as a prospective "fresh new Party member" (*naxin*), I was made vice-head of the Party Reconsolidation Group (the group was made up of both Party and non-Party members and the position as vice head was reserved for an activist from among the masses). After supper one night my close and trusted friend from the 3rd Platoon, Liang Beiquan, asked me the question: "Is it possible to apply the formula 'one divides into two' to Mao Zedong Thought?"[2] For some reason they had been arguing about this at the 3rd Platoon's discussion meeting as well. Liang Beiquan had maintained that Mao Zedong Thought, like everything else, could be "divided into two," and for this he had been opposed by the others. Not being able to win the argument, he had come to me. I immediately recalled the passages about absolute and relative truths in *On Practice* and told him: "Indeed, it's possible. Chairman Mao has made this very point himself." I went on explaining and analyzing the issue for maybe one or two hours and ended by saying: "If you have another argument with them, you now should be able to prove them wrong."

The next day at supper I went up to Liang Beiquan and asked him in a low voice: "So what happened? You won, didn't you?" He just lowered his head and continued eating, not saying a word. As I looked at the other comrades from the 3rd Platoon, I noticed that they too were silent and busy eating. What had happened? Right after supper the deputy political instructor called me to the company head's office. In a grave voice he asked me: "Zhao Yiming, ask yourself what kind of an attitude do you have toward our great leader Chairman Mao and

---

[1]Compare Document 17.

[2]For an account of the early 1960s controversy surrounding this slogan and its negation ("Two merge into one"), see Donald J. Munro, "The Yang Hsien-chen Affair," *The China Quarterly*, No. 22, April–June 1965, pp. 75–82.

toward Mao Zedong Thought?" I heard this big "bang" in my head as I realized what had happened. To have an "attitude problem"—In those days that was a major crime and tantamount to heresy! It turned out that on that very afternoon, Liang Beiquan and the others had started their debate again and Liang—with perfect assurance—had said: "Zhao Yiming says that Chairman Mao made precisely this point in *On Practice*." By chance, the deputy political instructor had been present and had taken notes on every word being said. Now he stared at me and warned me: "Your viewpoint is extremely reactionary. You oppose our great leader Chairman Mao and ever-victorious Mao Zedong Thought!" I was so baffled and scared that besides crying I could only say: "I am loyal to Chairman Mao!" The deputy political instructor made his point over and over again. It was only when he realized that I failed to get his point that he finally let me return to my bed.

Back in bed I started to calm down. I thought about it for a long time but still believed myself to be right. If I admitted to being wrong, it would mean admitting disloyalty to Chairman Mao, which was totally out of the question! The next morning, after breakfast, the deputy political instructor called on me again and talked to me well into the night. I quoted from *On Practice* and the *Quotations from Chairman Mao* to back up my argument and I insisted on two things: First, Chairman Mao had himself said that everything can be "divided into two." Second, I insisted that what I had meant by saying that Mao Zedong Thought can be divided into two was that it is both the absolute truth as well as the relative truth. On day three I was summoned by the political instructor, and although our conversation continued well into the night, I stood by my line of defense. On the fourth day old Zhang, the man in our regiment in charge of Party reconsolidation, tried to persuade me to admit my mistake. My relationship with him was quite good, so I said to him: "When I joined the army I wrote in my own blood the words 'Join the Liberation Army, Defend Chairman Mao.' How could I possibly oppose Chairman Mao!?" (Initially, because I was near-sighted, I had failed to meet the requirements for soldiers and only by writing such a "Blood Letter" had I finally been admitted into the army.) I was determined not to give in to his accusation. Two days after his visit, things started to calm down. The political instructor came around once more to warn me to take the whole incident as a lesson, but he no longer mentioned an "attitude problem." Of course, after this there was no longer any talk about me joining the

Party. A year later, when I was transferred to the regiment head office I found out that it was only thanks to old Zhang, who had put in a good word for me, that the incident had not been reported to the security section.

In 1978 I participated in a propaganda work conference concerning the criterion of truth, organized by the higher levels. At the meeting I heard that during the Cultural Revolution there had been quite a few men with the air force in my military region who had been punished for maintaining that the formula "one divides into two" may be applied to Mao Zedong Thought. Compared to some of them, I had been lucky.

70
Still Grieving

Citizens of Chongqing

Source: Excerpts from Chen Xiaowen, "Chongqing hongweibing mudi sumiao" (Sketch of a Red Guard Cemetery in Chongqing), translated by the editor and reprinted with permission of *Twenty-First Century* bimonthly (No. 30, August 1995, pp. 71–73).

[Memories, as told to Chen Xiaowen, an editor with the Chongqing Publishing House and historian of the Cultural Revolution, on Qingming, the holiday on which the Chinese traditionally visit and sweep the graves of their ancestors:]

Bao XXX, daughter of the man buried in grave No. 101, speaking on 5 April 1992:

> My father was a skilled worker who came to Chongqing during the War of Resistance when his factory was relocated here. At the time of his death he was one of only a handful of Grade 8 technicians in his factory. He was very skilled. He never involved himself in politics. All he cared about was making enough money to support his family. When the armed struggles began, he left his factory and took refuge in the Shangqiao city district. Suddenly one day a group of people showed up

and just dragged him off. A few days later we heard that he had been taken to Chongqing University. It was not until we got there, to ask for his release, that we heard that my father had been beaten to death. It turned out that someone had spread a rumor saying he was a member of the opposing faction—while in fact he was not a member of any faction at all. I don't know why those people hated him so. Our family immediately reported the matter to the police, who came and arrested the man responsible for the rumor. The Shapingba district where we lived was part of the 'August 15th' faction's turf and relatively peaceful, and as a consequence the public security and legal system was still just about operational and enjoyed the cooperation of the Red Guards. Later the man responsible was sentenced. He is still in jail!

Wang XXX, widow of the man buried in grave No. 40, speaking on 5 April 1992:

It's been quite some time since I retired. Hardly a day passes when I don't think about those events that took place twenty-five years ago. My man and I both worked in the Zhongliangshan coal mine, and we joined the rebel faction together. Our views were the same, and together we attended meetings, took part in debates, wrote big-character posters, published leaflets, and so on. He had gone out to give a friendly unit his support when he was killed in the intense fighting raging in the Panjiaping city district—You asked me if my man's death had any meaning? . . . It seems it should have some meaning. He supported the army and would always support the faction that had the backing of the army. Also, he responded to the call issued by Chairman Mao and the Party, to concern himself with affairs of state and to throw himself into the Cultural Revolution. Didn't all of that have a meaning? But by now the Cultural Revolution has all but been completely negated, in which case, does it still have a meaning? Once it's all been negated, what meaning does it have? Oh, I was afraid my son would be ill-treated by his stepfather so I never dared to marry again. Today I have come with my son and his new girlfriend to sweep the grave and to remind them of what it means to be an upright person. To let them know where we come from.

He XXX, son of He Xingui buried in grave No. 116, speaking on 5 April 1992:

I run the South Swallow Restaurant at 38 Rear Bridge Street in the Shipingqiao city district. My father was a construction worker, a Party member. He did not take part in the armed struggles, but had gone to get the wages for the people in his workshop. It happened on 1 August, the day the workers in workshop No. 45 were to get paid. Halfway there, he was killed by a seventeen-year-old student from the No. 35 Middle School who used him as a target while practicing how to use his rifle. This was not on the battlefield. After my father died, the factory never paid us a penny in compensation. With no real income, our life became miserable, like before Liberation. Finally, twenty years later, we succeeded in locating the person who had fired the rifle, in the commercial department of a construction factory. The head of his middle school knew what had happened. In 1987 I traveled to Beijing to raise the matter with the Cultural Revolution Complaints Office: Their answer was that the local authorities should work out a solution. Later they said that the time limit for bringing the matter to court had already passed and that legal action could therefore no longer be taken. Why when I first visited them, twenty years still had not passed! The murderer had been able to join the Party and had been promoted to cadre status all the same. They said his record was all white and clean. It was as if none of this had ever happened! In short, they're always right. As far as compensation after the Cultural Revolution was concerned, they would simply pass the buck from one department to another. They simply refused to be bothered. It was as if they had a secret agreement, they all said the same things. In the end, the lawbreaker remains free and beyond the reach of the law, while the innocent victim is languishing in the nether world. Do you think you could help us and make an appeal? Or did our father just simply die in vain?

Zhu XXX, older brother of Zhu Benwu, who is buried in grave No. 29, speaking on 5 April 1993:

Benwu went to Zishui Middle School in Wulidian, north of the river. He was called in by the East Sichuan Petroleum Bureau in Yuntai, Changshou County, to participate in the armed struggles. They had been fighting for seven days and seven nights when he was struck by a bullet in the head. He was eighteen when he died. I traveled to Changshou to retrieve the corpse. The county hospital was filled with the bodies of the dead and wounded. Dozens had died. We wrapped the body in white silk fabric (we rarely cremate the dead in these parts), dressed in a woolen Zhongshan suit. My father came to dig the grave. We set two lines of stones along the bottom of the grave, with a space in the middle for the coffin. When we buried him, we were unable to put a stone on his grave. The Petroleum Bureau said they had no money. They too had been driven out to become vagrants. Later, they said, when we have the money, we will put up a stone. But of course they never did. In 1992, the person who had been in charge of the burial even came to see me to ask for a receipt, saying he needed one to prove what had happened to the few hundred yuan they spent on the funeral.

Xi XXX, oldest son of Huang Peiying, who is buried in grave No. 98, speaking on 5 April 1994:

Back then I was a very active Red Guard in the Guanjing Alley Middle School. Actually, my mother had already succeeded in breaking out of the encirclement, but then she came back again. She took me with her, retreating by way of Tanzikou in the direction of Jiulongpo, when she was hit by a stray bullet. I was right behind her at the time. The blood just came gushing out, coloring the sandy road red. My mind went all blank, and all I could think of was: My mother won't be able to talk to us anymore, won't be able to care for us anymore. We spent three months on the grave. My second brother came and took charge of everything. He stayed at Chongqing Teacher's College. They had Rebel to the End faction POWs do all the hard labor. The POWs were brought here blindfolded to dig the pit, to fill it with earth, and to cover the grave. Then they were blindfolded once more and taken back to where they'd come from. I stood in front of the grave of my mother when the grave stone was set. I remember thinking how utterly meaningless all that factionalism was. It was as if at that moment I suddenly realized a lot of things. After that I withdrew from politics. To this day, when there's a problem or when I feel depressed, I often come here alone to sit for a while and have a smoke.

71
Walls

Zhang Zhiyang

Source: "Qiang," as translated by Nancy Liu and Lawrence Sullivan and published in *Chinese Studies in Philosophy,* Vol. 25, No. 3, Spring 1994, pp. 6–11, 19–30. The author is a philosopher currently employed by the Social Sciences Research Center at Hainan University.

The walls are solid and mighty. Constantly gazing at them causes me to hallucinate. Three years have passed, yet this unreal feeling still strikes back at me as I occasionally cast a quick glance at the walls. Is this a prison? Who can prove to me that it's real? Perhaps it's real, or maybe unreal. Perhaps it is a punishment for evil, and yet perhaps it is evil itself. . . . Alas, it is evil only when it becomes an object of judgment and then it is even more distinct, just like at an exhibition where people wearing white gloves point at things and say: "See this here, see that there." However, once it becomes experience itself, filling the space between the wall and me, how can a judgment be made? Am I the "criminal"? I tore up the list of "regulations governing criminals." When the cadre questions me: "What the hell are you doing?" I reply: "You know in the past when I wrote the character for 'criminal' I never paid much attention, and now I just noticed that it contains the 'dog radical' and I hate it." The cadre starts yelling: "Criminals are not humans. They are dogs."

Criminals are dogs. This is the first lesson I have learned in my solitary cell. Whenever in a sudden spark of consciousness I look at the walls, I hear its indifferent indictment: "Criminals are dogs."

But I haven't yet become a total cynic.

It's incredibly easy to turn a person back into an animal. It's simply a matter of repeating time itself over and over again until no time is left. The "East Is Red" blasts over the loudspeaker and it's time to get up. Water and breakfasts are passed out and bowls are collected. Water and lunch are passed out, bowls are collected, commodes emptied. The "Internationale" reverberates through the air and it's time for bed, leave the lights on. Idling away time is the only true rest: eat, shit, and sleep.

Sleep? Oh no, in German it is pronounced "Schlaf, der Schlaf," and the verb is "schlafen,"—the meaning is explicit and specific: merely to go to bed or to fall asleep—unlike the ambiguous Chinese word for "sleep" *(shuijiao)* [which carries a connotation of activities involving more than just sleep, namely having sex, as in the English phrase "to sleep with"—Ed.] Ah Q told Nanny Wu to "sleep" and Nanny Wu is frightened to death. The German Ah Q says "schlafen," and the German Nanny Wu is unmoved, continuing to cobble her shoe.

Idling away time turns life into an abstraction. It is abstract not only because it is a single person, a single protein, but also because it is the formation of a single thought, that is to say, a kind of existence that can only be displayed by thinking. A retreat from Husserl to Descartes's "I think, therefore, I am."

Is that the purpose of the prison?

One evening, supper is over and the commodes emptied. This abstract space of existence still abides by the law of the conservation of energy. "I am, therefore I think." "I think, therefore I am." The huge differences that marked the history of philosophy are nowhere to be found in my little abode. I sit on the edge of the bed, leaning against my chair attached to the desk. I'm right, the chair attached to the desk is on the bed that covers almost one half of the twelve-square-meter cell. Vertically, it covers one twelfth of the four meters. My bed is located in the lower right-hand corner just below the window. And the book desk—yes, the book desk, I lean against the edge of the bed when eating in order to maintain the purity and holiness of the book desk—is located in the left-hand corner also just below the window.

I sit silent with my back upright, and at times shudder a bit. What's on my mind? Perhaps memorizing adverbs in German. I work out the proper spelling in my head, and avoid saying the words out loud as I have no voice. Over the past three years, apart from the interminable interrogations in the first half of year one, I have remained almost completely silent. It has become a habit as I now go out of my way to safeguard this right of silence.

"What are you doing?" The guard questions me through the peep hole. The guards are rotated every two months. The new ones from Henan Province look extremely vigilant.

"I said what are you doing?" "Bang!" The peep hole whips open. The so-called peep hole is actually nothing but a small ventilation aperture in the cell door, fifteen centimeters in width and twenty-five centimeters in length. It is used to watch and spy on, and to deliver water, food, and newspapers to the inmate. In the summer months, it is usually shut tight with only a crack left open for peeping so as to prevent mosquitoes from flying in.

Guards impatient, angry, or fond of showing off usually thrust it open and then slam it shut, producing a crashing sound that reverberates through the hallway and the cells. But I am oblivious to any sound, light or heavy, footsteps or jostling of keys, or even bayonets being sheaved or fixed. Accustomed to all of these sounds, I soon become immune to them. It's weird that ears here are both the most sensitive organ and the most retarded. Perhaps I gave the guard a look, no to be more exact it was a kind of physiological reaction out of fear that mosquitoes would squeeze their way in. The cell is without a mosquito net, and the peep hole lacks a protective screen. I have to try to get rid of all the mosquitoes that gather on the cell window at dusk. How come those mosquitoes that survive by sucking my blood all amass at the window at dusk? To discard the darkness and throw themselves into brightness? Or, for fear of the heat and in a need for a cool breeze? No, neither. They are there fooling around in communal matrimony and reviewing the old dream of the "species." Oh God, you always arrange everything in such a neat, rational way, allowing them to take turns in sucking my blood and then going off together to pro-create, thereby offering me a bit of rest. Such fairness! Otherwise, my blood would not suffice to keep their proliferation going. Such an ecological equilibrium has no moral character to it, for prisoners should have the right to exist as prisoners. Otherwise, the sentence rendered by the mosquitoes would substitute for God's final judgment long before the prisoner serves out the sentence of his political term. Of course, I need not think of all that. The most pressing issue is the need for sleep, or rather to fall asleep. Without getting rid of the mosquitoes it's impossible to fall asleep in the evening. Especially when the cycle of bodily urges set in, insomnia quickly sets in. Once a mosquito buzzes in the ear, the rock that has just been pushed up to the top of the mountain suddenly begins to come crashing down. And to bring back peaceful rest, one has to traverse the whole cycle all over again. Such routine punishment was far more frightening than the final judgment.

"Your eyes are vicious, you cunning enemy! How dare you come here? I'll let you have it!"

"Bayonet"—"A solitary cell filled with long-drawn out loneliness. The advent of autumn is accompanied with obsolescence. The chill blade is reflected by the door, and the frost of moonlight is condensed on the window. . ."

I developed the habit of putting my words in order, not because I was in a mood for writing lüshi [a poem of eight lines, each containing five or seven characters, with a strict tonal pattern and rhyme scheme—Ed.], but simply because this makes them easier to remember. Thus feelings or emotions that appear in my mind in an instant can be recalled again and be mulled over. Having heard my roar, the cadres come over, and without asking anything, shut the peep hole and take off.

The next morning, it is my turn to enjoy a breath of fresh air, a privilege that was only recently granted. One hour daily, once in the morning and once in the afternoon, all at the behest of the cadres. Holding the basin, I am on my way to the sink to do some washing. The courtyard in which the prisoners take a breath of air is about sixty square meters—I've figured that out by marching it off. There are four poplar trees, one Chinese parasol tree, and two Rose of Sharon bushes, along with a deep water well. In the summer, the cadres often lower watermelons down in the well for them to cool.

All of a sudden, I sense that a few soldiers are approaching, and suddenly they surround me in a semicircle.

"Come over here!"

I take a towel and wipe the soap off my hands and turn around and lean on the sink, intuitively tightening my arms against my ribs.

"Stand upright, and come to attention!"

I stand there and don't move an inch, refusing to come to attention since there was no reason for doing so. My feet remain apart, parallel to my shoulders.

"I told you to come to attention!"

The soldier on my left kicks my left ankle with his leather shoe, and the soldier on my right does the same to my right ankle.

Still, I stand there, not moving an inch. But my lips are numb as beads of sweat stream down my forehead. I take the soldier standing in front of me as the squad leader since the order—in loud voice and with great authority—was barked out by him. The young man appears very strong and has no special facial features except that his eyes are a bit swollen, which makes his eyelids droop a little. He slowly takes off his military belt and before I notice whether he will use it with one hand or both, he thrusts his right leg forward and slaps my right cheek with his right hand. All of a sudden my right ear becomes fiery hot as if cut by a knife. At that instant, however, I am unaware of whether the pain is excruciating or ceasing, for the ankle bones of both of my feet have been exposed by the kicking, and that pain counteracts the pain coming from the belt. Fortunately, the chief cadre comes over just in time and puts a stop to it. In such a situation, the silence of a prisoner is sufficient to cause the arrogant soldiers to go berserk.

Human beings are sometimes humble creatures—if I were outside the prison, it would have taken months for the injury to heal. However, since I am in jail, it heals in less than a month, leaving only two scarlet red scars similar to a birth mark. Ever since then, whenever I sneeze, light or heavy, I experience a sparkling tinnitus.

Despite all this, the incident does not arouse any particular hatred or dislike in me, for it is too trivial. That is to say, an object that is too insignificant cannot become the object—for what is there to mull over? Those soldiers live as a "concept" *(guannian)* and they took me as a "concept" as well; however, I am not a "concept." If I had considered their actions so serious as to resist them, then I would have turned myself into a concept to prove their concept, or to put it another way, they would have used me to disguise and reinforce their concept that was hypocritical to begin with. I always remember a joke told by Marx: David Ricardo turned humans into a hat, Hegel turned the hat into a concept, and now Mr. Proudhon attempted to turn the concept into humans. I would like to venture in adding a point, namely, when the hat was turned into the concept, the conceptual "hat" gained a double-edged function: revealing and concealing. And so when the concept is turned back into humans once again, great caution must be taken in order to avoid disguising the very thing that was supposed to be revealed. In this regard, most of those involved were unaware of what was going on.

And what of myself? What kind of person am I after all? Have I been changed from a concept? What did I do to put myself in a situation where I have to take the walls as my proof of existence? I stare at the walls. They are silent, indifferent, and cold . . .

I am someone who lives relying on imagination, and therefore, I am good at discerning the truthfulness of others' imagination. I have time and again said to the judges of the Joint Special Case Committee of the Military Region and the Garrison Headquarters: "What you demand I don't possess, and what I do have you don't want."

My own humble life was full of imagination; however, their great spirit lives in a deeper imagination than my own. Nevertheless, my own imagination is an endless debt—I pay back those who do not need me, and their imaginations are unsatisfied exploitation, exploiting the exploited whom they created from time to time. Thus, our difference is that others exploit my imagination while I myself do not exploit myself in my own imagination. I give my imagination to others while they not only imagine how to exploit others, but also imagine themselves to be part of the exploitation, which places themselves in the midst of exploitation, that is, to exploit the exploitation. Such is the logic of self-exploitation. Didn't Marx warn you? The year 1971, it was no longer a prophecy, but it wasn't words of mourning either. It was merely a statement by an observer.

In so many years, the rendering of imagination has always been accompanied by my being evacuated from school and out of a job. I know that I am someone with no personal character whatsoever. To put it more precisely, I do not possess anything to demonstrate my personal character. Despite the fact that my imagination crawled across lost articles, they were never able to reveal a secret known by everyone as an unselfish sacrifice and win self-sublimation as with the Lei Feng–style diaries. Thus, although the military representatives searched through my diaries and books, including *Mother's Death* and *The Bells of the Evening Service of Verona,* they found nothing and said nothing, as if the purpose of searching was not to examine the diaries and books themselves, but the darts, daggers, bombers, and banners hidden in between the pages . . .

It seems that my statement did not win deliverance for me at my trial. You possess an unexplainable stubbornness. What can you give? Who wants your renderings? For things that are ignored by people in ordinary life, how can you, as a prisoner, have the right to request of the judge that he not only assess your innocence and kindness in this trial, but also your sublimeness and perfection? Even this is imagination. If it is not so weak that it borders on begging, then it must be high-sounding and impracticable in an unlimited way.

However, I could only gain emancipation in the renderings of my imagination. I must prove my refusal and surmount the walls. Even if the proof fails to convince the walls, at least I will try to convince the resistance that itself results from resistance—to continue to resist. You see when I caress my injuries, I worry whether they can sustain the corruption and poisoning brought on by such violence. And whether they can sustain the impotence sired by the violence and suppression. Would they sink in memory or wake up in memory?

Across from my solitary cell is a prisoner with an artificial leg fabricated in the Soviet Union—his real leg had been accidentally shot by one of the guards. With medical conditions so bleak, there was no alternative except to remove the leg from the thigh down, leaving a single foot still retaining its dignity. That old Bolshevik and old revisionist was said to be an old backstage hand. His rank was one level higher than mine. Nevertheless, I did not know him at all. Recently he's been acting a bit strange.

Before supper, it was time to clean the nightstool. Since my cell is right next to the toilet and across from his cell, I could not escape the glorious mission of assisting him after cleaning my own nightstool. Of course, this was under orders from the cadre, who conceived of it as such a glorious thing. The real advantage was that I could walk inside his cell and gaze at him leaning against the wall with one foot on the floor and his hands clasped before his chest in a bowing manner. His lips were shivering and the gray hair shone with a gentle glare. The corners of his eyes were long and narrow, filled with a smile. I noticed the words murmuring in his lips but never uttered out: "Many thanks, thanks, thanks . . ."

Recently, when the time came for another cleaning up of the nightstool, he clamped on his artificial leg and dressed up in tidy clothes. Soon after I removed the stool from his cell, he pursued me with awkward steps into the cell next door and pushed open the peep hole. . . . The result was not hard to imagine. He was no longer a sixth-rank cadre, instead he was a prisoner whom any soldier or cadre could berate or curse at and push around at will. Even a slap on the face was something natural.

"Why did you arrest my son? Why did you arrest my son? Why. . .?"

His door slammed shut. The old man was still screaming in his cell, "Why did you arrest my son? Why. . .?"

The doors of the cells were unlocked one by one, and the thirteen prisoners whose names were listed by the Central Committee came out one after another. "Pa, pa, pa" went the steps. "Quick, quick! Damn it, move it, move it!" the cadre yelled.

The surrounding walls echoed my heartbeat. What has happened today? Run too fast? No, he was shaking, the seventy-year-old man, staggering against the wall standing on one foot. . . . It was no joke, no show, no viewing a movie, it was not a misunderstanding, not protective detention, nor individual investigation. It was the prison, the special prison among model prisons with solitary cells. If during the cleaning of the nightstools anything out the ordinary occurred, a whole squad of soldiers would rush in like lightning with loaded guns and bayonets. A guard every five steps and a post every ten steps, all the soldiers stand with legs apart while holding guns fixed with bayonets. They were approaching closer and closer as if to suppress a riot.

How is it that fate has brought me to this predicament? Others thrust the bayonet against my throat, forcing me to admit: "You are not me.

You are merely yourself," while I try very hard to think, "I am not myself. I am you," or "I am not you, but I am not the I that you force me to admit." Isn't it true that between you and me there is no room for it?

No, I am not it, and it is not me. I am you, the same as me. Even if you sentence me, you cannot change the facts inside my heart. I know full well that the reason you bring one or two of the red-colored announcements listing those executed as well as the list of 117 names crossed out by a red pen is merely to threaten me to admit that I am not you. There have been too many monkey kings squeezed into your stomach, and the most urgent thing for you to do is to spit out the non-me inside me, and you inside me. It fears you more than meeting the enemy face to face.

In such a way, the battlefield of class struggle has to shift to the inside, to the rear, there engendering the tension of a full battleground, the kind of total war situation that turns humans into wolves. Class struggle indeed was a baton with two ends, one beating the enemy and the other beating oneself, just as Lenin had predicted. Since the enemies are among ourselves, it's hard to avoid not hitting oneself when hitting the enemy. Those who beat always think with full confidence that they are beating the enemy, only those who are beaten know what is self and what is the self forced to be the enemy.

Suddenly I thought about a letter by Bukharin: "Comrades, please do not forget that on the banner of communism that you hold high, there is Bukharin's blood, my blood." The unstrained tears stream down to my lips, the saltiness makes me feel that I am weeping. I am moved by my own sobbing, for in the bitter tears, I find the evidence of a non-Party Bolshevik.

Damn it! You are putting on a show again! Others acting in a genuine fashion, but you are merely acting, and never forgetting to act. You fear distinguishing, but you do not fear perceptual pain, but merely ask for the peace of rationality. On the one hand, you position the differences presented by the sharp criticisms in the same unity, that is, you place them into the theory of "continuing revolution," supporting the forbidden soul with unity, and are full of complaints and moaning about the exploitation that comes from the reality of differences. But on the other hand, you insist upon the right of independent thought within the differences, and no matter how benevolent you try to defend that right, there is no way to hide the sharpness of the weapons of criticisms. And thus the reward gained from the weapons of criticisms should not be full of complaints and blame. All in all, since you rest your case on the differences, then you shouldn't cheat yourself with the unity. Is it possible to attack people with differences and cease the attacks with the unity?

The wall is the boundary and what it proves is the reality of the differences. As for the degree and nature of such differences, it is purely a matter of experience. For a person, what he feels is what he can feel; therefore, the satisfaction of his feelings is not confined by the amount of feelings, but is only limited by the ability to feel. He can only feel so much, and when he feels enough, he can no longer feel anymore. To a third person, he might make comparisons as to the size of the differences. To those who actually experience the feelings, however, since both sides have reached the limit of satiation, they are the same. No one would make requests based on how much he feels, but he does agonize on the basis of the limit that he can undertake. Thus, since the limit has become the evidence, do not except the limit of others' feelings to compete with yours. Those who have limited tolerance cannot alleviate their insufferable pain brought on by feelings from the limit simply because of their limit of tolerance. In other words, since that person has reached the limit of tolerance, he can only take you as his enemy. What else can it be?

There is something special during the Spring Festival this year. During the cleaning of nightstools it has become very clamorous. Along with the yelling "Why did you arrest my son?" from the artificial leg, prisoners with heavy shackles on their legs trudge around making people feel as if fireworks during the festival were firing in their hearts.

I could not hold back the associations filling my mind. Irrespective of whether the present reality is iron or blood, nothing could stop the dramatization of itself. As for whether the matter itself is dramatic, or it has become dramatized in the emotional shifts in my heart, it is all the same to me.

Perhaps I'm fragile and frightened, unable to undertake the reality, and so I seek relief by escaping into my imagination.

Perhaps I have never belonged to reality and reality has never belonged to me. Imagination is my only shelter in life that not only protects me from being ridiculed and exploited, but also reminds me that the reason reality forces people to accept its solid constitution is because it feared its own fragility and falsehood. Escaping into imagination is thus a kind of numbness toward reality and eventually it is the call of reality's deceit.

Perhaps imagination itself is self-deception, for it neither views reality as reality nor cares about how reality is dismantled by this very imagination, whether it becomes white or black, astringent or bitter, empty or null. . . . No matter what, the solid ice of reality quietly melts away, and the reality that makes me disappear is also disappearing along with me.

> Covered by ink I came to this world,
> Heaven granted me a sky full of snow.

I was born along with the fireworks of the Lunar New Year. Apart from that pure coincidence of which I can boast, till now the past twenty or so years were prosaic as a gray dot. I myself have grown accustomed to it, and no matter how clamorous and glorious is the world, I only enjoy retreating into my own world, observing as if whatever this world possesses, I also have. Even the loneliness and pain of being understood is taken as a kind of enjoyment that is quietly expressed in the melody of the violin at dusk.

Oh, if my gray dot has any moment of shining, it is the imagination in music. Oh, God, this is my fate. That which is most impossible is most likely to stimulate my imagination, which is different from those who possess everything but imagination. My plain and worldly family background provided me no attachment to music whatsoever. In middle school, apart from being forced by taller classmates to play the generally evaded position of goalie, I didn't do anything that I really liked or disliked. In other words, I did not have any hobbies. It would have been fine if I had had everything, and it would also have been fine if I had nothing. I did not have any academic talent, and I lacked the industry to seek improvements. "So-so" seemed to become my personal motto. Despite my unusual interest in mathematics, I was too slow to catch on and sustain the willpower. However, something happened during my college math entrance examination that till this day I can't figure out whether it was advantageous or disadvantageous.

My school was one of the most famous high schools in the entire province, and thus, even with my "so-so" attitude I was assured of being admitted into at least an ordinary college. Plus the fact that the first exam was mathematics, and that was my bailiwick. God had arranged a favorable opportunity. The exam was scheduled in a woman's school located in the former "German concession." It was quiet and pleasant with a Gothic-style church in the back with a steeple aiming toward the sky. To a muddle-headed high school student, although the absence of God deprived the enlightenment of soul, it helped me hold back wild thoughts and thus was helpful to my exam.

Unexpectedly, soon after I opened the exam booklet, the sound of a violin came from afar as if there were numerous countless threads swinging around my ears and no matter how I struggled to get rid of it, I couldn't. As a result, I skipped half of the questions and didn't have the slightest idea about how to answer the other half. When the proctor came to collect the papers, looking at her, the first thought that entered my mind was: "I must have met this teacher somewhere . . ."

Failing the entrance exam was not unexpected. What was more embarrassing was that only two students out of the entire class failed. One suffered from epilepsy. As for me, the entire class berated me for becoming an idiot soon after I had eyed that female teacher.

Many years passed. And finally when I was able to afford to buy a violin with the money I made by doing chores, I played the song that determined my fate to become a violin teacher. I was told that it was Bach's *Aria on the G.*

Oh, perhaps, my whole life would have to be fixated on the string of G. Recalling, recalling. I always recall after things have happened weirdly. It was as if what belonged to my life was nothing but recalling. However, it wasn't even recalling. What is recalling? You are like a donkey who with eyes covered is being sold on the market. Apart from the sound of the hawker selling you, what else can you recall? Ears are your world, and so except for sound there is nothing else. Where are my eyes? Where are my eyes?

"Huh!"

The wall stands there coldly, and in the dim light my iron dark face is reflected and becomes brighter and brighter. As the shining light spreads, the windows, the door, and the ceiling all disappear—between the sky and earth, there exists only that one whitish wall.

"What about your eyes!"

Yes, what about your eyes? The wall is erected there for eyes and the wall is the truth of eyes. In the history of the human prison, these eight characters are written:

"The wall is the truth of eyes!"

"Move it. . . , move it . . ."

All of a sudden, there comes some yelling and shouting, distant and suffocating.

"Move it. . . , move it . . ."

"Bang," obviously the armed guard opened the peep hole.

"Move it. . ., move it. . .," the shouting comes from the front of the building like the whirling of gold coins.

"Shut up! Stop yelling!"

"Move it. . . , move it . . ."

Mad! All of a sudden, my heart becomes so tense that my entire body starts to shiver and my teeth chatter.

"Hua—" the iron shackles went flying as if they fell on my head and following that the "hua, hua" sound swirled above my head.

"Move it. . . , move it . . ."

"Hua . . ."

The distant and mincing "move it" sound from a distance is like dark lightning peeking through the roaring thunder. It hurts my eyes and reflects thousands upon thousands of sparkles on the peeling concrete ceiling, spreading. I feel dizzy and the ground under the bed starts shaking. I can't tell whether it is the bed or my heart. I hold fast to the bedding as if holding on to the two sides of a boat.

"The East Is Red" wakes me up and another day of life has resumed. Is it resumption or a repeat?

Repeat, for today is exactly the same as yesterday with the only difference being that it is more quiet. The cadres are on their annual New Year vacation and are probably out buying holiday fare. The number of armed guards both upstairs and down has, however, been doubled. The criminals who pass out the water and food still wear their wooden faces. I do not recognize the cadre who delivers the newspaper. The peep hole rolls open and slams shut, opening and shutting and opening and shutting, boring and monotonous like the pendulum on a clock. When it comes time to clean out the nightstool, I can't help but prop myself on my hands and take a look at the stairs through the glass window at the top of the door. In the past, it was the one wearing leg shackles that cleaned out the nightstool. But today the young man who for nearly half the night has been shouting "move it" is the last to do it. It appears as if his physical development is not yet mature. The gray and black prisoner coat fits him like a tent and his bare neck is as pale as newly sprouted narcissus. The skin on his head is dark and the pair of gold-framed spectacles reflect the sun like residual snow. It makes his entire face unclear. The nightstools he carries are too big for him, and as he descends the stairs holding the two leaves of the nightstool his body swaggers from right to left. I worry that he will fall right down the stairs.

Is he crazy? I can't believe it and I can't be sure whether what happened last night had indeed occurred. Later, when he turned around, he started shouting again: "Move it, move it." His voice is stiff, without the slightest color. It's a pure voice with its tone completely bereft of any meaning. It's weird. Perhaps the unique acoustics of the prison play a filtering role. I'm a bit disappointed.

I am familiar with all kinds of voices, of course, including that particular kind. What it gives you is dead silence. To put it another way, once you hear it you feel as if you have actually experienced silence. However, how was it that the yelling and shouting by this madman was so empty, carrying neither any communication nor meeting my expectations. It was just like a voice indifferent to anything sliding in the hallway just as if it was sliding through a deserted wilderness. Where did it come from and where would it go? How many such blind voices were wandering in the universe? Perhaps we shouldn't describe it as wandering since in having no desire it had absolutely nothing to lose! It was merely an extension of itself, timeless and without original sin.

That voice rigidly refused any expectations from me just like Gottfried Wilhelm Leibniz's "solitary cell" with neither windows nor doors. No exit, no entrance. Impossible to approach. Four days have passed and on each night I am so frustrated by it that I find falling asleep impossible. It is the nihilistic voice that is most irritating and can only be felt but never expressed and that always makes me doubt if I have really indeed heard it. Each time I hear it, it is different. And what I hear is merely the act of listening. Thus I have gone from expecting to hear people to expecting to hear voices, and from expecting to hear voices that have been spoken to hearing voices that have not been spoken. As a result, what I expect is merely expectation itself. I have no idea what I expect, I merely know that I have expectations.

I am anxious and hyper. This nameless expectation suddenly explodes on the fifth day, when not one voice is heard splitting the air. The walls suppress my nerves and suffocate my heart. My ears tremble so much that they stiffen to the point that I can't lay my head on the pillow or turn from side to side. My entire body suffers from excruciating pain as if all the muscles are suddenly cramped. Pain spreads throughout my neck, chest, and lower limbs, crackling like a fire. I can do nothing but violently jump up and down until I am so exhausted that I collapse on the floor like a corpse.

All has passed.

I do not know how I have wiled away that period of time. Perhaps nothing has happened. There was no need to think, no need to question, just march around twenty-two steps in a circle. And besides eating, from morning till night as soon as the "Internationale" was played I just kept walking despite the shouting and yelling from the soldiers until I could walk no more and I realized that I had taken my last step . . .

It has been thirteen years now, and it seemed that all of this had disappeared from my memory. I'm even unclear why it never even entered into any one of my confessions. Till finally a friendly stranger described to me his own personal experience and cried his heart out to me, all of a sudden it was like a lightning bolt that shone on the hidden wound of my own experience. My face did not flush nor did my heart jump. I was totally calm, as if its reemergence had already been planned. Of course, a forty-something-year-old man with a mature rationality and rich feelings has sufficient power of self-control.

For whatever reason, and irrespective of whether it was consistent with any standard of morality, I am still grateful to that young friend who went mad. His going mad rescued me from the suppression of the walls.

In that world of six walls, appeals to kindness or benevolence or endless self-reflection and imagination were useless. Instead, it was persistence and willpower to ignore the walls that counted most. Only this persistence and willpower could establish the living existence that belonged solely to myself and had nothing to do with the walls. In that living space, there must be no walls. There must neither be a deterioration as a result of affirming the wall, nor hyper anxiety as a result of negating the wall. One must know that the wall was built solely for the purpose of forging the abnormality that comes from deterioration or hyper anxiety. Going mad is the proof and also the signal. Honestly, no matter what emotions I exhibited at that time, here I must admit my basic emotional state: I was full of glee. In the beginning, the glee was unclear and even carried a sense of sin. Gradually, the glee became as clear as an azure sky and a peaceful setting.

If you do not possess the power to exist, confinement will destroy you. Let the moral consolation come later.

However, I must admit the crime forced on me in order to become a free human being.

72
Letter to Chen Yun, Deng Xiaoping, and Hu Yaobang

Wang Li

Source: Wang Li, *Lishi jiang xuangao wo wuzui* (*History Will Pronounce Me Innocent*) (N.p., 20 November 1993), p. 38. This source is a privately printed côllection of letters and documents concerning Wang Li's expulsion from the CCP. I wish to thank the author for sharing it with us.

Comrades Chen Yun, Xiaoping, and Yaobang:

Having pondered the matter for an entire week, I respectfully ask the Party Center to reconsider its disciplinary action against me.

I have grown to maturity through the Party's nurturing since the age of fourteen. The Party's profound loving kindness to me over the past fifty years remains forever engraved in my mind. I cannot even begin to describe the pain that I feel now as I am being asked to leave the Party. I did commit serious errors and remain in debt to the Party, yet proceeding from the Party's standpoint, I remain hopeful that you will give me a chance to remain a member and to continue my transformation.

Among the key members of the Central Cultural Revolution Group, from the outset I was regarded as a "holdover," and I was also the only person to be excluded from the Case Examination Group that persecuted older cadres. From a policy point of view, the Party would be justified in taking this distinction into account when deciding on how I am to be dealt with.

As far as I am concerned, I remain committed to clearing up thoroughly the theoretical chaos—in particular the theses of the so-called "continuing revolution under the dictatorship of the proletariat" and the so-called "basic line of the Party throughout the entire historical stage of socialism"—which I participated in creating in the course of the Great Cultural Revolution. Because those theoretical errors were of such great magnitude, it is still possible to feel their impact. They may even impact on the future. I ask of the Party Center to allow me to remain inside the Party and to let me play—in the act of clearing up [theoretical errors]—the role of a negative example.

Ever since my release from Qincheng Prison, I have devoted myself to the study of how the Party Center has developed Marxism-Leninism-Mao Zedong Thought since the Third Plenum. The correct line, and long- and short-term policies, of the Party Center are all being continuously enriched and developed. Unless I am able to take part in the life of the Party organization, it will be hard for me to stay in tune with the pulse of the Party and to make the most of the light and heat that still remain within me on behalf of the Party.

Wei Zheng of the Tang dynasty said: "We must judge the beauty of the form by studying its reflection in still water; we must judge politics by whether or not it imperils the survival of the realm." Of course, one cannot say that the nation perished in the Great Cultural Revolution, but the lessons to be learned are bitter indeed. In certain respects, I perhaps sense this more strongly than others. Perhaps I can be of some use to the Party if I am allowed to remain inside the Party to denounce myself by summing up the bitter negative experiences in which I took part.

Hoping that the Party Center Standing Committee will be able to consider my request,

I extend my most sincere greetings!

Wang Li
3 March 1984

Organizational Charts

Central State Organs, May 1966

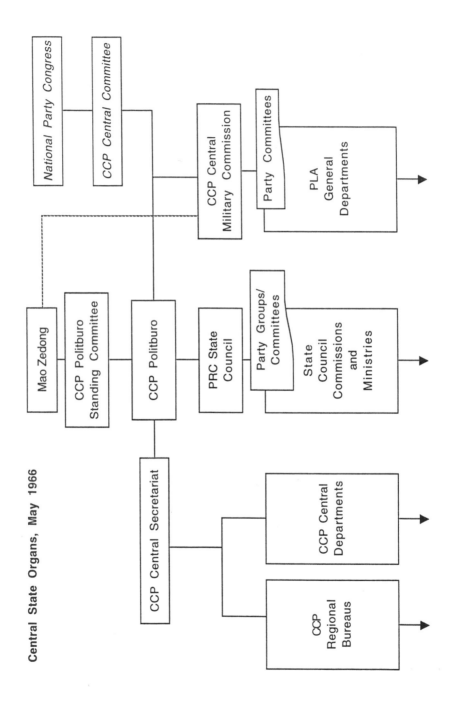

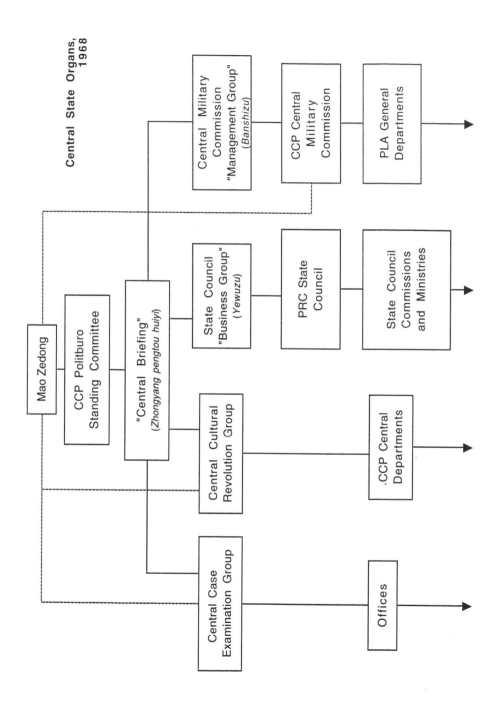

Central State Organs, 1968

Mao Zedong

CCP Politburo Standing Committee

"Central Briefing" *(Zhongyang pengtou huiyi)*

Central Military Commission "Management Group" *(Banshizu)*

CCP Central Military Commission

PLA General Departments

State Council "Business Group" *(Yewuzu)*

PRC State Council

State Council Commissions and Ministries

Central Cultural Revolution Group

CCP Central Departments

Central Case Examination Group

Offices

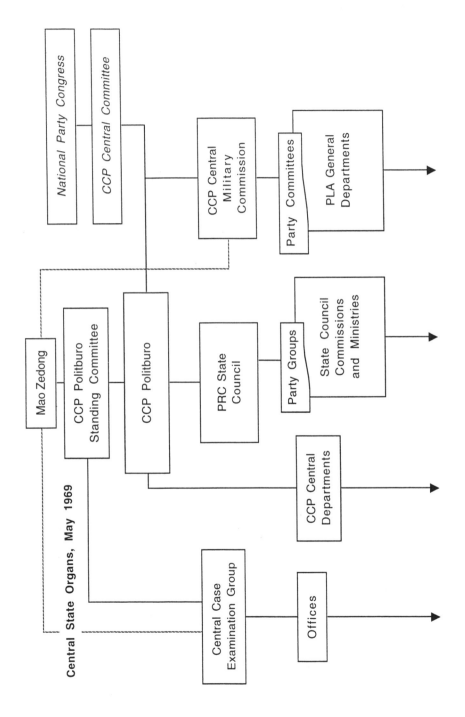

Central State Organs, May 1969

National Party Congress

CCP Central Committee

CCP Central Military Commission

Party Committees

PLA General Departments

Mao Zedong

CCP Politburo Standing Committee

CCP Politburo

PRC State Council

Party Groups

State Council Commissions and Ministries

CCP Central Departments

Central Case Examination Group

Offices

Chronology*

1965

November: Mao Zedong prepares the ground for what will be called the Great Proletarian Cultural Revolution by having the young literary critic Yao Wenyuan attack a play by Beijing's vice mayor, Wu Han, in a Shanghai newspaper; by replacing the director of the Central Committee General Office, Yang Shangkun, with his own trusted lieutenant and chief bodyguard, Wang Dongxing; and by taking steps, together with Lin Biao, toward removing PLA Chief of Staff Luo Ruiqing from his post. Mao leaves Beijing for east China, citing security concerns as one of the reasons for his departure from the capital.

December: Luo Ruiqing is purged at an enlarged Politburo meeting in Shanghai, chaired by Mao. In Beijing, Mayor Peng Zhen (concurrent head of the Party's ad hoc group of five in charge of culture) tries to protect his deputy Wu Han by insisting that any "mistakes" he may have committed are purely academic. Wu Han publishes a self-criticism, and Mao agrees to postpone the passing of a political verdict on him by two months. The Central Propaganda Department restricts media debate to historical and literary matters.

---

*The sources consulted in the preparation of this chronology include: Wang Nianyi, *Da dongluan de niandai* (*Years of Great Turmoil*) (Zhengzhou: Henan renmin chubanshe, 1988); Ma Qibin et al., eds., *Zhongguo gongchandang zhizheng sishi nian 1949–1989* (*The CCP Forty Years in Power 1949–1989*) (Beijing: Zhonggong dangshi ziliao chubanshe, 1989); "Beijing shi 'Wenhua dageming' dashiji" (Record of Major Events in the "Great Cultural Revolution" in Beijing Municipality), serialized in extra issues of *Beijing dangshi ziliao tongxun* (*Beijing Party History Materials Newsletter*), 1987; *Tianfan difu kai er kang—Wuchanjieji wenhua dageming dashiji* (*Heaven and Earth are Moved with Emotion—Record of Major Events in the Great Proletarian Cultural Revolution*), revised ed. (Beijing: Beijing dizhi xueyuan, 1967).

1966

January: With Lin Biao's blessing, Mao's wife Jiang Qing begins work on a highly critical review of the "struggle" in the literary and art field in China since 1949. The review, the text of which is finalized by Mao and released as an intra-Party document in April, concludes that a "great socialist revolution on the cultural front" has to be launched to eliminate a long dominant "dictatorial anti-Party anti-socialist black line."

February: Peng Zhen's group of five submits a report to Mao on the so-called "academic debate" in progress since November. Mao at first neither endorses nor rejects the report, the text of which is released for study as an intra-Party document. Soon, however, he turns against the (relatively) moderate views espoused in it and calls for it to be revoked.

March: In Beijing, the purged Luo Ruiqing attempts suicide. In Hangzhou, Mao Zedong maintains that if the Party Center were to turn "revisionist," provincial leaders would be under obligation to rebel against it. Two divisions loyal to the acting PLA chief of staff, Yang Chengwu, are ordered to move on the capital, ostensibly to "reinforce" the Beijing Garrison.

April: At a meeting of the Central Party Secretariat in Beijing, Zhou Enlai and Deng Xiaoping accuse Peng Zhen of having committed mistakes in line and of opposing Mao. In Hangzhou, a Politburo session chaired by Mao decides to dissolve Peng's group of five and to organize a new ad hoc group, directly under the Politburo Standing Committee, that will draft a policy document spelling out the new direction of the movement. Lu Dingyi, the director of the Central Propaganda Department, is implicated in the arrest of his wife on charges of slandering Lin Biao's wife.

May: The Politburo holds an enlarged session in Beijing, chaired by Liu Shaoqi, at which Peng Zhen, Luo Ruiqing, Lu Dingyi, and Yang Shangkun are dismissed from their posts. Lin Biao makes a sensational speech in which he, echoing Mao's fears, implies that the four dismissed leaders had been plotting a coup d'état. The Politburo issues a notification (the so-called "May 16th Circular") declaring war on "representatives of the bourgeoisie who have sneaked into the Party, the government, the army, and the various spheres of culture." A newly created Central Cultural Revolution Group is put in charge of the public side of the movement, while a special Central Case Examination Group is set up to manage the purge of senior "counter-revolutionary revisionists." Zhou Enlai henceforth chairs the meetings of both groups. There is growing unrest on campuses all over China as big-character posters attacking supposedly "reactionary" academics and cultural officials appear.

June: A task force led by the head of the Central Cultural Revolution Group, Chen Boda, takes over the *People's Daily* and publishes a Beijing University big-character poster in which the Party authorities in the capital are attacked by name. Total chaos on university campuses ensues, prompting Liu Shaoqi and Deng Xiaoping to dispatch so-called "work teams" in a futile attempt to restore order and reassert Party control. Mass rallies and kangaroo courts replace ordinary classes. In Beijing's middle schools, the children of the Party elite secretly organize themselves into so-called Red Guards.

July: Mao swims the Yangzi River and then finally returns to Beijing. He expresses extreme displeasure with the "erroneous leadership" exercised in his absence by Liu Shaoqi and Deng Xiaoping. The first work teams, dispatched in June, begin to be recalled after Mao insists that 95 percent of them have committed "errors in line." The members of the Central Cultural Revolution Group tour Beijing's campuses, urging the students there to "make revolution."

August: The Eighth CCP Central Committee convenes its Eleventh Plenum. Mao writes a big-character poster attacking Liu Shaoqi and sends a letter to the Red Guards, expressing his support for rebellious youth. The Politburo is reorganized, and Lin Biao replaces Liu in the number two position. The Central Committee announces its "Decision Concerning the Great Proletarian Cultural Revolution," officially launching the movement. The authorities expel more than 77,000 residents of "bad" class background from Beijing. In Tiananmen Square, the first of eight Red Guard rallies presided over by Mao takes place on 18 August. Police and army are ordered not to interfere as the Red

Guards go on a rampage in cities across China in search-and-destroy missions directed at the so-called "four olds" ("old ideas, old culture, old customs, and old habits").

September: The Cultural Revolution turns increasingly violent, and by the end of the month, 33,695 households have been "ransacked" and 1,772 persons killed by Red Guards in Beijing. Red Guards begin traveling across China in what becomes known as the "great exchange of revolutionary experience." Destruction of public property continues while frantic attempts are made by local officials to prevent the movement from interfering with the autumn harvest, industry, and the national economy.

October: Local Party leadership of the movement is suspended by order of the CCP Center, and "mass" organizations with direct links to the Central Cultural Revolution Group grow increasingly powerful. Mao Zedong convenes a work conference in Beijing and calls for intensification of the struggle against the so-called "bourgeois reactionary line" symbolized by Liu Shaoqi and Deng Xiaoping. Liu and Deng produce self-criticisms, but Red Guards call for their dismissal. Students and teachers from Beijing Teachers' University ransack Confucius's ancestral home in Qufu, Shandong, exhuming corpses and defacing more than 2,000 graves.

November: Mao Zedong endorses the formation of rebel workers' organizations after an incident in which workers from Shanghai disrupted train traffic in protest against not being allowed to travel to Beijing. The Central Case Examination Group involves a growing number of university students in a nationwide search for "renegades," and archives and libraries are occupied by Red Guards sifting through documents in search of incriminating evidence.

December: The CCP Center announces contradictory guidelines for extending the Cultural Revolution to all sectors of society, including rural villages. In utmost secrecy, the Central Case Examination Group begins building a file on Liu Shaoqi. A number of senior "counterrevolutionary revisionists" are rounded up and confined to special prisons in Beijing. Torture is henceforth used extensively by the Central Case Examination Group to extract confessions during interrogation.

In Shanghai, more than 100,000 people clash in a major street brawl. In Beijing, on his seventy-third birthday, Mao toasts the unfolding of a nationwide all-round civil war!

1967

January: Beginning in Shanghai and with Mao's support, rebelling representatives of the "masses" "seize power" from local authorities. The PLA is ordered to support the power seizures and does so, albeit reluctantly. In-fighting between contending factions makes the creation of new structures of political power (so-called Revolutionary Committees) possible in only a handful of provinces. Vice Premier Tao Zhu, number four in the Party hierarchy, falls from power and is put under house arrest in Zhongnanhai. Hundreds of children of high-ranking CCP cadres stage repeated sit-ins in the Ministry of Public Security, protesting against the harsh treatment accorded them and their parents.

February: When Mao criticizes members of the Central Cultural Revolution Group, senior military and State Council leaders seize the opportunity to call the wisdom of the entire Cultural Revolution undertaking into question. Mao turns on them angrily and responds by no longer convening the Politburo. From now on, the functions of that body are assumed by informal "briefing sessions" chaired by Zhou Enlai and attended only by leaders unconditionally loyal to Mao personally. In Sichuan, Inner Mongolia, and other provinces, local PLA commanders come down hard on unruly "mass" organizations. Revolutionary Committees set up in Shandong, Shanghai, and Guizhou receive official endorsement.

March: The CCP Center convenes a major conference of military leaders in an effort to explain the rationale behind the purge of Liu Shaoqi. The nationwide hunt for "renegades" intensifies as the Center issues an intra-Party circular describing the alleged treachery of key Party leaders in the 1930s. The local PLA unit massacres civilians occupying the newspaper premises in Xining, capital of Qinghai. Widespread chaos, exacerbated by failure to set up Revolutionary Committees, forces central authorities to impose direct military rule in Qinghai, Anhui, Guangdong, Guangxi, Jiangsu, Zhejiang, and Yunnan. Red Guard travel to "exchange revolutionary experience" is formally suspended.

April: Red Guards subject Liu Shaoqi's wife, Wang Guangmei, to public humiliation at a mass rally on the Qinghua University campus. On Mao's orders, the children of senior leaders arrested during sit-ins in the Ministry of Public Security in January are released. A Beijing Revolutionary Committee is set up under the chairmanship of General Xie Fuzhi. Direct military rule is imposed in Fujian and Inner Mongolia. Provincial military commanders are ordered by the Center to desist from suppressing the "revolutionary Left."

May: Increasing signs of unrest become visible within the PLA. The military in Guangdong and Hunan are forced to produce public self-criticisms. Main force units loyal to Beijing are ordered to take control of Gansu and Sichuan. Fighting in an air force plant in Chengdu leaves 48 dead and 127 wounded. PLA representatives are put in charge of key ministries and commissions in a first step toward extensive militarization of the State Council bureaucracy. A riot during a stage performance in the Beijing Exhibition Center becomes an excuse for the purge of non–Lin Biao supporters in the PLA General Political Department.

June: One-time CCP leader Li Lisan commits suicide while in the custody of the Central Case Examination Group. A gradual descent into a state of near civil war continues as thousands of civilians die in pitched battles between opposing "mass" organizations in Sichuan, Jiangxi, Zhejiang, Henan, Anhui, Ningxia, Hubei, and Shanxi. In Wuhan, clashes between members of two large mass organizations result in at least 103 dead and 2,774 wounded.

July: Mao leaves Beijing for an extended tour of central and eastern China. During his absence, Liu Shaoqi, Deng Xiaoping, and Tao Zhu—who have been under house arrest since the beginning of the year—are "struggled against" by Zhongnanhai staff. In Wuhan, central emissaries Xie Fuzhi and Wang Li are kidnapped by members of a "conservative" mass organization, the Million Heroes, supported by PLA Unit 8201, the provincial public security contingent. Zhou Enlai succeeds in arranging the release of Xie and Wang, who are promptly spirited back to Beijing, whereupon PLA main force units disarm Unit 8201 and begin hunting down sympathizers of the Million Heroes. In the weeks that follow, some 66,000 people are wounded and 600 killed in and around Wuhan. In conversation with the new military leadership,

Lin Biao claims that the "greatest, greatest, greatest" victory of the Cultural Revolution has been secured at the "tiniest, tiniest, tiniest" cost. Jiang Qing calls upon radicals to "attack with reason, defend with force!"

August: Having successfully brought China to the very brink of the "all-round civil war" to which he had toasted on the eve of the New Year, Mao pulls back and placates military leaders by sacrificing Guan Feng and Wang Li, two radical members of the Central Cultural Revolution Group. Guan is said to be behind recent calls for the ouster of senior officers ("Drag out a small handful in the army!") and Wang is held responsible for the sacking of the British legation and the crisis in China's foreign relations. Widespread fighting and violence nonetheless persist. In central Beijing, Xidan Market is looted and forced to shut down. In Shanghai, close to a thousand people are wounded, eighteen die, and property valued at an estimated 3.55 million yuan is destroyed as rival worker organizations clash at the Shanghai Diesel Engine Plant. In northern Ningxia, the PLA quells instances of serious ethnic unrest, killing hundreds. In Pingyao, Shanxi, close to ten thousand civilians are involved in violent factional battle.

September: In Zhuji County, Zhejiang, the PLA occupies a train station and summarily executes 146 civilians in order to secure the safe passage of Mao's special train. Fighting in Luzhou in Sichuan for the second time in two months leaves hundreds dead. A nationwide witch hunt for alleged members of the so-called ultra-Leftist "May 16th" conspiracy directed at Zhou Enlai and the PLA begins. The search continues off and on for almost a decade and results in the arrest of an estimated 3.5 million people.

October: Mao is quoted in a Party circular as saying that "the situation throughout the country is not just good but excellent" and "in a few months time, it will be even more excellent." The State Council releases statistics showing the disastrous decline in industrial production since May. Mao calls upon "mass" organizations to unite. Provincial leaders are called to Beijing to negotiate formation of Revolutionary Committees. Schools remain in a state of chaos as attempts to resume classes meet with limited success. Local Party branches begin resuming regular activities.

November: In Inner Mongolia, a Revolutionary Committee under the leadership of a Han general is set up and a regionwide campaign to denounce Ulanfu—a Mongol and the regional strongman before 1966—is launched. In Beijing, Jiang Qing announces the commencement of a nationwide movement to "cleanse the class ranks." In most parts of China, the movement continues well into 1969. In Zhejiang, its final toll is 9,198 dead.

December: The CCP Center orders the PLA to take control of China's public security and legal apparatus. Some 34,400 policemen and cadres are targeted, and over 1,100 subsequently die in a nationwide purge. The Center endorses the creation of Revolutionary Committees in Tianjin and Jiangxi. Chen Boda goes on record with the claim that the CCP underground in eastern Hebei may in fact have been controlled by KMT agents prior to 1949, whereupon the authorities in Tangshan respond by launching a major investigation (resulting in 2,955 dead) into 84,000 cases of suspected "treachery." The NCNA announces that 350 million copies of *Quotations from Chairman Mao* were published in 1967.

1968

January: Central authorities initiate a nationwide clampdown on economic speculation. Zhao Jianmin, a member of the Yunnan CCP Secretariat, is arrested in Beijing and accused of being a KMT special agent. Some 14,000 people with links to an alleged "spy ring" he is said to have controlled are rounded up and executed. Revolutionary Committees are set up in Gansu and Henan. Qi Benyu, a member of the Central Cultural Revolution Group, is purged and accused of being (together with Wang Li and Guan Feng) behind the "May 16th" conspiracy.

February: Central authorities call for urgent spending cuts. Bank accounts are frozen. Jiang Qing takes personal control of the investigation of Liu Shaoqi. Revolutionary Committees are set up in Hebei, Hubei, and Guangdong.

March: Lin Biao's power within the PLA is strengthened as Yang Chengwu, acting chief of staff; Yu Lijin, air force political commissar; and Fu Chongbi, commander of the Beijing Garrison are purged, and Lin's followers are allowed to dominate a reorganized Central Military

Commission Secretariat. The Central Case Examination Group team investigating purged Marshal He Long is given permission by Mao to look into Deng Xiaoping's political past. Revolutionary Committees are set up in Jilin, Jiangsu, and Zhejiang.

April: Mao, commenting on the assassination of Martin Luther King on 4 April, issues a statement in support of the "Afro-American struggle against violent repression." In Wuzhou, Guangxi, fighting between the PLA and the rebel organization 22 April Grand Army results in destruction of the city and the deaths of several thousand Red Guards. Revolutionary Committees are set up in Hunan, Ningxia, and Anhui.

May: Red Guards on the Qinghua University campus become bogged down in a bloody turf war that lasts for two months and results in ten dead and hundreds wounded. Revolutionary Committees are set up in Shaanxi, Liaoning, and Sichuan. The Central Case Examination Group inquiry into Deng Xiaoping's past is intensified.

June: Cotton and cloth rations are reduced as the economic situation continues to worsen. In what are highly exceptional circumstances, even in the Cultural Revolution, cannibalism ("human flesh banquets") flourishes as part of the ritual of "struggle" in Wuxuan County, Guangxi. Deng Xiaoping begins writing a major self-criticism in an (ultimately successful) attempt at preventing his expulsion from the CCP at the upcoming Central Committee Plenum.

July: Mao demobilizes the Red Guards and sends the first contingents of so-called worker-soldier propaganda teams to universities in Beijing. The PLA is ordered to bring an end to the widespread "mass" violence in Shaanxi and Guangxi. In Shaanxi, a semblance of order is restored after two months, during which 70,000 weapons and 4 million pieces of ammunition are confiscated. In Guangxi, sections of Nanning are reduced to rubble in pitched battles with tanks, heavy artillery, and napalm. The Beijing Revolutionary Committee collects photographs of 680 pretty middle school students as part of a secret citywide search for a suitable bride for the son of Lin Biao.

August: After months of chaotic negotiations between rival factions, Revolutionary Committees are finally set up in Fujian, Yunnan, and

Guangxi. As new authorities attempt to bring the situation there under control, some 300,000 suspected "counter-revolutionaries" are arrested (and some 37,000 of them are killed) in Yunnan. In Guangxi, the number of soldiers and civilians killed is estimated at between 90,000 and 300,000 as the state of civil war is finally brought to a close. With permission from the Central Case Examination Group, some sixty-five sons and daughters of senior "revisionists" are detained for ten months by the Beijing Public Security Bureau and attempts are made to make them denounce their parents.

September: As the last provincial-level Revolutionary Committees are set up in Tibet and Xinjiang, the *People's Daily* declares the entire country "with the exception of Taiwan" to be "red." At a rally in Beijing, Zhou Enlai cites Mao's recent instruction "The working class must exercise leadership in everything," and thousands of workers continue to be dispatched to schools all over China to "exercise leadership" and restore order.

October: The Eighth CCP Central Committee convenes its Twelfth Plenum, expelling Liu Shaoqi (but—upon Mao's insistence—*not* Deng Xiaoping) from the Party. A new draft constitution is prepared and submitted to the Party for discussion. A nationwide drive to send large numbers of cadres to so-called May 7th Cadre Schools—most of which are in fact recently evacuated labor camps—gets under way with the publication of Mao's dictum that "doing manual work is an excellent opportunity to study once again."

November: Mass rallies are convened all over the country to celebrate the Central Committee decision to "expel from the Party, once and for all, the renegade, traitor, and scab Liu Shaoqi." (Liu has been under house arrest since 1967 and is now left to die a slow and agonizing death—finally passing away in November 1969—under the watchful eye of the Central Case Examination Group.) In a report to CCP Center, the Beijing Revolutionary Committee claims that since the beginning of the Cultural Revolution, some 80,100 "class enemies" have been uncovered in the city, including close to 80 percent of all leading personnel employed by the original municipal administration.

December: The rural resettlement of urban youth intensifies. Between 1968 and 1978, a total of more than 16 million urban youths are "sent down" to China's countryside. In institutions of higher learning in Guangxi and elsewhere, teachers of bourgeois class background are labeled "birds and beasts" and put on public display in so-called "class struggle education exhibits." A CCP drive to recruit new members gains momentum.

1969

January: In its New Year editorial, the *People's Daily* declares decisive victory in the Cultural Revolution to have been won and total victory to be close at hand. Mao is quoted as calling for simultaneous intensification and moderation of the "cleansing of class ranks" movement. In Beijing, that movement continues through the spring, claiming, among other victims, 3,512 deaths through suicide.

February: A national planning conference puts top priority on development of agriculture and on allocations to the military sector. Targets include a 6 percent increase in grain production in 1969 to make up for the past two years during which output had failed to keep up with population growth. The conference also announces the forthcoming publication of volumes five and six of the *Selected Works of Mao Zedong,* which does, however, not take place.

March: Fighting breaks out between Chinese and Soviet border troops on the Ussuri River. Both sides suffer casualties in what the Chinese press describes as a Soviet act of "armed provocation." The Soviets propose negotiations to settle the conflict. In Inner Mongolia, the "cleansing of the class ranks" culminates in a clampdown on *Neirendang*—described as a "counter-revolutionary" underground organization of ethnic separatists. Conservative estimates put the number of victims of the clampdown at 346,000, including over 16,000 dead.

April: The CCP convenes its Ninth Party Congress. Mao Zedong, presiding, calls the congress a meeting of unity, yet significantly the congress reelects only 19 percent of the members of the Eighth Central Committee. A new Party constitution, describing Lin Biao as Mao's successor, is adopted. In its quarterly chronicle, *The China Quarterly* (September 1969) claims that the congress "indicated clearly that the radicals were no longer a powerful element in Peking." The calm presaged by the congress is short-lived as tensions grow between army and Party, between coteries of leaders, and eventually between Lin Biao and Mao himself. Lin dies in a plane crash in Mongolia in September 1971 and is denounced as a "counter-revolutionary conspirator." It is not until after Mao's death and the landmark Third Plenum of the Eleventh Central Committee in 1978 that the Cultural Revolution and all it stood for are officially relegated to the dustheap of history.

In the political report to the Ninth Party Congress, Lin Biao quotes Mao Zedong as saying:

> We have won great victory. But the defeated class will still struggle. These people are still around, and this class still exists. Therefore, we cannot speak of final victory. Not even for decades. We must not lose our vigilance. According to the Leninist viewpoint, the final victory of a socialist country not only requires the efforts of the proletariat and the broad masses of people at home, but also depends on the victory of the world revolution and the abolition of the system of exploitation of man by man on the whole globe, upon which all mankind will be emancipated. Therefore, it is wrong to speak of the final victory of the revolution in our country; it runs counter to Leninism and does not conform to facts.

Biographical Sketches*

An Ziwen (1909–1980): Member of Eighth CCP Central Committee and director of the Central Organization Department. Purged in Cultural Revolution as one of the so-called "Sixty-One Renegades," a group of CCP cadres released from KMT prisons on the eve of the Sino-Japanese War.

Bethune, Norman (1890–1939): Canadian surgeon who worked for the Communists in Yan'an during the Sino-Japanese War. Died of septicemia and was immortalized by Mao in "In Memory of Norman Bethune," one of the Cultural Revolution's so-called "Three Constantly Read Articles" (*lao sanpian*).

Bo Yibo (1908–): Alternate member of CCP Politburo, vice premier, and director of the State Economic Commission. Purged in Cultural Revolution as one of the so-called "Sixty-One Renegades," a group of CCP cadres released from KMT prisons on the eve of the Sino-Japanese War. Returned to influence following Mao's death.

Chen Boda (1904–1989): Alternate member of CCP Politburo, editor of *Red Flag,* and one of Mao Zedong's ghostwriters. Appointed director of the Central Cultural Revolution Group in May 1966. Promoted to Politburo Standing Committee at Eleventh Plenum. Member of Central Case Examination Group. Officially number four in the Party hier-

---

*Offices are those held at the beginning of the Cultural Revolution, unless otherwise indicated. The sources consulted in preparation of these biographical sketches include: Sheng Ping, ed., *Zhongguo gongchandang renming da cidian* (*Large Biographical Dictionary of the CCP*) (Beijing: Zhongguo guoji guangbo chubanshe, 1991); *Zhongguo gongchandang lishi da cidian* (*Large Encyclopedia of the History of the CCP*) (Beijing: Zhonggong Zhongyang dangxiao chubanshe, 1991); *Lijie Zhonggong Zhongyang weiyuanhui renming cidian* (*Biographical Dictionary of the Members of Successive CCP Central Committees*) (Beijing: Zhonggong dangshi chubanshe, 1992); *Dubao shouce* (*Newspaper Reader's Handbook*) (N.p., 1969).

archy after the Ninth Party Congress. Purged in 1970 and subsequently accused of being a follower of the disgraced Lin Biao. Imprisoned until 1988.

Chen Shaomin (1902–1977): A member of the Eighth Central Committee, she was the only one of fifty-nine full and alternate members present at the Twelfth Plenum who did *not* vote in favor of permanently expelling Liu Shaoqi from the Party. Not reelected to the Ninth Central Committee.

Chen Yi (1901–1972): Member of CCP Politburo, vice premier, and foreign minister. In the Cultural Revolution, Chen's career quickly took a turn for the worse, but as a PLA marshal who enjoyed Mao's protection, he managed to hold on to his Central Committee membership. Died of cancer.

Chen Yonggui (1914–1986): Party secretary of Dazhai brigade in Xiyang County, Shanxi, and *the* role model that peasants were told to emulate in the movement In Agriculture, Learn from Dazhai, launched on the eve of the Cultural Revolution. His career peaked in the mid-1970s when he was a member of the CCP Politburo. Retired in 1980.

Chen Zaidao (1909–1993): General and commander of the Wuhan Military Region. Implicated in the so-called "Wuhan Incident" in the summer of 1967, when members of a conservative mass organization together with officers and men under his command kidnapped emissaries from the Center. Imprisoned but released soon after the 1971 "Lin Biao Incident."

Deng Tuo (1912–1966): Member of the Beijing Municipal Party Secretariat. A talented essayist with a knack for the satirical, he was attacked at the very beginning of the Cultural Revolution. Committed suicide in May 1966.

Deng Xiaoping (1904–): General secretary of the CCP and vice premier. Deng was purged in the winter of 1966 as the "second biggest Party-person in power taking the capitalist road." After a period of internal exile during which he worked in a tractor plant in Jiangxi, he was formally rehabilitated in 1973. After alienating Mao a second time, he again fell from power in 1976. After Mao's death, he went on to become the most powerful man in the CCP and the architect of the Party's turn away from the Cultural Revolution.

Fu Chongbi (1916–): Major general and commander of the Beijing Garrison. Purged in March 1968 together with Yang Chengwu and Yu Lijin.

Gao Yangyun (1905–1968): Vice chairman of the Hebei People's Political Consultative Conference and concurrent party secretary of Nankai University. Purged in Cultural Revolution as one of the so-called "Sixty-One Renegades," a group of CCP cadres released from KMT prisons on the eve of the Sino-Japanese War.

Gong Xiaoji (1950–): Student in the middle school attached to Beijing University and cofounder of the conservative Red Guard United Action Committee.

Guan Feng (1919–): Deputy editor of *Red Flag* and an authority on classical Chinese philosophy. Member of the Central Cultural Revolution Group and Central Case Examination Group. Purged as an ultra-Leftist in August 1967. Imprisoned for over fifteen years. Now living in retirement in Beijing.

Han Aijing (1946–): Originally a student at the Beijing Aeronautical Institute, Han rose to national fame as the founder and leader of the *Beihang* Red Flag Combat Team, a university Red Guard organization with close links to the Central Cultural Revolution Group. Arrested after 1968. Now in Shenzhen.

He Long (1896–1969): Member of CCP Politburo, vice premier, and vice chairman of the Central Military Commission. A PLA marshal who ran afoul of Mao at the beginning of the Cultural Revolution, he was imprisoned and falsely accused of having planned to assassinate Mao. His premature death was brought on by what was almost certainly intentionally botched medical treatment.

Hu Qiaomu (1912–1992): Alternate member of CCP Central Secretariat, editor of Mao's *Selected Works,* and one of Mao's ghostwriters. In semiretirement for health reasons at beginning of Cultural Revolution. Returned to influence in 1975.

Hua Guofeng (1921–): A deputy governor of Hunan province at the beginning of the Cultural Revolution, Hua rose quickly through the ranks. Elected to the Central Committee at the Ninth Party Congress in 1969; promoted to Politburo membership in 1973; and chosen to succeed Zhou Enlai as premier and Mao as Party chairman in 1976. Increasingly powerless after 1978, he went into semiretirement in 1981.

Huang Yongsheng (1910–1983): PLA general and alternate member of Eighth CCP Central Committee. Appointed PLA chief of staff in 1968 and promoted to Politburo at the First Plenum of the Ninth CCP Central Committee. Member of the Central Case Examination Group. Arrested soon after the "Lin Biao Incident." Remaindered in custody for the rest of his life.

Jiang Qing (1914–1991): Wife of Mao Zedong. Ranking deputy director and de facto head of the Central Cultural Revolution Group. Member of the Central Case Examination Group. Promoted to Politburo at the First Plenum of the Ninth CCP Central Committee. Arrested immediately after her husband's death in 1976 together with Zhang Chunqiao, Yao Wenyuan, and Wang Hongwen (the "Gang of Four"). Famous for her role in promoting the so-called Revolutionary Beijing Opera. Committed suicide in prison while serving a commuted death sentence.

Kang Sheng (1898–1975): Alternate member of CCP Politburo and member of Central Secretariat. Appointed leading member of the Central Case Examination Group and adviser to the Central Cultural Revolution Group in May 1966. Promoted to Politburo Standing Committee at Eleventh Plenum. Officially number five in the Party hierarchy after Ninth Party Congress. Died of bladder cancer. Posthumously stripped of his party membership and held personally responsible for the persecution of hundreds of leading Party cadres in the Cultural Revolution.

Ke Qingshi (1902–1965): Member of CCP Politburo, vice premier, and mayor of Shanghai.

Kong Xiangzhen (1904–1986): Vice minister and party secretary of First Ministry of Light Industry. Purged in Cultural Revolution as one of the so-called "Sixty-One Renegades," a group of CCP cadres released from KMT prisons on the eve of the Sino-Japanese War.

Kuai Dafu (1945–): Student at Qinghua University. Rose to national fame as founder and leader of the Jinggangshan Regiment, a university Red Guard organization with close links to the Central Cultural Revolution Group. Arrested after 1968. Currently an engineer with a joint-venture firm in Shenzhen.

Lei Feng (1940–1962): PLA soldier who died in a car accident. In his lifetime, he allegedly performed countless good deeds, and beginning in 1963, he became the focus of a nationwide campaign to "Learn from Lei Feng."

Li Chuli: Deputy director of CCP Central Organization Department. Purged in Cultural Revolution as one of the so-called "Sixty-One Renegades," a group of CCP cadres released from KMT prisons on the eve of the Sino-Japanese War.

Li Xuefeng (1907–): Member of CCP Central Secretariat and First secretary of North China Bureau. Replaced the disgraced Peng Zhen as first secretary of the Beijing Party Committee in June 1966. Promoted to alternate membership of Politburo at Eleventh Plenum. Made chairman of the Hebei Revolutionary Committee in 1968. Purged at the end of 1970; rehabilitated in 1982.

Li Zuopeng (1914–): Lieutenant general with historical links to Lin Biao. Appointed first political commissar of the navy in 1967 and promoted to Politburo at the First Plenum of the Ninth CCP Central Committee. Arrested soon after the "Lin Biao Incident."

Liao Luyan (1913–1972): Alternate member of Eighth CCP Central Committee and minister of agriculture. Purged in Cultural Revolution as one of the so-called "Sixty-One Renegades," a group of CCP cadres released from KMT prisons on the eve of the Sino-Japanese War.

Lin Biao (1907–1971): PLA marshal, vice chairman of the CCP, vice premier, minister of defense, and vice chairman of the CCP Central Military Commission. At Mao's insistence promoted to the number two spot in the Party hierarchy at Eleventh Plenum of Eighth Central Committee, replacing the disgraced Liu Shaoqi. Largely a passive figure who did not seek enhanced power for himself and who never challenged Mao politically. Officially designated "Chairman Mao's successor" in the Party constitution adopted at the Ninth Party Congress. After 1969, Mao grew increasingly weary of Lin, who died under mysterious circumstances in a plane crash in Mongolia in September 1971 (the so-called "Lin Biao Incident").

Lin Liguo (1945–1971): Lin Biao's son, alleged to have planned to assassinate Mao Zedong in 1971. Died in plane crash in Mongolia with his parents.

Liu Lantao (1910–): Alternate member of CCP Central Secretariat and first secretary of North-West Bureau. Purged in Cultural Revolution as one of the so-called "Sixty-One Renegades," a group of CCP cadres released from KMT prisons on the eve of the Sino-Japanese War.

Liu Ren (1909–1973): Alternate member of Eighth CCP Central Committee, vice mayor of Beijing, and second secretary of the Beijing Municipal Party Secretariat. Purged together with Peng Zhen at beginning of Cultural Revolution. Formally arrested in January 1968. Died in prison.

Liu Shaoqi (1898–1969): Vice chairman of the CCP and president of the People's Republic of China. Demoted at the Eleventh Plenum and subsequently purged as the "biggest Party-person in power taking the capitalist road." Expelled from the CCP by the Eighth Central Committee at its Twelfth Plenum. The most senior victim of the Cultural Revolution, Liu died in November 1969 from medical neglect and physical abuse at the hands of Central Case Examination Group staff. Fully rehabilitated posthumously in 1980.

Liu Xiwu (1904–1970): Vice secretary of the CCP Central Committee's Control Commission. Purged in the Cultural Revolution as one of the so-called "Sixty-One Renegades," a group of CCP cadres released from KMT prisons on the eve of the Sino-Japanese War.

Liu Yingjun (1945–1966): PLA soldier who died in a car accident while trying to avoid hitting six small children. Hailed as a hero and outstanding pupil of Chairman Mao during the Cultural Revolution.

Liu Zhijian (1912–): Lieutenant general and deputy director of the PLA General Political Department when the Cultural Revolution started. Appointed deputy director of the Central Cultural Revolution Group in May 1966. Purged at the beginning of 1967.

Lu Dingyi (1906–1996): Alternate member of CCP Politburo, member of CCP Central Secretariat, vice premier, minister of culture, and director of the CCP Central Propaganda Department. Purged in May 1966 as member of the so-called Peng-Luo-Lu-Yang Clique. Survived years in prison and returned to influence following Mao's death in 1976.

Lü Yulan (1941–): Nationally famous peasant and labor hero from Shandong, elected to Central Committee at Ninth Party Congress.

Luo Ruiqing (1906–1978): PLA marshal, chief of staff, member of CCP Central Secretariat, and vice premier. Purged at the beginning of the Cultural Revolution, accused of opposing "giving prominence to Mao Zedong Thought" and of trying to "seize power" from Lin Biao. Arrested and sent to prison. Returned to influence following Mao's death in 1976.

Mai Xiande (1945–): PLA soldier, severely wounded in the head during engagement with KMT Navy. Described in Party media as a hero and outstanding Activist in the Study of Chairman Mao's Works.

Mao Zedong (1893–1976): Cofounder of CCP and Party chairman from 1943 until his death in 1976. Fiendishly clever, ruthless, and unpredictable politician. Launched the Cultural Revolution in what the Party media then described as an attempt to "combat and prevent revisionism" but what is now referred to by his successors as the biggest single mistake of his political career. Together with Joseph Stalin and Adolf Hitler, Mao appears destined to go down in history as one of the great tyrants of the twentieth century.

Nie Yuanzi (1921–): CCP general branch secretary in the Department of Philosophy at Beijing University. An influential Red Guard leader, she was made an alternate member of the Central Committee at the Ninth Party Congress but fell from power quickly thereafter and was imprisoned. Presently a consultant to the China Tian Lun Economic Development Corporation.

Niu Wanping: Student in the middle school attached to Beijing University and cofounder of the conservative Red Guard United Action Committee.

Peng Dehuai (1898–1974): Outspoken minister of defense and CCP Politburo member, purged in 1959 for criticizing Mao and the Great Leap Forward. Recalled from Sichuan to Beijing at the end of 1966, he was arrested and eventually died in prison. Rehabilitated posthumously in 1978.

Peng Xiaomeng (1948–): Student and Red Guard in the middle school attached to Beijing University. Singled out for praise by Mao in his "Letter to the Red Guards of Qinghua University Middle School" in August 1966.

Peng Zhen (1902–): Powerful member of the CCP Central Secretariat, mayor of Beijing, first secretary of the Beijing Municipal Party Committee, and head of the CCP Center's ad hoc group of five in charge of culture. Purged in May 1966 as member of the so-called Peng-Luo-Lu-Yang Clique and attacked, inter alia, for having said (just possibly with reference to Mao Zedong) that "everyone is equal in front of the truth." Survived a decade in prison and returned to influence following Mao's death in 1976.

Qi Benyu (1931–): Staff member of the Central Committee General Office who replaced Tian Jiaying as Mao's secretary in May 1966. Junior member of the Central Cultural Revolution Group and Central Case Examination Group. Arrested and purged as an ultra-Leftist in January 1968. Now living in retirement in Shanghai.

Qiu Huizuo (1914–): Lieutenant general with historical links to Lin Biao. Appointed director of the PLA General Logistics Department in 1968 and promoted to Politburo at the First Plenum of the Ninth CCP Central Committee. Arrested soon after the "Lin Biao Incident."

Tan Houlan (1940–1982): Originally a student at the Beijing Teacher's University, she rose to national fame as the founder and leader of the Jinggangshan Commune, a university Red Guard organization with close links to the Central Cultural Revolution Group. Arrested after 1968. Died of cancer while in prison.

Tan Zhenlin (1902–1983): Member of CCP Politburo and vice premier. Purged as a "capitalist roader" in the winter of 1966–67. Returned to power in 1973.

Tao Zhu (1908–1969): Member of Eighth CCP Central Committee, vice premier, and first secretary of Central-South Bureau. Transferred to Beijing at beginning of Cultural Revolution to replace Lu Dingyi as director of Central Propaganda Department. Promoted to number four position on Politburo at Eleventh Plenum. Adviser to Central Cultural Revolution Group and Central Case Examination Group. Purged in early 1967 and put under house arrest in Zhongnanhai. Died of cancer while in the custody of the Central Case Examination Group. Rehabilitated posthumously in 1978.

Tian Jiaying (1922–1966): Mao Zedong's personal secretary. Committed suicide in May 1966 after having been accused of "tampering with Mao's works."

Wan Li (1916–): Vice mayor of Beijing and member of the Beijing Municipal Party Secretariat. Purged in October 1966. Returned to power in 1973.

Wang Dabin (1946–): Student at the Beijing Geological Institute and nationally famous Red Guard leader of the *Diyuan* East Is Red Commune. Arrested after 1969. Currently said to be working in Shenzhen.

Wang Dongxing (1916–): Mao's chief bodyguard, who replaced Yang Shangkun as director of the Central Committee General Office in November 1965. Member of the Central Case Examination Group. Elected alternate member of CCP Politburo at First Plenum of Ninth Central Committee. Rose steadily in the ranks to become vice chairman of the CCP. Carried out the arrest of Mao's widow and the other members of the "Gang of Four." Clashed with Deng Xiaoping in 1978 and was forced into semiretirement in early 1980s.

Wang Guangmei (1921–): Wife of Liu Shaoqi and staff member of CCP Central Committee General Office. Purged along with her husband. Survived the Cultural Revolution in prison. Released and rehabilitated after the Third Plenum of the Eleventh Central Committee in 1978.

Wang Hongwen (1932–1992): Security guard in No. 17 Cotton Mill who rose to fame as "rebel" labor leader during Cultural Revolution. Appointed to Central Committee in 1969 and groomed by Mao as possible successor in early 1970s. Vice chairman of the CCP at the time of his arrest as one of the "Gang of Four" in 1976. Sentenced to life in prison in 1981.

Wang Jie (1942–1965): Young PLA soldier who died a hero's death in an explosion in 1965. Focus of Cultural Revolution campaign to "Learn from Wang Jie!"

Wang Li (1922–): Deputy director of the CCP International Liaison Department and Politburo ghostwriter. Appointed to the Central Cultural Revolution Group in 1966. Purged as an "ultra-Leftist" in August 1967. Incarcerated for fifteen years. Lives in retirement in Beijing.

Wang Renzhong (1917–1992): Alternate member of Eighth Central Committee and second secretary of CCP Central-South Bureau. Appointed deputy director of the Central Cultural Revolution Group in the summer of 1966. Purged and denounced as a "capitalist roader" in early 1967. Returned to influence following Mao's death in 1976.

Wu De (1913–1995): Alternate member of Eighth CCP Central Committee. Transferred from Jilin Province to become second Party secretary and acting mayor of Beijing in 1966. Elected to Central Committee at Twelfth Plenum in 1968. Succeeded Xie Fuzhi as chairman of Beijing Revolutionary Committee in 1972. Fell from grace after death of Mao, when he clashed with Deng Xiaoping.

Wu Faxian (1915–): Lieutenant general with historical links to Lin Biao. Commander of the PLA Air Force at the beginning of the Cultural Revolution. Promoted to Politburo membership at the First Plenum of the Ninth CCP Central Committee. Arrested soon after the "Lin Biao Incident."

Wu Han (1909–1969): Prominent historian and vice mayor of Beijing. The first public target of the Cultural Revolution, Wu died a broken man after being subjected to two and a half years of endless public "struggle" rallies, physical abuse, and severe maltreatment in prison.

Wu Xiuquan (1908–): Member of the Eighth Central Committee and deputy director of the CCP International Liaison Department. Attacked by Red Guards at the beginning of Cultural Revolution. Imprisoned in 1968. Released and rehabilitated in 1974.

Xie Fuzhi (1909–1972): Member of Eighth CCP Central Committee, vice premier, and minister of public security. Member of the Central Case Examination Group and deeply involved in the purge of countless senior Party figures. Promoted to alternate membership of Politburo at Eleventh Plenum and to full membership at First Plenum of Ninth Central Committee. Buried with honors after dying of cancer, he was posthumously expelled from the CCP in 1980 for his role in the Cultural Revolution.

Xu Bing (1903–1972): Alternate member of Eighth CCP Central Committee and director of CCP Central United Front Department. Purged in the Cultural Revolution as one of the so-called "Sixty-One Renegades," a group of CCP cadres released from KMT prisons on the eve of the Sino-Japanese War.

Xu Xiangqian (1901–1990): PLA marshal and vice chairman of the Central Military Commission, elected to CCP Politburo at the Eleventh Plenum of the Eighth Central Committee. Appointed head of the All-Army Cultural Revolution Group in January 1967, but for health reasons only sporadically active in that capacity. Criticized in the wake of the July 1967 "Wuhan Incident" but never purged.

Yang Chengwu (1914–): Alternate member of Eighth CCP Central Committee, PLA general, and deputy chief of staff. Became acting PLA chief of staff in 1966, after the fall of Luo Ruiqing. According to Zhou Enlai, instrumental in guaranteeing Mao's personal safety during early stages of Cultural Revolution. Member of Central Case Examination Group. Purged in March 1968 together with Yu Lijin and Fu Chongbi.

Yang Shangkun (1907–): Alternate member of CCP Central Secretariat and director of the Central Committee General Office (until November 1965). Purged in May 1966 as member of the so-called Peng-Luo-Lu-Yang Clique, allegedly for bugging Chairman Mao's quarters. Returned to influence after Mao's death. Made president of the PRC in 1988.

Yang Xianzhen (1896–1992): A member of Eighth CCP Central Committee and former president of Central Party School who was the target of a major public ideological controversy in 1964. Purged in Cultural Revolution as one of the so-called "Sixty-One Renegades," a group of CCP cadres released from KMT prisons on the eve of the Sino-Japanese War.

Yao Wenyuan (1932–): Radical Shanghai literary critic and polemicist who wrote "On the New Historical Play *Hai Rui Dismissed from Office*," commonly referred to as the first salvo of the Cultural Revolution. The youngest member of the Central Cultural Revolution Group. Member of the CCP Politburo after 1969. Arrested as one of the "Gang of Four" after the death of Mao in 1976. Sentenced to twenty years in prison in 1981, Yao now lives in Shanghai.

Ye Jianying (1897–1986): CCP Central Committee member, PLA marshal, and secretary general of the Central Military Commission. Elected to the Politburo by the Eighth Central Committee and to its standing committee by the Ninth Central Committee. Remained in power throughout the Cultural Revolution and masterminded the arrest of the "Gang of Four" soon after Mao's death. Retired for health reasons in early 1980s.

Ye Qun (1917–1971): Wife of Lin Biao and his acting representative on the Central Case Examination Group. Elected to CCP Politburo at the First Plenum of the Ninth Central Committee. Implicated in her son's alleged plot to assassinate Mao. Died in plane crash in Mongolia with her husband and son.

Yu Lijin (1913–1978): Lieutenant general and political commissar of the PLA Air Force. Purged in March 1968 together with Yang Chengwu and Fu Chongbi.

Zhang Chunqiao (1917–): Shanghai Party newspaper editor and senior propaganda official. Rose to fame as member of Mao's inner circle and deputy director of the Central Cultural Revolution Group. Elected to the CCP Politburo in 1969. Arrested as a member of the "Gang of Four" in 1976, at which point he was chairman of the Shanghai Revolutionary Committee and vice premier of the State Council. Sentenced to death with a two-year reprieve in 1981.

Zhang Pinghua (1908–): Alternate member of the Eighth Central Committee and member of CCP Central-South Bureau. Promoted to post as executive deputy director of the CCP Central Propaganda Department in summer of 1966. Fell from grace a few months later. Appointed deputy chairman of Shanxi Revolutionary Committee in 1971. Returned to influence following Mao's death in 1976.

Zhou Rongxin (1917–1976): One of Premier Zhou Enlai's closest aides at the beginning of the Cultural Revolution, involved inter alia in managing the logistics of nationwide Red Guard travel in 1966. Purged in 1967 but subsequently reinstated, promoted, and appointed Minister of Education in January 1975. Suffered from a heart condition and died after being attacked by the "Gang of Four" for "obstructing revolution in education."

Zhou Enlai (1898–1976): Without Zhou's help, Mao Zedong would never have been able to carry out the Cultural Revolution. China's premier and number three in the Party hierarchy, the charming and ruthless Zhou chaired not only the regular meetings of the State Council's inner cabinet, but also those of the Central Cultural Revolution Group and the Central Case Examination Group. Implicated in the inquisition and purge of thousands of senior leaders. Died of cancer.

Zhou Zhongying (1902–1991): Deputy director of the State Economic Commission. Purged in Cultural Revolution as one of the so-called "Sixty-One Renegades," a group of CCP cadres released from KMT prisons on the eve of the Sino-Japanese War.

Zhu Chengzhao: Student at the Beijing Geological Institute and now largely forgotten Red Guard leader who founded the "Third Headquarters," the most important Red Guard umbrella organization in Beijing. Denounced by radicals when he turned against the Central Cultural Revolution Group in 1967. Ultimate fate unknown.

Further Readings*

General & Politics

Ahn, Byung-joon. *Chinese Politics and the Cultural Revolution: Dynamics of Policy Processes.* Seattle: University of Washington Press, 1976.

Barnouin, Barbara, and Yu Changgen. *Ten Years of Turbulence: The Chinese Cultural Revolution.* London: Kegan Paul International, 1993.

Baum, Richard, ed., with Louise B. Bennett. *China in Ferment: Perspectives on the Cultural Revolution.* Englewood Cliffs, N.J.: Prentice-Hall, 1971.

The Cambridge History of China, Vol. 15, *The People's Republic, Part 2: Revolutions Within the Chinese Revolution,* eds. Roderick MacFarquhar and John K. Fairbank. Cambridge: Cambridge University Press, 1991.

Chang, Parris H. *Power and Policy in China.* University Park: Pennsylvania State University Press, 1978.

Dittmer, Lowell. *Liu Shao-ch'i and the Chinese Cultural Revolution: The Politics of Mass Criticism.* Berkeley: University of California Press, 1974.

Johnson, Chalmers A., ed. *Ideology and Politics in Contemporary China.* Seattle: University of Washington Press, 1973.

Joseph, William A., Wong, Christine, and Zweig, David, eds. *New Perspectives on the Cultural Revolution.* Cambridge, Mass.: Council on East Asian Studies, 1991.

Karnow, Stanley. *Mao and China: A Legacy of Turmoil.* New York: Penguin, 1990.

Kau, Michael Y.M., ed. *The Lin Biao Affair: Power Politics and Military Coup.* White Plains, N.Y.: International Arts and Sciences Press, 1975.

Lee, Hong Yung. *The Politics of the Chinese Cultural Revolution: A Case Study.* Berkeley: University of California Press, 1978.

Lewis, John Wilson, ed. *Party Leadership and Revolutionary Power in China.* Cambridge: Cambridge University Press, 1970.

Leys, Simon. *The Chairman's New Clothes: Mao and the Cultural Revolution.* New York: St. Martin's Press, 1977.

Lifton, Robert Jay. *Revolutionary Immortality: Mao Tse-tung and the Chinese Cultural Revolution.* New York: Random House, 1968.

Liu Guokai, *A Brief Analysis of the Cultural Revolution.* Armonk, N.Y.: M.E. Sharpe, 1987.

---

*In addition to the book titles listed here, the reader is strongly advised to consult the major journals in the field (e.g., *The China Quarterly, Australian Journal of Chinese Affairs*—now *The China Journal*) in which numerous articles on all aspects of the Cultural Revolution have been published over the years.

MacFarquhar, Roderick. *The Origins of the Cultural Revolution, 1: Contradictions Among the People 1956–1957.* New York: Columbia University Press, 1974.

———. *The Origins of the Cultural Revolution, 2: The Great Leap Forward 1958–1960.* New York: Columbia University Press, 1983.

———. *The Origins of the Cultural Revolution, 3: The Coming of the Cataclysm 1961–1966.* New York: Columbia University Press, forthcoming 1996.

———, ed. *The Politics of China, 1949–1989.* New York: Cambridge University Press, 1993.

Scalapino, Robert A., ed. *Elites in the People's Republic of China.* Seattle: University of Washington Press, 1972.

Schram, Stuart R. *The Thought of Mao Tse-tung.* New York: Cambridge University Press, 1989.

Teiwes, Fred, and Sun, Warren. *The Tragedy of Lin Biao.* London: C. Hurst, 1996.

Wedeman, Andrew. *The East Wind Subsides: Chinese Foreign Policy and the Origins of the Cultural Revolution.* Washington, D.C.: Washington Institute Press, 1987.

Yan Jiaqi and Gao Gao. *Turbulent Decade: A History of the Cultural Revolution.* Edited and translated by D.W.Y. Kwok. Honolulu: University of Hawaii Press, 1996.

Society

Bernstein, Thomas P. *Up to the Mountains and Down to the Villages: The Transfer of Youth from Urban to Rural China.* New Haven, Conn.: Yale University Press, 1977.

Chan, Anita. *Children of Mao: A Study of Politically Active Chinese Youths.* Seattle: University of Washington Press, 1985.

The Cultural Revolution in the Provinces. Cambridge, Mass.: East Asian Research Center, Harvard University, 1971.

Forster, Keith. *Rebellion and Factionalism in a Chinese Province: Zhejiang, 1966–1976.* Armonk, N.Y.: M.E. Sharpe, 1990.

Gong Xiaoxia. "Repressive Movements and the Politics of Victimization." Cambridge, Mass.: Harvard University, Department of Sociology, Ph.D. thesis, 1995.

Granqvist, Hans. *The Red Guard: A Report on Mao's Revolution.* New York: Praeger, 1967.

Gray, Sherry. "Bombard the Headquarters: Local Politics and Citizen Participation in the Great Proletarian Cultural Revolution and the 1989 Movement in Shenyang." Denver: University of Denver, Graduate School of International Studies, Ph.D. thesis, 1992.

Hinton, William. *Hundred Day War: The Cultural Revolution at Tsinghua University.* New York: Monthly Review Press, 1972.

Kwong, Julia. *Cultural Revolution in China's Schools, May 1966–April 1969.* Stanford, Cal.: Hoover Institution Press, 1988.

Lin Jing. *The Red Guards' Path to Violence.* New York: Praeger, 1991.

Nee, Victor. *The Cultural Revolution at Peking University.* New York: Monthly Review Press, 1969.

Perry, Elizabeth J., and Li Xun. *Organized Disorder: Shanghai Workers in the Cultural Revolution.* Boulder, Colo.: Westview Press, forthcoming.

Rosen, Stanley. *Red Guard Factionalism and the Cultural Revolution in Guangzhou (Canton).* Boulder, Colo.: Westview Press, 1982.

Walder, Andrew G. *Chang Ch'un-ch'iao and Shanghai's January Revolution.* Ann Arbor: Center for Chinese Studies, University of Michigan, 1978.

Wang Shaoguang. *Failure of Charisma: The Cultural Revolution in Wuhan.* Hong Kong: Oxford University Press, 1995.

White, Lynn T., III. *Policies of Chaos, The Organizational Causes of Violence in China's Cultural Revolution.* Princeton: Princeton University Press, 1989.

Wu Di. *The Cultural Revolution in Inner Mongolia: Extracts from an Unpublished History.* Edited by Michael Schoenhals. Stockholm: Center for Pacific Asia Studies, 1993.

Zheng Yi. *Scarlet Memorial.* Boulder, Colo.: Westview Press, 1996.

Culture

Barnstone, Willis, ed. *The Poems of Mao Tse-tung.* London: Barrie & Jenkins, 1972.

Bergman, Pär. *Paragons of Virtue in Chinese Short Stories during the Cultural Revolution.* Skrifter utgivna av Föreningen för Orientaliska Studier, 16. Stockholm: Stockholm University, 1984.

Wagner, Vivian. "Die Lieder der Roten Garden" (Songs of the Red Guards). M.A. thesis, University of Münich, 1995.

Economics

Naughton, Barry. "The Third Front: Defense Industrialization in the Chinese Interior," *The China Quarterly,* No. 115, September 1988, pp. 351–86.

Perkins, Dwight H. *China's Economic Policy and Performance during the Cultural Revolution and Its Aftermath.* Cambridge, Mass.: Harvard Institute for International Development, 1984.

Zweig, David. *Agrarian Radicalism in China.* Cambridge, Mass.: Harvard University Press, 1989.

Memoirs and Firsthand Observations

Bennett, Gordon A., and Montaperto, Ronald N. *Red Guard: The Political Biography of Dai Hsiao-ai.* Garden City, N.Y.: Doubleday, 1971.

Chen, Jack. *Inside the Cultural Revolution.* London: Sheldon Press, 1976.

Chen Jo-hsi. *The Execution of Mayor Yin and Other Stories from the Great Proletarian Cultural Revolution.* Bloomington: Indiana University Press, 1978.

Cheng Nien. *Life and Death in Shanghai.* London: Grafton Books, 1986.

Feng Jicai. *Voices from the Whirlwind: An Oral History of the Chinese Cultural Revolution*. New York: Pantheon Books, 1991.

Fokkema, D.W. *Report from Peking: Observations of a Western Diplomat on the Cultural Revolution*. London: C. Hurst, 1972.

Frolic, B. Michael. *Mao's People: Sixteen Portraits of Life in Revolutionary China*. Cambridge, Mass.: Harvard University Press, 1980.

Gao Yuan. *Born Red: A Chronicle of the Cultural Revolution*. Stanford, Cal.: Stanford University Press, 1987.

Hunter, Neal. *Shanghai Journal: An Eyewitness Account of the Cultural Revolution*. Boston: Beacon Press, 1969.

Li Zhisui, with the editorial assistance of Anne F. Thurston. *The Private Life of Chairman Mao*. New York: Random House, 1994.

Liang Heng and Shapiro, Judith. *Son of the Revolution*. New York: Knopf, 1983.

Ling, Ken. *The Revenge of Heaven: Journal of a Young Chinese*. New York: Putnam, 1972.

Lo Fulang. *Morning Breeze: A True Story of China's Cultural Revolution*. San Francisco: China Books and Periodicals, 1989.

Lo, Ruth Earnshaw. *In the Eye of the Typhoon*. New York: DaCapo, 1980.

Luo Ziping. *A Generation Lost: China under the Cultural Revolution*. New York: H. Holt, 1990.

Milton, David, and Milton, Nancy Dall. *The Wind Will Not Subside: Years in Revolutionary China, 1964–1969*. New York: Pantheon Books, 1976.

Min Anchee. *Red Azalea*. New York: Pantheon, 1994.

Niu Niu. *No Tears for Mao. Growing Up in the Cultural Revolution*. Chicago: Academy Publications, 1995.

Rittenberg, Sidney. *The Man Who Stayed Behind*. New York: Simon and Schuster, 1993.

Ross, James. *Caught in a Tornado: A Chinese-American Woman Survives the Cultural Revolution*. Boston: Northeastern University Press, 1994.

Thurston, Anne F. *Enemies of the People: The Ordeal of the Intellectuals in China's Great Cultural Revolution*. New York: Knopf, 1987.

———. *Chinese Odyssey: The Life and Times of a Chinese Dissident*. New York: Scribner's, 1991.

Wen Chihua. *The Red Mirror: Children of China's Cultural Revolution*. Boulder, Colo.: Westview Press, 1995.

Witke, Roxane. *Comrade Chiang Ch'ing*. Boston: Little, Brown, 1977.

Yang Jiang. *A Cadre School Life*. Hong Kong: Joint Publications Service, 1982.

Yue Daiyun and Wakeman, Carolyn. *To the Storm: The Odyssey of a Revolutionary Chinese Woman*. Berkeley: University of California Press, 1985.

Zhai Zhenhua. *Red Flower of China*. New York: Soho, 1992.

Zhelokhovtsev, A. *The "Cultural Revolution": A Close-Up*. Moscow: Progress Publishers, 1975.

Index

Michael Schoenhals received his Ph.D. in Sinology from Stockholm University and is currently associate professor at the Center for Pacific Asia Studies, Stockholm University. A specialist on Chinese politics, he has been a post-doctoral fellow and visiting scholar in the John King Fairbank Center, Harvard University, and a visiting assistant research linguist at the Center for Chinese Studies, University of California, Berkeley. He is the author of *Doing Things With Words in Chinese Politics* (1992) and *Saltationist Socialism: Mao Zedong and the Great Leap Forward* (1987).